The What, Where, When, How & Why
of Gardening in New Mexico

New Mexico
GARDENER'S
GUIDE

JUDITH PHILLIPS

COOL
SPRINGS
PRESS

Nashville, Tennessee

A Division of Thomas Nelson, Inc.
www.ThomasNelson.com

ACKNOWLEDGMENTS

THE NAMES AND KIND DEEDS OF THE PEOPLE who in one way or another led me to write this book could themselves fill a book. My parents made sure my siblings and I learned to love and respect nature by taking us to beautiful places and allowing us the freedom to explore them. I owe Emmett Koehler, the gentleman and scholar who gave me my first nursery job, the high standards I have worked toward in the nearly thirty years since he so patiently answered my first million questions about growing plants. Often his responses to my queries were a sprig of the plant and the invitation to watch it grow.

Because New Mexico is such a diverse place, and gardeners only really know their own plots in any exacting way, I rely on the skill and insights of many friends across the state to fine-tune my understanding of how things work in their backyards. Ongoing plant conversations of many years' duration with Ellen Reed, whose garden is a magnificent blend of Western wildflowers and exotics from heather to hellebore, provide a global view of horticulture that balances my local focus. My visits with Ellen Wilde of Santa Fe have helped remind me of what a difference clay soil, real winter, and somewhat reliable summer rain can make in one's garden choices. Greg Magee, a Las Cruces landscape architect devoted to nature as a model for effective design, provided clarification and suggestions for southern New Mexico gardens. David Salman of Santa Fe Greenhouses and High Country Plants makes a career of enlarging the plant palette for Western gardeners and is generous with his time and information as well. Ty Curtis of Curtis & Curtis Seed on the eastern plains filled the gaps in the turfgrass information. In my crusade to limit soil disturbance, I've grown out of touch with many annuals, and Sherry McAnally of Bell's Greenhouse in Albuquerque provided input on those vital garden plants.

New Mexico

GARDENER'S GUIDE

CONTENTS

INTRODUCTION

Gardening in New Mexico

*S*TANDING ON A MOUNTAIN RIDGE in the company of thousand-year-old bristle cone pines, looking out across hundreds of miles of desert grassland interrupted only by the sinuous green Rio Grande, I feel very, very small. When I first came to New Mexico, the sheer expansiveness of this place intimidated me. I arrived in July during a very good monsoon year. It seemed to rain almost every afternoon, yet the marigolds I planted still dried up and died. *Marigolds* died? I was humiliated.

Summer mellowed into autumn and was followed by, according to my Eastern and Midwestern standards, a mild winter. The soft, gray sages and salt bush, the tawny oaks, and the deep-green creosote bush, mountain mahogany, and pinyon provided just the right contrast for the unexpected richness of the color of dried grasses and seedheads of dormant wildflowers—subdued rust and platinum, gold and silver. I started feeling less lost in the grandeur, more comfortable with sparsity.

Then came spring. Winds battered my budding confidence, and hordes of grasshoppers and chest-high weeds swallowed my garden. I began to look at untended gardens to see what was surviving without a loving hand and running hose. I saw that most plants I thought needed full sun seemed a lot happier in afternoon shade. I also realized that while there was very little diversity in the gardens, an amazing bounty of beautiful plants prospered out in the desert and mountain foothills. Why were the gardens of a place as dramatically different as New Mexico so similar to those of New York and Indiana? I took classes that taught me that if I worked hard enough and long enough, I could grow almost anything I wanted to grow here. In the newly germinating Native Plant Society of New Mexico, I found a small group of knowledgeable advocates for wild plants and formed friendships that have become as deeply rooted as mesquite. The more I compared wild landscapes with carefully tended gardens, the more it seemed that a hybrid of the two would be the most interesting place to grow. I began stalking the desert and foothills, collecting seeds for wildflowers that might grow in my garden.

D. H. Lawrence wrote that "it was New Mexico that liberated me from the present era of civilization." My first attempts to garden in

Introduction

New Mexico began to liberate me from the homogeneity of urban horticulture, and it seems I wasn't alone in my discontent with the struggle to grow the same few plants coast to coast. There has been a surge of regionalism in gardens across America. As nature is squeezed by development, we have come to value those remaining fragments of wilderness that let us know we are in New England or the Midwest. Rather than cultivating only the few plants that are so broadly adapted they will survive nearly anywhere, some nurseries have begun to seek out plants that are particularly suited to regional climates and local microclimates.

In the Southwest, a rapidly expanding population draws on a very limited supply of water. This is a wonderful place to live; it's no wonder that so many people visit and decide to stay. New Mexico is a place of contrasts. You can take a foot trail west of bustling Albuquerque into one of the canyons of the Petroglyphs National Monument, and a ten-minute walk will bring you to where thousands of prehistoric designs adorn the rocks. Silence and bird song mark the absence of traffic sounds, and you are alone in nature. Even in the middle of town, you need only look past the buildings around you to see the contrasting raw desert and ancient mountains. The cities themselves are old adobe blended with modern concrete and steel, but park at the edge of just about any town in New Mexico and you can walk a short distance into cottonwood bosque or rocky foothills, brittle desert or marshlands. You can be basking in the 65-degree Fahrenheit sunshine of a December afternoon and a few hours later have the temperature bottom out at -10 degrees Fahrenheit. You can ski in the morning and play golf or plant bulbs in the afternoon. You can start the day 700 feet below ground at Carlsbad Caverns, still 2400 feet above sea level, and end it on Wheeler Peak 13,000 feet in the sky.

HIGH AND DRY:
ACCLIMATING TO THE NEW MEXICO LANDSCAPE

To a Southwestern gardener, altitude has enormous significance. Every 1000-ft. gain in altitude yields a 3-degree drop in temperature, and at least a few inches' increase in annual precipitation.

Introduction

New Mexico spans 370 miles north to south, and if latitude were the only influence, there would be only a 1-degree Fahrenheit decrease for every 100 miles you traveled north. If altitude were not a factor, Las Cruces in the south would vary from northern Farmington by less than 4 degrees Fahrenheit. Yet Las Cruces has a growing season 2 months longer with nearly twice as many days above 86 degrees Fahrenheit as Farmington has.

Cold-hardiness zones based on potentially lowest temperatures are difficult to apply to New Mexico because there may be episodes of -20 degrees Fahrenheit that last only a few hours and occur only once in a decade. This unpredictability affects plants much differently than would a routine occurrence or longer spells of comparable cold. Whether a cold snap comes in early November, when plants are just entering dormancy, or in mid-January, when they are well and truly numb to cold, also makes a world of difference. Some perennials that suffer in winter in the warmer desert areas breeze through winter where there is an insulating blanket of snow during the coldest weather. Conversely, since moist air absorbs heat from plant tissues more quickly than dry air does, our dry cold has less physical effect on plants than the same degree of cold in wetter climates. Still, many Mediterranean plants can take the ultimate high and low temperatures of central and southern New Mexico, but they just can't tolerate the occasional 70-degree shifts within a span of a few hours.

To survive anywhere in our state, plants need at the very least to adapt to 40-degree swings in daily temperatures. The lack of substantial cloud cover and a humidity level that is commonly less than 25 percent at 5 p.m. cause heat to dissipate quickly at night. In summer, this rapid cooling makes life after sundown a refreshing reward for having endured the day's heat. In spring and autumn, it may sound a death knell for plants that can't make the transition.

THE LAY OF THE LAND

New Mexico is divided roughly in half north to south by the tail end of the Rocky Mountains. Our Sangre de Cristo, Sandia, Manzano, Oscura, Capitan, Sacramento, and finally the southern-most Guadalupe Mountains keep most of the severe winter Arctic storms that barrel down the east face of the Rockies out on New Mexico's eastern plains. The mountains also act as a barrier to summer thunderstorms generated by dying hurricanes in the Gulf of Mexico. Storms drop most of their moisture on the plains and east slopes of the mountains, making them lush and green compared with the sun-baked west slopes. As a result, towns on New Mexico's east plains, the southernmost extent of the Great Plains shortgrass prairie, average nearly double the precipitation of communities west of the mountains.

The northwestern quadrant of the state is the edge of the arid Colorado Plateau, a plains area of quite a different nature. Eroding slick-rock sandstone mesas and looming volcanic chimneys lie in the rain shadow of the Rockies on the east and the Cascades and Sierra Nevadas further west. The moisture from both summer and winter storms falls in the mountains. What remains are the howling winds that shape the high plateau desert landscape. The Navajo Nation occupies much of this area; Farmington, Gallup, and Grants are the largest Plateau towns.

The communities nestled in the northern, central, and southern mountains easily capture the most rain and nearly all the snow that falls on New Mexico. Taos, Santa Fe, and Ruidoso are all communities at 7000-ft. elevation, but because latitude and altitude are not the only variables in our climatic mosaic, there is a dramatic difference in the moisture they receive. The height of the surrounding mountain peaks and east- or west-slope exposure influences both daytime temperature and annual precipitation. Taos is sheltered by taller peaks that capture more of the moisture from storms, so it is the driest of the three, even though it is the furthest north. Ruidoso is surrounded by old weathered peaks that share the wealth of rain and snow more generously, so even though it is farthest south it has the shortest growing season and can be twice as wet. Santa Fe occupies a southwest-facing slope, capturing a long day of sun even in winter. Moreover, the cold drains downslope and pools in the basin below the city where the growing season may be a few weeks shorter than it is in Santa Fe itself.

The northernmost expanse of Chihuahuan Desert covers central, southern, and western New Mexico. This desert is also a result of

Introduction

the rain shadow effect of mountains. Only the most powerful tropical storms from the Pacific are able to breach the barrier of the Mexican Sierra Madres. The southwest bootheel of New Mexico receives the benefit of Pacific storms first. Those of us in the central desert are further shielded by the Black Range as well as the San Mateo and Magdalena Mountains, so we tend to be drier still. Likewise, only the most moisture-laden Gulf Coast hurricanes surmount our southern Rockies to dampen the desert beyond. Most precipitation falls in summer as brief torrential thunderstorms, but there are usually a few episodes of Arctic lows pushing south to collide with Gulf moisture streaming north. This leaves a dusting of snow a few times each winter, even in the low elevations.

Though similar in elevation, Silver City in the foothills of the southern Gila Mountains receives nearly twice as much rain as Albuquerque in north central New Mexico. Albuquerque, 70 miles north of the limits of true Chihuahuan Desert, is the state's largest urban area. With its concentration of buildings and paving, the city has become a heat island with a climate more typical of the desert a few hundred miles to the south. The other dramatic example of climate-altering human development is Truth or Consequences, which enjoys the longest frost-free season in the state because of its proximity to Elephant Butte Lake. This lake was a flood control and irrigation project that, when completed in 1916, was the largest manmade lake in the United States. Forty miles long with 200 miles of shoreline, the lake absorbs enough heat in the summer to lengthen the growing season by nearly a month compared to Las Cruces and El Paso, 75 and 115 miles south respectively. (Although El Paso is technically in Texas, we tend to annex it horticulturally because its gardeners are so friendly and we share a similar climate. Because it is downstream along the Rio Grande, El Paso also shares some of the same water with us.)

DIRTY TRICKS: COPING WITH NEW MEXICO SOILS
Given this rumpled canvas as the backdrop, there are some general conditions that apply fairly broadly to the whole of New Mexico. Because of the pervasive dryness and intense sunlight, soils lack organic matter. The subsoil is variably porous bedrock of volcanic

origin, the limestone and sandstone of ancient seas, or granite upthrusts from the time the mountains were formed. The topsoil is the eroded, decomposed granite, sands, and clay that wind and water have deposited for our garden beds. Topsoil, in the rich, loamy, organic gardening sense of the word, materializes only after years of consistent effort on the part of gardeners. New Mexico soils are rich in calcium and other minerals, and moderately to strongly alkaline because there isn't enough rainfall to leach out mineral salts or to break down organic matter that would mellow mineral concentrations. Even in areas above 10,000 ft. where rain and snow consistently contribute more than 20 in. of moisture and a mantle of conifer forest adds a litter of needles, the subsoil usually has a pH of 6.5, though the top 12 in. may be slightly more acidic. The strong light intensity and UV exposure at high altitudes destroy organic matter before microbes can make it into earth, so regardless of elevation, climatic conditions conspire to keep soils high in pH and low in humus.

Many of the plants profiled in this book are described as preferring well-drained soil. Plant roots require oxygen as well as water to thrive, and good drainage is the healthful balance of moisture and air in the soil.

In foothills areas, the soil is usually either fairly coarse, decomposed granite or cement-like limestone silt; both are well-drained soils unless overirrigated. Coarse, sandy soils and fine, silty sand make up the broad plains that dominate the middle elevations. Sands absorb water quickly and also lose it rapidly to evaporation. Immediately after rain or irrigation, water fills the pore space in the soil. As plants absorb moisture and evaporation dries the soil surface, the water that is wicked away is replaced with air, restoring the soil's oxygen balance.

Drought-adapted plants, having evolved in a climate where rain is infrequent but liable to fall in torrents when it finally comes, require definite cycles of irrigation and aeration. When soil pore spaces are consistently filled with water or have been compressed mechanically by being driven over during construction, oxygen levels in the soil become too low to support root growth. New transplants fail to root out and the roots of established plants die off, causing the plants to decline.

Calcium carbonate *caliche* is common in New Mexico soils, and interferes with drainage only when it is compacted. *Caliche* hardpans form naturally where looser topsoil accumulates on top of less-permeable subsoil. Such subsoil occurs where a layer of sandy soil caps a subsurface of basalt laid down by volcanoes a thousand years ago, or where eroding decomposed granite buries huge subsurface slabs of solid rock. Water filters through the looser surface soil and pools on top of the rocky subsoil, eventually forming a crust of calcium carbonate that slows the penetration of water even more. Hardpans can also develop in gardens if the soil is not allowed to dry between waterings, and if water is applied shallowly, compressing soil particles and fertilizer salts into an impermeable layer. Gardeners have few options in dealing with hardpan. If it exists naturally, break through it as much as possible, and grow plants that will adapt. Prevent hardpans from developing by applying water slowly so it penetrates at a rate the soil can absorb. Water as deeply as needed to satisfy the plants, and occasionally water beyond the root zone to flush accumulating salts.

In the bottomlands, soils are usually a mixture of coarse sugar sand and heavy clay. Because the soil was laid down over centuries as rivers changed course and meandered across the floodplain, clay and sand deposits are often layered on top of and ribboned alongside each other. Clay is the most difficult soil to garden because it absorbs water slowly and stays sticky-wet too long for many plants. As it dries, clay reaches a stage where it rewets itself by pulling moisture from the plants growing in it. It is difficult to know when to water because while the clay still feels damp, plants may begin to wilt from reverse osmosis. When it dries, clay cracks open; this is nature's way of aerating poorly drained desert soil. The surge of air into the cracked soil also dries out the roots of plants not adapted to this radical regime. To add insult to injury, concentrations of salt crust collect on the surface where the clay drains most slowly, making gardening nearly impossible. Thoroughly mixing gypsum into tight saline clay will cause the fine clay particles to clump together so that water can be used to flush the salts below the root

zone of garden plants. Mulches help by reducing surface evaporation, thus slowing the rise of salts by capillary action.

Working copious amounts of organic matter into heavy clay soil
is one of the best ways to make clay soil a fit medium for gardening. Humus improves the drainage of clay enough to greatly
increase the variety of plants that will grow well, though not
enough to suit plants that require high levels of soil oxygen.

Soil testing and amending assume that you need to alter existing
conditions. The results of a soil test will confirm what you may
already suspect: the soil is alkaline, and it lacks organic matter and
nitrogen. The supplement recommendations you receive with soil
test results are usually based on the needs of garden plants from
more-temperate climates: vegetable crops, lawns, and perhaps roses.
The many plants that are adapted to dry climates and are now
available for use in water-conservative landscapes have not evolved
to grow in richly organic soils. How much of your garden soil will
require a major overhaul depends on the plants you choose to grow.
There is a range of adaptation within the palette of xeric plants. At
the arid end of the spectrum, drought-requiring plants are the camels
of horticulture; they have evolved in the most extreme conditions of
intense sunlight, heat, and wind, which rapidly evaporate what little moisture may be available. These chronic xerics will decline in
soils enriched with organic matter because compost releases carbon
dioxide as it breaks down, displacing the oxygen these plants
require. Just as too much water in the soil can deprive drought-
adapted plants of oxygen, too much organic matter can be harmful
to plants that have evolved to thrive in gritty, mineral-rich soils.

Plants adapted to more consistently moist conditions are at the
opposite end of the xeric spectrum. These are plants native to the
wetter areas in arid climates, such as canyon bottoms and high
mountain meadows; or to the transitional areas between desert and
temperate climates, such as prairies and savannas. In gardens, these
plants readily adapt to soil amended with compost. The rich humus
acts as a sponge, absorbing whatever moisture is available. Plants of
this type also benefit from deep mulching, which prevents the rapid
evaporation that can kill their network of fine absorbing roots. As
you read through the plant profiles you will find the chorus of a

song that goes "dig generous holes, only as deep as the rootball, but several times its diameter . . ." The verses that follow will tell you which plants prefer amended soil and which require only that the existing soil be loosened well. I hope that the "dig generous holes" refrain echoes through your mind as you work the soil, urging you to chip away a little further. This is hard work! Your plants will thank you with vigorous roots that will make you both look good. There are also variations on the theme of mulching, because some plants prefer a fibrous mulch that stays cooler on the surface, while other plants need the aeration or flood resistance of gravels.

JUST ADD WATER

Whether you are gardening on a blank canvas scraped bare for construction or renovating an older garden, it helps to think of the whole garden as a series of plant combinations intended to look good and grow well together. Within the garden, plant groupings fit together like the interlocking pieces of a puzzle. While each grouping has its own focus, shared elements such as the type of paving used, the repetition of silver foliage, or variations of a flower color woven through all the spaces will unify the whole.

Garden spaces also sort themselves out according to how they are used. Where shade is needed, the planting might be dominated by a tree or grove of small trees. Trees that are thirstier and more shallowly rooted will need moisture-tolerant groundcovers within their root zones. These groundcovers will create moist soil pockets that the young transplants can extend roots into as they grow. Mature, shallowly rooted trees require moisture-loving groundcovers planted at the perimeter of the tree canopy, where the trees' absorbing roots are most likely concentrated. The most drought-tolerant trees need companions that will thrive with reduced watering once all plants are established. Compatible evergreen and deciduous shrubs may be clustered to provide privacy or wind protection, to create a warm winter microclimate, or to frame a distant view.

An overall plan emerges from matching plants to the places they're needed. The outdoor living and play spaces—lawns, shade trees, patios, and front entryway gardens—are oases in the garden. They are the most densely planted, may be the most colorful, and

Introduction

will require the most water to maintain. Surrounding the living spaces are plant groupings nearly as lush that provide privacy and wind protection. The driest zones are usually the perimeter spaces where the priority is either to blend into the surrounding native ecosystem (if you live out of town) or to beautify the space while minimizing weeds (if you garden in the city). The USDA Zones for hardiness and the relative water ratings of low, moderate, or ample are general indications of compatibility. Suggestions for the depth and frequency of watering once plants are well established are also given to make it easier to choose suitable companions. The maintenance watering recommendations are keyed to temperature to help adjust for altitude, since the same plant will use less water in cooler, high-elevation gardens than it does in the hot low-desert areas.

The amount of water new transplants require may vary tremendously depending on the weather, the size of the plant, and the type of soil. Spring winds are an element of our arid climate that can be part blessing and part curse. Unless small amounts of water are applied frequently to compensate, wind will quickly dry the soil and wither tender, emerging leaves. When temperatures drop, however, wind mixes the air, preventing damaging late frosts in low pockets in the garden. Wind also picks up loose, sandy soil and sandblasts soft new growth to pulp. Using row covers, erosion fencing, and wind-resistant mulches around new plants that are not sheltered by garden walls or buffered by other plants will help reduce the damage. The rootballs of transplants should be damp at planting time, and water should initially be applied where the rootball meets the backfill so that both the existing roots and the soil they will extend into are kept moist. The quantity of water applied varies with the size of the plant. It is generally best to water so that moisture permeates the rootball and filters more deeply and laterally to encourage roots to extend downward as well as outward.

A rule of thumb for all but the most drought-loving plants is to keep the soil as evenly moist as possible while new transplants adjust to the garden and begin to root out. Water more frequently at first, especially in late spring through summer when surface moisture evaporates quickly in the heat. Make a gradual transition to deeper watering as new roots develop. The most heat- and drought-loving plants such as cactus, succulents, and many of the plants noted as low water users need benign neglect, even as new transplants. While their root zone should not dry out completely, they should be watered less often even when first planted. Ultimately, how often a plant needs water depends on a host of variables including the plant's stage of development, root mass, and overall vigor, as well as the soil type, exposure to wind, light intensity, the innate adaptation of the species, and the vigor of the individual plant. Irrigation systems may be as simple as a length of good-quality garden hose or as sophisticated as a multi-valve drip and sprinkler system with an automatic timer. No matter how water is delivered, it should be applied slowly so that it penetrates the soil without running off, and it should be limited to the amount really needed by the plants. Exactly when and how much to water is one of the most difficult gardening lessons to learn, and thoughtful observation of how plants respond is the best teacher.

WHY THESE PLANTS?

Like gardens, gardening books can include only so many plants. Culling, selecting the best of the best, is a trying chore for writer and gardener alike. What makes a plant worthy of words on the page or a place in the soil? My criteria for both is similar. Some plants are included for their all-around adaptability and near indestructibility. These are the easiest to grow under a variety of extremes and often become the framework of the garden. Other plants are valuable for their suitability for certain specific situations such as dry shade under trees, moist shade under canales (roof drains) and gutters along north- and east-facing walls, south-facing sunbaked sidewalk borders, and the seams between flagstone pavers or boulders. Some plants are noteworthy for their affinity for the colder, moister niches both in individual gardens and in northern and high-elevation locations of New Mexico. Other plants are included because they thrive in the hot, dry, south and west garden beds, and more generally on the mid-elevation central plains and desert mesas of the state. Some plants are valued for brief but spectacular blooming, while others are irresistible because they continue to flower through much of the growing season. To be at its finest, a garden needs a blend of textures and colors, evergreen foliage and sculptural forms, dazzling flower displays and serene leafy bowers.

Because of the high elevation and lack of cloud cover in New Mexico, some plants grown here require more shade than they do when grown in other places. I have provided symbols for the amount of sunlight suitable for each plant's growing requirements. The following symbols indicate full sun, partial shade, and shade.

Full Sun   Partial   Shade
Shade

Most of the plants described here prefer alkaline soil. If they don't all laugh in the face of our erratic weather, they at least smirk a bit at drought, heat, and cold. Given the harshness of our climate, it is surprising how many horticultural standards can be grown here if they are placed well. Many older landscapes that are being renovated to make them more up-to-date and water conservative have well-established firethorn, barberries, Washington hawthorn, blue spruce, rose-of-Sharon, and other good-quality plants that can be maintained as part of a new garden. I have included a tried and true sampling with caveats that might help you manage them more conservatively.

Some garden standards that have been widely grown in New Mexico have been passed over in favor of better adapted, less thirsty newcomers. For lawns, the newer fescue cultivars are more deeply rooted, heat tolerant, and disease resistant than bluegrass. Blue grama and buffalograss are a softer green, more in character with other arid-adapted ornamentals, and they are more water conservative still. Water demand isn't the only reason I abandon some old standbys. Coreopsis is host to powdery mildew, and since yellow-flowering perennials are a dime a dozen in our plant palette, why cultivate an ongoing problem? A similar situation exists with *Euonymous* and scale insects, though well-adapted broadleafed evergreens are not as easily replaced.

Pest problems are often related to planting too many individuals of too few species and the environmental stresses that result, particularly when the species are poorly adapted. Sycamore trees have been planted heavily in Albuquerque, and why not? They are long-lived giants that give generous shade. My affection for sycamores is rooted in the majesty of their massive forms and their beautiful bark. Yet the Albuquerque sycamore forest is under attack by several pests including scale, bagworm, and horntail borer; and sycamore decline actually begins when adolescent trees need to extend their roots to support their growing canopies and find only hard dry soil beyond their planting holes. Because their needs far exceed what the average urban planting space can provide, they are doomed to suffer. Tortured trees first show signs of distress in the form of burnt leaf margins and chlorosis, which soon progress to dieback in the canopy. None of us intends our garden to be a haven for pestilence, but nature doesn't take such a parochial view. Ailing plants are valuable hosts for insects and disease microorganisms that exist to turn ill-adapted species into food for better-suited ones. Life goes on, and our gardens evolve to meet practical limitations and changing tastes.

It takes living with plants to really know them, and we all experience attitude adjustments regarding the planting choices we have made over the years. Reassessing those choices may mean removing plants when they become liabilities. One of the things I enjoy about writing on a word processor is the delete key. If only it were as easy to eliminate bad ideas in the garden!

DIVERGING GARDEN PATHS: NEW MEXICO STYLE

Gardening is ultimately about beauty, and realizing the need to conserve water in New Mexico has led us to begin to cultivate many styles of beauty as we diversify the garden palette. Instead of working so hard to change the desert to suit plants from wetter climates, we're being selective and gardening with the many plants that meet us halfway. I walked out our back door today and continued on into the desert. Small birds twittered nervously in the denser tree and shrub planting at the heart of the garden as a hawk rode the thermals above. The dialogue between the huge flocks of cranes and geese wintering along the Rio Grande reached me in breaking waves from two miles away. After a while I turned to look back home, and saw that the mountains had disappeared under charcoal-colored clouds. Our garden was still in sunlight, the grasses and

Introduction

sage pale against the dark sky. The trees glowed copper and gold, and the hawk continued its lazy circles. Odds are that when the clouds disappear, the ridges will be white with snow. Other days I've taken this same path and turned to see a double rainbow arched across our garden, the desert soft green and fragrant after rain. I continue to feel very small in this landscape, but now I savor the sensation. It's liberating to tend a garden of plants that respond to my gesture of occasional watering with brilliant flowers, nectar for butterflies, and seeds for songbirds. I will always be in awe of the sweep of the New Mexico landscape, and my garden flourishes since I have learned to compromise, to cultivate plants that want to be here as much as I do.

Surrounded by desert, I have chosen to live in a garden that looks deceptively wild: native shrubs and wildflowers mingle with Mediterranean herbs and trees from China and Russia. City gardeners might cultivate many of the same plants, avoiding the rampant rooters that help bind the dunes in my garden but are potential weeds in their more confined spaces. City gardeners might also choose to prune more than I do. Their motive might be to limit reseeding, to satisfy a need for control, or to fit more plants into the space. Wild-looking isn't the same as wild, however, and many of the native plants described in the profiles are quite self-contained. Shadscale, blackfoot daisy, desert sage, creeping dalea, and algerita look controlled with very little effort on our part, while some of the shrub roses and climbers will grow quite wild unless they are reined in periodically. There is also a distinction to be made between xeriscapes and desert gardens. Water-efficient xeric plants can be used lavishly or with great restraint to create any number of garden styles. Desert gardens are inspired by natural, arid ecosystems; they may be stark and austere or have the filmy translucence of a mirage, but they are obviously dry places. We can choose to celebrate the desert or temper it a bit, or do both in different parts of the garden. Our gardens are dynamic mirrors of our evolving relationship to our world. We can make lush oases that use surprisingly little water, or pay tribute to the prairie with a dramatic sweep of ornamental grasses. We can build a rock garden that makes us feel 10,000 feet high, or plant a soothing meditation garden that draws us inward. Isn't it this wealth of possibility that keeps us growing?

CHAPTER ONE

Annuals and Biennials

*B*Y THEIR NATURE, ANNUALS AND BIENNIALS ARE
THE MOST TEMPORARY elements of any garden design.
Their short but merry life allows them to be generous with their color.

Annuals germinate, bloom, and set seeds all in one growing
season. Their seeds often have a strong preference for certain temperatures. The warming of soil to temperatures in the mid-fifties can
trigger the sprouting of many species, but some seeds sprout when
the soil has warmed only a bit above freezing, while others don't stir
until the soil is a toasty 70 degrees Fahrenheit or warmer.

Biennials are plants that usually take two years to flower from
seed. Their seedlings are genetically programmed to require a certain
number of hours of light and darkness as well as a certain amount
of cold before they set flower buds. The seeds sprout and a rosette
of leaves develops, but biennials bloom only after they have been
primed by light, dark, and cold. Biennials sown early in fall to allow
seed to germinate and the rosette of leaves to form before the onset
of winter cold will bloom the following spring or summer.

In extreme climates like that of New Mexico, wildflowers adopt
a strategy of holding out for the most opportune conditions before
expending their energy. Seeds germinate when seedlings have the
best chance of finding enough moisture to root extensively. They
then flower when they have the roots to support the effort.

Ecologically, annuals and biennials are the healers of the Earth's
minor and major catastrophes. Whenever there is significant soil
disturbance, annuals and biennials are the pioneers that move in
and repair the damage. Unfortunately for gardeners, many of these
storm troopers are weeds. Though we do not till the soil on their
behalf, weeds often take advantage of the work we do for more
highly regarded plants.

In gardens, annuals and biennials fill seasonal niches. Some come
on strong as soon as hard freezes ebb in spring, continuing until

heat triggers a push for seed production. Others need heat to begin flowering and wane as nights grow longer at summer's end. Still others provide a blaze of late-season glory and bloom in late summer until frost triggers their rush to seed. Plant profiles give the specific temperature preferences that determine the best planting times for each plant.

Soil preparation is the basis of strong color display, whether it means loosening the soil so that new roots can easily gain ground, or tilling compost into the bed to satisfy the needs of less desert-adapted plants. In dry climates like that of New Mexico, seeds sown right where plants are to grow develop extensive roots uninterrupted by transplanting, creating plants that flower with greater abandon.

New gardeners sometimes lack the confidence to start from scratch, and even those of us who live in our gardens cannot resist a display of blooming plants in the nursery. Sometimes a bit of indulgence is worth the price. Tender perennials that we grow as annuals may take so long to develop from seed to flowering that our frost cuts them down just as they reach their most colorful. Purchasing robust plants that have not yet begun to flower is a good compromise between immediate gratification and giving the plants time to grow the roots needed to support a long and colorful bloom phase.

No matter where in New Mexico you garden, the soil should have a moisture reserve that penetrates a foot below the surface before planting. After a dry winter, it may take a few waterings to build up an adequate reservoir.

Annuals and biennials that need organically amended garden soil will also need fertilizing to sustain a long color season. Blood meal, kelp, fish emulsion, four-month time-release formulas, and granular fertilizers are all useful. The organic sources promote long-term soil health, while chemical sources yield fast temporary results. Granular fertilizers need to be dosed carefully to avoid burning tender roots and creating a salt buildup in the soil. The most desert-adapted annuals and biennials will grow well without fertilizer in unamended soil. Too much additional fertilizer is likely to produce abundant foliage instead of flowers.

African Daisy

Dimorphotheca sinuata

Height: 12 in.
Color: Yellow, apricot, orange, or white
Bloom Period: April to August
Water: Moderate to low

Light Requirement:

*T*his South African native likes warmth and comes on strong when the soil warms up in spring. Plants spread at least as wide as they grow tall. In bloom for several months, their 2-in. daisies appear in pastel shades of yellow, apricot, orange, and white and have contrasting dark eyes that seem to shimmer above the mound of narrow leaves. The satiny petals fold up at night and on cloudy days. If African daisy likes where it is growing, it tends to naturalize. Though it doesn't always stay exactly where it was originally planted, it is not an aggressive threat to local wildflowers—our relatively cold winters and persistent periods of drought limit self-sowing to warm niches in the garden where a bit of extra water is available.

WHEN TO PLANT
Warm soil temperature induces seeds to sprout, so sow the seeds in early spring. Transplant greenhouse-grown plants after all chance of frost has passed.

WHERE TO PLANT
African daisy will grow best in light, well-drained, alkaline soil that is low in organic matter. It prefers places that grow warm early in spring. It makes a great filler for those groundcovers (such as cotoneaster and creeping dalea) that take a few years to fill in. In new gardens where the shade of young trees doesn't cover much ground, watering drifts of African daisy at the perimeter of the tree root zone creates a moist soil area for tree roots to extend into. As the shade canopy expands, a shade-tolerant annual such as pansy or a perennial such as dwarf plumbago can replace the daisies.

HOW TO PLANT
There are about 15,000 seeds per oz., and 1 oz. seed raked 1/2 in. deep into 150 to 200 sq. ft. of tilled soil will give a strong showing. Seeds take 2 weeks to a month to sprout when the temperature is in

the preferred 60- to 70-degree Fahrenheit range. Because seeds take a while to sprout, African daisy is often transplanted from containers. Combining seeds and transplants not only gives those of us who can't wait faster results, but the seeded plants will prolong the show after the transplants have faded in the heat. Loosen the soil well in the area to be planted. Rake the seeds into the soil, then set out clusters of started plants 12 to 24 in. apart in the seeded area. Water well to settle the soil around the seeds and roots.

ADVICE FOR CARE

Keep the seedbed damp until seeds germinate; then begin gradually to water more deeply and less often to encourage the seedlings to root more extensively. While the plants are in bloom, water to a depth of 18 to 24 in. only as often as it takes to keep plants vigorous. Cultivating the soil before planting exposes weed seeds to light, inducing them to sprout; water provided for the daisies also encourages the weeds to grow. Pull weeds from the seedbed when they are very small so that they don't steal moisture from the daisies. Waiting until weeds have developed extensive roots before pulling them disturbs more soil and exposes new weed seed to light, starting the cycle again. Many tender young seedlings look similar enough to make weeding a confusing chore. If you're not sure which seedlings are weeds, take samples to your favorite nursery and get them identified. No gardening professional will find your questions silly— we've all pulled up enough of the wrong plants during our gardening careers to appreciate your efforts to avoid doing the same.

SPECIES, CULTIVARS, OR VARIETIES

'Glistening White' African daisy (*Dimorphotheca pluvialis*) is a brilliant all-white variety.

REGIONAL CONSIDERATIONS

In southern New Mexico, African daisy may bloom as early as March and continue through May; in the northern part of the state, it may not begin to bloom until May and will continue blooming throughout the summer.

California Poppy

Eschscholzia californica

Height: 12 in. **Color:** Orange **Bloom Period:** Mostly spring **Water:** Low to moderate	**Light Requirement:**

*A*native wildflower from warmer areas in the Southwest, California poppy begins as a rosette of delicate blue-green leaves. New seedlings are incredibly cold tolerant, surviving brief temperature drops to well below zero as long as the soil is not too wet. While the weather is cool, the lacy leaves develop into a vigorous clump 12 to 18 in. across, and as spring arrives, the cup-shaped orange flowers burst into bloom. Slender seedpods form with the onset of hot weather. California poppy is listed as an annual, biennial, or short-lived perennial, depending on when and where it is planted. As an annual with one long season of color and the likelihood of reseeding, this plant is a winner for New Mexican gardens.

WHEN TO PLANT

Because seedlings usually need a period of cold in order to bloom abundantly, it is best to sow seed in either autumn or late winter. Seeds that don't sprout within a few weeks of fall sowing may germinate early in spring. Greenhouse-grown seedlings can be set out in spring for an instant show, but they generally won't be as vigorous as those sown where they are to grow in the garden.

WHERE TO PLANT

California poppy adapts to most soils in full sun and can be sown in drifts in a prairie planting or used as a filler for early color in perennial beds. Mixed with blue flax, it's a great way to celebrate the arrival of spring. California poppy does well in the light shade of acacia, mesquite, or desert willow, but too much shade will limit blooming. The flowers also close at night and on cloudy days.

HOW TO PLANT

Scratch the small round seeds into premoistened loosened soil: 1/2 oz. seed covers 100 sq. ft. of bed or prairie. Transplant container-grown plants 10 to 18 in. apart, watering thoroughly to settle the soil around the roots.

ADVICE FOR CARE

Because its seed germinates in cool weather, California poppy can be established with occasional watering. Several good soakings while they are in bloom may be necessary to keep the plants productive; removing the seedpods as they form will also ensure a longer bloom period. To encourage reseeding, let seedpods form toward the end of the season. In sandy or gravelly soil, seeds may find a niche in the soil and establish new plants. Where the soil is heavier or compacted on the surface, light tilling or raking in the seeds will help continue the cycle. Cultivating the soil before planting exposes weed seeds to light, inducing them to sprout; water provided for the poppies also encourages the weeds to grow. Weed the seedbed when weeds are small so that they don't steal moisture from the poppies. Waiting until weeds have developed extensive roots before pulling them exposes more weed seed to light, starting the cycle all over again. California poppy seedlings look very much like the winter annual mustard weeds, so be sure you're removing unwanted plants, not the poppies themselves.

SPECIES, CULTIVARS, OR VARIETIES

In February and March, Mexican gold poppy (*Eschscholzia mexicana*) covers acres of hillsides in southern New Mexico, especially in years of ample winter and early spring rain. Its flowers are smaller and bright yellow-gold rather than orange, but its garden virtues are the same as those of its western cousin. Several cultivars of California poppy are available in various shades of orange, some with semidouble flowers, but none seem as reliable as the species.

Cosmos

Cosmos bipinnatus

Height: 3 to 4 ft.
Color: Pink, rose, burgundy, or white
Bloom Period: Midsummer to autumn
Water: Moderate

Light Requirement:

*C*osmos is a Mexican wildflower made bigger, brighter, and bolder by plant breeders' careful selection. The fine spring-green foliage grows tall to support the flowers that have 2- to 3-in.-wide petals in shades of pink. The combination of sturdy stems and large open-faced flowers attracts butterflies, and the feathery leaves are a perfect foil for the cheerful flowers. Cosmos cuts well for bouquets if stems with newly opened buds are harvested early in the morning. The unpretentious flowers of cosmos against an adobe wall or weathered peeled-post coyote fence embodies the charm of New Mexico.

WHEN TO PLANT

Sow in spring after all chance of frost is past and soil temperatures are in the 65- to 80-degree Fahrenheit range. Seeds take only a week or so to germinate, and plants bloom 2 to 3 months later. Potted seedlings can be set out in late spring, but undisturbed seedlings are much more vigorous.

WHERE TO PLANT

Cosmos is not fussy about soil, but tilling compost into the seedbed, especially in sandy or gravelly soils, improves water retention and produces lusher, more colorful plants. Cosmos can be used as a filler for roses, dwarf butterfly bush, or evergreen shrubs; as a border along fences; and as a backdrop for perennial beds. If the only vegetables you grow are a few tomato plants each year, cosmos makes a good alternating crop to help prevent wilt diseases in the tomatoes.

HOW TO PLANT

Be moderate when amending the soil with compost, since too rich a soil or too much nitrogen fertilizer will produce abundant foliage and few flowers. Till the soil thoroughly so that new roots will have an easy time gaining ground. 1 oz. seed covers 150 to 200 sq. ft. For stronger plants, thin seedlings to a foot or more apart.

ADVICE FOR CARE
Cosmos may need watering deeply once a week while budding and in bloom. Cultivating the soil before planting exposes weed seeds to light, inducing them to sprout; water provided for the cosmos also encourages the weeds to grow. Pull weeds from the seedbed when they are very small so they won't steal moisture from the cosmos. Rooting weeds out early disturbs the soil less; waiting until weeds have developed extensive roots before pulling them exposes more weed seed to light, starting the cycle all over again. Once the cosmos is thinned to a foot apart and about a foot tall, adding a mulch of grass clippings or fine bark will help suppress weeds. Pulling spent plants up after frost and shaking the seed around will help cosmos self-sow, though usually not well enough to forego a planned annual seeding in spring.

SPECIES, CULTIVARS, OR VARIETIES
'Sonata Dwarf' is shorter with stouter stems and rose-pink or white flowers; it is a good choice for very windy sites. *Cosmos sulphureus* hybrids come in a range of single, double, and semi-double flowers in red, orange, or gold on 3-ft.-tall plants with coarser, dark-green foliage. 'Sunny Red' is a dwarf cultivar with vermilion blooms on 12-in. stems.

Cowpen Daisy

Verbesina encelioides

	Light Requirement:
Height: 1 to 4 ft. **Color:** Yellow **Bloom Period:** July to October **Water:** Low to moderate	

*T*his summer-blooming member of the large clan of native yellow daisies gets its name from its tendency to colonize corrals. It also grows along roadsides and fence rows where the soil is disturbed seasonally and extra moisture is likely to accumulate. The lower portions of the stems are hidden by triangular gray-green leaves 2 to 4 in. long and half as wide. The flower stalks are leafless with one flower per stem. Blooms are 1 in. in diameter, and both the toothed ray petals and the discs are yellow. Cowpen daisy begins to show color in July, but it is most impressive in late summer when it has reached its maximum size and forms a mass of golden flowers. Early settlers used a tea brewed from the leaves to relieve insect bites.

WHEN TO PLANT

Sow seed in fall or in early spring while the soil is still cool.

WHERE TO PLANT

Cowpen daisy is not fussy about soils and is undemanding when it comes to watering. It can get out of hand when cultivated in good garden soil. Coarse and a bit rangy, it is at its best in naturalized areas. Mix it into shrub borders for summer color among sumacs, Apache plume, fernbush, vitex, and junipers. Songbirds harvest the seeds, and when mixed with grasses such as sand lovegrass, little bluestem, and sideoats grama, cowpen daisy provides a colorful way to reclaim roadsides, septic leach fields, and drainage swales.

HOW TO PLANT

1 oz. seed will cover 200 sq. ft. of tilled soil. Rake the seeds in to a depth of 1/2 in. and tamp the surface lightly. If winter is unusually dry and seeds sown in fall don't sprout, scratch up the area with a rake and water deeply a few times before reseeding in spring. The moisture and disturbance may stimulate dormant seeds to sprout.

ADVICE FOR CARE

Cultivating the soil before planting will expose weed seeds to light, inducing them to sprout; water provided for the daisies also encourages the weeds to grow. Pull weeds from the seedbed when they are very small so they won't steal moisture from the daisies. Rooting weeds out early will disturb the soil less; waiting until weeds have developed extensive roots before pulling them will expose more weed seed to light, starting the cycle again. Many tender young seedlings look similar enough to make weeding a confusing chore. If you're not sure which seedlings are weeds, take samples to your favorite nursery and get them identified. Once cowpen daisy is a foot tall, it is usually strong enough to hold its own among weeds. Mow down the frost-killed stalks with a brush mower or hard-bladed string line trimmer after the birds have cleaned up the seeds. If the litter is left as mulch, a reseeding stand of cowpen daisy may develop with no other effort. If the stalks are cleared away, you may need to lightly till and reseed each spring. Sometimes tilling alone will aerate the soil and induce dormant seeds to sprout.

SPECIES, CULTIVARS, OR VARIETIES

There are no other species in cultivation.

REGIONAL CONSIDERATIONS

Cowpen daisy thrives with no extra watering at northern elevations of 7000 ft. and on the eastern plains of New Mexico where annual rainfall is 14 in. or more. Plants growing along a driveway, road, or along a drainage channel may harvest enough runoff to be self-sufficient. Occasional deep watering will be necessary in hotter, drier locations, especially when the plants start to flower.

ANNUALS AND BIENNIALS

Creeping Zinnia

Sanvitalia procumbens

Height: 4 to 6 in.	**Light Requirement:**
Color: Yellow or orange	
Bloom Period: Summer to frost	
Water: Low to moderate	

Creeping zinnia is an undemanding little plant, naturally trim and tidy looking, and willing to bloom for months if given any encouragement at all. Native in Mexico, where it has crept into gardens from the roadsides and is invited to stay, creeping zinnia brightens the gaps between paving stones and tumbles over the edges of stone walls. Plants grow as a trailing carpet of thin stems spreading 18 in. across the sun-baked soil. The mat of small, green, oval leaves is dotted with small, 1/2-in. daisies that have orange or yellow rays and dark-purple centers. Heat seems to be this plant's growing impetus, and it will even grow well in pots as long as it is watered regularly. Though creeping zinnia is recommended for draping from hanging baskets, New Mexico's incessant wind makes hanging baskets a bit of a hazard except when they are tied up securely in enclosed courtyards.

WHEN TO PLANT
Sow outdoors in spring as soon as frost is past.

WHERE TO PLANT
Creeping zinnia prefers well-drained soil. It will adapt to alkaline clay as long as it is not kept too wet, but it will be slower to fill in and may not self-sow. A great filler between boulders or flagstones, creeping zinnia is also used as a living mulch at the base of shrubs, especially in new gardens where it adds color and a lush feeling until shrubs get established.

HOW TO PLANT
Seeds are small (50,000 per oz.) and require light to germinate, so they should be pressed onto the surface of loosened soil. Germination takes a week or two when the soil temperature is 70 degrees Fahrenheit.

ADVICE FOR CARE

Though well suited to heat and drought, creeping zinnia makes a more attractive garden plant if it is watered occasionally. Once established, the plants cover densely enough to exclude most annual weeds, but initial weeding will be necessary. The cultivating done to prepare the soil for planting exposes weed seeds to light and induces them to sprout. Remove weeds while they are small so that they will have little opportunity to establish extensive roots or shade out the low-lying zinnia. Weed seedlings have an uncanny way of blending with desirable seedlings like secret agents in a suspense thriller; garden professionals at your favorite nursery or the local County Extension Service can help you sort the "good guys" from the "bad guys."

SPECIES, CULTIVARS, OR VARIETIES

'Mandarin Orange' has bright-orange flowers and is a bit more mounded, growing 8 in. tall and twice as wide. 'Golden Carpet' has tiny pumpkin-yellow flowers, and 'Yellow Carpet' is lemon yellow. Most true zinnias are extremely susceptible to mildew, but cultivars of *Zinnia angustifolia*, also sold as *Zinnia linearis*, are disease free and very prolific. 'Crystal White' has white daisies with golden eyes on plants 5 in. tall and 10 in. wide; 'Star Gold' has yellow flowers with fewer ray petals; the flowers of 'Golden Orange' are pumpkin yellow. All bloom in 6 to 8 weeks from small seeds (70,000 per oz.) sown when the soil is 70 degrees Fahrenheit.

REGIONAL CONSIDERATIONS

Because of its heat-loving nature, creeping zinnia does best at lower elevations and in the south and central areas of New Mexico.

Desert Marigold

Baileya multiradiata

Height: 12 to 18 in.
Color: Yellow
Bloom Period: All seasons except winter
Water: Low

Light Requirement:

One of New Mexico's most garden-worthy wildflowers, desert marigold starts life as a small rosette of woolly white leaves. After a period of cold (vernalization) that is necessary to set the buds, the basal leaf cluster enlarges to a tidy 8 or 10 in., and sturdy down-covered stems emerge, each stem topped with 1-in.-diameter semidouble daisies. The petals and discs make a brilliant yellow contrast to the silver leaves and stems. Within a few weeks the plant develops from a low rosette to a bright mound of color, and will continue to bloom for months with occasional rain or watering. Since plants usually grow in large groups and reseed well once a seed source is established, desert marigold can become a lovely low-water, low-maintenance filler. A couple of avid gardeners once told me that they credit their dogs with developing the beautiful dense planting of desert marigold that covers nearly an acre of sunny space between the trees in their valley garden. The dogs like to chase the sulfur butterflies that visit the flowers, and while running through the plants they scuff up the soil, shake ripe seeds loose, and push them into the surface in one fun and easy operation. Of course my gardening friends weed out any undesirable plants that encroach on the scene, but because so little water is needed for the desert marigold, not many weeds find it hospitable.

WHEN TO PLANT

Sow seeds any time from autumn to early spring. Seedlings started in autumn will bloom the following spring, while spring seedlings may not bloom until late summer. Transplant container-grown plants in mid-spring.

WHERE TO PLANT

Desert marigold is best adapted to loose sandy or gravelly soil, but it will grow in most soils if not kept too wet. It can be used as a filler in xeric flower borders with torch lily, Russian sage, and gayfeather, or between desert shrubs such as Texas sage, creosotebush, fairy duster, and shadscale. Desert marigold usually won't persist very long in a dense planting of prairie grasses, but it can be used for color until the grasses fill in.

How to Plant
Loosen the soil and rake the seed lightly into the surface. 1 oz. seed will cover 500 to 1000 sq. ft. Occasional watering during cool weather will help germinate seeds. Infertile, gritty soils produce the best stands, so compost is recommended only if you are trying to lighten heavy clay. Container-grown plants can be set out 18 to 24 in. apart to establish an instant display, and though they won't flower as well as seedlings started in place, they may shed enough seeds to establish a colony.

Advice for Care
In the wild, flushes of bloom follow significant rainfalls. In gardens, the woolly leaves and stems don't respond well to regular overhead sprinkling, so watering should be done only occasionally. Transplants may be drip-irrigated, but since plants don't persist in the same place, new ones will have to be planted each year. After several hard freezes or a prolonged dry spell, the withered plants can be mowed off or pulled up. If plants are pulled, scattering seeds in the soil disturbed in the process will help develop a strong future display.

Species, Cultivars, or Varieties
There are no other species in cultivation.

Regional Considerations
In southern New Mexico, plants sometimes survive the winter after flowering and rebloom the following spring.

Gazania

Gazania splendens

Height: 6 to 12 in.	**Light Requirement:**
Color: Varies	
Bloom Period: Summer	
Water: Low to moderate	

*G*azanias are native to arid South Africa and have been part of the bedding plant scene for years, spawning many cultivars that are available each spring in a range of container sizes. Everything about this plant is appealing. The foliage is coarse enough to be interesting, but with its dark-green tops and silver undersides, it is still quite refined. Plants clump twice as wide as they grow tall. The large 3- to 4-in. flowers are held on stout leafless stems just beyond the leaves. Blooms come in a broad range of colors from creamy white to yellow, orange, red, mahogany, and shell pink. The flowers look individually painted; their petals resemble the fine plumage of a rare tropical bird.

WHEN TO PLANT
Transplant greenhouse-grown plants in spring after the last frost.

WHERE TO PLANT
Plant in any well-drained soil, including good garden soil not too high in organic matter. Gazanias can be grown in flower borders along paths and patios, or in large pots. I like them where their amazing detail can be fully appreciated, but they are equally beautiful planted en masse in drifts underplanted with creeping sedum or desert zinnia.

HOW TO PLANT
Most gazanias are grown from papery fringed seeds, 15,000 seeds per oz., which sprout in about 2 weeks at 60 degrees Fahrenheit. Light can inhibit germination; seeds must be covered well. Since seedlings develop rather slowly, most gardeners prefer to transplant readily available potted starts. Gazanias set out from 4-in. to 1-gallon pots transplant well and flower abundantly. Loosen the soil well and water thoroughly to settle the soil around the rootball.

Advice for Care

Gazania usually does well when watered every week to 10 days while in bloom. If grown in unamended sand or decomposed granite soil, plants may be lightly fertilized a few times in summer. Because it is so self-contained and distinct looking and doesn't compete well with invasive plants, gazania should be weeded as often as necessary to maintain a clean growing area. Trim off old stems and leaves when necessary.

Species, Cultivars, or Varieties

There are several cultivars, including 'Mini-Star', a compact plant 8 in. tall and wide with 3-in.-diameter self-cleaning flowers. 'Tangerine' is an all-orange selection, and 'Sunshine' is a mix of bicolor blooms in a range of colors including rust with an olive-green band near the center. Trailing gazania (*Gazania rigens* var. *leucolaena*) makes a mat of fresh silver foliage topped with yellow flowers competitive enough to be used as a groundcover in beds. It is usually grown from cuttings. *G. linearis* 'Colorado Gold' grows 4 in. high and 12 in. wide and has golden-yellow flowers. It is reliably cold hardy to Zone 5, most productive in lightly composted soil, and needs water once a week when grown in full sun and temperatures are above 90 degrees Fahrenheit. In the hotter low desert it holds up better with afternoon shade.

Regional Considerations

Gazania may be a short-lived perennial in southern New Mexico; in the central part of the state, it may survive mild winters in urban areas to 6000-ft. elevation where the heat reflected from buildings and pavement moderates the climate.

Globe Amaranth

Gomphrena globosa

Height: 12 to 24 in. **Color:** White, pink, or red **Bloom Period:** Summer **Water:** Moderate	**Light Requirement:**

*T*hough it usually makes sense to look to places with climates similar to our own for plants to complement our own wildflowers, globe amaranth is different. It comes from the Asian tropics but also does very well here. It is not only colorful but easy, tolerating our heat and wind like a native. Its stiff, upright branches form a leafy mound at least 18 in. wide. Each stem is topped with round, papery, 1-in. clover-like flower heads. Flower colors range from pure white and pale lavender-pink to deep magenta and orangy red.

WHEN TO PLANT
Transplant or sow outdoors after all chance of frost is past.

WHERE TO PLANT
Plants are most compact and colorful when grown in sunny warm spots in fast-draining soil without much organic matter. Globe amaranth is a mainstay of annual beds, looking fresh and vigorous when other plants are waning.

HOW TO PLANT
Globe amaranth is grown from seeds, but since it transplants easily, it is usually either transplanted from plants started 2 months early indoors or from plants purchased from a nursery. Seeds are 12,000 to the ounce and germinate best in the dark at 70 degrees Fahrenheit. Seedlings require bright light to develop strong foliage and stems. Loosen the soil well before planting so that new roots can gain ground easily.

ADVICE FOR CARE
The cultivating done to benefit the amaranth will also induce weed seeds to sprout. Pull weeds while they are small to avoid repeatedly disturbing the soil and exposing more weed seeds to light. Because

globe amaranth flowers so profusely for such a long time, it helps to apply mild doses of fertilizer monthly, or you can work a 4-month-formula time-release fertilizer into the soil at planting time. The flowers dry on the plants. Only the red-colored specimens will look weathered enough to prompt removing, though plants will flower longer and more strongly with occasional deadheading.

SPECIES, CULTIVARS, OR VARIETIES
'Gnome' is a dwarf cultivar with white, rose-magenta, or pink flowers on plants growing only 8 to 10 inches tall and wide. 'Strawberry Fields' is a red cultivar that fades to a bleached-looking orange unless it receives some shade in the afternoon. Too much shade will reduce flowering, so it may be necessary to try this one in a few places before you find the ideal spot.

REGIONAL CONSIDERATIONS
While globe amaranth takes little water at higher elevations and in the northern third of the state, it needs regular watering in the southern lowlands. The key to its success in the south is its heat-loving nature.

Hollyhocks

Alcea rosea

	Light Requirement:
Height: 2 to 5 ft. **Color:** Varies **Bloom Period:** June to July **Water:** Low to moderate	

*H*ollyhocks are often listed as short-lived perennials, and they may bloom a second season if they are grown in place from seed and if their spent flower stalks are removed promptly. Even as annuals with a fairly short bloom period, they are widely grown for their old-fashioned charm. Few plants look as good against an adobe garden wall. Hollyhocks start from seeds, progress to a clump of big, rough, rounded leaves, and finally grow strong stems 5 ft. tall. The stems are graced with large tubular or double ruffled flowers in a rainbow of colors from white to creamy yellow, pale pink, peachy apricot, rose, and deep wine with nearly black shading.

WHEN TO PLANT

Sow in mid-spring when the soil warms to at least 60 degrees Fahrenheit, up until the time when summer soil temperatures reach 90 degrees Fahrenheit; or transplant young seedlings after the last frost. Seed-grown plants will bloom the following spring.

WHERE TO PLANT

Though they develop strong stems if grown in full sun, hollyhocks withstand the wind best when grown with the extra protection of a wall or fence. Hollyhocks adapt to most soils, but good garden soil with some organic matter worked in retains moisture and produces the most consistent results.

HOW TO PLANT

Seeds can be sown where the plants are to grow, and plants produced this way seem to be stronger, less susceptible to disease, and more likely to last two blooming seasons. Flowers produce so much pollen that cross-pollinating can be prevented by simply grouping different colors separately from each other. Save seeds of especially nice varieties to grow the following year and to share with friends. Seeds are large, only 3000 to the ounce, and germinate best in warm soil. Plant seeds at least $1/8$ in. deep to exclude light. Hollyhocks take about 2 to 3 weeks to sprout; transplants should be a few months old before they are planted outdoors.

ADVICE FOR CARE
Because plants get so large, it is better to avoid self-sowing in small garden spaces like patio courtyards; remove spent flower stalks nearly down to the ground before they set seed. This may spur a second bloom in late summer. Remove any rust-infected leaves as soon as you notice them. Water deeply while the plants are flowering, and every 2 weeks to monthly during the rest of the year.

SPECIES, CULTIVARS, OR VARIETIES
'Summer Carnival' is a double variety with large flowers, and although many people find them beautiful, I prefer the simple beauty of open single flowers. Doubles seem too frilly to be real. Some yellow hollyhocks are actually a different species, *Alcea rugosa*. This species is distinct because its foliage is a deep olive green, it has the texture of fine sandpaper, and its leaves are more deeply lobed and more rust resistant.

REGIONAL CONSIDERATIONS
In northern and high-elevation gardens where plants are subject to frost heaving, set the crown of the plant a little below the soil surface when transplanting, or mulch seed-grown plants to avoid exposing the crown buds and roots to drying winter wind.

Moss Rose

Portulaca grandiflora

Height: 4 to 6 in.
Color: Varies
Bloom Period: All summer
Water: Low to moderate

Light Requirement:

*M*oss rose is a compact Brazilian native that has enjoyed a hallowed place in the bedding plant palette for at least a hundred years. It is low spreading with succulent stems and plump little cylindrical leaves that make a cushion 8 to 10 in. across. Moss rose flowers open in the sunlight, one at a time at the ends of the stems, and close at night. They are 1 to 2 in. in diameter and come in a rainbow of jewel-bright colors, including true red, rose, coral, pale pink, orange, yellow, and white. Flowers may be single or double. Rabbits and quail find moss rose a delicacy, so although it can be grown in harsh, dry places, you may need to keep it within garden walls if you live on the outskirts of town or farther out in the desert. Moss rose often reseeds, usually reverting to single flower forms.

WHEN TO PLANT

Sow after all chance of frost is past and the soil has warmed to 70 degrees Fahrenheit. Cell-pack and 4-in.-pot greenhouse-grown plants also need warm, frost-free soil.

WHERE TO PLANT

Moss rose is at its best in infertile, well-drained soil. It likes it hot, so southwestern exposures in rock gardens, along paths, and between paving stones are appropriate places to grow moss rose. They are also good for edging xeric flower borders, in cactus gardens for extra color, and in containers on sunny patios.

HOW TO PLANT

Seeds are tiny, 280,000 per oz.; whether sowing them in containers for later transplanting or directly in the garden, the planting process is the same. Press seeds lightly into the soil surface and water gently to avoid washing seeds away or burying them too deeply. If transplanting from containers, loosen the soil well when digging the planting holes, and backfill with unamended soil. Thin the seedlings or space transplants 6 to 12 in. apart. Fine gravel is a better mulch than bark, especially if you want to encourage self-sowing.

ADVICE FOR CARE

Other than occasional watering and weeding, moss rose is undemanding and will continue to bloom without trimming. Too much fertilizer or organic matter in the soil can actually reduce flowering. When planting in previously undisturbed desert soil, weeds may not be much to worry about. Where the soil has been disturbed repeatedly and weed seed is abundant, the cultivating done to prepare for planting will probably produce a flush of weeds. Remove them promptly before they can shade out the tender young moss rose.

SPECIES, CULTIVARS, OR VARIETIES

Since it has been cultivated for such a long time, there are many cultivars of moss rose, including several with names such as 'Sundance', 'Sunglo', and 'Sundial', reminders of its favorite position in the garden. 'Afternoon Delight' was selected for flowers that stay open longer in late afternoon.

REGIONAL CONSIDERATIONS

Moss rose will grow in hot sunny spots anywhere in New Mexico, but the season is quite short above 8000 ft. in elevation. Plants need regular watering in the southern half of the state and at lower elevations.

Mullein

Verbascum bombyciferum 'Arctic Summer'

Height: 3 to 6 ft.	**Light Requirement:**
Color: Lemon yellow	
Bloom Period: Summer	
Water: Low to moderate	

*M*ullein is a Mediterranean relative of our wild snapdragons, the *Penstemon*. As is true of penstemon, any apparent resemblance to snapdragons stops with the upright form of mullein's flower spikes. Mullein is much valued for its foliage, huge basal rosettes of leaves with unusual color and texture. Most species are biennial, producing their wonderful foliage the first season and prominent flower and seed stalks the following summer. 'Arctic Summer' is a striking plant with foot-long silver leaves and 1¹/₂-in. clear yellow flowers. Fine white down resembling spun sugar cloaks the thin, 4-ft.-tall stems.

WHEN TO PLANT

Seeds germinate best when soil temperatures reach 70 degrees Fahrenheit. Greenhouse-grown plants can be transplanted as soon as danger of hard freeze is past.

WHERE TO PLANT

Because it is not fussy about soil, mullein will grow nearly anywhere, but bright light and lean conditions produce the best-looking plants. Mullein poses a design dilemma; the first-year foliage rosettes are too striking to be consigned to the back of the border, but the following year's tall flower stems are out of place in front. Using the plants clustered in the middle ground seems the best compromise. A group of 3 to 7 plants, depending on the space available, can be used as a focal point occupying the same space a shrub might; or groups of 3 to 5 plants can be scattered through a new groundcover planting of cotoneaster or prostrate sumac to add interest until the shrubs fill out.

HOW TO PLANT

Seeds are very fine, thousands per ounce. They need light to germinate, so they should be pressed into the surface of a tilled seedbed or container and misted lightly to avoid washing them too deeply into the soil. If transplanting from containers, loosen the soil well when digging the planting holes and backfill with unamended soil.

ADVICE FOR CARE

At 7000-ft. elevations and above, mulleins need little or no supplemental watering. Farther south, regular deep watering is required, especially while the plants are blooming. Resist being too generous with water or the plants will become loose and floppy. Like penstemon, mulleins are promiscuous; most produce copious amounts of seed. Species and varieties cross-pollinate with abandon, so to produce true seed they must be very widely separated. To avoid self-sowing, trim off the flower stems routinely.

SPECIES, CULTIVARS, OR VARIETIES

Verbascum thaspus, the roadside weed, is attractive in wild gardens but greedily invasive in cultivated spaces. It is easy to be seduced by its fuzzy pale-green leaf rosettes, and even the stout, strongly vertical flower spikes can be appreciated, but the image tarnishes when flower spikes turn a burnt-out brown and millions of seeds scatter across the garden. There are several other biennial mulleins that are both beautiful and less aggressive, including moth mullein (*V. blattaria*), which has a smooth green leaf rosette 12 to 18 in. across. Its greenish white flowers with purple stamens grow clustered on 3-ft.-tall stems. *V. densiflorum* has bright-green fuzzy leaves and for most of the summer, burnished yellow flowers 2 in. across. *V. undulatum* has large velvety leaves with wavy margins in rosettes 2 ft. across. The rosettes look as if they were frosted with gold. If grown in good garden soil with ample water, the plant will lose its distinctive character, so be sure to grow it dry, lean, and in full sun. There are species that are perennial in Zones 6 to 8, including *V. phoeniceum*, which is native to the Caucasus and Iran. It blooms in partial shade from early summer into fall on 3-ft. spikes in shades of pink, salmon, violet, and white. 'Pink Domino' has pink flowers with maroon centers on 4-ft. stems. Dwarf mullein, *V. dumulosum*, has woolly leaves and yellow flowers with purple centers on 1-ft.-tall stalks. Flowers bloom in midsummer.

Nolana

Nolana paradoxa

Height: 10 in. **Color:** Blue **Bloom Period:** Summer **Water:** Moderate	**Light Requirement:**

olana is a fairly recent introduction to the bedding plant market and an excellent choice for water-conscious gardeners. Originally from the seacoast areas of Chile and Peru where rainfall may be scarce and moisture is available mostly in the form of condensation, nolana requires heat and tolerates drought and salty soil. Its trailing stems spread 18 to 24 in. and are covered with fleshy leaves that glisten in bright sunlight. Its 2-in. funnel-shaped flowers are a cool morning-glory blue with white throats.

WHEN TO PLANT

Sow seeds or transplant started plants in spring after all chance of frost is past and soil temperatures reach 70 degrees Fahrenheit.

WHERE TO PLANT

Nolana prefers infertile sandy or gravelly well-drained soil. It makes a good border plant or filler between desert shrubs mixed with desert marigold and wildflowers such as bubblegum mint, blanket flower, and desert penstemon. Because it tolerates shifts in temperature, needs heat to flower well, and vines enough to cascade over the edge of pots, nolana is well suited for use in large patio tubs where less heat-tolerant plants quickly fade. Whether grown in pots or in the ground, nolana is lusher and flowers best when shaded from the relentless afternoon sun.

HOW TO PLANT

Sow seeds lightly covered with soil at 70 to 75 degrees Fahrenheit for germination in 10 days. Because seedlings may get off to a slow start if soil doesn't warm quickly in spring, seeds can be started indoors 2 months early, or you can set out 2- to 4-in.-pot greenhouse-grown plants in cultivated soil.

ADVICE FOR CARE

When plants are held in the greenhouse for too long they become aphid farms, so try to time seeding to produce plants that can be put outdoors when they are 8 to 10 weeks old. Once the plants are outdoors, pests don't seem to find them attractive. Seeds develop inconspicuously and new flowers continue to form without dead-heading. Plants do self-sow, but not in such numbers that they get out of hand. A small amount of a 4-month-formula time-release fertilizer worked into the soil at planting time sustains the long season of color, but too much compost, water, or nitrogen will pro-duce foliage at the expense of flowers. During the hottest weeks of summer, nolana grown in full sun should be watered once a week; plants grown in afternoon shade may go a bit longer between water-ings. Plants in pots less than 12 in. in diameter may need water every day or two when temperatures reach 90 degrees Fahrenheit.

SPECIES, CULTIVARS, OR VARIETIES

Nolana humifusa has smaller blue flowers with dark-violet throats and veining; overall it seems more silver, less vivid, and less robust than *Nolana paradoxa*.

REGIONAL CONSIDERATIONS

Nolana probably won't have the heat needed to produce abundant blooms in the northern part of the state or anywhere above 7000 ft. in elevation. It takes volunteer seedlings so long to develop in cen-tral New Mexico gardens that they are usually cut down at their height of color by frost; it is best to set out potted plants each spring.

Pansy

Viola × *wittrockiana* cultivars

Height: 6 in. **Color:** Varies **Bloom Period:** All seasons except summer **Water:** Moderate to ample	**Light Requirement:**

*T*his is one of the old favorite bedding plants that fills a valuable niche in the garden. It provides winter color in a climate where people often spend quite a bit of time outdoors, except on those blessedly rare days that are cold and ugly enough to make polar bears feel at home. Pansies are water efficient because they bloom at a time when evapo-transpiration—moisture loss by evaporation from the soil and transpiration from plant tissue—is lowest, so they lose relatively little of what they're given. They grow best in partial shade, root out faster in early autumn when days may still reach 90 degrees Fahrenheit, and bloom longer in spring when temperatures again begin to spike. If you've recently moved to the desert and miss familiar garden flowers but don't want to watch your favorites shrivel and fade, try a sweep of pansies or other violas during cool weather.

When to Plant

Pansies are cool-season plants that are best transplanted in the shorter days of early autumn. This allows them to root well before they are exposed to extreme cold. They can also be sown in fall for spring blooms, or transplanted in early spring.

Where to Plant

Pansies give a better show when planted in compost-amended soil. They are most water efficient and colorful when mass planted in partial shade in borders or edging paths. Plant under trees such as New Mexico olive, redbud, hawthorn, fruit or flowering trees, or honey locust for winter color.

How to Plant

Pansies are grown from seeds, but because they transplant easily they are usually either set out as plants started 2 months early indoors, or as plants purchased from a nursery. Seeds are 20,000 to the ounce, and take nearly 2 weeks to germinate in the dark at 60 degrees Fahrenheit. Seedlings need bright light and cool air temperatures to develop strong foliage and stems before transplanting. Cultivate the soil well, adding compost to help keep soil more evenly moist.

ADVICE FOR CARE
A woodsy-looking mulch such as shredded bark or pine straw helps retain soil moisture and minimizes frost heaving in colder areas. Removing spent flowers regularly will keep plants blooming longer. Avoid disturbing plants when they are frozen.

SPECIES, CULTIVARS, OR VARIETIES
Selections that perform well in our extremes of heat and cold include the 'Imperial Hybrids': 'Silver Blue' and 'Orange Prince', ice blue and apricot respectively, with 3-in. flowers; 'Maxim Hybrids', bred for uniformity in size with slightly smaller flowers in a wide range of shades including bicolors, all with blotched faces; 'Crown Hybrids', all large-flowered with single-color unblotched faces; 'Regal Hybrids', similar to 'Crown Hybrids' but with blotched faces; 'Universal Plus Hybrids', updated selections of an old standard known for long color display and weather resistance; and 'Baby Lucia', a miniature selection with 1-in. bright-blue flowers on compact 4-in. plants. 'Johnny Jump-up' and other cultivars of *Viola cornuta* are even easier to grow, and since seeds germinate well in warmer soil, these cultivars are more reliable when sown directly where the plants are to grow. They grow as sprawling mounds 8 in. high and 12 in. wide, covered with 1-in. flowers in a range of colors and bicolors including blues, violets, lavenders, and yellows. Plants grown in good garden soil in the shade may reseed.

Skyrocket

Ipomopsis rubra

Height: 2 to 4 ft.	**Light Requirement:**
Color: Screaming scarlet	
Bloom Period: Summer	
Water: Moderate	

kyrocket is an amazing biennial. Its first phase is a 4-in.-diameter tuft of finely divided silver-green leaves that resemble one of grandma's lace doilies. After weather has been cold enough to cause the plant to set bud, a strong vertical stem densely cloaked in the same fine, soft foliage emerges from the expanded lacy basal rosette. Tubular flowers clustered in the leaves cover nearly half the stem length, their scarlet color seeming both more intense and less brassy in comparison to the pale foliage. The strong color and narrowly columnar form calls up a plethora of fireworks metaphors, and since the plant can bloom any time from May to September, depending on when the seed germinates, chances are good that hummingbirds will be celebrating July 4th with sips of skyrocket nectar.

WHEN TO PLANT
Seeds germinate best in warm soil, and can be sown in late summer or early autumn to bloom the following season. Seeds sown in mid-spring or early summer will remain lacy leaf rosettes until late the next spring.

WHERE TO PLANT
Skyrocket is not fussy about soil, and any fairly well-drained garden soil will yield good results. Use its drama to advantage by planting it against a wall, or fly patriotic colors by interplanting skyrocket with blue salvias, woolly veronica, or Russian sage for contrast. Dark evergreen foliage such as pines or 'Hillspire' junipers, or soft-green foliage such as silverberry also make effective backgrounds.

HOW TO PLANT
Seedlings quickly develop a deep taproot, making them difficult to transplant, so it is better to sow seed where the plants are to grow. 2 oz. seed will cover 500 sq. ft. of bed or border space. Rake the seed lightly into tilled soil that has warmed to near 70 degrees

Fahrenheit. Germination usually takes 2 to 3 weeks, and can be evened out a bit by refrigerating seeds mixed with damp perlite in a plastic bag for a few weeks prior to sowing.

ADVICE FOR CARE

Increase watering from every 2 weeks to weekly when plants are in bloom. Skyrocket will usually self-sow if spent flower stalks are left in place to set seed. Since seedlings tend to come up where they are not wanted (such as between paving stones in pathways), let seeds ripen, but harvest them before they shatter, and sow the harvested seeds where you want them to grow. Alternatively, you can let nature take its course and weed out the strays. The soil disturbance needed to start annuals and biennials also induces weed seeds to sprout by exposing them to light. Remove weeds while they are small to avoid stimulating further weed germination and to keep weeds from shading the *Ipomopsis*. Skyrocket seedlings look very much like annual mustards, so make sure that what you are eliminating is a weed.

SPECIES, CULTIVARS, OR VARIETIES

Scarlet gilia (*Ipomopsis aggregata*) is a New Mexico wildflower found along road cuts, forest slopes, and in open meadows, mostly in sunny, drier niches up to 9500-ft. elevation in the southern mountains, and as low as 5000 ft. on the northern plains. The flowers resemble those of skyrocket, but individual flowers dangle from open, widely branching 2-ft.-tall-and-wide plants. Where skyrocket screams, scarlet gilia whispers.

Sweet Alyssum

Lobularia maritima

Height: 3 in. **Color:** White, pink, or purple **Bloom Period:** Varies **Water:** Moderate	**Light Requirement:**

Sweet alyssum was probably used as a bedding plant by Julius Caesar's gardener. It is nearly as old as time and has not changed much. Because it is so crisp and cheery, grows so easily, and demands so little, its future, likes death and taxes, seems assured. Mounds of fine light-green leaves are covered with flat clusters of tiny honey-scented flowers that elongate into lacy racemes as the season progresses.

WHEN TO PLANT

Sow seeds very early in spring, since seedlings can withstand considerable frost and seeds will germinate when soil temperatures are 50 to 70 degrees Fahrenheit. Wait until later in spring to set out plants grown indoors unless they have been hardened off.

WHERE TO PLANT

Sweet alyssum will grow in just about any soil where some moisture is available. It is used in beds, borders, and pots as foreground edging or filler. Use the color variation to advantage by pairing purple varieties with soapwort or dianthus, and by combining white varieties with salvias or pineleaf penstemon. Because alyssum is so adaptable, it can be used to weave a thread of continuity through various areas in the garden. The sweet fragrance can become a bit cloying in enclosed spaces, but it is very pleasant when caught wafting on the breeze along a path.

HOW TO PLANT

Seeds are very fine, 90,000 to the ounce, and need light to germinate, so they should be pressed into the surface of a tilled seedbed or container and misted lightly to avoid washing them too deeply into the soil. Tilling 3 or 4 in. of compost into the soil prior to planting will improve moisture retention in sandy or gritty soil, and will help improve drainage in heavy clay. Alyssum is more likely to self-sow in good garden soil than in unamended or compacted soil.

ADVICE FOR CARE

Shear spent blooms periodically to prolong flowering and limit self-sowing. Plants that began flowering in early spring will usually decline when temperatures stay in the 90s, and can be cut off at soil level at this time. Cultivating the soil to plant alyssum will also stimulate weed seeds to sprout by exposing them to light. If the area to be planted has been disturbed repeatedly and weed seed is abundant in the soil, cultivating repeatedly to germinate and destroy weeds before planting can help reduce weeding after planting.

SPECIES, CULTIVARS, OR VARIETIES

'Carpet of Snow' is the white sweet alyssum; 'Rosie O'Day' is a deep pink; 'Royal Carpet' is deep purple.

REGIONAL CONSIDERATIONS

When planted below 7500 ft. throughout central and southern New Mexico, sweet alyssum will bloom from spring into summer until hot weather sets in and plants decline. At high elevations and in the northeastern corner of the state, plants may bloom in June and last until frost.

Verbena

Verbena tenuisecta 'Imagination Purple'

Height: 12 in. **Color:** Dark violet-purple **Bloom Period:** Spring to frost **Water:** Low to moderate	**Light Requirement:**

*S*outh American verbenas are frost sensitive enough to be considered annuals throughout New Mexico, and even the natives here are erratic and short-lived enough to be thought of as annual plants. The brevity of their life may be due to its intensity, for few flowers bloom as continuously regardless of heat and drought. Verbena's wiry stems sprawl to 2 ft. and are covered quite densely with small rough leaves. The flowers are actually clusters of small florets closely crowded into flat-topped umbels. 'Imagination Purple' is a luxuriant purple that will not fade in our intense sunlight.

WHEN TO PLANT

Transplant in spring after all danger of frost is past. Sow seeds when soil temperatures warm to 65 to 75 degrees Fahrenheit.

WHERE TO PLANT

Verbena likes it hot. Though it is not a fussy plant, it is most productive in lean, well-drained soil. Its color intensity and low profile make verbena excellent for lining pathways, spilling over the edge of pots and retaining walls, or highlighting entryways. It is good as foreground for taller perennials and shrubs, or as a temporary filler where newly planted perennial groundcovers need time to grow out. The color stops traffic, especially when planted with 'Moonshine' yarrow, 'Burgundy' gaillardia, or desert penstemon.

HOW TO PLANT

Two oz. seed will cover 500 sq. ft., taking 3 weeks or more to germinate. Seeds are fine; they should be covered to a depth of $1/16$ in. because they need darkness to sprout. Refrigerating the seeds mixed with damp perlite or vermiculite in a plastic bag for a week or two before sowing can make germination more uniform, if not faster.

ADVICE FOR CARE

Too much water, especially in compost-amended soil, can reduce blooming. Removing spent flowers will prolong the bloom period, and if plants start to flag in extreme heat, trimming stems back can produce a new surge of growth. A mild fertilizer such as blood meal or time-release types worked into the soil at planting time can help sustain blooming. Like too much water, too much nitrogen can produce more foliage and few flowers. Cut plants down to the ground during winter garden cleanups. Some may return in spring.

SPECIES, CULTIVARS, OR VARIETIES

'Peaches and Cream' is an apricot-and-pale-yellow variety that is more compact than 'Imagination'. *V. canescens* 'Homestead Purple' is a plains native selection that will form a carpet of deep-purple flowers throughout the growing season if watered every week during summer's heat. It is used as a groundcover for pockets of color, especially in contrast with silver foliage or pink or yellow wildflowers, and may persist for several years in Zone 6 and 7 gardens. *V. rigida* is an Argentine native with coarse, thistle-like foliage and deep-purple flowers. 'Polaris' is a pale-lavender selection. New Mexican natives include fernleaf verbena, *V. bipinnatifida*, with pink-purple flowers, and *V. wrightii*, which is similar but more upright in form. *V. peruviana* 'Red Devil' has wiry stems that lie flat on the soil and spread 18 in. wide. It is beautiful interwoven among blackfoot daisies, perky sue, and other compact perennials. 'Red Devil' may persist for several seasons if kept warm and dry in winter in Zones 5 through 8.

REGIONAL CONSIDERATIONS

In southern New Mexico, many of these plants will persist for at least two or three years. They can be cut back severely in winter to clean up the garden.

CHAPTER TWO

Bulbs, Corms, and Rhizomes

$\mathcal{B}$ULBS, CORMS, AND RHIZOMES are all plants with
enhanced storage capacities, so it's no surprise that many are
native to our desert Southwest and to similarly arid climates around
the world. They evade drought by being seasonal—blooming early
in spring when temperatures are cooler, or blooming during the
summer monsoons when rain is most likely to fall. Most are leafy
for only a short time before and after flowering, when they are
renewing the reserves spent to produce this season's foliage and
flowers and recharging themselves for the next growing season.
Bulbs, like tulips and daffodils, are clusters of overlapping underground leaves that enclose the already-formed buds of future stems
and flowers. Corms, such as crocus, are underground stems that are
sometimes covered with layers of starchy scales. Rhizomes are prostrate underground stems that form roots and stem buds at nodes
along their length. Some irises are bulbs, and some are rhizomes.
For simplicity's sake, I'll refer to all bulbs, corms, and rhizomes as
bulbs unless otherwise noted.

One of the advantages of living in New Mexico is that we can
grow plants that require winter cold to bloom (as many of the
spring bulbs do), yet in much of the state our winters are mild
enough for us to leave some of the more tender bulbs in the garden
in winter as long as we mulch them well. Our dormant season is
long enough to make the early spring color of tulips, daffodils,
grape hyacinths, and spring crocus a most welcome sign that winter
is near an end. Planting spring bulbs in autumn is taking the future
in hand and affirming the renewal of life. It is an act of hope that
even though nature seems to be dying all around us, she will
reemerge with a flourish a few months from now.

Even in the smallest, most cultivated settings, all bulbs look best
when they are planted en masse, in great sweeping drifts or filling

Chapter Two

whole beds. There's nothing more forlorn than a narrow band of daffodils or tulips marching across the garden like the lost platoon. If your budget is tight, choose bulbs that are well suited to your garden and group them in places visible from windows and along the most-used pathways. They will multiply in time and give you offsets to expand your range. The more generous the display of color, the more unsightly foliage you will have to hide after flowering has finished and the bulbs are restoring themselves. Wait until the bulb leaves wither completely before removing them. Choose companion plants that are late to come out of dormancy such as dwarf plumbago or warm-season ornamental grasses. Allow enough space between groups of waning bulbs and later successional plants to give the bulb foliage adequate light to photosynthesize and renew itself. Most hybrid bulbs have flowers larger than those of their wild ancestors, so even if they were originally from dry climates, they will tolerate soils moist enough to maintain other xeric plants while they are dormant as long as the drainage is good.

Those of us who garden on the frontier have to protect our gardens from marauding deer, voles, rabbits, pocket gophers, and other varmints who would rather eat our flowers than look at them. In extreme situations, bulbs may have to be planted in hardware mesh baskets in the soil, with chicken wire pinned on top of the soil under the mulch so that the bulbs grow totally enclosed in wire fencing. If you buy bulbs early, take care not to store them in the refrigerator with fruit; the ethylene gas released by ripening fruit can kill the flower buds in the bulbs.

There are so many bulbs to choose from that most retail nurseries carry a limited assortment of the old standards and some of the most recent introductions. For minor species and native bulbs you'll have to check with specialty growers. Some of the Mediterranean species tulips, daffodils, and crocuses are rare in the wild because of the overcollecting that continues even though international laws ban their commerce. Since wild-collected bulbs are usually more dried out and of poorer quality than cultivated bulbs, which are freshly harvested and stored under controlled conditions, gardeners can learn which suppliers are reputable and avoid black market dealers.

Crocus

Height: 4 in.
Color: White, yellow, or purple
Bloom Period: Early spring or autumn
Zones: 4 to 8
Water: Low

Light Requirement:

*C*rocuses frame the gardening season like colorful bookends. With the possible exception of skiers, New Mexicans have usually had enough of winter by February. The spring-blooming corms of Dutch crocus (*Crocus vernus*) are the welcome first signs of the coming of spring. Dutch crocuses bloom in a variety of colors including blue, violet, yellow, and white. Some are purple-and-white striped. The violet-purple flowers of autumn crocus (*Crocus speciosus*) appear in September and October to mark the mellow ebb of the growing season.

WHEN TO PLANT

Plant Dutch crocus in autumn when the soil has begun to cool down and days are noticeably shorter. Autumn crocuses are planted in late summer, usually sometime in August, and they bloom soon afterwards.

WHERE TO PLANT

Crocuses are not particular about the soil; our gritty decomposed granite and sand are ideal for them, and even valley clay will do as long as it is not kept too wet; this is especially important while the corms are dormant. Crocuses make beautiful additions to rock gardens among soapwort, Greek yarrow, fleabane, and stonecrops; or they may be grouped along paths and the edges of perennial borders with blue fescue, desert zinnia, or blue spurge. Crocuses are also planted in broad sweeps in buffalograss lawns.

HOW TO PLANT

Set out new corms in tilled soil, or spade the soil to loosen areas within an established planting. To create more natural-looking drifts, put the corms in a box, basket, or large pot and gently toss them out across the area to be planted, digging them in where they fall. Be sure to turn them bud side up and dig them in about 2 in. deep. Crocus may also reseed and produce offsets.

ADVICE FOR CARE

Trim off the spent flowers, but leave the foliage. Photosynthesis will continue in order to renew the corm for the next bloom season. Trim off the leaves when they have withered naturally. Carefully forking the bed while corms are dormant in summer will help dislodge cormlets and spread them out.

SPECIES, CULTIVARS, OR VARIETIES

There are several species of crocus available through specialty bulb growers, including deep-purple *Crocus chrysanthus*, the source of the Dutch hybrids. The species has smaller deep-purple flowers and blooms earlier than the hybrids do. Mixing the species with the hybrids will extend the bloom period in spring. Blooming in October, the culinary delicacy saffron (*C. sativus*) has cupped, deep-purple buds with yellow anthers and three-lobed scarlet stigmas. Stigmas are the valued part; it takes 4000 flowers to make an ounce of saffron. *C. sativus* is hardy in Zones 6 to 8. Greek crocus (*C. goulimyi*) is an autumn species that is unmatched for its fragrant, intense blue-purple blooms suffused with pink. It is the least cold hardy of the species mentioned here and is reliable only in Zones 7 and 8.

Daffodils

Narcissus species and hybrids

Height: 6 to 20 in.
Color: Yellow, white, pink, apricot, or bicolors
Bloom Period: Early to late spring
Zones: 4 to 8
Water: Moderate

Light Requirement:

*D*affodils are among the first plants that were cultivated as ornamentals. As a result of their long history of breeding, garden narcissus are now divided into twelve divisions as determined by the Royal Horticultural Society and the American Daffodil Society. Each group has distinct characteristics based on the depth and the form of the central trumpet, cup, or corona: when the center of the flower is at least as long as the petal segments, it is a trumpet; when it is shorter than the petal segments it is a cup; and when the cup is replaced with petals, is highly fluted, or filled with stamens that look like petals, it is a corona. The form and size of the petals and sepals, the height of the stems, and the number of blooms per stem are other distinguishing traits. Larger, taller types and double-flowered specimens do best in more protected courtyard beds, while smaller, short-stemmed types hold up satisfactorily when exposed to our spring winds. The pink- and orange-toned cultivars keep their color best in partial shade. All make good cut flowers. The *tazetta* varieties are used for forcing because they require less cold to bloom well.

WHEN TO PLANT
Set bulbs out in mid-fall when the soil has begun to cool.

WHERE TO PLANT
Daffodils perform better if the soil is amended with compost to improve drainage and water retention. They are used in beds and borders, or interplanted with groundcovers such as periwinkle, dwarf plumbago, or Mexican evening primrose under spring-blooming trees that require moderate watering. In northern and high-elevation gardens, daffodils can be naturalized with cool-season meadow grasses, and will often bloom through late snow cover.

How to Plant

Mix compost thoroughly into the soil before planting. To create more natural-looking drifts, put the bulbs in a box and gently toss them out across the area to be planted, digging in bulbs where they fall. Be sure to place them nose up. Plant larger types 6 in. deep, miniatures 3 in. deep. Planting masses of one color is a grand gesture, while mixing several types together in an area has a spontaneous charm. In either case, more is better.

Advice for Care

Trim off the spent flowers, but allow the leaves to continue photosynthesizing until they wither naturally. This renews the bulbs for the next season.

Species, Cultivars, or Varieties

'King Alfred' is a 16-in. yellow that is nearly a century old. It is probably still the most widely planted cultivar. 'Mount Hood' is similar in size and form, but is white blushed with a hint of yellow. With my propensity for wildflowers, I love the triandus types such as 'Thalia', a 16-in. fragrant, white, mid-season, multi-flowered cultivar as elegant as it is easy; the fragrant jonquillas, also multi-flowered in a range of yellows, pinks, and bicolors; and the commercially propagated species, wild forms and wild hybrids such as 'Yellow Hoop Skirts', a 5-in.-tall multi-flowered variety with widely flared trumpets. One of the most reliable and prolific miniatures is 'Tête-a-Tête', an 8-in.-tall early yellow with narrow petals that are swept back from slender trumpets with 2 flowers per stem. The species and miniatures are less cold hardy; they are reliable only in Zone 6 and warmer zones. The more robust varieties perform best at higher elevations and in the northern third of the state.

Grape Hyacinth

Muscari armeniacum

Height: 6 in.
Color: Purple, blue, or white
Bloom Period: Early to mid-spring
Zones: 4 to 8
Water: Low to moderate

Light Requirement:

*G*rape hyacinths are by far the easiest and most reliable spring bulbs for naturalizing in New Mexico. If bulbs are planted 3 to 4 in. apart, they will reseed and offset to form a dense seasonal groundcover. Their grassy foliage appears in late summer and remains green through winter. The bloom stalks of grape hyacinth, like tiny clusters of grapes, start poking through the leaves after the crocus have faded, just in time to contrast with the earliest tulips.

WHEN TO PLANT

Plant grape hyacinths in autumn when the soil is cooling down and days are shortening noticeably. Bulbs can be kept refrigerated for a brief period of time if the soil is still too warm for roots to develop when the bulbs arrive. Established stands can be thinned and replanted elsewhere in late summer when the leaves reappear.

WHERE TO PLANT

Grape hyacinths do well in any soil as long as it doesn't stay too wet. They will increase more readily if the soil is softened with compost. Use them as edging for paths and perennial borders, or as an alternate-season groundcover interplanted with dwarf plumbago or 'Rosy Glow' sedum. Plant three bulbs per 4-in. pot of plumbago or sedum. Because the leaves are dark green throughout fall and winter, grape hyacinths will look out of place in dormant buffalograss.

HOW TO PLANT

An old trick for creating more natural-looking drifts is to put bulbs in a box, basket, or large pot and gently toss them out across the area to be planted, digging bulbs in where they fall. Be sure to place them bud side up and 2 to 3 in. deep. In more formal settings, a section of 4-in. welded wire fencing can be used to space bulbs in a grid pattern, 1 bulb per square. Grape hyacinths increase readily by seeds and offsets, so the gaps in a geometric pattern will fill in after a few seasons.

ADVICE FOR CARE

Trim off the spent flowers if you want to prevent reseeding, but allow the leaves to continue photosynthesizing until they wither. This renews the bulbs for the next bloom season. One of the advantages of interplanting grape hyacinths with a groundcover is that the emerging growth of the groundcover will hide the declining bulb foliage.

SPECIES, CULTIVARS, OR VARIETIES

Both 'Blue Spike', a medium-blue, double-flowered form, and 'Saffier', a dark-blue selection, are sterile, making them good choices for small protected spaces where the more robust species might become weedy. Though these cultivars won't reseed, they do offset a little. Feather hyacinth (*Muscari plumosum*) has threadlike pale-purple flower clusters on 8-in. stems. *M. neglectum* is the most prolific of the grape hyacinths. It has longer leaves with lower florets that are very dark blue with white rims, while the florets at the tip of the spike are pale blue.

Iris

Iris species and hybrids

Height: 8 in. to 3 ft. **Color:** Varies **Bloom Period:** Late spring **Zones:** 4 to 8 **Water:** Low to moderate	**Light Requirement:**

*B*earded irises are the choice of most New Mexican gardeners. They grow so easily and bloom briefly but spectacularly in May in nearly every color imaginable, including deep jewel tones of purple, wine, blue, yellow, pink, apricot, and butterscotch; muted pastels of the same; and blends of those colors. The flowers may be 6 in. overall. The form of the flowers is classic, with three inner, upward-curving petals called "standards" and three outer sepals called "falls." The falls curve downward, unfurling brushy "beards." The pale-green, sword-shaped leaves are 2 in. wide and 18 in. long. Siberian irises bloom later in spring on slender 30-in. stems above clumps of narrow, dark-green leaves. The flowers are smaller in shades of dark violet-blue, pale blue, and white, but the foliage is handsome throughout the growing season, and the plants tolerate quite a bit of shade.

When to Plant
Bearded iris can be planted from containers anytime, but established plants should be divided and reset in late July and early August. Siberians can be divided any time after blooming: in late summer or fall at lower elevations, or in spring in colder areas.

Where to Plant
Plant bearded types in full sun in infertile sandy or gritty soil that drains well. Use them as accents in drier borders to continue the color display begun with spring bulbs; or plant in clumps between flowering or evergreen shrubs. Mixing bearded iris with daylilies, 'Moonshine' yarrow, or ornamental grasses will help hide the ratty fading foliage. Though Siberian irises need more water, they are quite drought tolerant once well established, especially if grown in shade. They prefer more humusy soil, and may become iron deficient in unamended New Mexican grit. The best sites for Siberian

iris are in runoff swales from canales or gutters on the north and east sides of walls.

How to Plant

Plant rhizomes shallowly, especially in heavier soil and colder locations. When making divisions, let the cut roots dry before resetting plants.

Advice for Care

If drip irrigating, place emitters to the side of the plant, not right above the rhizome. Water bearded types thoroughly once every 1 or 2 weeks from the time when growth begins in spring up until 6 weeks or so after flowering. Water monthly while dormant. Lift and divide rhizomes every 5 years. Siberians prefer weekly watering while in bloom, twice a month while leafy, and monthly while dormant. The only major pest is iris borer, which is easy to recognize by the wet streak it leaves on leaves as it eats its way down toward the rhizome. Removing affected leaves and roots is the surest control.

Species, Cultivars, or Varieties

The native Rocky Mountain iris (*Iris missouriensis*) is rhizomatous, forming clumps of narrow dark-green leaves with deep-blue flowers on 2-ft.-tall stems. It is usually found growing along streams between 7500 and 10,500 feet in elevation. Several bulbous types grow well in New Mexico. They should be planted 3 in. deep and divided only when flowering declines. Juno iris (*Iris bucharica*) is native to Afghanistan and Turkistan and grows 12 to 16 in. tall. It produces 5 or more blooms to a stem in a blend of yellow, cream, and rust above corn-like glossy-green leaves. Two extremely cold-hardy dwarf irises are *Iris danfordii*, which blooms in early spring with yellow flowers spotted with brown on stems 4 to 6 in. high; and *Iris reticulata*, which has violet-blue flowers blotched yellow on the falls. Dwarf types can also be planted in buffalograss lawns for early color.

Meadow Saffron

Colchium autumnale

Height: 6 in. **Color:** Lilac-pink **Bloom Period:** September **Zones:** 4 to 8 **Water:** Low to moderate	**Light Requirement:**

*S*ometimes confused with autumn crocus, meadow saffron has the curious habit of sending up 1-ft.-tall leaves in spring that wither and disappear by June, then blooming in September with 4-in. chalices of purplish pink. Depending on the cultivar and location, it may leaf out after flowering instead of in the spring, but either way, the huge blooms seem to appear out of nowhere. This is fitting for a plant named for Colchis, the mythological source of the Golden Fleece. In the slanting light of early morning or late afternoon, the flowers glow as though lit from within. Undisturbed clumps may produce a dozen or more flower stems.

WHEN TO PLANT

The bulbs are dormant only in July and August. Set them out promptly; if you delay planting, they may flower in the sack or on the shelf. This may seem a miracle at the time, but it will exhaust the bulb.

WHERE TO PLANT

As its name suggests, meadow saffron can be planted in occasionally mowed buffalograss or sheep's fescue meadows, though the coarse green foliage in spring looks rather weedy in still-dormant buffalograss. Colchium adapts best in partial shade; it can be mixed with low-growing artemesias, catmint, soapwort, or dwarf plumbago for contrast.

HOW TO PLANT

Set out new corms in tilled soil, or loosen spots with a spade when planting into established cover. Be sure to place them bud side up and about 2 to 3 in. deep.

ADVICE FOR CARE

Meadow saffron is the essence of easy. Other than planting with an ally to back up its silken blossoms and hide its waning foliage, little care is needed. If flowering diminishes, lift and separate the corms in summer while they are dormant. Plants and corms contain colchicine, a potentially toxic alkaloid used in the treatment of gout. Animals seem to know better than to eat these plants; meadow saffron is one of the few bulbs that don't need shielding from wildlife.

SPECIES, CULTIVARS, OR VARIETIES

Colchicum bornmuelleri has 5- to 8-in. fragrant, pale-pink flowers that deepen to lilac rose at the tips as they mature. *C. byzantinium* is the earliest and most fragrant of these species. It has lilac-purple blossoms with a spidery pattern of white lines that radiates like a star from the center of the blossom. *C. speciosum* produces 4-in. raspberry-pink flowers in September and October. Its bulbs are larger than those of the other species, and it is so robust that it may need lifting and resetting every few years.

Ornamental Onions

Allium species

Height: 6 to 24 in. **Color:** White, pink, or lavender **Bloom Period:** Summer **Zones:** 4 to 8 **Water:** Moderate in sun	**Light Requirement:**

An easy way to conserve water in the garden is to cultivate plants that serve more than one purpose. Chives and garlic chives are grown for their savory leaves, but they are beautiful garden flowers as well. The fine grassy leaves of *Allium schoenoprasum* add a nice touch of onion to summer meals, and when combined with sour cream elevate a lowly potato to gourmet status. The globular rose-pink flower heads make an interesting foil for early salvias and the blue spikes of veronica. Garlic chives (*Allium tuberosum*) are more robust and have wider leaves and a stronger flavor. The white flower umbels bloom in August atop 18-in.-tall leafless stems. The seedheads persist into winter. They resemble snowflakes and make a fine addition to the wreath-maker's palette. In more temperate climates, garlic chives have a nasty reputation for creeping into lawns and swallowing flower beds whole, but in the arid New Mexican landscape they extend only as far as moist soil and afternoon shade allow.

WHEN TO PLANT

Seeds germinate best in cool soil near 50 degrees Fahrenheit. Plants can be transplanted from containers at any time during the growing season, but it's best to avoid planting when temperatures are above 90 degrees Fahrenheit, especially if planting in full sun.

WHERE TO PLANT

Alliums are not particular about soil. Chives add interesting texture to herb gardens mixed with salvias, rosemary, and thymes. Garlic chives make a good groundcover under fruit trees or in any shady spot where their tendency to reseed is an asset.

HOW TO PLANT

Allium seed sprouts like a lawn on open soil, especially when compost has been tilled into the soil for better moisture retention.

Established plants may be lifted and divided in spring or fall. To set out plants or divisions, loosen the soil well, place starts at the same level they had been growing previously, and water thoroughly to settle the soil.

ADVICE FOR CARE

Chives may need watering once a week while actively growing, especially while flowering and if being cut for kitchen use. If grown in the shade, garlic chives can be watered at most every 2 weeks in summer after plants are well established. Cut the old stems back to the ground some time before they begin regrowth in spring.

SPECIES, CULTIVARS, OR VARIETIES

Swirling onion (*A. senescens* var. *glaucum*) forms a 3-in.-high and 6-in.-wide clump of narrow blue-gray leaves that swirl outward from an open center like a cowlick. The swirl is most pronounced when plants are grown in full sun, but it also adapts to moderate shade. Globular lavender flower heads appear on 8-in. stems in midsummer. Swirling onion will self-sow in moist garden soil if not deadheaded promptly. *A. tanguticum* 'Summer Beauty' is a rhizomatous plant with 2-in.-diameter clusters of deep-lavender florets borne on 12-in. stems above 1/4 in.-wide bright-green leaves. Blooms last a month or more when plants are grown in sun or partial shade. Nodding onion (*A. cernuum*) is native in the mountains of New Mexico, where it grows in grassy meadows in pine forests. The rose-pink clusters of florets droop from the limber stems. At lower elevations plants require shade and flower color tends to fade.

Rainlily

Zephyranthes longiflora

Height: 12 in. **Color:** Yellow, white, or pink **Bloom Period:** Summer **Zones:** 6 to 8 **Water:** Low to moderate	**Light Requirement:**

A week or so after rain falls on the arid hills and mesas of central and southern New Mexico, grassy leaves 6 to 8 in. long appear from the newly moistened sands, followed soon after by single funnel-shaped yellow flowers on leafless stems. Aptly named, rainlilies are just one of the desert's many surprises. During a year when the rains come, the rocky slopes and sandy lowlands become a garden of wildflowers. Desert marigolds and zinnias jostle globemallow, blackfoot daisies, and evening primroses, all in a rush to flower and set seeds as insurance against the inevitable drought. The bulbs of rainlily give it an edge; though they are small teardrops hardly an inch in diameter, they store sufficient food and moisture to push up leaves and flowers as soon as enough rain falls to nudge them awake. In very good years, there's enough rain to germinate seeds and start still more bulbs. In bad years, bulbs remain dormant, conserving stored energy until times are better.

WHEN TO PLANT

Sow seeds or plant dormant bulbs in early summer when soil temperatures have reached 70 degrees Fahrenheit. Transplant potted plants while foliage is actively growing.

WHERE TO PLANT

Rainlily does best in well-drained sandy or gravelly soil. Its compact size and showy flowers make it a good addition to rock gardens and dry perennial borders. It also works well when clustered between sage, rosemary, lavender, fairy duster, woolly butterfly bush, and other blooming or evergreen arid-adapted shrubs. Rainlily can be planted in warm-season native grass prairies, but it may need extra water if the grass is very dense.

How to Plant

Loosen the soil well so that new roots can expand easily; organic amendments are unnecessary. Set bulbs 2 in. deep, clustered 2 or 3 in. apart in groups of at least five for immediate impact. Seed germinates in 4 to 7 days at 70 degrees Fahrenheit, but roots develop below ground shortly before the first leaves appear.

Advice for Care

Let the soil dry a bit between waterings. If it gets too dry, the plants will go dormant until added moisture stimulates a rebound. As with all bulbs, let the leaves wither naturally so that the bulb enters dormancy with plenty of reserves for the future.

Species, Cultivars, or Varieties

The yellow form of *Zephyranthes longiflora* is the wild species. There are three horticultural cultivars: *Z. candida* is white, *Z. citrina* is a somewhat larger yellow, and *Z. rosea* is pink. There are also two more recent hybrids, 'Apricot Queen' and 'Prairie Sunset', that are yellow suffused with pink and coral. *Z. drummondii* is another rainlily native to the eastern plains of New Mexico; its grassy foliage also appears with the first summer rain. The small bulbs of *Zephyranthes* lie 6 to 12 in. below the soil surface. Pink buds open to fragrant single white funnel-form flowers on leafless stems 12 in. tall. Growing conditions are similar for all rainlilies.

BULBS, CORMS, AND RHIZOMES

Starflower

Ipheion uniflorum

Height: 6 in.
Color: Blue
Bloom Period: Late spring
Zones: 5 to 8
Water: Moderate

Light Requirement:

Starflowers are Argentine natives. Their small bulbs produce several stems, each topped with a single blue flower 1½ in. across. The sweet fragrance of the flowers drifts on the warm spring air. The grassy foliage smells faintly of onions if crushed. The bulbs are covered with a fiber mesh and bloom best when crowded. They are modestly priced, and even in plots the size of postage stamps, more is better. Two dozen bulbs per sq. ft. will give a good show the first spring, and will become a luxuriant azure carpet in a few years' time. Starflower has the charm of a wildflower and the self-contained habits and colorful intensity of a refined garden flower.

WHEN TO PLANT

Set bulbs out in mid-fall when the soil has begun to cool down.

WHERE TO PLANT

Starflower does best in well-drained soil, and its fine texture and rich color work well in rock gardens, for edging pathways, or in perennial beds mixed with soapwort, creeping baby's breath, species tulips, and mat daisy for contrast. It is one of the rabbits' favorite selections at the spring salad bar. In rural areas, *Ipeion* should be planted in fenced or walled gardens or new buds may be shaved off down to stubble. Repeated cropping exhausts the bulbs. Starflower is one of the later-flowering bulbs and can be paired with pineleaf penstemon or mat daisy and sidebells penstemon.

HOW TO PLANT

Cluster bulbs an inch or two apart for a strong color show, planting 2 to 3 in. deep in loosened soil. Starflower neither requires nor resents organically amended soil, but it will require less fertilizing and watering when planted in good garden soil.

ADVICE FOR CARE

Leave the foliage to fade naturally so that the bulbs are restored for the next season. Starflowers rarely if ever need thinning.

SPECIES, CULTIVARS, OR VARIETIES

'Wisley Blue' has flowers that are larger and darker blue than those of the species. Starflower is also known as *Brodiaea uniflora* and *Triteleia uniflora*. There are several species of *Brodiaea* and *Triteleia* native to the West Coast from California to British Columbia. They differ from *Ipheion* in that they have sparser foliage and produce umbels of flowers on stems up to 16 in. tall. Though most of the western natives bloom for 2 to 3 months from mid-spring into summer, their color display is less intense, and they are less tolerant of water during their dormant summer phase.

REGIONAL CONSIDERATIONS

In Zone 5, keep bulbs well mulched to ensure that they overwinter reliably.

Tulips

Tulipa species and hybrids

Height: 4 to 28 in. **Color:** Varies **Bloom Period:** Spring **Zones:** 4 to 8 **Water:** Low to moderate	**Light Requirement:**

Tulips have a history rich in drama and intrigue. The first tulip seeds were sent to Vienna in the early 1550s by the Austrian ambassador to the Sultan of Turkey, who reported paying dearly for the seeds of plants growing in a Constantinople garden. The Turks had selected and cultivated native species tulips for centuries, so much so that many of the tulips growing wild in the 1500s were actually escaped garden cultivars and hybrids. Clusius, one of the earliest European tulip breeders, was robbed of his choicest stock, which fueled the Dutch fever "tulipomania." Wild speculation in tulip "futures," the breeding of new colors and forms, rocked the European economy in the mid-17th century, establishing Holland as the leader in the cultivation of tulips, a distinction that is still claimed today. The wind and early heat here in New Mexico can make life difficult for the tall hybrids that have been bred for temperate European gardens. If you want the bold color and large flowers of the modern hybrids, the Kaufmanniana and Greigii types perform beautifully, are more perennial, and have interesting foliage as a bonus.

WHEN TO PLANT

Set bulbs out in fall when the soil has cooled. If the soil is too warm and wet, bulbs will rot instead of rooting.

WHERE TO PLANT

Tulips require well-drained soil. The diminutive species types are beautiful when used to fill the seams between boulders in a rock garden, when massed along paths, or when used to edge perennial borders. The more robust types can be used with dwarf iris and crocus to brighten dormant buffalograss in early spring. The hybrids are bold in their own right, but create an even grander show when mixed with blue spurge or grape hyacinths for contrast.

How to Plant

Loosen the soil well to a depth of 12 in. Incorporate a small amount of compost to lighten heavier soils or to improve water retention in sand. Plant the species bulbs to a depth of 2 to 3 in.; plant hybrids 4 to 6 in. deep. Cluster bulbs in groups of five or in extravagant masses of 105. Because substantial variation in the depth of the bulbs will stagger flowering time and diminish the intensity of the display, plant the bulbs at the same depth for a more controlled effect. Broadcast bulbs in grand sweeps for a more natural appearance.

Advice for Care

Water tulips deeply when they are in bloom and until the foliage fades naturally. This allows the bulbs to be restored for the next season. Working a slow-release fertilizer into the soil at planting time or topdressing with a quick-release fertilizer in spring when the foliage first emerges may help hybrid tulips perennialize. Voles and ground squirrels can destroy tulip beds overnight. Planting bulbs in hardware cloth baskets sunken in the soil sometimes slows the animals down, but the situation often becomes a choice between wildlife and garden.

Species, Cultivars, or Varieties

One early cultivar of *Tulipa kaufmanniana* is 'Shakespeare', whose flowers are carmine red on the outside and red blended with salmon and yellow when fully opened. Stems are 6 to 8 in. tall. 'Red Riding Hood', a midseason cultivar of *T. greigii*, has scarlet blooms with a black base and stands 8 in. tall. *T. greigii* cultivars are also available in apricot, rose, and pink shades. Species tulips lack the brass of the hybrids but compensate with a tendency to increase reliably over the years. Three of the best are *T. tarda*, 4 in. tall with flowers that bloom within the leaves and are white blushed with green; *T. batalini*, 6 in. tall, the species of which is soft yellow, while cultivars are rose, pink, peach, or coral; and 'Lipstick Tulip' *T. clusiana*, 8- to 12-in.-tall plants with white, broadly red-striped flowers on very slender, tapered buds. This species is rhizomatous and can get out of hand in good garden soil. One of the smallest species is *T. linifolius*, which has pointed red petals and black centers on stems only 4 in. tall. Its narrow prostrate leaves have subtle red margins.

CHAPTER THREE

Cacti and Succulents

$\mathcal{C}$ACTI AND SUCCULENTS are truly remarkable plants. Faced with surviving where rains are few and far between, these drought lovers root extensively and often quite shallowly so that they might absorb every drop of precious moisture. The misers of the plant world, they plump up their waxy-skinned bodies, and hold that moisture quite efficiently.

Cacti and succulents test the paradigms of garden design with their spiky forms, barbed stems, lack of leaves, and ephemeral display of brilliant flowers. These are not plants that fit into an English-style cottage garden, though there is a drama about agave, sotol, and yucca that works in formal garden settings. Cacti and succulents can weave the intricate patterns of a knot garden, or create the spare serenity of a Japanese-style garden. Spiny plants are also excellent foundation plantings because they require minimal watering and few thieves are tempted by cactus-shielded windows.

New Mexico's cold desert denies us the use of most of the cacti that have strong architectural impact. To survive persistent sub-freezing winter temperatures, cold-hardy cacti and succulents have evolved as relatively small plants. The towering saguaros and fire-plug-sized barrel cacti of the Sonoran Desert survive only in the low deserts of southern New Mexico, and even there an unusually cold, wet winter spells trouble for those giant jelly rolls. Ocotillo and tree-form yuccas are our most statuesque succulents. Most of our cold-hardy cacti range from pincushions less than six inches high and wide to cane chollas that occupy as much space as a large shrub. When the nights grow longer, these plants stop absorbing water so that there will be room within the cell walls for the remaining fluids to expand. As temperatures drop, cold-hardy cacti and succulents concentrate sugars in their sap, which acts as antifreeze. Externally these changes are subtle: plants turn a duller color and sag a bit. The pads of the largest prickly pear recline on the ground, while the cholla stems shrink and droop. With the return of warm days in spring, plants recover quickly.

The drought-requiring nature of these plants limits their close companions to species of similar adaptation, but my favorite gardens where cacti grow are not cactus gardens. They are a blend of desert trees and shrubs that provide a tracery of fine branches and leaves made even more delicate looking by the rugged contrast of plump prickly pear pads. Such a desert garden may have fairy duster clambering through stems of ocotillo, and bird-of-paradise masking the dried leaves that insulate the trunks of soaptree yucca. The smallest cacti may be tucked between boulders in a rock garden, purple prickly pear may be surrounded by red iceplant, and pencil cholla might punctuate a sweep of desert marigold and verbena.

When blending spiny plants with leafy ones, keep the cacti on higher ground to ensure good drainage and to keep leaf litter from collecting in the spines, creating a painful cleanup chore. Combine prickly plants with companions that require only seasonal cleanup. Since cacti, ocotillo, agave, and many yuccas are not people-friendly plants, allow plenty of space to accommodate their mature sizes plus a bit of wiggle room so that you can work around them safely.

Other than locating large specimens a comfortable distance from paths and play areas, the way cacti and succulents are used in gardens can vary with the taste of the gardener. They may be used in the hotter, drier spots throughout the landscape, reserved for accent use, or figured prominently in a low-maintenance arid zone bordering the more cultivated parts of the garden.

Regardless of the place they occupy within the garden, nothing expresses the fierce fragility that is the paradox of New Mexico better than these magnificent plants lit by slanting sunlight. Don't contribute to the degradation of wild ecosystems by purchasing collected plants unless you are sure they have been salvaged from areas about to be bulldozed or from private land with the owner's permission. Specialty nurseries propagate the plants described here; these patient growers deserve our patronage.

Beargrass

Nolina species

Height: 2 to 5 ft.	**Light Requirement:**
Flowers: White	
Foliage: Evergreen	
Bloom Period: Spring or summer	
Zones: 6 to 8	
Water: Very low	

Young seedlings of beargrass look like rather coarse-bladed clumps of grass, but unlike true grasses, the leaves live for several years. As the clumps grow, the leaves harden to a glossy olive green, become stiffer, and in three or four years might be mistaken for yucca. Beargrass, like yucca, is a lily, but its leaves are slender, less than 1 in. wide and 3 to 5 ft. long. Triangular in cross-section, the leaves arch gracefully to form clumps twice as wide as they are tall. The individual flowers are tiny, but appear by the hundreds on densely branched, plumelike flower spikes. While yuccas are often found in large colonies on the desert plains, beargrass is almost always found on slopes. It grows in large groups that are sometimes spread over miles of rocky terrain. The women of the southern pueblos weave beautiful, flat open baskets from the leaves.

WHEN TO PLANT
Beargrass seeds germinate best in spring when the soil is warm but before really hot weather sets in. Young seedlings grow faster if they are partially shaded. Container-grown plants can be transplanted any time of year, but be sure to acclimate plants to full sun or cold if they are to be set out during the extremes of summer or winter.

WHERE TO PLANT
Nolina needs fast-draining soils and is often planted among boulders in accent groupings. Its evergreen leaves complement other succulents and cacti as well as mesquite, live oaks, prostrate sumac, cliffrose, desert marigold, and sand lovegrass. Because the leaves are not barbed, beargrass is often used for a tropical look around swimming pools in xeric gardens.

How to Plant

Loosen the soil well in an area 3 times the width of the rootball. Be sure the plant doesn't settle after watering, burying the crown deeper than the plant had been growing. Gravel is preferred as mulch because it will keep the crown drier while helping to maintain moisture in the soil.

Advice for Care

If plants are growing near a pool where seed litter might be a problem, prune off the flower stems after the plants bloom. If environment is a higher priority, leave the seedheads on until the birds have harvested their fill. The dried basal leaves may be trimmed off in more cultivated garden settings. Water May through August to a depth of 3 ft. once or twice a month. Keep plants dry in winter to avoid root rot.

Species, Cultivars, or Varieties

Nolina texana leaves are 1/2 in. wide and 2 to 3 ft. long in clumps 4 to 5 ft. wide. The flower spikes barely extend beyond the leaves. The densely clustered flowers are massed in heads 6 in. across. *N. texana* is native to the foothills of the mountains bordering the Rio Grande and Pecos River in central and southeastern New Mexico and West Texas; it may survive Zone 5 winters if established early in summer and kept dry in winter. The southwestern New Mexico and Arizona species is *N. microcarpa*, a much larger plant with leaves up to 5 ft. long in clumps 5 to 8 ft. wide. Its flower stems arch 3 ft. above the mound of leaves.

CACTI AND SUCCULENTS

Century Plant

Agave species

Height: 18 in. **Flowers:** Red-and-yellow **Foliage:** Evergreen **Bloom Period:** Summer **Zones:** 5 to 8 **Water:** Very low	**Light Requirement:**

There is considerable variation in size and leaf color among the more than 100 species of agave. They are similar in that they all have a dramatic rosette form made of broad fibrous leaves radiating out from a central growing point, and their leaves bear hooked barbs along their margins and are spine-tipped. Calling agave "century plant" is an exaggeration. A plant develops to maturity within 10 to 50 years depending on growing conditions and species. When it's ready to flower, it devotes all its energy to producing a prodigious flower stalk that may reach 6 in. in diameter at the base and 15 ft. in height, topped with a tiered candelabra of clustered red-and-yellow florets. Hummingbirds and bats visit the nectar-laden flowers. Agave usually develops small plants at the base of the main rosette; these offsets replace the original plant when it dies.

WHEN TO PLANT

Agave is best transplanted when the soil is warm, but it can be set out any time of year as long as it has been acclimated to cold and is kept dry during the winter months.

WHERE TO PLANT

Agave is a natural work of art and is very effective when displayed as such. Desert marigold, iceplant, verbena, lantana, creeping dalea, desert zinnia, blue spurge, and Greek germander all make good groundcovers around century plant. Fairy duster, manzanita, shadscale, sages, and yellow bells are interesting shrub companions. Because of their sharp leaf tips, it is best to locate century plants away from high-traffic areas, especially away from active play spaces.

How to Plant

Loosen the soil well in an area 3 times the width of the rootball so that plants can root out easily. Be sure the plant doesn't settle after watering, burying the crown deeper than the plant had been growing. Gravel mulch helps keep the crown dry while maintaining moisture in the soil.

Advice for Care

Water agave once a month in summer and keep the plants dry during cold weather. After they have flowered, don body armor and remove the spent plants entirely.

Species, Cultivars, or Varieties

Many agave are cold hardy only in Zone 7 or warmer zones, but New Mexico agave (*A. neomexicana*) and Parry's century plant (*A. parryi*) are two very cold-tolerant species. New Mexico agave grows 15 in. high and 24 in. wide and usually produces many offsets. It is native up to 7000 ft. in the mountains of southern New Mexico. Its wide, gray-green, wedge-shaped leaves are 3 in. wide at the base, tapering to a brown spine at the tip. The leaves curve slightly outward. Parry's agave grows 18 in. tall and wide and resembles a giant blue artichoke. The leaves are 4 in. wide at the base and taper to a black spine at the tip. *Agave lechuguilla* is one of the smallest agaves, with gray-green leaves only 10 in. high on compact upright plants less than 1 ft. wide. It rootsprouts aggressively, forming dense colonies, and is a good barrier and erosion-control plant in wild gardens in Zone 6 and warmer. The slender flower stems of lechuguilla grow 8 ft. tall; the florets are yellow tinged with purple.

Cholla and Prickly Pear

Opuntia species

Height: 1 to 6 ft. **Flowers:** Yellow or pink **Foliage:** None **Bloom Period:** Early summer **Zones:** 5 to 8 **Water:** Very low	**Light Requirement:**

Though not as architecturally impressive as warm desert plants like saguaro and barrel cactus, the cholla and prickly pear of the cold deserts are interesting for their range of shapes, stem forms, spine colors, spine textures, and satiny flowers in a range of pale to brilliant colors. Their spiny stems are a safe haven for many nesting birds, and hummingbirds work the flowers. Cholla and prickly pear are our largest cacti.

WHEN TO PLANT

Prickly pear and cholla are best transplanted when the soil is warm but can be set out any time of year as long as plants have been acclimated to cold and are kept dry during the winter months. Shield new plants with poultry netting if rabbits gnaw on them in pursuit of their stored moisture.

WHERE TO PLANT

Shrubby cacti will grow in any soil that can be kept dry. They combine well with other succulents, desert shrubs, and wildflowers in borders and as accent groupings. Give these plants plenty of space and site them away from paths and play areas.

HOW TO PLANT

Opuntia can be grown from seeds, but large plants are grown more quickly from cuttings. Sever pads or canes cleanly with a sharp blade. Lay the pieces in a shaded place for a week or so until the cuts dry. Set the cuttings in loosened soil and don't water them. For seasoned gardeners, the hardest part of rooting cacti is leaving them alone. Kitchen tongs make handling the spiny plants easier. When transplanting container-grown specimens, loosen the soil well so that plants can root out easily. If the plant settles after watering, the stems will still root as long as the soil is not kept too wet.

ADVICE FOR CARE

Cholla and prickly pear can be watered monthly during hot weather, but once well-rooted they require no supplemental watering. There are two insect pests to watch for: cocchineal and borers. Cocchineal are scalelike insects. The adults are covered with a white cottony substance and when crushed bleed a beautiful magenta fluid that is prized by weavers as a source of dye. Control cocchineal in the garden in summer by regularly hosing off affected plants. Borer adults are large, black, smooth-bodied insects with long antennae. They can be found feeding on the outer surface of *Opuntia* in the early morning. The unseen larvae do the most damage, devouring the soft tissue inside the pads and canes until portions of the plant collapse. The best control is to remove the adults by hand whenever they appear, and to remove discolored portions of the plant with the larvae inside as soon as they are noticed.

SPECIES, CULTIVARS, OR VARIETIES

Christmas cholla (*O. leptocaulis*) grows 3 ft. high and wide with slender, dark-green stems armed with long gold spines. Its pale-yellow flowers appear in early summer; the marble-sized, bright-red fruits persist into winter. Candle cholla (*O. kleiniae*) is similar but grows at least twice as large. It has dusty-pink flowers and spines that aren't as pretty but are just as sharp. Cane cholla (*O. imbricata*) grows 4 to 6 ft. high and wide; it has starlike clusters of gray spines on its 1¹/₂-in. dull-green canes that are indented with bumps called "tubercles." Large magenta flowers appear in June and are followed by yellow fruits in late summer. Gold cholla (*O. davisii*) grows 2 ft. high and 3 to 4 ft. wide with short, pale-green canes that are densely armed with pale-gold paper-sheathed spines that glow when backlit by the sun. The small yellow-green flowers bloom in early summer. Silver cholla (*O. echinocarpa*) is similar, but its spine sheaths are silver. Both gold and silver cholla are cold hardy to Zone 6. Purple prickly pear (*O. macrocentra*) grows 18 in. high and twice as wide with 5-in. rounded blue-green pads armed with 2-in.-long dark-brown spines at the top edge. In early summer it produces large yellow flowers, each with a red ring around the gold stamens; its pads turn shades of purple during cold weather. Engelmann's prickly pear (*O. engelmannii*) is the largest of the cold-hardy prickly pear, growing 4 ft. high and 8 ft. wide. Its 12-in. circular green pads are armed with 2-in. white or gray spines. Yellow flowers 2 in. across fade to a pale orange and are followed by large, juicy purple fruits. The flavor of the fruits varies; some are quite tasty.

Hardy Tiger Jaws

Chasmatophyllum musculinum

Height: 1 in.
Flower: Yellow
Foliage: Evergreen
Bloom Period: Summer
Zones: 5 to 8
Water: Low

Light Requirement:

ardy tiger jaws is one of a choice group of cold-tolerant succulents from the mountains of South Africa that are being introduced to American gardens through the Denver Botanic Gardens. It forms a dense-spreading mat of smooth, pale-green leaves 12 in. across. Individual leaves are oblong, wedge-shaped, and paired opposite each other on the prostrate stems. The name "tiger jaws" is suggested by the ridges on the paired leaves, which actually look nothing like the yawning mouth of a savage beast. We gardeners are an imaginative group, and common names often reflect our whimsy as much as they describe the character of plants. The leaves of tiger jaws are so closely crowded that its thick woody stems are not visible. Flowers are daisylike with pale-yellow satiny petals surrounding frilly stamens of the same color.

WHEN TO PLANT

Hardy tiger jaws are best transplanted when the soil is warm, but they can be set out any time of year as long as the plants have been acclimated to cold and are kept dry during the winter months.

WHERE TO PLANT

These plants prefer coarse, gritty soils. Tiger jaws can be grouped with pineleaf penstemon, Greek germander, Persian rockcress, and the small species of cactus in xeric rock gardens. Plant it between flagstones in pathways or use it for edging along patios. Rabbits love the moisture-filled leaves and will chew plants down faster than they can regrow, so it is best to grow tiger jaws in walled or fenced gardens.

How to Plant

Plants are grown from seed pressed lightly into the surface of sharp sand or other gritty, warm soil. Clusters of leaves attached to a short section of stem also root easily in warm, well-aerated soil. To transplant container-grown stock, loosen the soil well in an area 3 or 4 times the width of the rootball so that plants can root out easily. Be sure the plant doesn't settle too much after watering, burying the crown too deep. If the crown and stems are buried only slightly, they will still root as long as the soil isn't kept too wet. Gravel is preferred as mulch because it will keep the crown drier while helping to maintain moisture in the soil.

Advice for Care

Hardy tiger jaws may need summer watering to a depth of 18 to 24 in. every 2 weeks. Water monthly in spring and fall, and once or twice in winter if there has been no rain or snow.

Species, Cultivars, or Varieties

There are no other species in cultivation at this time.

Regional Considerations

At the cold-hardiness limits of its range, it is best to transplant tiger jaws in spring or early summer, allowing plenty of time for the plants to root before the onset of winter.

Hedgehog Cactus

Echinocereus species

<table>
<tr><td>

Height: 4 to 8 in.
Flower: Pink or red
Foliage: None
Bloom Period: Late spring and early summer
Zones: 5 to 8
Water: Very low

</td><td>

Light Requirement:

</td></tr>
</table>

*H*edgehog cactus starts as a single columnar stem a few inches in diameter. As the plant grows, offsets develop along the main stem, and it eventually becomes a compact mound with many heads in clumps 12 in. or more in diameter. Each head, or growing tip, produces brilliantly colored cup-shaped flowers. All hedgehogs have flowers that last only a few weeks, but they are so spectacular that even gardeners who thought they didn't like cactus find themselves wondering where they might plant a few. Luckily the plants are relatively small and grow very well in pots, so there is always room for them.

WHEN TO PLANT

Hedgehog cactus is best transplanted when the soil is warm, but it can be set out any time of year as long as the plant has been acclimated to cold and is kept dry during the winter months.

WHERE TO PLANT

Smaller types should be placed in the foreground of rock outcroppings or desert gardens and paired with xeric flowers and shrubs that are equally self-contained to ensure that the hedgehogs are not shaded out by their companions. Claret cup grows large enough to be appreciated at a distance as well as up close. Desert zinnia, gazania, moss rose, rainlily, blue spurge, blackfoot daisy, creeping baby's breath, Greek germander, pineleaf penstemon, woolly thyme, fairy duster, lavender, shrubby salvias, and shadscale all make good garden companions.

HOW TO PLANT

Hedgehogs are grown from seeds sown in very warm, fast-draining soil. It may take 5 years for seedlings to bloom for the first time. To transplant container-grown specimens, loosen the soil well so that plants can root out easily. Be sure the plant doesn't settle any deeper than it was growing previously.

ADVICE FOR CARE

As long as the soil is aerated and dries quickly between waterings, young plants can be watered every few weeks in summer to speed their growth. Mature plants should only be watered monthly in summer if at all.

SPECIES, CULTIVARS, OR VARIETIES

Green hedgehog (*E. viridiflorus*) has clusters of 2-in.-wide, 4-in.-tall stems with red-and-white spines. It produces green, citrus-scented flowers and is cold hardy to Zone 4. Fendler hedgehog (*E. fendleri*) grows 8 in. tall. It is slow to form offsets, so the plants are usually taller than they are wide. The dark-green stems are armed with central spines surrounded by smaller white spines with reddish markings. The pink flowers are 3 in. long and are followed by large, red, spiny fruits. The subspecies *E. fendleri* ssp. *kuenzleri* has strawberry-scented fruits. Lace hedgehog (*E. reichenbachii*) grows 6 in. high in mounds 6 in. wide. Its starlike spines lie close to the stems; the rose-pink flowers are nearly as large as the stems that produce them. Claret cup hedgehog (*E. triglochidiatus*) grows 12 in. high in clusters 18 in. across. The 3-in.-thick green stems are angular and armed with gray spines on the ribs. A profusion of scarlet flowers nearly hides the plant body in early summer.

Ocotillo

Fouqueria splendens

Height: 6 to 15 ft.
Flowers: Red
Foliage: Deciduous
Bloom Period: Spring and summer
Zone: 7 and 8
Water: Very low

Light Requirement:

Ocotillo is hard to characterize in garden terms. Technically it's a shrub, very obviously of desert origin. It stores water in its stems and roots to get through times of drought. Flushes of small oval leaves are produced along its thorny whiplike stems in spring and after summer rains, disappearing quickly when the soil dries again. Long, unbranched stems radiate upward from a crown at ground level to form a broad vase shape. A 15-ft. stem might be 2 in. thick at the ground and taper to ³/₄ in. at the tip. Tubular red flowers sprout from the branch tips like flames on a candle, drawing hummingbirds to a feast of nectar. Like the leaves, the flowers come in flushes in response to rain. Ocotillo is native to rocky hillsides in central and southern New Mexico and could be the signature plant of our Chihuahuan desert, as the saguaro cactus is of the Sonoran desert.

WHEN TO PLANT

In central New Mexico, plant in spring and early summer so that ocotillo has time to root before cold weather. In the southern low-desert areas it can be planted any time of year.

WHERE TO PLANT

Ocotillo needs well-drained gravelly or sandy soil. Because it has such a striking profile, it is planted as an accent plant against south- and west-facing walls where it basks in the reflected heat. In desert gardens it can be grouped with violet silverleaf, bird-of-paradise, red yucca, prickly pear, cholla, creosote bush, fernbush, or sages. Plant it with red iceplant, lantana, or creeping dalea as filler at ground level.

How to Plant

Loosen the soil well in an area 3 or 4 times the width of the rootball but only a few inches deeper so that plants can root out easily. If you bury the crown a little deeper than it was planted previously in order to stabilize a large plant, be sure not to keep the soil too wet at the base until new roots have had time to form along the buried stems. Gravel is preferred as mulch because it will keep the crown drier while helping to maintain moisture in the soil. Seeds germinate easily in warm soil. The hard part is waiting for a sizable plant to develop. Green stem cuttings also root easily in a very well-drained aerated medium with bottom heat. More ocotillo are wild collected than nursery grown. Buy from a reputable dealer to avoid plants that may have been stolen from public or private land. Ocotillo should also be source identified; plants from much warmer southern and Sonoran sources will not be as cold hardy as locally native or higher-elevation plants.

Advice for Care

Although ocotillo is very drought tolerant once established, new transplants may be watered twice a month during the first summer to help develop new roots. Established plants may be watered deeply once or twice a month in summer to keep them leafy. Stop watering in August and let nature take its course so that plants go into cold weather hardened off. If branches break or stems are arching into a pathway, cut them back all the way to the ground to maintain the natural form of the plant.

Species, Cultivars, or Varieties

No other species is cold hardy in New Mexico.

Regional Considerations

At the cold-hardiness limits of its range, it is best to allow the plant plenty of time to root before the onset of winter. An elevation of 6500 ft. is probably the upper extent of ocotillo's cold hardiness in central New Mexico and southward.

Pincushion Cactus

Escobaria species

Height: 3 or 4 in.	Light Requirement:
Flowers: Pink	
Foliage: None	
Bloom Period: Summer	
Zones: 4 to 8	
Water: Very low	

*P*incushion cactus are delicate-looking plants. Tiny, succulent, blue-green buttonlike stems are overlaid with a lacy pattern of small spines. The vase-shaped flowers hint at this plant's resilience. They are nearly the size of the plant and come in shades of pink ranging from soft salmon to screaming magenta. Unfortunately, hikers rarely stumble upon these gems along the trails any more, as overcollecting has stripped the hillsides of the slow-growing plants. Nursery-grown plants are available from specialty growers; buying these plants allows gardeners to tuck pincushion cactus into sunny niches without despoiling the remaining wild populations.

WHEN TO PLANT

Plant in spring so that pincushions will have plenty of warm rooting time before the return of cold weather.

WHERE TO PLANT

Pincushion cactus is finely sculpted and must have space in the fore-ground apart from other plants that would otherwise crowd and shade it. When nestled among boulders it thrives in the reflected heat, and condensation from the stone encourages rooting. It is easy to grow in pots or in rockery troughs.

HOW TO PLANT

Plants grown from seeds may take 5 years to bloom for the first time. To sow seeds, press them into very warm fast-draining soil. The sideshoots of older plants can be cut cleanly, allowed to callous, and then rooted in aerated, barely moist soil. To transplant con-tainer-grown specimens, loosen the soil well in an area 3 times the width of the rootball so that plants can root out easily. Be sure the plant doesn't settle too much after watering, burying the crown too deep. If the crown and stems are buried only slightly, they will still root as long as the soil isn't kept too wet. Gravel is preferred as mulch because it will keep the crown drier while helping to maintain moisture in the soil.

ADVICE FOR CARE

Once established, pincushion cactus needs careful weeding to keep larger plants from taking over. It will tolerate occasional watering, but water no more than monthly in summer. This drought-requiring plant thrives on neglect; attempts to force growth with fertilizer and water can weaken it.

SPECIES, CULTIVARS, OR VARIETIES

Lee's pincushion (*E. leei*) grows 3-in.-high, 6-in.-wide clusters of several dozen stems. Salmon-pink flowers bloom on the oldest, largest stems. This plant is particularly endangered by overcollecting, and growing it from nursery-produced seeds or plants in the garden will help preserve a native jewel. New Mexico pincushion (*E. vivipara* var. *neomexicana*) grows in clusters 4 in. high and 6 in. wide. The green plant body is covered with a filigree of white, red-tipped spines. Brilliant magenta flowers cover the small plants in early summer. Plain's pincushion (*E. missouriensis*) grows only 2 or 3 in. high but forms the largest clusters of the three types mentioned here. Mature plants produce clumps nearly a foot across. Plain's pincushion has small white flowers, fewer spines, and tolerates the most moisture and cold (to Zone 4).

Purple Iceplant

Delosperma cooperi

Height: 1 to 6 in.
Flower: Deep-magenta with yellow eyes
Foliage: Somewhat evergreen
Bloom Period: Summer
Zones: 5 to 8
Water: Low

Light Requirement:

The hardy iceplants are a select group of carpet-forming succu-lents, mostly South African in origin, that will survive the cold winters of the high desert. Their fleshy leaves, 2 in. long and ¼ in. thick, are clustered densely on the prostrate woody stems. The daisy-like flowers are brilliantly colored and so profuse at times that they hide the foliage. In milder climates, iceplant is used as a large-scale groundcover, but in New Mexico gardens it is more reliable as a filler in medium-sized spaces. Purple iceplant is a robust plant that spreads up to 24 in. wide in just a few summers; it is one of the most cold tolerant and easy to grow of the hardy iceplants. Its flowers are 1-in. deep-magenta daisies with yellow stamens. In protected gardens, the foliage is semi-evergreen, but in harsher exposures the blue-green leaves will wither entirely by midwinter.

WHEN TO PLANT

Cuttings need warm soil to root; plants establish most quickly when planted after the temperature moderates in spring. Iceplant can be transplanted in full bloom in the heat of summer as long as it is watered regularly. Late spring or summer is the ideal time to relo-cate volunteer seedlings. It is best to forego planting in winter.

WHERE TO PLANT

Iceplant is well suited to gritty infertile soil but adapts to most soils if not kept too wet. Rabbits love the moisture-filled leaves and will chew plants down faster than they can regrow, especially in winter, so it is best to use them in walled or fenced gardens. Purple and red iceplants blend well with blue and purple flowers such as giant four o'clock, blue mist, salvias, buddleias, Texas and Russian sages, and lavender. They flower most profusely when grown in full sun. Yellow and white iceplants are more vigorous when grown in partial shade.

How to Plant

Iceplant's modest above-ground growth is little indication of the deep, shrublike root system that established plants develop. Cuttings root easily as long as there is a section of woody stem attached. To transplant container-grown plants or rooted cuttings, loosen the soil well in an area 3 or 4 times the width of the rootball so that plants can root out easily. Gravel is preferred as mulch because it will stay drier on the surface while helping to maintain moisture in the soil.

Advice for Care

Iceplants thrive on deep watering 2 or 3 times a month when temperatures are 90 degrees Fahrenheit or above. Water monthly or less when the soil is cool. Fertilizer is not needed. Plants do not bloom as well when grown in nitrogen-rich garden soil.

Species, Cultivars, or Varieties

Red iceplant (*Malephora crocea*) has plump evergreen leaves and grows 6 in. high and 30 in. wide. It produces large red daisies with yellow centers. The least cold tolerant of the hardy iceplants, it grows best in Zones 7 and 8. Shrubby iceplant (*Ruschia pulvinaris*) grows 4 in. high and 12 in. wide with slender, 1-in.-long leaves. Its magenta daisies are 3/4 in. wide with white centers. Flowers bloom for a month in early summer. Trailing iceplant (*Ruschia hamata*) grows 6 in. high and 18 in. wide and has small, tubular leaves on long, slender stems. Hot-pink flowers contrast with the blue-green leaf color. Yellow iceplant (*D. nubigenum*) has 1-in.-thick, bright-green, wedge-shaped leaves that turn red in winter and are reliably evergreen. The 3/4-in. yellow flowers bloom most heavily in late spring and spottily throughout summer. Yellow iceplant is most vigorous in partial shade.

Sotol

Dasylirion wheelerii

Height: 5 ft. **Flowers:** White **Foliage:** Evergreen **Bloom Period:** Early summer **Zones:** 6 to 8 **Water:** Very low	**Light Requirement:**

Sotol is a lily native to the Chihuahuan desert. Like its kin, bear-grass and yucca, it produces slender evergreen leaf blades that grow in a large clump from a central crown. Sotol is also called "saw-tooth yucca." Its leaf margins are bordered with fine hooked teeth and look much like double-edged saw blades. The 30-in.-long, 1/2-in.-wide leaves are pale blue or green with yellow margins. The crown initially grows at ground level; young plants resemble clumps of grass. As it matures, sotol develops a short trunk that elevates the fan of leaves and gives the plant a bold silhouette. Bolder still is the flower stalk, which emerges from the crown and pushes skyward 10 or 12 ft., unfolding masses of tiny white florets.

WHEN TO PLANT
Sotol roots fastest into warm soil. It is very heat loving and may be planted any time from spring through late summer. Cold-acclimated plants can be set out in fall or winter as long as they are kept dry.

WHERE TO PLANT
Sotol grows slowly but consistently to a massive 6-ft. spread. Like all spiny plants, it should be given a bit of extra space as a safety zone. In the foothills and lava beds of south and central New Mexico where sotol grows wild, desert willow, littleleaf sumac, creosote bush, cholla and prickly pear, Apache plume, fairy duster, and turpentine bush are all companions. They make a pleasing mix in gardens as well. Clumps of sotol and *Opuntia* planted together as a border will provide a dramatic and formidable barrier.

HOW TO PLANT
It takes patience to grow sotol from seeds; sow the seeds on warm well-drained soil. Nursery-grown plants are available in large sizes.

To transplant container-grown specimens, loosen the soil well in an area 3 or 4 times the width of the rootball, so plants can root out easily. Be sure the plant doesn't settle after watering, burying the crown deeper than the plant had been growing. Gravel is preferred as mulch because it will keep the crown drier while helping to maintain moisture in the soil.

ADVICE FOR CARE

If a controlled appearance is desired, or if plants are growing near a pool where seed litter would be a problem, prune off flower stems immediately after the plants bloom. If habitat is a higher priority, leave the seedheads on until the birds have harvested their fill. Hummingbirds use the stalks as roosts. The oldest basal leaves may be trimmed off in more cultivated garden settings. Speed young plants' growth by watering to a depth of 3 ft. once or twice a month from May through August. Be sure to keep plants dry in winter to avoid root rot.

SPECIES, CULTIVARS, OR VARIETIES

Dasylirion leiophyllum is very similar to *D. wheelerii*. The most obvious distinction between the two is the difference in the barbs on the leaf margins: those on *D. leiophyllum* angle downward along the leaves, while the barbs on *D. wheeleri* angle toward the leaf tips.

REGIONAL CONSIDERATIONS

When transplanting sotol at the cold-hardiness limits of its range, it is best to plant in spring or early summer. This will allow plenty of time for the plant to root before the onset of winter.

Yucca

Yucca species

Height: 3 to 15 ft.	**Light Requirement:**
Flowers: White	
Foliage: Evergreen	
Bloom Period: Early summer	
Zones: 4 to 6	
Water: Low	

With their spearlike leaf blades, dramatic silhouettes, and elegant tiered flower candelabra, yucca plants are the cornerstone of the desert garden. Their waxy, bell-shaped white flowers are pollinated by small chalk-white *Pronuba* moths whose larvae consume some of the seeds in exchange for the adults having carried the pollen from flower to flower.

WHEN TO PLANT

Plant the less cold-tolerant species in spring or summer so that plants will have plenty of warmth to establish themselves before the onset of cold weather. The more cold-tolerant types can be planted any time as long as the plants have been acclimated.

WHERE TO PLANT

Yuccas are undemanding as long as there is plenty of light and the soil remains fairly dry. Single plants or groups of a single species create an austere, minimalist planting. For a softer, lusher garden, yuccas can be grouped with Texas sage, bird-of-paradise, creosote bush, fernbush, fairy duster, desert willow, acacia, mesquite, iceplant, 'New Gold' lantana, verbena, or creeping dalea. Red yucca will grow and bloom well in partial shade and requires more water to thrive.

HOW TO PLANT

If grown from seeds sown in very warm fast-draining soil, it may take more than 5 years for seedlings to bloom for the first time. To transplant container-grown specimens, loosen the soil well in an area 3 times the width of the rootball so that plants can root out easily. Be sure the yucca doesn't settle after watering, burying the crown deeper than the plant had been growing. Gravel is preferred as mulch because it will keep the crown drier while helping to maintain moisture in the soil.

ADVICE FOR CARE

In more cultivated garden settings, you may wish to prune off the flower stems immediately after plants bloom. Scale insects sometimes feed on the ends of the leaves. They rarely do enough damage to warrant control. A light application of horticultural oil in spring will smother scale crawlers (the mobile juvenile form of the insect). Tender new leaves can be vulnerable, so be sure to test the spray on a few leaves first to ensure that it will not burn the foliage. To speed young plants' growth, water to a depth of 3 ft. once a month from May through August. Keep plants dry in winter to avoid root rot.

SPECIES, CULTIVARS, OR VARIETIES

Soaptree (*Y. elata*) grows 15 ft. tall and produces a stout trunk sheathed in dried leaves. The 24-in.-long, $1/2$-in.-wide leaf blades arch away from the crown. The flower stalk grows at least twice the height of the plant. Soaptree is hardy in Zones 6 to 8. Soapweed (*Y. glauca*) is a scaled-down model of soaptree. Mature plants are rarely taller than 4 ft. and have shorter leaves and flower stems. Soapweed is hardy in Zones 4 to 8. Spanish dagger (*Y. baccata*) grows 3 to 4 ft. high with multiple heads of green leaves that are $1^1/2$ in. wide and 2 ft. long. The flower spikes grow just beyond the leaves; sweet 6-in.-long fruits develop from the flowers. Spanish dagger is hardy in Zones 5 to 8. Joshua tree (*Y. brevifolia*) is a multi-headed plant that grows to 20 ft. tall. Stiff, light-green leaves $3/4$ in. wide and 12 in. long are sharply pointed and clustered in dense heads. Each head produces several flower stalks in an impressive display of creamy-white flowers. Joshua tree is hardy in Zones 6 to 8. Red yucca (*Hesperaloe parviflora*) is so different from the others that it is in a separate genus. It has narrow basal leaves 1 in. wide and 3 ft. long in clumps 4 to 5 ft. wide. Both the leaves and flower spikes are limber; the entire plant is softer in character than other yuccas. The coral or yellow flowers bloom from May through September and are pollinated by hummingbirds. Red yucca is hardy in Zones 5 through 8.

CHAPTER FOUR

Groundcovers

$\mathcal{G}$ROUNDCOVERS IS A CATCHALL GARDEN CATEGORY. When I began to garden in New Mexico and looked to nature for clues to cope with the harsh climate, my concept of groundcover was one of the first to undergo a shift in meaning. Nearly any low-growing plant can be considered a groundcover if it densely cloaks the soil surface over a relatively large area.

When you closely examine any wild plant community that hasn't been altered significantly by overgrazing, clearcut logging, or natural disasters, one of the first things that becomes apparent is that many different species make up the plant community in even the smallest spaces. Usually there are a few dominant species, such as beargrass and sumac in the foothills, or sage and dalea in the low deserts, that provide the obvious cover. Look more closely and you will see dozens of companion species that fill the gaps between the predominant plants. It is the richness of these associates that makes a wild landscape stable and capable of adapting to change.

The horticultural definition of groundcover is a monoculture, a single plant variety covering a relatively large space, but such uniformity is not natural, and at times may even be unhealthy. An insect pest or disease can have a devastating impact, both visually and functionally, on the space as a whole. The design role of groundcovers in the garden is to provide neutral space, those uncluttered sweeps that offset the plants that are used as focal points. Mixes of plants can work just as well as an extensive planting of a single species as long as the mix is subdued and there is enough repetition to suggest a pattern. In cultivated gardens, giant four o'clock paired with cotoneaster, and creeping dalea combined with desert zinnia are refined blends. At the opposite end of the spectrum, a mix of prairie grasses is the ultimate example of a wildly diverse groundcover.

Native grasses are enjoying a renaissance nationwide. Sometimes water conservation is the motive for growing them, but just as often the motive is to retire the lawn mower and gain freedom from weekly maintenance chores. Economics also comes into play— native grass groundcovers make excellent dollar sense when a large area needs to be covered. Since prairies are grown from seed, the planting cost per square foot is low. The initial planting cost may be similar to turfgrasses, but once established, a mix of warm-season native grasses can get by with no fertilizer and only one or two annual mowings; it will stay reasonably green if watered deeply twice a month from April through September.

The plants I've included in the profiles are vigorous, fairly low-growing with a spreading form, and easy to grow under a range of conditions. They form a dense cover in a reasonable amount of time, are long-lived, and stop just short of being weedy. If used in a border in good garden soil, in fact, some of them would be too invasive.

Long-time New Mexico gardeners might wonder why spreading junipers are not among the groundcovers profiled. They provide tough, long-lived, dense cover with a modest amount of water, and they are evergreens that come through a freeze-drying winter look-ing good. Nurseries will supply, and gardeners will buy, spreading junipers whether I extol their virtues or not, but for diversity's sake I wanted to devote space to plants that haven't been used so much. Before dismissing them as redundant, there are a few points I should make about junipers in high-desert gardens. 'Wilton Carpet', or 'Blue Rug', is a beautiful female *J. horizontalis* that grows quite well as long as it is shaded in the afternoon. The *J. sabina* cultivars usually do better than those of *J. horizontalis* in resisting pests such as scale and spider mite, yet 'Calgary Carpet' is a *sabina* that draws mites like a magnet. There are at least a hundred cultivars of spread-ing junipers, and many of them are female clones that produce no irritating pollen. The very prostrate forms tend to be more robust and pest resistant when mulched with shredded bark, pine straw, or pecan hulls, probably because those mulches reflect less heat.

Soil preparation varies for different groundcovers, but one thing is basic: Because a degree of uniformity is desired even when a vari-ety of plants are used, the more consistent the growing conditions, the more the plants will respond in kind. Completely remove all other vegetation from the area before preparing the soil, and keep shrubby groundcovers mulched to suppress weeds as much as possible.

Creeping Dalea

Dalea greggii

Height: 6 in.	**Light Requirement:**
Flowers: Purple	
Foliage: Evergray	
Bloom Period: Summer	
Zones: 7 and 8	
Water: Low to moderate	

*C*reeping dalea is native to the limestone slopes of southern New Mexico at elevations between 2500 and 6000 ft. where annual rainfall is just 8 to 10 in. per year. The thin, wiry stems are densely covered with tiny, silver leaves. Stems trail along the soil and root where they touch soft ground, eventually creating a mounding carpet 3 ft. across. The globular flower heads, clusters of purple flowers only $^1/_2$ in. in diameter, are inconspicuous at a distance and a nice surprise up close. Dalea is a very subdued groundcover that makes a carefree foil for bolder, more colorful plants. It is noteworthy for its drought and heat tolerance.

WHEN TO PLANT
Plant when the soil is warm. The small, self-shading leaves make transplanting in summer possible in the low desert, but at the high-elevation limits of its range, creeping dalea needs ample time to root before cold weather.

WHERE TO PLANT
Dalea tolerates a range of soils but is best adapted to well-drained rocky or sandy soil. Its fine texture and low profile make creeping dalea excellent for planting between boulders; draping over the edge of retaining walls; as a base for the sculptural forms of cacti, agave, and yuccas; and as filler between desert wildflowers and shrubs, especially those with coarser or darker foliage such as Jerusalem sage, Arizona rosewood, sumacs, Mexican buckeye, and algerita.

HOW TO PLANT
Recent research has demonstrated that the best soil preparation for container-grown plants, even deeply rooting desert shrubs like

dalea, is to dig holes only as deep as the rootball, but four to six times its diameter. A plant's long initial taproots are forced to branch laterally when it is potted, and loosening the soil around the roots will encourage a stronger root system. Backfill soil requires no amendment. A fine gravel mulch will encourage root development along the stems.

ADVICE FOR CARE

Water deeply during the growing season at least every 2 weeks until plants fill in. Establishment usually takes 2 years. Once well-established, creeping dalea can be maintained with deep monthly watering during the growing season and an occasional watering in winter. Limiting water to only what plants require helps minimize weed invasion. If plants overgrow their space or if unusually cold weather causes some winter dieback, trim out the oldest woody stems. Shorten stems overall to encourage new growth in spring.

SPECIES, CULTIVARS, OR VARIETIES

Feather dalea (*Dalea formosa*) is semi-evergreen and twiggy, growing 2 ft. tall and wide with wine-colored flower clusters. Feathery seedheads give the plant a hazy look. Broom dalea (*Psorothamnus scoparius*) forms a 2-ft.-high, 3-ft.-wide mound of slender blue stems. It blooms heavily through the month of August with fragrant clusters of wine or indigo-purple flowers. Both these plants require well-drained soil.

REGIONAL CONSIDERATIONS

Feather dalea is cold hardy to at least 7000 ft. throughout New Mexico, while broom dalea prefers the longer season of hot weather in the central and southern portion. Creeping dalea is best adapted to the hot southern desert.

Creeping Germander

Teucrium chamaedrys 'Prostrata'

Height: 6 in. **Flowers:** Rose-pink **Foliage:** Evergreen **Bloom Period:** Summer **Zones:** 5 to 8 **Water:** Moderate	**Light Requirement:**

*L*ike roses, salvias, artemisias, and penstemons, teucriums have few black sheep in the family. Creeping germander is a low-spreading, root-sprouting groundcover that tolerates heat and spreads out at least 2 ft. when watered deeply. It is grouped with the ground-covers because it is aggressive enough to resist weed encroachment and will swallow up any nearby, less-vigorous perennials if planted in good garden soil. The glossy dark-green leaves are small, about $1/2$ in. long, with notched margins. They grow closely spaced on short, upright stems. The rose-pink flowers are crowded in spikes 2 to 4 in. above the foliage, producing a sheet of color that lasts for several weeks in summer. Blooming is somewhat less intense but lasts longer when plants are grown in partial shade.

WHEN TO PLANT

Plants can be transplanted from containers any time; in winter, set out only those plants that have been acclimated to cold. Divisions transplant easily in spring and late summer or in early fall. Seeds germinate when the soil has warmed to at least 60 degrees Fahrenheit.

WHERE TO PLANT

Creeping germander adapts easily to most soils. It makes a good filler in large rock gardens and works well as a groundcover under both deciduous and evergreen trees. Plant creeping germander along paths and patios with 'Bowles Mauve' wallflower, English lavender, curry plant, Texas sage, and other compact, silver-leafed plants.

HOW TO PLANT

When transplanting container-grown plants or divisions, dig gener-ous holes, loosening the soil so that new roots will have an easy time breaking ground. When plants are to be spaced 18 to 24 in. apart, it is easier to rototill the entire planting area and set plants out in the tilled soil. Backfill soil requires no amendment. A generous topdressing of mulch will keep the soil more uniformly moist and more moderate in temperature. Seeds should be sown on tilled soil; cover lightly. Germination takes 7 to 14 days.

ADVICE FOR CARE

Creeping germander requires very little care. Shear off the spent flower stems in late summer, and pull those few weeds that manage to muscle their way into an established stand. Water to a depth of 2 ft. every 2 weeks from May to September when temperatures are above 80 degrees Fahrenheit; water monthly the rest of the year.

SPECIES, CULTIVARS, OR VARIETIES

Teucrium chamaedrys, the species, is not evergreen. It grows taller than creeping germander, often reaching more than 1 ft. There are so many intermediate forms of this plant that planting selections and culling out the least attractive may be the way to develop the best groundcover for your needs. Bush germander (*Teucrium fruticans*) grows 4 ft. high and spreads twice as wide with small, silver leaves and soft lavender flowers on slender, arching stems. Native to rocky slopes in the Mediterranean foothills of Spain and North Africa, bush germander is very heat and drought tolerant once established. In southern New Mexico, however, it is reliably cold hardy only in Zone 8.

Daylily

Hemerocallus hybrids

Height: 1 to 4 ft.
Flowers: Broad spectrum of colors
Foliage: Herbaceous
Bloom Period: Varies
Zones: 3 to 8
Water: Moderate to high

Light Requirement:

*D*aylilies are included with groundcovers because they grow densely enough to exclude weeds and are most impressive if planted in large groups. There are so many cultivars that generalizing is difficult. All have large, funnel-shaped flowers in a range of colors from creamy white to yellow, gold, orange, coral, pink, red, and bicolor mixes. The time and duration of bloom period depends on the variety. Flowers appear any time from spring to late summer and last from a few weeks to a month. Planting a mix of cultivars can extend the color through the whole season. The narrow, strap-like leaves are $^1/_2$ to 1 in. wide and at least 1 ft. long. They arch over to create a lush base for the elegant flowers. The tetraploid hybrids are the largest and most water intensive of the hybrids. They produce leathery flowers in a broad range of colors. Dwarf forms of daylily bloom the longest and are the most water conservative. The so-called evergreen varieties are herbaceous but dormant only briefly in warmer areas.

WHEN TO PLANT
Set out potted plants in spring, late summer, or autumn. Divide and reset established plants in late summer or autumn. Seeds germinate in a range of soil temperatures.

WHERE TO PLANT
Daylilies are much more productive in soil that has been generously amended with compost. They are most effective in large sweeps of a single color, varieties of different shades of the same color, or a combination of a few strongly contrasting colors. Daylilies make an impressive foreground when planted between flowering shrubs of contrasting color, i.e., apricot, orange, or yellow massed around vitex, or late-blooming pink shades with crape myrtle. Plant them as groundcover under open canopy trees such as jujube or hawthorn.

How to Plant

Dig generous holes, loosening the soil so that new roots will have an easy time breaking ground, and set plants 12 to 18 in. apart. Mix compost into the backfill soil and use more as mulch to keep the soil cool and more uniformly moist. Water thoroughly at planting time; in warmer parts of the state, be sure to water at least once a week during the growing season. Seeds germinate more uniformly if they are refrigerated in a damp vermiculite mixture for one month prior to sowing in spring.

Advice for Care

Trim off the spent flower stalks near their base after the last flower fades, and cut the leaves to the ground after hard freezes in fall. Because of their vigorous growth and coarse, fleshy roots, daylilies need to be divided every 3 to 5 years to maintain prolific flowering. Fertilizer should be unnecessary if the soil is amended every time beds are reworked. If leaves show signs of iron deficiency (a yellowing between the veins, which remain green), add chelated iron or iron sulfate.

Species, Cultivars, or Varieties

Lemon lily (*Hemerocallus flava*) is an old favorite with fragrant yellow flowers that bloom in May on 30-in. stems. 'Stella d'Oro' is a dwarf cultivar with yellow flowers on 12- to 18-in. stems. It blooms continuously from May to September. 'Black-eyed Stella' is similar with a dark-red throat.

Regional Considerations

Daylilies bloom most vigorously in the northern and higher elevation areas in New Mexico when planted in full sun. In the southern and low-desert areas, they will need regular watering and afternoon shade.

Desert Zinnia

Zinnia grandiflora

Height: 6 in. **Flowers:** Yellow **Foliage:** Deciduous **Bloom Period:** Summer **Zones:** 5 to 8 **Water:** Low	**Light Requirement:**

*N*ative to all the southwestern deserts as well as to the short-grass prairie and foothills of the Rockies, desert zinnia is the best choice for low cover and color in hot, dry places. It is noteworthy as a groundcover not because it is aggressively competitive, but because it is so drought tolerant and long-lived. The pale-green mounds of grassy foliage grow 6 to 10 in. wide, appearing when the soil warms in spring. Individual plants spread by slender rhizomes to form colonies. By June or early July, 1-in. flowers with 5 wide ray petals and small orange or yellow clusters of disc flowers cover the plants. Fading flowers become papery and remain on the plants.

WHEN TO PLANT

Sow seeds or transplant container-grown plants when the soil warms in spring. Heat-loving desert zinnia can be planted in mid-summer as long as the soil is kept moist until plants root out.

WHERE TO PLANT

Places that are oven-like nightmares for most plants are made to order for desert zinnia. Plant along sidewalks, in parking strips, at the edges of buffalograss mixed with winecups or flameflowers, or on south and west exposures between flagstones. Desert zinnia blooms continuously for several months in summer.

HOW TO PLANT

Seeds germinate erratically, so seed heavily for denser coverage. The seeds are attached to the ray flowers, but whole dried flower heads collected in autumn can be raked into tilled soil without cleaning the seeds. Flower heads should be stored cool and dry in paper sacks until spring soil has warmed to 70 degrees Fahrenheit. For faster coverage, transplant small container-grown desert zinnias.

Place plants 8 in. apart to cover the area in one year, or 12 in. apart to cover by the second growing season. Loosen the soil well so that transplants can root laterally. No soil amendments are needed. Weeds will be less of a problem initially if the soil is lean and mean.

ADVICE FOR CARE

Once established, desert zinnia will grow without supplemental watering, though it will only flower after rains. If watered deeply once or twice a month, it will bloom continuously throughout the summer. Excessive watering in heavy soil can lead to root rot. Too much water in lighter soils increases the likelihood of weed invasion. Water should penetrate 12 to 18 in. deep. Desert zinnia can be mowed in late winter to tidy up the planting.

SPECIES, CULTIVARS, OR VARIETIES

Cultivars of the annual *Zinnia angustifolia*, also sold as *Zinnia linearis*, are mildew-free and very prolific. 'Crystal White' has white daisies with golden eyes on plants that grow 5 in. tall and 10 in. wide; 'Star Gold' has yellow flowers with fewer ray petals; and 'Golden Orange' produces pumpkin-yellow 1-in. daisies that stand out against the small, dark-green leaves. Plants are more compact when grown dry and more sprawling when grown in good garden soil with regular watering. They are not nearly as drought adapted as desert zinnia.

REGIONAL CONSIDERATIONS

Because there is less heat to stimulate growth, desert zinnia is slower growing in the north and at elevations above 7000 ft. Too much winter moisture can lead to root rot.

Dwarf Plumbago

Ceratostigma plumbaginoides

Height: 6 in.
Flowers: Cobalt blue
Foliage: Herbaceous
Bloom Period: July to September
Zones: 5 to 8
Water: Moderate

Light Requirement:

---

*D*warf plumbago forms a dense groundcover that provides three seasons of interest. The shiny, apple-green leaves appear late in spring looking fresh and lush. By midsummer, sheets of round, 3/4-in. cobalt-blue flowers cluster at the ends of the stems. They cover the foliage, creating a refreshing oasis in the summer heat. Foliage turns red with the shorter days of autumn, then drops, leaving the short wiry stems to face winter alone. Dwarf plumbago looks so cultivated and refined as a groundcover, and its jewellike color is so vibrant, that it is tempting to mix it into flower beds. What really separates groundcovers from other herbaceous perennials anyway? The best answer to that question is plenty of space. Once plumbago digs in and starts to grow, only another groundcover of equal tenacity will be able hold its own in plumbago's company.

WHEN TO PLANT

Transplant potted plants or divide established clumps after soil has warmed in spring and danger of frost is past. Dwarf plumbago is one of the last perennials to leaf out in spring.

WHERE TO PLANT

Dwarf plumbago grows best as a groundcover in compost-amended soil under trees that take moderate to heavy watering. Fruit trees, honey locust, bur oak, and Texas red oak are all compatible selections. Fill the winter gap in its coverage by underplanting plumbago with grape hyacinths. When given a reasonable amount of water in our arid valley gardens, sweeps of dwarf plumbago and garlic chives under groves of trees create the feel of a cool forest glade.

How to Plant

Dig generous holes, loosening the soil so that new roots will have an easy time breaking ground. Till 3 or 4 in. of compost into the entire area to be planted and set plants 12 to 18 in. apart in the amended soil. Use shredded bark, pecan hulls, or more compost as mulch to keep the soil cool and more uniformly moist. Water thoroughly at planting time and at least once a week during the first growing season.

Advice for Care

Water at least every 2 weeks once plants are well-rooted. When temperatures exceed 90 degrees Fahrenheit, even established plants may need water once a week, especially while they are flowering. Water monthly in winter if there is no rain or snow. For cleanup, mow dwarf plumbago while it is dormant. If the groundcover is underplanted with grape hyacinths, set the mower blade high to leave the bulb foliage uncut; mow as soon as the plants go dormant in autumn. Once it has formed a dense network of roots, dwarf plumbago will resist weed invasion well.

Species, Cultivars, or Varieties

Ceratostigma griffithii grows 2 to 3 ft. tall. *C. willmottianum* can reach 4 ft. with limber, wiry stems. Its leaves and flowers are similar to those of dwarf plumbago. Neither plant gives the brilliant flower show of dwarf plumbago; both require more water.

Regional Considerations

Be sure to transplant plants grown in Zone 5 as soon as they begin growth in spring so that they will have adequate establishment time before cold weather returns. At higher elevations, dwarf plumbago can be planted in full sun. At lower elevations and in southern New Mexico, plant in full shade.

Giant Four O'Clock

Mirabilis multiflora

Height: 12 to 18 in.	**Light Requirement:**
Flowers: Magenta	
Foliage: Herbaceous	
Bloom Period: May to September	
Zones: 5 to 8	
Water: Low to moderate	

*M*irabilis means wonderful, and that's what giant four o'clock is as a groundcover. Though it dies back completely to the ground each autumn, its extensive root system and 3- to 6-ft. spread above ground make giant four o'clock shrublike in effect. As the soil warms in spring, thick stems densely covered with lush-looking, arrow-shaped leaves sprawl across the ground. Within a month, hundreds of 1½-in. tubular flowers will open each afternoon, drawing hawk moths and hummingbirds to drink. Flowers close by mid-morning the next day, reopening again after four in the afternoon. The starchy roots are sometimes more than 4 in. in diameter; after a few years they easily penetrate the soil 4 ft. deep. Mirabilis is a common New Mexican wildflower, especially in the pinyon- and juniper-dotted foothills between 5000 and 7500 ft.

WHEN TO PLANT
Sow seed and transplant young plants in spring when the soil has warmed to 70 degrees Fahrenheit.

WHERE TO PLANT
Giant four o'clock needs plenty of space in well-drained, infertile, sandy or gravelly soil. Compost retains too much moisture to be beneficial. In heavy clay soils, root rot can be a persistent problem. Even long-established plants can suffer occasional setbacks after unusually wet winters, emerging very late and flowering sparsely. Giant four o'clock looks great draping over the edge of retaining walls. Planting it in raised beds solves the drainage problem better than organic soil amendments can; amendments can also encourage rank, soft growth. Mass plants at the edge of the canopy of pines, cedars, and junipers. Giant four o'clock makes a striking contrast to blue mist or Russian sage. Plant it near patios that are used in the

morning or evening (when the flowers are open) so you can witness the steady parade of hawk moths and hummingbirds.

How to Plant

Sow the large, round seeds where the plants are to grow. Seed that has been mixed with damp perlite and refrigerated for 1 month will germinate in 7 days if sown in warm soil. Container-grown seedlings are very brittle. Unpot the plants carefully and disturb the fleshy roots as little as possible.

Advice for Care

In hotter, drier locations, plants are most colorful and lush when watered deeply once or twice a month during active growth. Established plants grown in cooler areas may rarely need supplemental water. Frost kills the top-growth, and the stems detach cleanly from the root soon afterward. Whole plants can be lifted with a garden fork and moved to the compost pile, or shredded and used as mulch where more plants are desired. Birds love the seeds and may drop them, primed to germinate, beneath trees where they roost. Uproot any unwanted seedlings promptly to prevent a much more difficult chore later.

Species, Cultivars, or Varieties

Marvel of Peru (*Mirabilis jalapa*) is the old garden four o'clock. It is not used much anymore because it is invasive, difficult to contain, and its colors are brassy.

'Gro-low' Sumac

Rhus aromatica 'Gro-low'

Height: 2 ft.
Flowers: Red fruits
Foliage: Deciduous
Bloom Period: Spring
Zones: 3 to 7
Water: Moderate

Light Requirement:

'Gro-low' sumac is a fast-growing shrub with smooth russet stems and glossy, dark-green leaves divided into three leaflets. 'Gro-low', a selection of a widespread native shrub called "fragrant sumac," is noteworthy for its low-spreading form and red fall foliage. Although it produces clusters of sticky red fruits in summer, it is layered or grown from cuttings, since seedlings revert back to the common taller form.

When to Plant

Container-grown plants can be transplanted any time the temperature is below 90 degrees Fahrenheit. Rooted layered stems should be moved in spring or fall while the top growth is dormant.

Where to Plant

'Gro-low' sumac is not fussy about soil. It requires less water when planted in clay and loams. Allow for at least 6 ft. of spread when planting near walkways. Its red fall color makes 'Gro-low' sumac striking as a foreground for conifers, especially blue spruce, blue atlas cedar, and columnar junipers.

How to Plant

Dig generous holes, loosening the soil so that new roots will have an easy time breaking ground. Recent research has demonstrated that the best soil preparation for container-grown shrubs is to dig holes only as deep as, or at most a few inches deeper than, the depth of the rootball, but 4 to 6 times its diameter. This is because most plants develop lateral, absorbing roots first and rely on those roots for initial establishment and long-term survival. Backfill soil requires no amendment. A generous mulch will keep the soil cooler and more uniformly moist, and it helps suppress weeds until the sumac fills in.

ADVICE FOR CARE

As long as they are given enough space to spread, the graceful arching stems of 'Gro-low' require no pruning. Tip-pruning, cutting the ends of individual branches back to the first laterals while plants are young, develops a network of finer branches. New plants can be made with a technique called "layering": year-old stems are pinned to the soil in late summer. The layers will usually be rooted by the following spring or summer and can be severed from the parent stock and transplanted in autumn or the following spring.

SPECIES, CULTIVARS, OR VARIETIES

'Autumn Amber' is similar to 'Gro-low', but its leaves are usually smaller and less glossy. Fall coloration is not as consistent as that of 'Gro-low'. 'Autumn Amber' rarely produces fruits, and those that do form are hollow, so plants must be propagated by cuttings or layering. It is decidedly more heat and drought tolerant than 'Gro-low' because it is actually a prostrate sport of threeleaf sumac (*Rhus trilobata*), a native of the hotter, drier climate of the Southwest. Threeleaf sumac is considered by some to be a xeric subspecies of fragrant sumac (*Rhus aromatica*). Fragrant sumac has a native range covering much of the temperate United States; its broad distribution makes it an extremely variable plant.

REGIONAL CONSIDERATIONS

Because 'Gro-low' is better adapted to cooler, moister climates, and has consistently beautiful scarlet fall color, I use it in more protected, cultivated niches in the low-desert areas. I use 'Autumn Amber' in the hellish spots such as street medians and exposed south or west slopes. 'Gro-low' works well throughout the state at elevations above 6500 ft.

Himalayan Fleeceflower

Persicaria affinis

Height: 6 to 18 in. **Flowers:** Pink **Foliage:** Semievergreen **Bloom Period:** Summer **Zones:** 4 to 7 **Water:** Moderate to heavy	**Light Requirement:**

*F*leeceflower starts the growing season as a mat of narrow green leaves streaked with red. In summer, the wiry flower stems stand well above the foliage carpet. Small, light-pink flowers are tightly clustered along the stems; while they are not individually showy, the impact of the numerous stems, lacy flowers, and colorful foliage is quite powerful. Leaves turn red in the fall and persist well into winter.

WHEN TO PLANT

Fleeceflower transplants well from containers any time the temperature is below 90 degrees Fahrenheit. Winter planting in milder winter areas is fine as long as the plants have been hardened off. Mulch helps prevent frost-heaving in cold weather and keeps soil cooler and moister in hot weather. New plants can be made by division in early spring.

WHERE TO PLANT

If you give fleeceflower rich garden soil and lots of water, it will go on a rampage. When planted in our typically infertile soil with controlled watering, it is a well-mannered groundcover under trees or combined with ornamental grasses. It does especially well with robust plants such as muhly, maiden grass, blue avena, and feather reedgrass.

HOW TO PLANT

Because seed dormancies make germination erratic, fleeceflower is usually propagated by division. Dig generous holes, loosening the soil so that new roots will have an easy time breaking ground. Since plants are usually spaced 18 to 24 in. apart, tilling 3 in. of compost into the area to be planted and then setting plants out in the loosened soil will be easier than digging individual holes. A generous topdressing of compost, shredded bark, or pecan hulls as mulch will keep the soil more uniformly moist and more moderate in temperature, accelerating the development of a dense groundcover.

ADVICE FOR CARE

For a neater winter appearance, trim the spent flowers in fall; cut them off just above the mat of leaves. In hotter locations, an iron supplement may be needed for at least the first few summers until fleeceflower becomes well established. Water to a depth of 2 ft. once a week when the temperature is above 90 degrees Fahrenheit, twice a month when temperatures are 60 to 90 degrees Fahrenheit, and monthly if there is no rain or snow in winter.

SPECIES, CULTIVARS, OR VARIETIES

There are two color variations: 'Border Jewel', with deep rose-pink flowers, and 'Darjeeling Red', which blooms crimson.

REGIONAL CONSIDERATIONS

Fleeceflower is more drought tolerant and vigorous when grown in partial shade at lower elevations.

New Gold Lantana

Lantana × 'New Gold'

Height: 1 ft.	**Light Requirement:**
Flowers: Yellow-gold	
Foliage: Deciduous	
Bloom Period: Late spring through summer	
Zone: 8	
Water: Low to moderate	

'New Gold' is a hybrid lantana that has been performing well in the warmest gardens of New Mexico. Plants have a compact form, with stems trailing to make a mound 4 ft. across. The leaves are dark green, 1 in. long with toothed margins, and provide a good background for the bright golden-yellow clusters of small, tubular flowers. 'New Gold' is not aggressive enough to cover large areas, but once it is well established it will bloom profusely over several months with very little water. It is one of the few shrubby groundcovers that will thrive in southern desert gardens.

WHEN TO PLANT

Container-grown plants may be transplanted in spring, after all chance of frost is past, until midsummer, well before the onset of cold weather. This will ensure that plants have plenty of time to root out while the soil is warm.

WHERE TO PLANT

'New Gold' lantana prefers well-drained soil and is most robust in hot, protected microclimates. It is striking when paired with Texas sage, Russian sage, or other summer-flowering plants along sidewalks and courtyard patios.

HOW TO PLANT

Dig generous holes, loosening the soil so that new roots will have an easy time breaking ground. Recent research has demonstrated that the best soil preparation for container-grown shrubs is to dig holes only as deep as, or at most a few inches deeper than, the depth of the rootball, but 4 to 6 times its diameter. This is because plants develop lateral, absorbing roots first and rely on these roots most for initial establishment and long-term survival.

Advice for Care
Once plants are well rooted, deep infrequent watering promotes the best balance of foliage and flowers. Too much water and fertilizer yields fewer blooms. A generous topdressing of compost or fine gravel as mulch will keep the soil more uniformly moist and more moderate in temperature, accelerating root development. Geotextile weed-barriers fabric used under 3 or 4 in. of mulch will suppress weeds until lantana can fill in. The geotextile is especially helpful in areas with a history of persistent weeds, because even when it is mature, lantana is open enough to allow weeds enough light to get started. Keep plants young and vigorous by cutting back the oldest, most weathered stems in spring as new growth begins.

Species, Cultivars, or Varieties
No other species or cultivar of *Lantana* is as cold tolerant or as colorful as 'New Gold'.

Regional Considerations
Lantana may be grown as an annual as far north as Albuquerque, but it is robust enough to be considered a groundcover only in the low desert of southern New Mexico.

Periwinkle

Vinca minor

Height: 6 in. **Flowers:** Blue **Foliage:** Evergreen **Bloom Period:** Spring **Zones:** 4 to 7 **Water:** Moderate to high	**Light Requirement:**

On the eighth day God said, "Let there be vinca!" and it has been used in gardens ever since. The small, dark-green leaves on slender stems form a dense evergreen carpet that is punctuated with clear-blue flowers in early spring. Periwinkle, an old standby that is long-lived and reliable in gardens across the country, is of limited use in the desert southwest. As a controlled, low-maintenance, evergreen groundcover for shade, it occupies a niche in the garden palette that is shared with few other plants. In cooler, high-elevation gardens, as well as in shaded oases at lower elevations, it is usually touted for "dry shade." I hesitate to make that claim here, though in wind-protected areas periwinkle can be a water-efficient groundcover.

WHEN TO PLANT

Vinca may be planted from containers any time the temperature is above freezing and below 90 degrees Fahrenheit. Cold-season planting is hard on evergreens; planting at least 6 weeks before extreme cold, or waiting until temperatures stabilize in spring, will help prevent loss due to frost desiccation. When the soil is frozen, roots cannot absorb moisture to replace what winds steal from the foliage. New plants can be made by division in early spring.

WHERE TO PLANT

Vinca will establish faster and requires less water over the long term if generous amounts of compost are tilled into the soil before planting. Its best use is as a groundcover under deciduous trees in walled courtyards. Underplanting with dwarf daffodils or weaving a ribbon of woolly lamb's ears through a bed of vinca makes it more seasonally interesting.

How to Plant

To cover an area quickly, plants should be spaced 12 to 18 in. apart.
Till 4 in. of compost into the entire area to be planted, then set plants
out in the amended soil. A generous topdressing of compost, shredded bark, or pecan hulls as mulch will keep the soil cooler and more
uniformly moist, hastening vinca's spread. Mulch also prevents
frost-heaving in cold weather and helps suppress weeds until the
vinca is thick enough to resist invasion.

Advice for Care

Once it is well-established, vinca can be maintained with weekly
watering when temperatures are above 90 degrees Fahrenheit, deep
watering every 2 weeks in spring and fall, and monthly watering in
winter. It may take 3 years of ample watering before water use can
be reduced. Mow vinca every 3 or 4 years in late winter to rejuvenate a mature planting.

Species, Cultivars, or Varieties

Vinca minor 'Bowles' is a cultivar with larger flowers. There are
also forms with white leaf margins, but variegated foliage takes a
beating in the desert, even when grown in wind-protected shade.
Variegations are the result of non-functioning chromatophores in
the leaf that cannot make starch and sugar, and they essentially
weaken the plant. This can be compensated for in more temperate
climates, but here the variegated tissue may burn. *Vinca major* is a
coarse, sprawling, deciduous version of periwinkle. It requires close
cropping every winter to keep it from building up a mass of dead
growth under the current season's greenery.

Prairie Grasses

Bouteloua et al

Height: 18 to 30 in. **Flowers:** Inconspicuous **Foliage:** Light green **Bloom Period:** Summer **Zones:** 5 to 8 **Water:** Low to moderate	**Light Requirement:**

*G*rasslands of the high plains and desert are a paradox. They are both fragile and resilient. The grasses described here for creating prairie groundcover differ from the ornamental grasses in that they could easily become invasive in a cultivated setting. Wildflowers can be added in broad sweeps for seasonal color and garden appeal, but grasses are the plants that provide a stable, weed-resistant surface.

WHEN TO PLANT

Most prairie grasses grow, bloom, and set seed when the soil is warm. At elevations below 7500 ft., these grasses germinate well between early May and late August. At lower elevations and in southern New Mexico, the season is extended by about 3 weeks in both spring and fall. If you are planting above 7500 ft., cool-season grasses are usually a better option; these can be seeded in spring or late summer.

WHERE TO PLANT

Prairie grasses are ideal groundcovers for large areas (several thousand sq. ft.) of open soil that are in need of reclaiming, where foot traffic is occasional, and a relaxed, sweeping, wild look is desired.

HOW TO PLANT

If the site has been scraped and compacted during construction (as is usually the case), rototill the area to be seeded. No soil amendment is necessary. Heavy seeding rates and regular watering during the first season will ensure that a thick stand of grass develops. When soil temperatures are at least 65 degrees Fahrenheit, and if the seeded area is watered daily, germination will usually take 1 to 2 weeks.

ADVICE FOR CARE

Once the fine threads of grass are an inch tall, begin watering more deeply and less often. Maintain a weekly watering schedule until

September, gradually increasing the depth of watering to 12 in. From after the first frost until the soil rewarms in April, water every 4 to 6 weeks to a depth of 2 feet. From May to September, water deeply every two weeks to keep the grasses green. After the first two years, watering becomes optional. Prairie grasses should not be cut closer than 4 to 6 in. during the growing season. Mow as often as needed during the first two summers to keep weeds from reseeding and overshadowing the grass. Prairies are usually mowed short some time in winter after the seedheads have weathered.

SPECIES, CULTIVARS, OR VARIETIES

The following is a sampling of the many native grasses available from specialty seed suppliers. Alkali sacaton (*Sporobolus airiodes*) has fine leaf blades arching to 12 in. The airy, 24-in. seedheads are pale green, fading to pale blond when they become dormant. Alkali sacaton adapts to most soils including valley clays high in salts. A pound of seed covers 4000 sq. ft. of soil. Indian rice grass (*Oryzopsis hymenoides*) is a cool-season grass that greens up early in spring, then flowers and ripens seed in early summer. The wiry leaves grow 1 ft. high and are topped by the 18-in. seedheads. Sow 1 lb. per 1000 sq. ft., covering seeds deeply to keep birds from stealing the seed before it sprouts. Little bluestem (*Schizachyrium scoparium*) has coarse, blue-green leaves to 12 in. tall and is very vertical in form. Fluffy rust-colored seedheads grow up to 24 in. tall. The plant cures a rich rust color after frost. A pound of seed covers 4000 sq. ft. Sand bluestem (*Andropogon hallii*) is very similar to little bluestem, but the seedheads are fluffy white and the leaves turn pink after frost. It is more heat and drought tolerant than little bluestem. A pound of seed covers 4000 sq. ft. Sand dropseed (*Sporobolus cryptandrus*) has upright arching leaves 18 in. tall and misty-purple flower heads to 24 in. tall. It looks windswept even on a calm day. A pound of seed covers 4000 sq. ft. Sideoats grama (*Bouteloua curtipendula*) has coarse, vertical leaf blades 12 in. tall topped with stiff stems and large seeds that hang to one side like pennants. Sow 3 lbs. of seeds per 1000 sq. ft. Spike muhly (*Muhlenbergia wrightii*) is a long-lived bunchgrass that forms fan-shaped clumps of narrow leaves 12 in. tall. The slender, constricted seed spikes grow to 18 in. tall. One lb. of seed covers 4000 sq. ft. and can be mixed with western wheat, sideoats grama, little bluestem, or blue grama as prairie groundcover at elevations above 6500 ft. Western wheat (*Andropyron smithii* or *Elymus smithii*) is another heat-tolerant, cool-season grass. Its coarse blue leaves grow to 18 in. tall and the stout seedheads reach up to 36 in. in summer. The rhizomes of western wheat form a thick sod. Sow 3 lbs. of seed per 1000 sq. ft. in March to April or August to September. Western wheat grown at lower elevations prefers heavy valley soils.

Prairie Sage

Artemisia ludoviciana

Height: 6 to 30 in.
Flowers: Inconspicuous
Foliage: Deciduous
Bloom Period: Summer
Zones: 4 to 8
Water: Low to moderate

Light Requirement:

*P*rairie sage is an aggressive groundcover that is as close to indestructible as a plant can be without being a noxious weed. Its rhizomes spread quickly and densely enough to exclude most other herbaceous plants. The coarse, silver carpet of foliage contrasts well with bold flower colors and brightens the shade beneath trees. Prairie sage flowers are inconspicuous but are borne on leafy stems that by midsummer have changed the profile of the plant from low filler to tall and stately.

WHEN TO PLANT

Prairie sage is so adaptable and easy to plant that it can be transplanted any time the soil is workable. In the heat of summer, new transplants will require ample watering to make the transition. Rhizomes can be divided in spring or fall.

WHERE TO PLANT

Any soil will suit prairie sage, though it can become invasive in good garden soil. Allow it space, and choose vigorous companions for interplanting. Try it with torch lily and gayfeather in sun; if planting in shade, combine it with yerba mansa, giant four o'clock, or Organ Mountain evening primrose. Because it adapts to a range of moisture levels, prairie sage can be grown under desert willow or fruit trees with equal success. The coarse silver foliage is attractive as filler at the base of evergreens.

HOW TO PLANT

Dig generous holes, loosening the soil so that new roots will have an easy time breaking ground. Recent research has demonstrated that the best soil preparation for container-grown plants is to dig holes only as deep as the rootball, but 4 to 6 times its diameter. This is especially appropriate for rhizomatous plants like prairie sage because it encourages lateral absorbing roots to develop. Since plants are usually spaced 2 to 3 ft. apart for coverage in one season, rototilling the areas to be planted is more efficient than digging individual holes. The backfill soil requires no amendment. A generous topdressing of compost, shredded bark, or pecan hull as mulch will help prairie sage fill in faster by keeping the soil more uniformly moist and more moderate in temperature.

ADVICE FOR CARE

Mow the flower stalks in late summer to stimulate a flush of soft new foliage, especially when the plant is used as a groundcover under trees. It will also be easier to rake fallen tree leaves in autumn if the sage is short. While prairie sage isn't evergreen, its leaves dry and curl to create an interesting dormant texture. Once plants are established, deep-water once or twice a month to support good leaf density.

SPECIES, CULTIVARS, OR VARIETIES

Roman wormwood (*Artemisia pontica*) has very finely cut silver-green leaves and grows 12 in. high and at least 18 in. wide. It is not nearly as vigorous as prairie sage and can be used as a filler in perennial beds and borders without overrunning other plants. Silver spreader (*Artemisia caucasica*) forms a soft mat of silky, silver-green foliage 3 in. high and 24 in. wide. It is a good groundcover in rock gardens because it requires sharp drainage and is compact enough to combine with smaller plantings without overwhelming them. Silver spreader is very vulnerable to excess watering, especially in summer.

Spreading Cotoneaster

Cotoneaster species

Height: 1 to 2 ft. **Flowers:** Small; followed by red fruit **Foliage:** Evergreen **Bloom Period:** Spring **Zones:** 5 to 7 **Water:** Moderate	**Light Requirement:**

*C*otoneasters are low-maintenance groundcovers for large spaces. They spread at least 6 ft. wide, but will cover 8 to 10 ft. if given a few extra years to fill the space. The glossy, rounded, dark-green leaves are $1/2$ in. or less in diameter. Clusters of small white or pink-tinged flowers grace the plants in spring, followed by a profusion of red-orange fruits in autumn. Still, I don't value the evergreen cotoneasters as much for their flowers or fruit as for their reliability as fillers. Planting just a few plants will create a lush sweep of cool green with very little effort on the gardener's part. Design-wise, groundcover cotoneasters create negative space, the monotonous counterpoint for the color of flowering shrubs, perennials, and annual borders. Lawns most often fill that role, but drip-irrigated spreading cotoneasters will produce a comparable rich, green cover using a fraction of the water; and they don't require the fertilizing or mowing lawns need. Of course you can't play soccer on cotoneaster, so if you need play space or love to push a mower around, see the turfgrass chapter for ideas on how to make lawn care more efficient.

WHEN TO PLANT

Transplant cotoneasters any time during the growing season. Don't let plants set out in the heat of summer dry out too much between waterings.

WHERE TO PLANT

Cotoneasters prefer well-drained soils. They must be given adequate space to grow. If I seem to be emphasizing this point, it's because nothing is worse than a beautiful planting in its prime that has had its branches lopped off to clear the sidewalk or half the patio. Most people have remarkably little faith that the small plants they nurture will generously reward their care. Satisfy your urge for immediate gratification with annuals or short-lived perennials as temporary fillers between widely spaced cotoneasters.

How to Plant

Cotoneasters that are held in containers for very long may become pot-bound. Either uncoil and loosen the roots, or score the rootball with a sharp knife in several places to encourage new root formation away from the tight root mass. Plant in holes only as deep as the rootball, but four to six times its diameter so that the lateral absorbing roots can quickly push into loosened soil. Backfill soil requires no amendment. To minimize weeding and keep soil cooler, use a 3- to 4-in. layer of shredded bark or pine straw mulch on geotextile in the area plants will eventually cover.

Advice for Care

When plants are given enough room to spread, only occasional pruning to remove broken branches is necessary. Unusually fast-growing, unruly shoots may sometimes need to be removed, but one of the cotoneaster's assets is its naturally graceful growth habit. Well-established plants should be watered to a depth of 2 ft. every 2 weeks. Full coverage usually takes 3 to 4 years.

Species, Cultivars, or Varieties

Bearberry cotoneaster (*C. dammerii*) has several valuable cultivars including 'Eichholz', which grows 1 ft. high and at least 8 ft. wide with red, orange, and yellow fall foliage color and pea-sized orange fruits; 'Coral Beauty', which grows 18 in. high and 8 to 10 ft. wide with bright-red fruits in autumn; and 'Low-fast', a faster-growing cultivar with less-dense foliage. It grows 8 in. high with a mature spread of at least 10 ft. Thymeleaf cotoneaster (*C. microphyllus* var. *thymifolius*) is more compact than the others, growing 18 in. high and only 6 ft. wide. Its oblong leaves are only 1/4 in. long and have silver undersides; it produces less-showy fruit. These cotoneasters are reliably cold hardy to at least 6500 ft. in elevation. They need partial shade and deep mulch to thrive in low-desert areas.

Yerba Mansa

Anemopsis californica

Height: 6 to 12 in.	**Light Requirement:**
Flowers: White	
Foliage: Deciduous	
Bloom Period: Summer	
Zones: 4 to 8	
Water: Moderate	

*Y*erba mansa leaves are rubbery, cool green, 2 in. wide and 6 in. long, and grow as rosettes that are flat in bright sunlight or upright when growing in shade. The rosettes become so densely clustered above the mat of rhizomes and pencil-thick deep roots that even the formidable bindweed will cede ground to yerba. Still, the plant does not extend relentlessly beyond its desired limits; it does not self-sow aggressively, and water is a controlling factor in its spread. Yerba mansa flowers are pure-white daisies borne on slender, nearly leafless, 12-in. stems. The petals droop like a scalloped skirt from the elongated central cone. The foliage turns red in autumn and dries to a deep rust color. Yerba mansa has a long history of use as a stomach remedy and tonic in the Southwest; the leaves produce a fresh astringent aroma when stepped on or raked.

WHEN TO PLANT
Established plants can be divided and reset in spring or fall; well-rooted containerized stock can be transplanted any time of year.

WHERE TO PLANT
Yerba mansa is native to low-lying water catchment areas, roadside swales, and under cottonwoods along major rivers from New Mexico to California. One of its best garden applications is as a groundcover in runoff basins below canales and roof gutters, where it absorbs excess water, suppresses weeds, and prevents erosion. Yerba can also be used as a groundcover under deciduous trees because even though it grows thick and lush, it doesn't deplete the soil of nutrients, nor does it compete aggressively for available water.

How to Plant

Plants of yerba mansa can be spaced 2 to 4 ft. apart for coverage in one or two seasons. Use the closer spacing for plants in 4-in. or quart-sized containers, and the wider spacing for well-rooted plants in gallon-sized pots. For the closer spacing, rototilling the areas to be planted is more efficient than digging individual holes. Backfill soil requires no amendment, but plants will fill in faster if compost is tilled into loose, sandy soil before planting. When starting yerba mansa in storm drainage basins and swales that will flood periodically, use coarse gravel as a mulch; lighter compost or bark will float. In more conventional garden spaces, shredded bark, pecan hulls, or gravel fines may be used as mulch to conserve moisture and suppress weeds until the yerba fills in.

Advice for Care

Water weekly until plants start sending out stolons, then water deeply once or twice a month to maintain dense cover. Once established in water catchments, yerba may not need any supplemental watering. Mow the groundcover with a mulching mower or string-line trimmer in winter, leaving the shredded stems and leaves as mulch. By the end of a dry winter, leaves and stems are brittle enough to rake up without mowing. Yerba mansa does not need fertilizing, but broadcasting granular fertilizer over the groundcover to supplement companion trees will have no adverse effect.

Species, Cultivars, or Varieties

There are no other species.

CHAPTER FIVE

Ornamental Grasses

*N*EW MEXICO IS A MOSAIC OF GRASSLANDS. Our highest mountains are home to alpine meadows; the river valleys and desert lowlands are cloaked in grasses; and the prairie on the eastern side of the state is the transition from Great Plains to Chihuahuan Desert. In autumn, we travel to the mountains to see the aspen and big tooth maples turn gold and crimson. The arroyos are awash with yellow chamisa and purple asters, and grasses throughout New Mexico turn shades of rust, rose, copper, and blond.

Living so close to such wealth, we tend to take grasses for granted. While we Westerners have always known that there's more to grass than lawns, until recently we were inclined to simply let the deer and cattle graze it. Growing numbers of us have begun to admire our grasslands as a basic element of who we are in horticultural terms. The subtlety of grasses—fluffy seedheads catching the rising or setting sun, mellow foliage bending in the winter wind—is a unique feature of our high desert.

When designing a landscape, the difference between turf and ornamental grasses can be seen as the difference between soldiers and artists. Turfgrasses are close cropped and regimented; individual personality is suppressed for the greater good of the sod as a whole. Ornamental grasses are free spirits; bold or demure, exuberant or elegant, self-expression is paramount. Because grasses grow so easily here, the natives are best allowed large spaces to colonize as they will. The many ornamental grasses from beach dunes and pampas that adapt well here are less likely to reseed invasively in more cultivated parts of the garden. The larger ornamental grasses may stand alone in place of shrubs, while the least invasive species can be mixed in perennial borders or grouped for accent.

Grasses can also signal the transition from more manicured to wilder areas in the garden, and their fast growth makes some grasses

Chapter Five

ideal for erosion control in storm runoff catchments. Sun or shade, dry or moist, large or small, there is an ornamental grass to fill every niche.

Suggestions for soil preparation, watering, and fertilizing are included in the profiles of the individual grasses. Ornamental grasses must be trimmed down at some point in the year. When they are trimmed depends on the species and, to a great extent, on the weather. A dry fall and winter will extend the ornamental season, while wet snow or rain will end the display early. All things to their season—the time to trim is when the dance is over. When the leaf blades and seedheads of the many late-summer and autumn revelers look frayed or matted from wind and snow, warm-season grasses are ready for the shears. Conversely, the steely blades of blue avena are at their prime in fall and winter. Their drying seedheads will have to be removed by midsummer. Nature's means of rejuvenating grasses is fire, and were it not for local fire codes and plastic irrigation equipment, the chore of ornamental grass garden cleanup would be a pyromaniac's sweetest dream. Use sharp shears to trim if you have only a few plants. A hard blade attachment on a weed whacker makes shorter work of more extensive plantings. Thick gloves, goggles, and a dust mask will make the task safer and more comfortable.

No matter where or how they are used, the strength of grasses is their softness. They add texture and grace to any setting. The slightest breeze starts grasses dancing, and the play of light on leaf blades and seedheads is even more effective because it reaches a crescendo when the rest of the garden is slipping into dormancy.

Blue Avena

Helictotrichon sempervirens

Height: 18 to 36 in.	**Light Requirement:**
Zones: 4 to 7	
Water: Moderate	

*B*lue avena is elegant in form and color. The clumping, rather stiff, steel-blue foliage holds its color throughout winter. Leaves are slender, 1/8 in. wide, and grow in tight, 18-in.-tall bunches that are held in a narrow 18- to 24-in.-wide fan shape. The seedheads are loose panicles borne on stems twice the height of the leaves; the flat seeds resemble oats and dry a pale straw color. Most of the seeds are empty, which prevents weedy self-sowing. The foliage is much more interesting without the dried seed stalks, so they can be removed any time. Blue avena is a cool-season grass, but it is fairly heat and drought tolerant once established, perhaps because of the limited evaporative surface of the narrow leaves and the pale, heat-reflecting leaf color.

WHEN TO PLANT

Blue avena is best transplanted or divided in cool weather while the root system is most active. Before I began to plant and divide it in April and September, I thought this was a fussy plant. If it establishes roots in cool weather, it will sail through summer unscathed.

WHERE TO PLANT

Blue avena must have porous well-drained soil to thrive. If grown in heavy clay soils and given too much water in summer, it will not survive. Its neutral color, fine texture, and controlled spread make blue avena an excellent garden companion for a wide range of plants. It makes a subtle color foil for bright blossoms such as gayfeather, dwarf solidago, purple coneflower, and penstemon, and is appealing clustered between evergreens such as Arizona rosewood, 'Arp' rosemary, compact mahonia, and 'Hillspire' juniper. Blue avena can also be part of a tone-on-tone monochromatic scheme with partridge feather and artemisias. The winter contrast with the rust seedheads of 'Autumn Joy' sedum is striking.

How to Plant

Plants are propagated by division. A mature clump easily breaks apart at the crown into 6 or 8 well-rooted sections. Burying the crown too deeply weakens the plants, so reset the new plants at the same depth they were growing previously. Dig generous holes, loosening the soil so that new roots will have an easy time breaking ground. When transplanting a large number of plants that are to be spaced 2 to 3 ft. apart, tilling the entire planting area is more efficient than digging individual holes. No compost is needed, though in very sandy soil it may help hold moisture and get plants off to a faster start, and in clay it can help improve drainage. A light topdressing of shredded bark or pecan hulls as mulch will keep the soil cooler and more uniformly moist, accelerating root development. Gravel mulch can also be used when plants are grown in the shade or along dry stream beds that carry runoff water.

Advice for Care

Where only a few plants are grouped as accents, remove old leaves with a pet grooming comb to give plants a neater, bluer look. For more extensive plantings, cut leaves down close to the ground in early spring to rejuvenate mature plants. To maintain a more manicured look, trim off the flower stalks as soon as they start to dry. Water to a depth of 2 ft. once a week when temperatures are 85 degrees Fahrenheit or above, every 2 weeks when temperatures are 60 to 85 degrees Fahrenheit, and monthly during cooler weather. Fertilizing is not usually necessary, but a small amount of a lawn fertilizer can be applied in fall.

Species, Cultivars, or Varieties

No other species are widely cultivated.

Regional Considerations

At elevations above 7500 ft., blue avena may produce more viable seed and self-sow. Plants at higher elevations are more vigorous when grown in full sun and can be more susceptible to rust when grown in deep shade.

Blue Fescue

Festuca ovina 'Glauca'

Height: 4 to 12 in. **Zones:** 4 to 7 **Water:** Moderate to ample	**Light Requirement:**

*B*lue fescue looks like miniature blue avena. It is also a cool-season bunchgrass, but its wiry, silver-blue leaf blades grow only 4 to 8 in. high in 6- to 10-in.-wide tufts. Blue fescue's flower spikes appear in early summer, forming a lacy fountain 4 to 6 in. above the foliage. The seedheads bleach to a pale straw color by midsummer and can seem out of place among all the other actively growing, blooming plants in the garden.

WHEN TO PLANT

Blue fescue is best transplanted or divided in cool weather while the root system is most active: in March, April, or September in Zone 7; and in May or August in Zone 4. Seed germinates best and seedlings are most robust in cool soil.

WHERE TO PLANT

Fragile as it may look, blue fescue tolerates most soils with little bother as long as it never stands in water. It provides a soft textural contrast in rock gardens and low perennial borders, mixing well with pineleaf penstemon, creeping baby's breath, Greek germander, sedums, or Greek yarrow.

HOW TO PLANT

Plants are mostly propagated by division to maintain the desired characteristics, especially good foliage color; the leaf color of seedlings is extremely variable. A 3-year-old clump easily breaks apart at the crown into 4 or more well-rooted sections. Loosen the soil so that new roots will have an easy time breaking ground. If plants are to be spaced 12 to 24 in. apart in large groups, tilling 3 in. of compost into the area to be planted and setting plants out in the amended soil is a more efficient way to plant than digging individual holes. Planting in regimented grid patterns is an interesting idea, but even when plants are of a fairly uniform cultivar, the idiosyncrasies of some individuals will make the planting uneven at best. Massing plants in ribbon-like drifts usually works better over the long term; even if a few plants die outright, the pattern will not be destroyed. A light topdressing of shredded bark or pecan hulls as mulch will keep the soil more uniformly moist and more moderate in temperature, accelerating root development. A fine gravel mulch can also be used when plants are grown in the shade or in runoff catchments.

Advice for Care

Cut back the dried seed stalks in midsummer. To keep the foliage soft and colorful, trim the whole plant back to 3 or 4 in. in early spring. After a few years, plants tend to die out in the center and should be lifted, divided, and reset at the same soil level they were originally growing. Blue fescue is low growing enough to be spray irrigated, a method of watering massed plantings that is more practical than using individual drip emitters. Blue fescue uses less water when planted in the shade below 6500 ft. Irrigate deeply once a week when temperatures are 80 degrees Fahrenheit or above, every 2 weeks when temperatures are 60 to 80 degrees Fahrenheit, and monthly during cooler weather. Established plants should be watered to a depth of 12 in.

Species, Cultivars, or Varieties

There are many cultivars, including 'Joseph', with 6-in. leaves and lacy, 12-in. flower spikes all in pale silver-blue; 'Elijah Blue', which is soft blue, not as silver, and a bit taller; and 'Sea Urchin', the smallest of the three.

Blue Lyme Grass

Elymus arenarius 'Glaucus'

Height: 12 to 24 in.
Zones: 4 to 8
Water: Moderate to ample

Light Requirement:

*P*lants native to coastal dunes often grow well in New Mexico gardens because they have evolved to thrive in loose, sandy soil in areas battered by winds and salt spray. Those conditions are easy to find in landlocked New Mexico, although our salty soil is a result of aridity rather than overspray. Blue lyme grass is native to the coastal dunes of Europe and Asia. Its salt tolerance makes it drought tolerant as well; plants that tolerate salinity do so in part by being able to efficiently retain and use the moisture they absorb. Salt draws water, and salt-tolerant plants are capable of maintaining high enough osmotic pressure in their cells to resist the reverse osmosis of the salt. If blue fescue resembles a miniaturized blue avena, then lyme grass is avena on steroids. In good garden soil, the plants will form mounded clumps and spread by rhizomes. The pale metallic-blue leaf blades grow $1/2$ in. wide and 12 to 18 in. long. The summer flower spikes are downright scraggly; it is best to dispose of them promptly.

WHEN TO PLANT

Divide blue lyme grass in late summer or fall if planting in the south; if planting in the north, divide plants in spring. This will allow them to root out during a period of moderate conditions before they are exposed to extreme heat or cold. Container-grown plants can be transplanted any time except when temperatures are above 90 degrees Fahrenheit.

WHERE TO PLANT

Although blue lyme grass evolved to stabilize loose dune sand, it will grow in almost any soil. It tends to run amok in good garden soil, so it should be clumped alone as an accent or grown with companions that are aggressive enough to hold their own. Sand lovegrass, red yucca, sumac, giant four o'clock, prairie sage, southernwood, and Organ Mountain primrose are comparably strong plants with contrasting colors, forms, and textures.

How to Plant

When planting blue lyme grass, it is best to ignore the standard recommendation to dig generous holes and loosen the soil so that new roots have an easy time breaking ground. The best soil preparation for container-grown plants is to dig a hole only as deep as, or at most a few inches deeper than, the depth of the rootball, and only twice its diameter. This will limit the progress of the rhizomes. No compost is advised. The rockier or more infertile the soil, the more compact and refined blue lyme grass will be.

Advice for Care

Even in the south, our winters are usually cold enough to ensure that the foliage eventually dies back. Plants can then be cut down close to the soil. Flower stalks should be removed as they appear. Water deeply once a week when temperatures are 85 degrees Fahrenheit or above, every 2 weeks when temperatures are 60 to 85 degrees Fahrenheit, and monthly during cooler weather. Established plants should be watered to a depth of 24 in. Fertilizing is not usually recommended unless leaves yellow in the summer's heat. Chelated iron or a granular iron-and-sulfur fertilizer can be used to restore good color.

Species, Cultivars, or Varieties

Siberian wild rye (*Elymus racemosus*) is quite similar to blue lyme grass but grows nearly twice as large, especially in sites where it receives more water or stays cooler in summer. It is also hardy to Zone 4.

Dwarf Fountain Grass

Pennisetum alopecuroides

Height: 12 to 24 in.	**Light Requirement:**
Zones: 5 to 8	
Water: Moderate	

*T*he fountain grasses are easily recognized as a group by their plush flowers and seedheads. Dwarf fountain grass is much more consistent and cold hardy than the other species. By midsummer, the slender bright-green leaves arch 12 to 18 in. tall in clumps at least as wide, and bushy spikes of rosy-brown flowers 5 to 8 in. long and 1 in. wide begin pushing up through the foliage. Late summer and autumn are the height of the season for these showy grasses, when the color fades to pink-blushed tan and the silken texture of the flowers becomes fluffier. Light reflected off the leaves and seedheads makes fountain grass glow, and even gentle breezes make the limber stems dance.

WHEN TO PLANT
Whether you are seeding, dividing existing plants, or setting out container-grown plants, these warm-season grasses respond most quickly when planted in soil that is between 70 and 85 degrees Fahrenheit.

WHERE TO PLANT
Dwarf fountain grass is not fussy about soils. It grows large enough to balance small shrubs in borders, yet it is subdued enough to mix with perennials such as salvias, Jerusalem sage, and gayfeather. After frost, dwarf fountain grass combined with rudbeckia is a study in shades of brown; the muted tans of the grass counter the deep sable cones of black-eyed susan.

HOW TO PLANT
Plants are propagated by seed or division. Seeds of dwarf fountain grass germinate in less than a week when the soil is warm. A 2- or 3-year-old plant can be cut in quarters with a sharp knife or shears. Set the new plants in the soil at the same level they were growing previously; burying the crown too deeply will weaken plants. Dig generous holes, loosening the soil so that new roots will have an

easy time breaking ground. When planting dwarf fountain grass in large groupings, till the entire area to be planted and set out the plants in the soft soil. In time, grasses will amend the soil they grow in with the compost of their sloughed-off roots, but 3 to 4 in. of compost spread across the planting area and tilled into the soil before planting can get fountain grass off to a faster start.

ADVICE FOR CARE
Cut plants down close to the ground when they start to look weathered. Water to a depth of 18 in. every 2 weeks when temperatures are above 65 degrees Fahrenheit; water monthly during cooler weather. Fertilizing is not usually necessary. Chelated iron or a granular iron-and-sulfur fertilizer can be used if leaves yellow in summer's heat.

SPECIES, CULTIVARS, OR VARIETIES
'Hameln' has arching leaf blades 1/8 in. wide and 20 in. long. The flowers are buff ivory with darker filaments. 'Little Bunny' forms a mound 1 ft. high and wide; the short flower spikes are buff tinged with pink. Purple fountain grass (*Pennisetum setaceum* 'Rubrum') is the largest and most striking variety. Its slender purple-tinged leaves create 3-ft.-wide fountains of foliage that are topped with graceful flower spikes up to 4 ft. tall. It is used as an annual in the higher and cooler central and northern areas; it is only reliably perennial in Zone 8 gardens. Dwarf feather-top (*Pennisetum villosum*) has slender, arching, bright-green leaves that grow to 18 in. high and wide; the fluffy ivory flower spikes are flecked with gold stamens.

REGIONAL CONSIDERATIONS
In southern New Mexico, fountain grass can reseed invasively.

Dwarf Pampas Grass

Cortaderia selloana 'Pumila'

Height: 4 to 6 ft.
Zones: 5 to 8
Water: Ample to moderate

Light Requirement:

*M*any gardeners find themselves in a love-hate relationship with dwarf pampas grass. They are seduced by the magnificent flower spikes that appear in early autumn. Standing well above the foliage, the silky panicles unfold into 6- to 12-in. creamy ivory plumes. The seedheads dry and persist impressively into winter. A wet snowfall can leave plants bedraggled and in need of trimming. This is when the trouble starts, as the gardener dons heavy, long-sleeved shirt, thick gloves, goggles, and dust mask or bandana to tame the huge mound of 3/4-in.-wide, 4-ft.-long leaves. The centers of established plants die out leaving an ever-widening ring of live foliage that requires plenty of space and a good share of water and work to maintain.

WHEN TO PLANT

Dwarf pampas is a warm-season grass and establishes roots fastest if transplanted or divided when the soil has warmed to 70 degrees Fahrenheit in spring.

WHERE TO PLANT

Use dwarf pampas grass where you want drama. A mature plant will require a space at least 6 ft. wide. Because of the strong presence of pampas grass from summer into winter, and its strong absence when the plants are cut to stubble, it is best used as accent among evergreens that can provide a backdrop while the grass is at its peak and supply interest while the grass is dormant. Site dwarf pampas grass on the sheltered side of the evergreens to keep the plumes showy for as long as possible. The sharp-edged leaf blades should be kept well away from high-traffic areas. One of the best places to use these majestic plants is in storm drainage catchment basins; they will benefit from the added water.

How to Plant

Dwarf pampas grass is selected all female, and it will not come true from seed, so plants are propagated by division. A mature plant can be divided into sections with a sharp axe. Dig generous holes, loosening the soil so that new roots will have an easy time breaking ground. No compost is needed, though it will help hold moisture in very sandy soil; it will also get plants off to a stronger start. A 3- to 4-in. layer of shredded bark, pecan hulls, or gravel as mulch will keep the soil more uniformly moist and more moderate in temperature, accelerating root development. Use coarse gravel as a mulch when pampas grass is planted in storm drainage catchments because finer, lighter materials will float when the basin floods.

Advice for Care

Dwarf pampas grass requires regular deep watering in summer. When plants need water, leaf color becomes gray and leaf margins curl to reduce their evaporative surface. Plants grown in open, exposed areas in loose, sandy soil may need water to a depth of 24 in. as often as once a week when temperatures are 85 degrees Fahrenheit or above, every 2 weeks when temperatures are 60 to 85 degrees Fahrenheit, and monthly during cooler weather. Work a small amount of a balanced lawn fertilizer into the soil around the perimeter of the plant each spring. Chelated iron or a granular iron-and-sulfur fertilizer can be added if leaves yellow in summer's heat. Cut dwarf pampas grass back as close to the ground as possible in winter or early spring. Once the plants have grown large, a hard-bladed trimmer makes the job as easy as it can be.

Species, Cultivars, or Varieties

The species grows larger, spreads to 8 ft., and has coarser leaves. Its slightly larger plumes vary in color from ivory to silver, sometimes tinged with pink. The variegated forms look iron deficient in our strong light.

Feather Reed Grass

Calamagrostis arundinacea 'Karl Foerster'

Height: 2 to 3 ft. **Zones:** 5 and 6 **Water:** Ample to moderate	**Light Requirement:**

*T*his cultivar of feather reed grass is named for a German nursery-man who pioneered the use of grasses as ornamental plants. It is a long-lived cool-season grass with leaves ¼ to ½ in. wide and 18 to 24 in. long. Plants are stiffly upright and arch slightly. In May and June, the flower stems stand nearly 2 ft. taller than the leaves. The narrow tapered plumes are soft green tinged with purple; they cure to a pale blond color after frost.

WHEN TO PLANT

At elevations of 7500 ft. and above, spring planting will ensure that plants are well established before cold weather returns. In milder areas, fall planting will allow roots to develop before the heat of the following summer.

WHERE TO PLANT

'Karl Foerster' is not particular about soil, but adding compost will improve water retention in sand or decomposed granite, and it will improve drainage in heavy clay. The strong vertical lines of feather reed grass are perfect in narrow beds where height is needed. The play of wind through the pale flower spikes will be emphasized by a weathered fence or dark evergreen backdrop. Plants grow well in dappled or afternoon shade, especially at lower elevations. Plants grown in more shade tend to relax to a more open, sprawling form.

HOW TO PLANT

Feather reed grass is propagated by division; a mature clump breaks apart easily at the crown into 6 or 8 well-rooted sections. Reset the new plants at the same level they were growing previously, as burying the crown too deeply will weaken them. Dig generous holes, loosening the soil so that new roots will have an easy time breaking ground. In a large grouping of plants spaced 2 to 3 ft. apart, tilling 3 to 4 in. of compost into the area to be planted and setting plants out in the amended soil is a more efficient way to plant than digging individual holes. A 3-in.-deep topdressing of shredded bark or pecan hulls as mulch will keep the soil cooler and more uniformly moist, accelerating root development.

ADVICE FOR CARE
Cut leaves down close to the ground in early spring to remove weathered foliage and rejuvenate established plants. To maintain a more manicured look, trim off the seedheads whenever they start to look weathered. Water deeply once a week when temperatures are 80 degrees Fahrenheit or above, every 2 weeks when temperatures are 60 to 80 degrees Fahrenheit, and monthly during cooler weather. Established plants should be watered to a depth of 18 in. Fertilizing is usually not necessary, but a small amount of a balanced lawn fertilizer may be applied in autumn, and chelated iron or a granular iron-and-sulfur fertilizer can be used if leaves yellow in summer's heat.

SPECIES, CULTIVARS, OR VARIETIES
'Karl Foerster' is the preferred cultivar, the one most widely grown in New Mexico.

REGIONAL CONSIDERATIONS
Feather reed grass is best adapted to areas above 6500 ft. in elevation and in the northern third of New Mexico. In hotter desert areas, heat is a limitation even if water is abundant.

Maiden Grass

Miscanthus sinensis

Height: 4 to 6 ft. **Zones:** 5 to 8 **Water:** Ample to moderate	**Light Requirement:**

*M*aiden grass, also called "eulalia," begins the season as a graceful fountain of slender green leaves emerging in late spring. It makes a soft foil for spring- and summer-blooming shrubs and flowers. With the first hints of cool, crisp autumn days, the grasses' feathery flower tassels take center stage in shades of white, tan, or rust-tinged pink or purple. The first frost turns the leaves complementary shades of tan, rust, or yellow. By midwinter, the foliage weathers to more muted tones, and seedheads bleach a soft silver. Maiden grass has been cultivated for more than a century in such diverse conditions that there are many cultivars, some more cold hardy than others.

WHEN TO PLANT
Maiden grass is a warm-season grass that establishes new roots in warm soil. Since it is adapted to cooler, wetter climates than our low desert, the grass is best transplanted or divided in spring when the soil is warm but before water use peaks in the heat of summer.

WHERE TO PLANT
Allow plenty of space for plants to mature. Maiden grass is most impressive when used as an accent among evergreens or against the backdrop of a wall. Since it is not even remotely drought tolerant until well established, planting maiden grass in drainage swales and basins to capture storm runoff will help meet its water needs.

HOW TO PLANT
Plants are propagated by division; a mature clump can be quartered with an axe into well-rooted sections. Burying the crown too deeply weakens plants, so set them at the same level they were growing previously. Dig generous holes several times wider than the rootball, loosening the soil so that new roots will have an easy time breaking ground. Thoroughly mixing compost into sandy soil will help hold

moisture and get plants off to a stronger start. A 3- to 4-in. mulch of shredded bark or pecan hulls keeps the soil more uniformly moist and moderate in temperature. Coarse gravel mulch should be used when plants are grown in drainage areas because lighter materials will float when the basins flood.

ADVICE FOR CARE

Cut old growth close to the ground at the end of winter, or sooner if wet snow weathers the plants. Water deeply once a week when temperatures are 85 degrees Fahrenheit or above, every 2 weeks when temperatures are 65 to 85 degrees Fahrenheit, and monthly during cooler weather. Water should penetrate 24 in. deep. A balanced lawn fertilizer may be worked into the soil around the plants in spring, and a granular iron-and-sulfur or chelated iron supplement should be applied if leaves yellow in summer's heat.

SPECIES, CULTIVARS, OR VARIETIES

Miscanthus sinensis 'Gracillimus' is one of the oldest varieties selected for fine leaf texture and russet fall color. It is very upright when young, becoming more open as it matures, with bronzy flower stems that may reach 6 ft. in early fall. Stems fade to silver in winter. 'Yakujima' is a smaller cultivar, 3 ft. tall and wide, with rusty-brown fall color and russet flowers that fade to ivory. Flame grass (*M. sinensis* 'Purpurascens') is compact, growing 4 ft. tall and slowly spreading 3 ft. wide. It has rusty-orange fall foliage and creamy-ivory seedheads. Porcupine grass (*M. sinensis* 'Strictus') is a variegated form, but the yellow color is banded horizontally across the leaf blades rather than vertically along the leaf margins. The plants grow 5 ft. tall, are stiffly upright, and are a full zone more cold hardy than the other maiden grasses. Zebra grass (*M. sinensis* 'Zebrinus') has leaf variegation similar to porcupine grass, but the form is softer and mounding, reaching 4 ft. tall and wide. Plant variegated cultivars where they will be sheltered from afternoon sun to reduce water use and shade the leaf banding. 'Puentchken' is a cultivar with more compact clumps of foliage that grow to 3 ft. tall and wide. Its 5-ft.-tall flower spikes stand well above the leaves.

Muhly Grass

Muhlenbergia capillaris

Height: 2 to 3 ft.	**Light Requirement:**
Zones: 5 to 8	
Water: Moderate	

As the growing season progresses, muhly grass forms dense clumps of narrow leaf blades arching in mounds 3 ft. wide. A warm-season grass native to coastal dunes in the southeastern United States, muhly's salt, heat, and wind tolerance make it well-adapted to the Southwestern deserts. In autumn, the leaves are obscured by clouds of airy, pink flower panicles. After frost, both leaves and seedheads fade to a pale straw color.

WHEN TO PLANT

Transplant potted plants any time the soil is warm, and divide established plants in spring so they will have time to root well before frost. Seeds germinate quickly once the soil has warmed to at least 70 degrees Fahrenheit, but seedlings are so variable in color and form that choice plants are increased by division. Many new cultivars are trademarked, and their vegetative propagation is restricted to licensed growers.

WHERE TO PLANT

While it is able to thrive in loose, infertile sand in New Mexico gardens, muhly does best in soil that retains water well, since we receive only a third of the rainfall it is used to getting on the southeast coast.

HOW TO PLANT

A mature clump easily breaks apart at the crown into 6 or 8 well-rooted sections. Dig generous holes only as deep as the rootball but several times its diameter, loosening the soil so that new roots will have an easy time breaking ground. Set the plants at the same level in the soil as they were growing previously, since burying the crown too deeply will weaken them. Compost is not strictly required, though it helps hold moisture and get plants off to a stronger start in sandy soil, and in clay it can help improve drainage a bit.

Advice for Care

To keep litter from blowing around the garden and to prepare for new growth in spring, cut the plants down close to the ground in winter when old growth becomes brittle and looks weathered. Water plants deeply once a week when temperatures are above 85 degrees Fahrenheit, every 2 weeks when temperatures are 65 to 85 degrees Fahrenheit, and monthly during cooler weather. Established plants should be watered to a depth of 24 in. Fertilizing is not usually necessary, but a small amount of a balanced lawn fertilizer may be applied in spring, and a granular iron-and-sulfur fertilizer can be used if leaves yellow in summer's heat.

Species, Cultivars, or Varieties

'Regal Mist' is a trademarked cultivar of *Muhlenbergia capillaris*; it is selected for darker, more profuse flowers and adaptability to desert heat and low humidity. Deer grass (*M. rigens*) is native to the foothills of the Sonoran Desert at elevations between 3000 and 7500 ft. It is cold hardy only in Zones 7 and 8. Its 20-in. gray-green leaf blades grow in 3-ft. clumps with tightly cylindrical 1/4-in. flower spikes held above the leaves from July to October. *M. lindheimeri* is larger and bolder than deer grass with 1/4-in.-wide blue-green leaf blades that are folded lengthwise down the middle. Flowers are narrow, upright silver plumes up to 5 ft. tall. After frost, the whole plant turns pale silver. Lindheimer's muhly is also limited by cold to Zones 7 and 8, and like deergrass, it is very drought tolerant once established. 'Autumn Glow' is a trademarked cultivar.

Prairie Dropseed

Sporobolus heterolepis

Height: 12 to 24 in. **Zones:** 3 to 7 **Water:** Moderate to low	**Light Requirement:**

*M*ost grasses are fast growing when compared with other herbaceous perennials, but it takes prairie dropseed about 3 years to mature and flower. While most grasses smell like, well—like new-mown grass, dropseed flowers are sweetly aromatic like honey, a subtle blend of fresh and pungent. Classified as a warm-season grass, prairie dropseed is native to the Great Plains, a much colder climate than the Southwestern deserts. When planted at 4500 ft. in central New Mexico, it greens up early in March. The leaves are bright green and softer than most desert grasses, but similarly fine textured. They grow 12 in. long and relax into cow-lick clumps similar to hard fescue. The flowers are lacy panicles borne on stiff 2-ft.-tall stems in August and September. Prairie dropseed goes dormant with the first frosts, turning burnished shades of gold and copper.

WHEN TO PLANT

Sow seeds when the soil has warmed to 65 degrees Fahrenheit. Established clumps are easily divided in mid-spring, and potted plants can be set out any time. Once temperatures top 85 degrees Fahrenheit, plants take more water and seem to do little rooting until late summer.

WHERE TO PLANT

Prairie dropseed is one of the best warm-season ornamental grasses for higher-elevation gardens, but the southern desert area of Zone 8 is a little too hot, even with afternoon shade. This grass prefers soil rich in organic matter, and in New Mexico that means good garden soil. The same characteristics that have placed prairie dropseed in jeopardy on its home turf—its slow growth and small stature—make it an excellent choice for interplanting with perennials in beds, borders, and rock gardens. In groups of at least 7 plants, the rippling pattern of its clumping form is emphasized. For summer fragrance, winter color, and year-round grace, use it at entryways, near patios, and in other places where people linger.

How to Plant

An ounce of seed will cover about 100 sq. ft., and while seed sprouts in a week or two when the soil is warm, the plants are very slow to fill in. Mature clumps break apart easily at the crown into 3 or 4 well-rooted sections. Reset the new starts at the same level they were growing previously, since burying the crown too deeply weakens plants. In beds where plants are spaced 1 to 2 ft. apart, tilling 4 in. of compost into the area to be planted and setting plants out in the loosened and amended soil is an easier way to plant than digging individual holes. A light topdressing of shredded bark, cotton burrs, or pecan hulls as mulch will keep the soil more uniformly moist and more even in temperature.

Advice for Care

Cut leaves down close to the ground in early spring to rejuvenate established plants. Trimming off the seedheads whenever they start to look weathered will emphasize the swirling pattern of the leaves. Water to a depth of 2 ft. once a week when temperatures are 85 degrees Fahrenheit or above, every 2 weeks when temperatures are 65 to 85 degrees Fahrenheit, and monthly during cooler weather. A small amount of a balanced lawn fertilizer may be applied in spring until plants become well established. Apply a granular iron-and-sulfur fertilizer if leaves yellow in summer's heat.

Species, Cultivars, or Varieties

The dropseeds native to New Mexico are described in the Ground-covers chapter with prairie grasses. They reseed too profusely to use in cultivated garden areas.

ORNAMENTAL GRASSES

Sand Lovegrass

Eragrostis trichodes

Height: 18 to 48 in. **Zones:** 5 to 8 **Water:** Low to moderate	**Light Requirement:**

I first saw sand lovegrass in early autumn, shimmering in the sun and wind, a sweep of 2-ft.-high, purple-and-amber seedheads floating like smoke above red-streaked leaves. It was love at first sight. As cold weather set in, the color turned from amber to gold and finally to pale strawberry-blond by winter's end. As often happens during the course of a love affair, that first infatuation has been tempered by a few things I've learned while living with sand lovegrass. It is a cool-season grass that adapts to most soils and moisture levels by adjusting its size and growth rate. The thin bright-green leaves are 1/8 in. wide and may form a dense mound 2 ft. high and wide. The mound can reach twice that size if provided with additional water. Flowers emerge in open, lacy panicles, first pale green, then reddish purple. The sheer number makes them showy; by late summer, the flowers have doubled the size of the plant. The form varies from a narrow upright fountain if plants are crowded, to an arching mound when they are more widely spaced. Each plant can produce 100,000 seeds a year (there are 1,500,000 seeds per lb.), and it seems that every seed will germinate if given any encouragement at all. The good news is that excess seedlings are easy to pull up, but I have learned to plant sand lovegrass only where its lust for life is an asset.

WHEN TO PLANT

Sow seeds in early spring when the soil is 50 to 80 degrees Fahrenheit. Dividing or transplanting can be done just about any time the soil isn't frozen. In the heat of summer, new transplants need ample water until they root out. In winter, transplants should be watered sparingly.

WHERE TO PLANT

Though it is called *sand* lovegrass, this plant will grow easily in most soils. If planted in good garden soil with ample water, it is guaranteed to run amok. It is well suited for use as as one of the prairie grasses as described in the Groundcovers chapter, but it can also be mixed in *dry* shrub and perennial borders for winter color. Use it in large, open spaces that are minimally irrigated or where reseeding will soften design lines; or plant it along a wrought-iron or split-rail fence. In most cases, if you want a dozen plants, start with three, and don't plant where the design concept requires hard edges and definite plant placement.

How to Plant

When transplanting sand lovegrass, preventing its life from being too easy can be a means of containing its growth. If you want to use a few plants as an accent, loosen the soil so that new roots will have an easy time breaking ground, and dig holes as deep as the depth of the rootball, but only twice its diameter. If you want a large sweep of plants, till the area to be planted and sow seed, 1 oz. per 200 sq. ft., in spring. Instead of raking, roll or drag the surface to press the fine seeds into the surface. No compost is needed.

Advice for Care

Cut the leaves down close to the ground in mid-spring just as new leaves begin to emerge. To maintain a more manicured look and limit reseeding, trim off the seedheads when they start looking weathered. Apply water to a depth of 2 ft. every 2 weeks when temperatures are above 70 degrees Fahrenheit, and monthly during cooler weather. Fertilizing is not usually necessary.

Species, Cultivars, or Varieties

'Lehmann's Lovegrass' (*Eragrostis lehmanniana*) is an African species that was introduced into the United States for erosion control, and it does the job well. Unfortunately, it aggressively swallows most native species in its path; in the southwest it has become the grass version of kudzu vine.

Threadgrass

Stipa tennuissima

Height: 12 to 24 in.
Zones: 5 to 8
Water: Low to moderate

Light Requirement:

*T*hreadgrass is aptly named, as the leaves most resemble dense clumps of fine green or golden thread. Though the leaves are soft and slender, they stand upright like the tips of artists' brushes, arching whichever way the wind was blowing last. The flowers and seedheads are equally filamented, temporarily fluffing out the tops of the plants. Its color is a striking feature of this warm-season New Mexico native. The leaves, flowers, and seedheads all change from bright green to pale blond-gold. Plants are usually a blend of both colors: more green in early and late summer, mostly gold in winter.

WHEN TO PLANT

Transplant potted plants any time the soil is warm; divide established plants in spring or summer so they will have time to root well before frost. Seeds germinate when the soil has warmed to 70 degrees Fahrenheit. Plants recover slowly when transplanted too early in spring, but transplants establish quickly when temperatures are near 100 degrees Fahrenheit.

WHERE TO PLANT

Threadgrass will tolerate almost any soil that doesn't stay too wet. It reseeds copiously in good garden soil. Its windswept form suggests casual settings, and it blends well with the jewel-toned flower spikes of Rocky Mountain penstemon, gayfeather, bubblegum mint, and skyrocket, or with low-spreading plants such as verbena, iceplants, and nolana. Heat-loving threadgrass grows best below 8000 ft. in the southern part of the state, and below 7000 ft. in the north.

HOW TO PLANT

Plants are propagated by seed and division. A two-year-old clump breaks apart easily at the crown into 4 or 5 well-rooted sections. Dig generous holes, loosening the soil so that new roots will have an easy time breaking ground, and reset the plants at the same level they had been growing. A plant will decline if the crown is buried too deeply. For a large grouping of plants spaced 18 to 30 in. apart, tilling the area to be planted and setting plants out in the loosened soil is easier than digging individual holes. An ounce of seed covers a 100-sq.-ft. area. Sow seeds on tilled soil in late spring. Instead of raking, roll or drag the surface to press the fine seeds into the soil. No compost is needed, though it will help improve drainage in clay soils. A 3-in. mulch of shredded bark or pecan hulls may suppress reseeding, while a fine gravel mulch will encourage it.

ADVICE FOR CARE

Rejuvenate established plants by shaving off leaves close to the ground in early spring. To maintain a more manicured look, comb off the seedheads with a fine rake or steel-toothed grooming comb when they start to tangle in matted clumps. Tangled seedheads can also be sheared off, but combing will leave the elegant silky foliage intact throughout the growing season. Water to a depth of 2 ft. every week or two when temperatures are 70 degrees Fahrenheit or above; water monthly during cooler weather. Fertilizer is not necessary. If plants are grown in good garden soil, volunteer seedlings will need to be weeded out once or twice a season. Threadgrass is not long-lived, but it reliably replaces itself with new seedlings, and culling out declining plants is easy.

SPECIES, CULTIVARS, OR VARIETIES

There are several other native *Stipa*, including needle-and-thread (*Stipa comata*) and New Mexico feathergrass (*Stipa neomexicana*). Both have coarse, pale-green leaf blades, beautiful silver awns that glow as they catch the sunlight on rocky hillsides, and irritating seed-heads that pierce clothing, skin, and pet fur. While these other species play an important role in reclamation planting, threadgrass is the most garden friendly of the group.

Tufted Hairgrass

Deschampsia caespitosa

Height: 2 ft. **Zones:** 4 to 6 **Water:** Ample to moderate	**Light Requirement:**

*O*ccurring throughout the Northern Hemisphere in areas receiving 24 or more inches of annual precipitation, tufted hairgrass enjoys a very wide natural distribution. In the Southwest, this cool-season grass grows in the mountains at 7500- to 9000-ft. elevations. It forms dense, upright clumps of 12.-in.-long, 1/8- to 1/2-in.-wide dark-green leaves that are folded lengthwise. The lacy yellow or white flower panicles are so profuse in late spring that they hide the foliage. Leaves turn golden orange in fall.

WHEN TO PLANT

Tufted hairgrass is best transplanted or divided during cool weather while the root system is most active. This is in March, April, or September in Zone 6 and in May or August in Zone 4. Seed also germinates best and seedlings are most vigorous in cool soil.

WHERE TO PLANT

Tufted hairgrass prefers soil rich in organic matter. It is most at home in cool, shady meadows. It is interesting mixed with *lamium* under trees in a shady courtyard. Use it to hide the declining foliage of spring bulbs. Plant more densely in areas that are unprotected by garden walls or fences, because rabbits just love tender hairgrass. Because seed-grown plants are variable in size and color, massing plants in ribbon-like drifts usually works better than regimented patterning.

HOW TO PLANT

Plants are propagated by seed and division. A 3-year-old clump easily breaks apart at the crown into 4 well-rooted sections. Dig holes only as deep as the depth of the rootball, setting the new plants at the same level they had been growing. Burying the crown too deeply will weaken the plants. If plants will be spaced 12 to 24 in. apart, till 4 in. of compost into the area to be planted and set plants out in the loosened soil. Drifts of hairgrass can also be established by sowing seed, 1 oz. per 100 sq. ft., on tilled soil in late summer or early fall. Instead of raking, roll or drag the surface to press the fine seeds into the soil. A light topdressing of shredded bark or pecan hulls as mulch will keep the soil cooler and more uniformly moist, accelerating root development.

ADVICE FOR CARE

Cut leaves down close to the ground at the end of winter to rejuvenate established plants. To maintain a more manicured look, trim off the seedheads when they start to look weathered. Water to a depth of 2 ft. once a week when temperatures are 80 degrees Fahrenheit or above, every 2 weeks when temperatures are 60 to 80 degrees Fahrenheit, and monthly during cooler weather. Fertilizing is not usually necessary, but a small amount of a balanced lawn fertilizer may be applied in autumn. A granular iron-and-sulfur fertilizer can be used if leaves yellow in summer's heat, but chronic chlorosis may be an indication that the spot is too hot for hairgrass.

SPECIES, CULTIVARS, OR VARIETIES

Most commercially grown specimens of tufted hairgrass are European cultivars that demand more water and resent our infertile soils. Seeking out plants grown from New Mexico and Colorado seed sources is worth the effort; plants will thrive with much less fussing. Native seed can be used for reclamation seeding in areas that get at least 20 in. of annual precipitation. The watering estimates above are for native selections; European plants may need twice as much.

REGIONAL CONSIDERATIONS

Tufted hairgrass is adapted only in north and central mountain gardens. At lower elevations, especially in the southern desert, you may as well sauté it as try to grow it. You can enrich the soil and water often, but short of air-conditioning the garden, nothing will enable hairgrass to survive the persistent heat.

CHAPTER SIX

Perennials

$\mathcal{M}$OST PERENNIALS ARE HERBACEOUS PLANTS that live at least three years. From that basic definition, the garden path tends to branch quite diversely. While it is true that perennials differ from shrubs in not having persistent woody stems, it is probably more accurate to say that perennials flower on the newest growth; even if they releaf on old stems, they look better in the garden if they are cut down to the ground each year. When that cutting is performed depends on whether the leaves persist after frost, and whether they are attractive if they do.

Perennials' lifespans vary from just a few years to more than a quarter of a century. Veronicas, gayfeather, Greek germander, bush penstemon, and giant four o'clock may easily outlive many shrubs. Blanketflower and some penstemon may decline after three prolific years. Longevity is genetically determined, but garden care can also have a great influence. Drought- and heat-loving plants and alpines may die if they are kept too wet in winter. Perennials from more temperate climates may decline if they are kept too dry. Most perennials have a preferred range of light intensity, and they will live long and prosper when they find themselves in comfortable surroundings.

Wildflowers used within their native range do better when the soil is not amended with organic matter; this is also true of many perennials that have evolved in arid climates worldwide. Perennial wildflowers used for reclamation within their native range usually need little water and no fertilizer once they are established, but when they are crowded in borders and expected to flower for an extended period of time, extra water will be needed. Mountain wildflowers planted in the desert, and desert perennials transplanted several thousand feet above their natural range, will suffer culture shock just as other exotics do when planted in New Mexico's harsh climate.

Most perennials develop more quickly than woody plants, so one of their roles in the garden is to provide cover and interest until the slower plants come into their own. Perennials offer more stability than annuals do, but most are not as permanent as trees and shrubs, so they allow a measure of flexibility. Enjoy them while they thrive, and when they decline you can use their space to try something new.

My favorite perennials bloom with gusto and have interesting foliage when not in bloom. Their array of leaf colors and textures adds the richness of fine brocade to garden borders. Many perennials are fragrant, and some lure hummingbirds and butterflies with their nectar. Perennials may have a shorter blooming season than that of annuals, but there are exceptions to that rule on both sides. Those that do flower over a period of several months usually enjoy a few weeks of saturated color followed by continuous light blooming or by flushes of stronger color interrupted by rest periods.

Perennials can be grown from seeds and cuttings, by dividing large established clumps, or by transplanting potted starts. The profiles suggest the methods that work most easily for each plant. While there are some tried-and-true techniques, don't be afraid to bend the rules a bit to fit your particular situation. Many perennials don't bloom the first year from seed, but again there are exceptions. When purchasing started plants, remember that you are really buying roots. The foliage should be healthy, but not so pumped up with fertilizer that it dwarfs the roots. If a plant is rootbound, it may not be a bargain unless it can be divided immediately.

The information in the profiles is offered as a starting point. You don't really get to know plants or how to grow them from books. Gardening is learned with a shovel, one hole at a time; as a group, perennials are good plants for experimentation. Friends who have extensive perennial collections may give you their volunteers and the benefit of their experience. Because many perennials can be grown from seed quickly, regardless of your budget or aptitude, anyone can afford to be lavish with them. There are so many wonderful plants to try that even if you don't succeed half the time, you'll still have much to show for your efforts. After twenty-five years of tinkering, I still find dozens of "new" perennials I want to try every season.

Artemisia

Artemisia species

Height: 6 to 36 in.	**Light Requirement:**
Color: Silver	
Bloom Period: Summer	
Zones: 4 to 8	
Water: Moderate to low	

*A*rtemisias vary in size and growth habit, but all are valued for their beautiful foliage. Their flowers are small, greenish-yellow, and inconspicuous at best, but the leaves, whether finely etched or softly lobed, silver blue or icy green, create an elegant garden fabric on which to embroider colorful annual and perennial flowers.

WHEN TO PLANT
Transplant or divide established plants in spring or early autumn. Potted plants may be set out any time.

WHERE TO PLANT
All artemisias prefer well-drained soil, but they tolerate most soils as long as they are not kept too wet. Plants will have stronger, more compact growth in soils lacking organic matter. 'Powis Castle' and beach wormwood are used in perennial beds, borders, and large rock gardens. Southernwood makes a beautiful large filler between roses and other dark-leafed shrubs. Artemisias provide subtle contrast for ornamental grasses.

HOW TO PLANT
The ground-hugging beach wormwood will root where stems touch the soil; rooted tips can be severed and transplanted elsewhere. 'Powis Castle' artemisia is easily started from cuttings of new shoots after the stems become a bit woody. Southernwood will self-sow with abandon if flower stems are left to set seed. Dig generous holes, loosening the soil so that new roots will have an easy time breaking ground. A 3-in. topdressing of shredded bark, pecan hulls, composted cotton burrs, or fine gravel as mulch will keep the soil more uniformly moist.

ADVICE FOR CARE

All artemisias benefit from hard pruning before spring; remove much of the old growth 3 to 6 in. from the ground. Southernwood and 'Powis Castle' are attractive most of the winter, but beach wormwood and silvermound go dormant early and can be cut back in late autumn. Though artemisias smell wonderful, making trimming a pleasant task, the pollen and the fine hairs on the leaves and stems can be irritating; you may want to wear a dust mask. Water to a depth of 2 ft. every week when temperatures are above 95 degrees Fahrenheit, every 2 weeks when temperatures are 70 to 95 degrees Fahrenheit, and monthly during cooler weather.

SPECIES, CULTIVARS, OR VARIETIES

Artemisia × 'Powis Castle' is a natural hybrid that first appeared in the gardens of Powis Castle in Wales. Plants mound 18 in. high and 24 to 36 in. wide with lacy, silver-blue foliage, a citrusy-lavender aroma, and few flower heads. Beach wormwood (*A. stelleriana*) is a coastal dune native of the southeastern United States that grows 12 in. high and nearly twice as wide. Its white leaves are deeply lobed. 'Silver Brocade' is an aptly named patented cultivar. Silvermound (*A. schmidtiana*) has very fine silver-green leaves that form a flat cushion 4 to 10 in. high and 12 to 18 in. across. Removing flower stems when they first appear will stimulate new growth and counter silvermound's unfortunate tendency to fall open in the center, exposing gray stems and withered foliage. Because the growing season is much shorter and cooler at higher elevations, plants grown there will stay soft and attractive with less cutting. Southernwood (*A. abrotanum*) grows 3 ft. high and wide with strong stems and dense, fragrant, silver-blue foliage. More finely cut than beach wormwood, but coarser than 'Powis Castle', southernwood's foliage turns steel gray after frost and persists well through winter.

Blackfoot Daisy

Melampodium leucanthum

Height: 10 to 14 in. **Color:** White with a yellow center **Bloom Period:** April to October **Zones:** 5 to 8 **Water:** Low	**Light Requirement:**

*I*f you're out hiking the foothills or mesas of New Mexico and you come across perfect bouquets of 1-in. white daisies with yellow eyes, chances are you've encountered blackfoot daisy. The linear leaves are usually less than 1 in. long and 1/8 in. wide. They are fairly sparse on the intricate network of wiry stems; the flowers make up the substance of the plant. In southern desert gardens, blackfoot daisy blooms in early April. In gardens at higher elevations and in the north, it will bloom in mid-May and flower until frost if watered occasionally. Plants growing wild bloom heavily in spring with a second bloom after ample rainfall in summer. Blackfoot daisy is easy to work into gardens of all kinds because it is so self-contained, cheery when in bloom, and gracefully inconspicuous at other times.

WHEN TO PLANT

Seeds germinate and plants establish roots best in warm soil. Container-grown plants can be set out any time when temperatures are above freezing as long as the soil is not kept too wet when it's cold, or allowed to dry out too much while plants are blooming.

WHERE TO PLANT

Blackfoot daisy is at home in very cultivated-looking gardens, yet it is so undemanding that it works equally well in wilder naturalized gardens. When planted in rock gardens, xeric flower borders, and along pathways and dry streambeds, the compact mounded form creates a gentle rhythm with other plants of similar size and shape. Try it with pineleaf penstemon, paperflower, the shrubby salvias, or the low-spreading iceplants, verbenas, and desert zinnia. At its northern and high-elevation range, grow blackfoot daisy in the hottest, driest niche in the garden.

How to Plant

Seed growth is erratic. Though they always germinate better when the soil is warm, freshly harvested seeds sometimes sprout in less than a week and sometimes take a month or more to germinate. Seeds stored cool and dry are even more inconsistent. To transplant potted plants, dig generous holes, loosening the soil so that new roots will have an easy time breaking ground. In a large grouping where plants are spaced 12 to 15 in. apart, till the area to be planted and set out plants in the unamended soil. A 3-in.-deep topdressing of fine gravel as mulch will keep the soil more uniformly moist and more moderate in temperature, accelerating root development. Shredded bark and other fibrous mulches can keep the crowns of the plants too wet.

Advice for Care

Tidy up the plants (if rabbits don't get to it first) by cutting blackfoot daisy down close to the tuft of new leaves near the crown any time from autumn to early spring. Water deeply every 2 weeks when temperatures are above 75 degrees Fahrenheit, and monthly or less during cooler weather. Well-established plants should be watered to a depth of 24 in. Fertilizing is unnecessary.

Species, Cultivars, or Varieties

There are two annual cultivars of *Melampodium paludosum* which are grown as bedding plants. 'Derby' grows 8 to 10 in. tall and wide with 1 1/2-in. yellow daisies, while 'Medallion' grows to 24 in. tall and wide with yellow daisies with orange centers. Both love the heat, though they are not nearly as drought tolerant as the perennial.

Blanketflower

Gaillardia grandiflora 'Burgundy', 'Goblin', 'Monarch'

Height: 12 to 24 in. **Color:** Red-and-yellow **Bloom Period:** May to frost **Zones:** 3 to 8 **Water:** Moderate to low	**Light Requirement:**

*B*lanketflower is a native New Mexican wildflower that has been cultivated and hybridized for at least 150 years. There are both annual and perennial forms of gaillardia. The double 'Lollipop' is derived from the wild annual *Gaillardia pulchella*, while the perennials are mostly hybrids of *Gaillardia aristata*. Blanketflower is outstanding for its long and colorful flowering season. Wiry, hairy flower stems emerge from a clump of pale-green leaves. The leaves are 1 in. wide, 4 or more in. long, rough-textured, hairy, and irregularly lobed and incised. The common forms have 3-in. daisylike flowers with tip-notched petals. Red and yellow bands surround the flower's red eye.

WHEN TO PLANT

Gaillardias are grown from seed or division, but most of the single-color hybrids don't come true from seed. They can be sown, transplanted, or divided in spring or late summer and autumn. If sown in spring, they will bloom the same summer. Potted plants can be set out any time in summer as long as they are watered regularly during establishment.

WHERE TO PLANT

Lean, well-drained soil produces the best results. Small amounts of compost tilled into the soil may help get plants off to a faster start, but avoid rich, fertile garden soil because blanketflower will reward your kindness with rank floppy growth and fewer flowers. It mixes nicely in flower beds with catmint, fleabane, Rocky Mountain or pineleaf penstemon, and 'Blue Queen' Salvia.

HOW TO PLANT

To transplant, dig generous holes, loosening the soil so that new roots will have an easy time breaking ground. Seed sown when the soil temperature has warmed to 70 degrees Fahrenheit will germinate within a week.

ADVICE FOR CARE

Remove seedheads as they dry to keep plants in bloom, and trim stems close to the ground any time after frost. Plants may self-sow if left untrimmed; seedlings will be variable. Water deeply every week or two when temperatures are 80 degrees Fahrenheit or above; water monthly or less during cooler weather. Too much moisture in winter can lead to root rot. Established plants should be watered to a depth of 24 in.

SPECIES, CULTIVARS, OR VARIETIES

'Burgundy' produces wine-red flowers on 18-in. stems. Plants grow slightly taller than they are wide. Though it is not as vigorous as the other cultivars, few others produce such gorgeous red color. 'Goblin' has red-and-yellow bicolor flowers that cover the compact, mounded plant. It grows 12 in. high and wide. 'Golden Goblin' is supposed to be an all-yellow strain, but it is unstable and often reverts to red-and-yellow flowers. 'Monarch' is one of the older red-and-yellow cultivars. It is a very robust plant, often growing 24 in. tall and nearly as wide. The wild species, *Gaillardia aristata*, is only 12 in. tall and produces flowers only 1 1/2 in. in diameter, but it is much more drought hardy and has a simple charm (hybrid-lovers might call it scrawniness) that is appealing in prairie plantings.

Blue Spurge

Euphorbia myrsinites

Height: 6 in.
Color: Yellow
Bloom Period: Early spring
Zones: 5 to 8
Water: Low

Light Requirement:

*E*uphorbia is a large and diverse genus whose cosmopolitan members include tree-form succulents from Africa, the Christmas poinsettia from Mexico, and at least 700 other related species. Blue spurge, also called myrtle spurge, has thick stems that emerge from the crown of the plant and curve along the ground. Its closely spaced leaves are crisp, wedge-shaped, and pale blue. Clusters of small flowers surrounded by chromium-yellow bracts form at the end of each stem in early spring. As the flowers fade, a host of new stems sprout from the crown. By conventional herbaceous perennial standards, blue spurge is odd in form and texture, but among desert-adapted plants with their stark profiles and waxy foliage, it looks quite at home.

WHEN TO PLANT

Transplant volunteer seedlings in spring or early autumn. Potted plants may be set out any time, but when temperatures are extreme, transplant only well-rooted specimens that have been hardened off outdoors.

WHERE TO PLANT

Blue spurge is not fussy about soil, but it establishes most rapidly when the soil is well drained and relatively dry. Its early blooms are outstanding when contrasted with Kaufmanniana or Greigii tulips. It also works well as a base for clumps of yucca or agave. Grow it naturalized along dry streambeds and pathways or in the light shade of desert willows or mesquite.

HOW TO PLANT

Blue spurge grows from seeds sown outdoors late in spring or seeds sown earlier indoors. Whether you plant indoors or out, warm soil is a must. Every small varmint for miles around, from field mice to ground squirrels, starlings to quail, will try to steal the large seeds, so protect them with row cover. Germination is erratic, with a few seeds sprouting at a time; the majority of seeds have germinated at the end of 3 weeks' time. To transplant, dig holes only as deep as the rootball, but 4 times its diameter. To start a large grouping of plants spaced 12 to 15 in. apart, till the area to be planted and set out plants in the loosened soil. A 3-in.-deep topdressing of shredded bark, pecan hulls, or fine gravel as mulch will keep the soil more uniformly moist and more moderate in temperature. Blue spurge tends to self-sow prolifically in gravel mulch.

ADVICE FOR CARE

After flowering, the bloom stems decline and need to be cut back to the crown. Ripe seeds pop off the plant and may form little colonies within shooting range of the original plant. Seedlings are easy to remove if too many crop up. The milky sap can be irritating,  strongly so to some people. Wear gloves while weeding or pruning, and don't rub your eyes. The toxins in the sap seem to make it virtually pest free. Rabbits won't even touch it! Once plants are established, water so that moisture penetrates to 24 in. deep. Water every 2 weeks when temperatures are above 70 degrees Fahrenheit, and monthly during cooler weather. Fertilizing is usually not necessary.

SPECIES, CULTIVARS, OR VARIETIES

Cushion spurge (*Euphorbia epithymoides*, also known as *E. polychroma*) has similar flowers in late spring on wiry, upright stems 12 in. tall. Its dark-green leaves turn red with frost and drop soon after. Not as drought or heat tolerant as blue spurge, it takes cold to Zone 4. Gopher spurge (*Euphorbia biglandulosa*, also known as *E. rigida*) is very similar to blue spurge but is a bigger, bolder plant that grows 2 ft. high and 4 ft. wide. It is less cold hardy than blue spurge. Though it can survive most winters in Zone 6, it is most robust in Zones 7 and 8.

REGIONAL CONSIDERATIONS

Because it tends to self-sow and is unpalatable once germinated, blue spurge can escape cultivation and invade wild ecosystems when planted at elevations between 6500 and 7500 ft. where rainfall is 16 in. or more.

'Bowles Mauve' Wallflower

Erysimum linifolium 'Bowles Mauve'

Height: 18 to 24 in.	**Light Requirement:**
Color: Pink-purple	
Bloom Period: All growing season	
Zones: 5 to 8	
Water: Moderate to low	

'Bowles Mauve' wallflower rewards very little work on the gardener's part with whorls of narrow, 1/2-in.-wide, 3-in.-long silver leaves that grow in starburst patterns on compact, mounded plants. The crisp, evergray foliage is offset by the many stiff spikes of pink-purple flowers. Flowers begin in mid-spring with a tremendous show, continuing in flushes until frost. 'Bowles Mauve' wallflower is propagated by cuttings and so is very consistent in leaf and flower characteristics, but because it adapts to such a range of growing conditions, gardeners' experience with the plant varies. At high elevations and in the low-desert areas it can be short-lived, while at mid-elevations it may be considered a mainstay shrub. If you consider the soil and cultural conditions that produce such varied results, there seem to be a few general trends. When plants are given abundant water and fertilized regularly, they may flower so heavily that after 3 or 4 years they are exhausted. They will need replacing at the end of their short but brilliant careers. Plants can be weakened by too much winter moisture at high elevations or too little winter moisture in the desert. All in all, the middle ground seems the most productive.

WHEN TO PLANT

Set out plants in spring after danger of hard freezes is past; this is especially important in colder areas. Late spring and summer planting also works if care is taken to keep transplants from getting too dry, especially when they are in bloom.

WHERE TO PLANT

'Bowles Mauve' grows best in well-drained soil. Its uniform, mounded form lends itself well to small manicured gardens, but it is equally at home in more informal settings. It combines best with yellow flowers, white flowers, and other red-toned purples. The pale foliage contrasts nicely with dark-green plants. A few possible companions are creeping germander, 'Mersea Yellow' pineleaf penstemon, golden columbine, Jerusalem sage, 'Profusion' fleabane, desert zinnia, and rosemary.

How to Plant

Dig generous holes, loosening the soil so that new roots will have an easy time breaking ground. In a perennial bed where plants are spaced 24 to 30 in. apart, tilling a few inches of compost into the area to be planted and setting plants out in the amended soil is a more efficient way to plant than digging individual holes. When transplanting individual plants, don't add more than 20 percent compost by volume to the backfill. A 3-in.-deep mulch of shredded bark, pecan hulls, or fine gravel keeps the soil more uniformly moist and helps suppress weeds.

Advice for Care

To maintain a more manicured look and keep plants blooming, trim off spent flower heads when they start to look weathered. Water plants deeply once a week when temperatures are 85 degrees Fahrenheit or above, every 2 weeks when temperatures are 65 to 85 degrees Fahrenheit, and monthly during cooler weather. Established plants should be watered to a depth of 24 in. Fertilize lightly with a 4-month time-release formula to sustain flowering without forcing rank growth.

Species, Cultivars, or Varieties

'Wenlock Beauty' is smaller than 'Bowles Mauve', growing 12 in. tall and 18 in. wide. As they open, flowers vary in color from pinkish buff to deep rose. Western wallflower (*E. capitatum*) is a common wildflower above 7000 ft. in open meadows. It has orange-to-mahogany flowers on stout, 2-ft. stalks.

Bubblegum Mint

Agastache cana

Height: 2 to 3 ft. **Color:** Rose-pink **Bloom Period:** Midsummer to frost **Zones:** 4 to 8 **Water:** Moderate	**Light Requirement:**

*E*ach spring, a small cluster of new leaves emerges from the ground. The leaves are less than an inch across, are spade-shaped with scalloped edges, and have the unexpected scent of bubblegum! By midsummer, flower stems have lengthened and whorls of tubular flowers have hummingbirds very interested. The show and fragrance continue until frost blackens the topgrowth. Bubblegum mint is unlike most mints both in its heat and drought tolerance and in its self-contained growth habit. It doesn't rootsprout or swallow up great gulps of garden space, but a single plant can cover a 2-ft.-square in one long growing season.

WHEN TO PLANT

The southwestern agastaches are all heat-loving and transplant best when the soil is warm. Plant any time from mid-spring to midsummer when plants begin to bloom.

WHERE TO PLANT

Bubblegum mint prefers well-drained soil, but it also grows well in organically amended garden soil. It contrasts nicely in perennial beds and shrub borders with Russian sage, pitcher sage, 'Moonshine' yarrow, dwarf butterflybush, English lavender, Texas sage, and Apache plume. Because of their scent and the hummingbirds they attract, I like to place plants near children's play spaces, and near patios and other high-traffic areas where big kids can enjoy them, too.

HOW TO PLANT

Seed will germinate well at 70 degrees Fahrenheit after a month of cold, moist prechilling. Press seed lightly into tilled soil. It is important to sow shallowly because the tiny seeds need light to germinate. To transplant from containers, dig generous holes only as deep as the rootball but 4 times its diameter. This will allow plants to develop the lateral, absorbing roots they rely on for initial establishment and long-term survival. Stems are brittle and break easily, so they need careful handling during transplanting. To start a large grouping of plants spaced 2 to 3 ft. apart, till 3 in. of compost into the area to be planted and set out plants in the amended soil. A 3-in.-deep mulch of shredded bark, pecan hulls, or fine gravel keeps the soil more uniformly moist and helps suppress weeds.

ADVICE FOR CARE

Trim off the faded flower heads to keep plants blooming vigorously. Cut frosted plants down to the ground any time from autumn to early spring—sooner rather than later if the area is highly visible. Though bubblegum mint will succumb to root rot easily in wet clay soil, it generally seems to perform best with regular watering. Water should penetrate to a depth of 24 in. Water once a week when plants are flowering or temperatures are 85 degrees Fahrenheit or above, every 2 weeks when temperatures are 65 to 85 degrees Fahrenheit, and monthly or less during cooler weather. In spring, a small amount of granular fertilizer may be applied to beds where plants are induced to bloom heavily. Use a granular iron and sulfur fertilizer if leaves yellow in summer's heat.

SPECIES, CULTIVARS, OR VARIETIES

Mexican lemon mint (*A. mexicana*) is very similar to bubblegum mint but its leaves are a bit smaller, brighter green, and have a delicious lemon fragrance. Licorice mint (*A. rupestris*) has narrow, anise-scented silver-green leaves. Flower spikes are a soft coral. Licorice mint is the most drought tolerant of the three plants listed here, but it still needs regular watering while in bloom.

REGIONAL CONSIDERATIONS

Though it is native to southern New Mexico, bubblegum mint is cold hardy to at least 7000 ft. throughout the state.

Candytuft

Iberis sempervirens

Height: 12 in.	**Light Requirement:**
Color: White	
Bloom Period: Spring	
Zones: 3 to 8	
Water: Moderate	

andytuft is a Mediterranean native with small, linear, dark-green leaves and short, wiry stems. Single plants form dense evergreen cushions 18 in. across. Its pure-white flowers are 1½-in. clusters of small florets so profuse that they nearly hide the foliage in spring. The seedheads that follow are pale green and contrast nicely with the leaves. Candytuft has a crisp, clean look that gives a planting a cultivated feel without too much effort on the part of the gardener.

WHEN TO PLANT

Seeds, 9000 per oz., germinate at 60 degrees Fahrenheit, so they can be sown fairly early in spring. Divisions can be made in spring, late summer, or fall; potted plants also transplant best when temperatures are cooler.

WHERE TO PLANT

Candytuft is not particular about soil, but some organic matter worked into the mix will help retain moisture and get plants off to a strong start. In lower-elevation gardens, candytuft looks lusher and takes less water if given afternoon shade. Plant it in rock gardens or use it for edging walkways, patios, and perennial borders. When combined with soapwort, grape hyacinths, dwarf daffodils, or blue flax, candytuft is a celebration of spring. Its foliage makes it an attractive filler year round.

HOW TO PLANT

Recent research has demonstrated that the best soil preparation for container-grown plants is to dig holes only as deep as the rootball but 4 times its diameter. This will allow plants to easily develop the lateral, absorbing roots they rely on for initial establishment and long-term survival. In beds and borders where plants are spaced 12 to 18 in. apart, tilling 3 to 4 in. of compost into the area to be planted and setting plants out in the amended soil is easier than digging individual holes. A 3-in.-deep topdressing of shredded bark, composted cotton burrs, or pecan hulls as mulch will keep the soil cooler and more uniformly moist, accelerating root development.

ADVICE FOR CARE

To maintain a more manicured look, trim off the seedheads when they start to look weathered. Cut stems close to the ground in early spring to clean up established plants before new growth emerges. Water deeply once a week when temperatures are 85 degrees Fahrenheit or above, every 2 weeks when temperatures are from 60 to 85 degrees, and monthly during cooler weather. Established plants should be watered to a depth of 18 in. Fertilizing is usually not necessary, but a small amount of granular or time-release fertilizer can be applied in spring until plants are well rooted. A granular iron-and-sulfur fertilizer can be used if leaves yellow in summer's heat.

SPECIES, CULTIVARS, OR VARIETIES

'Little Gem' is a dwarf form growing 6 in. high and 12 in. wide. It produces large white flower clusters. 'Autumn Beauty' and 'Autumn Snow' rebloom in fall.

REGIONAL CONSIDERATIONS

In central and southern New Mexico below 6000 ft., candytuft grows best in afternoon shade. Plants grown in this part of the state will need more water and may sunburn in midsummer.

Catmint

Nepeta × faassenii and *Nepeta mussinii*

Height: 12 to 18 in.	**Light Requirement:**
Color: Lavender-blue	
Bloom Period: April to November	
Zones: 4 to 8	
Water: Moderate to low	

The 18- to 24-in. mounds of small, silver leaves on wiry stems make catmint an asset in the garden even when it is not in bloom. Short spikes of soft purple-blue flowers are produced continuously from early spring to hard frost except when temperatures consistently top 90 degrees Fahrenheit. As a result of this heat tolerance, catmint suffers only brief doldrums in summer. A relative of catnip, catmint does not seem to be as attractive to felines, though there are individual cats who find it heavenly. In most gardens, catmint will grow vigorously enough to survive the damage caused by this affection.

WHEN TO PLANT

Nepeta mussinii is grown from seeds, 38,000 per oz., and often self-sows in gardens. Transplant seedlings or potted plants in spring or late summer and fall. Potted plants can be set out throughout the summer as long as they are watered regularly until new roots are established.

WHERE TO PLANT

Catmint is not fussy about soil. Compost amending can reduce water use in the short term, but it is not necessary. Catmint adapts to a range of watering regimes. It can be grown under small-leafed deciduous trees such as desert willow and honey locust and is robust enough to hold its own as filler among shrubs such as barberry, roses, sumacs, and turpentine bush. It blends well in perennial beds with 'Moonshine' yarrow, red valerian, bubblegum and licorice mints, gaura, Jerusalem sage, Mexican tarragon, and rudbeckia. If combining catmint with dwarf daffodils or tulips, allow enough space to keep it from smothering the bulb foliage.

How to Plant

Seed requires light to germinate; press seeds barely into the surface of the tilled soil and water gently. Refrigerating seed in a mixture of seed and damp vermiculite or perlite will prime it to germinate at 65 to 75 degrees Fahrenheit. To transplant, dig generous holes, loosening the soil so that new roots will have an easy time breaking ground. In perennial beds where plants are spaced 12 to 15 in. apart, tilling 2 or 3 in. of compost into the area to be planted and setting plants out in the amended soil is easier than digging individual holes. A 3-in.-deep topdressing of shredded bark, pecan hulls, or fine gravel as mulch will keep the soil more uniformly moist and more moderate in temperature, accelerating root development.

Advice for Care

Trim off the spent flower heads to stimulate another flush of bloom, to prevent weedy self-sowing, and to maintain a more manicured look. Cut leaves down close to the ground any time from autumn to early spring to rejuvenate established plants. Water to a depth of 24 in. every 2 weeks when temperatures are above 70 degrees Fahrenheit, and monthly during cooler weather. Fertilizing is usually not necessary, but a granular iron-and-sulfur fertilizer can be used if leaves yellow in summer's heat.

Species, Cultivars, or Varieties

Nepeta mussinii is the common, more cold-hardy species that is similar to *N. × faassenii* except that it reseeds prolifically. Reseeding can get out of hand in small gardens, but in larger spaces it will be somewhat limited to areas where a bit more water is available. A naturalized colony in bloom is a sight to behold. 'Six Hills Giant' is catmint on steroids, a super-robust sterile hybrid of *N. × faassenii*. It grows 3 ft. tall and wide with larger flowers on longer spikes. Hybrids 'Blue Wonder' and 'Snowflake' grow 12 in. high and 16 in. wide with longer bright-blue or white flower spikes. 'Six Hills Giant' seems to tolerate extra winter moisture best. Chinese catmint (*N. yunnanensis*) has linear leaves on plants 2 ft. high and 18 in. wide with short spikes of blue flowers. Remove spent flowers regularly for bloom throughout the summer.

Columbine

Aquilegia species

Height: 6 to 30 in.	**Light Requirement:**
Color: Blue or yellow	
Bloom Period: Spring	
Zones: 3 to 8	
Water: Moderate to ample	

"*A*quilegia" comes from the Latin for "water-bearer," and that is what you will need to be if you grow this plant that prefers evenly moist soil. Columbine's elegant flowers—long spurs swept back from crownlike faces—and lacy, lobed leaves on wiry stems are well loved. Although the plants are short-lived even when their demands are met, I thought it best to include them here with cautions. While most hybrid columbines rapidly succumb to heat and drought, golden columbine (one of the parents used to produce many of the fussier hybrids) is remarkably adaptable. It will grow well and flower profusely, even in low-desert gardens, as long as it is planted in the shade, mulched, and watered regularly for the month or so it is in bloom. Other hybrids are best reserved for the cool mountain gardens above 7500 ft., where summer rains and winter snowpack keep columbine happy.

When to Plant

Seeds may be sown indoors in February. Germination (at 70 degrees Fahrenheit) usually takes a few weeks. Seeds sown outdoors in April or May may take twice as long to germinate, and our spring winds will make it difficult to keep the seedbed moist enough. Container-grown plants can be set out when temperatures have moderated in spring, or in early autumn. Temperatures are too hot for summer planting at lower elevations.

Where to Plant

To give columbine the best chance possible, plant it in compost-enriched soil in protected niches where it will be shaded lightly all day (or at least from the hottest afternoon sun). Plants grown at higher elevations can be planted in full sun. Rock gardens and shady courtyards are ideal places to use columbines. Golden columbine contrasts nicely in shady gardens with catmint, veronicas, flowering onions, grape hyacinths, and cranesbill. Appropriate companions in upland gardens are Rocky Mountain columbine, soapwort, dianthus, candytuft, and veronicas.

How to Plant
Till 3 to 4 in. of compost into the area to be planted and set out plants in the amended soil. A 3-in.-deep topdressing of shredded bark, pine straw, or pecan hulls as mulch will keep the soil cooler and more uniformly moist, accelerating root development.

Advice for Care
To maintain a more manicured look and keep plants blooming longer, trim off the flower heads when they start to look weathered. Rejuvenate established plants by cutting leaves down close to the ground any time before new spring growth. Keep plants consistently moist while budded and in bloom. When plants are shaded and mulched, it may be enough to water deeply once a week when temperatures are 70 degrees Fahrenheit or above until plants stop blooming. Water every 2 weeks when temperatures are 60 degrees Fahrenheit or above, and monthly during cooler weather. Water should penetrate to a depth of 18 to 24 in. once established. Fertilizing is usually not necessary if the soil has been amended with compost, but a granular iron-and-sulfur fertilizer can be used if leaves yellow in summer's heat.

Species, Cultivars, or Varieties
Golden columbine (*A. chrysantha*) produces a lacy mound of leaves 12 in. high and 15 in. wide with flower stems that reach 30 in. Flowers are clear yellow. Rocky Mountain columbine (*A. caerulea*) grows 12 in. tall and wide with blue-and-white flowers held just above the airy foliage. It blooms for most of the summer when planted in full sun above 8000 ft. elevation; when grown in shade above 5000 ft., flowers last through spring.

Cranesbill

Geranium species

Height: 12 in. **Color:** Shades of pink or purple **Bloom Period:** Spring and summer **Zones:** 4 to 8 **Water:** Moderate to ample	**Light Requirement:**

*S*ince my garden is at 4500-ft. elevation—low by New Mexico standards—I had written off true geraniums as impossibly thirsty and difficult until my husband brought a few plants home. Was I wrong! While they are montane and north temperate zone natives, some geraniums are remarkably easy to grow here. Deeply divided leaves are clustered on thick stems, forming tight mounds that spread up to 18 in. wide. Plants are dormant only briefly in midwinter. The flat, open-faced flowers nod above the foliage on slender stems, appearing early at lower elevations and blooming in midsummer in the mountains. Cranesbill develops thick, deep roots that partially explain its adaptation to drier conditions. The name "cranesbill" comes from the shape of the plant's long, tapered seed capsule.

WHEN TO PLANT
Seeds stored dry over the winter lose viability quickly, so it is best to sow fresh seed in late summer for germination the following February to April. Plants develop new roots faster when the soil is cool, so transplanting in spring or fall is best, especially at lower elevations.

WHERE TO PLANT
Geraniums grow best in well-drained, humusy soil. They can be planted under large deciduous trees such as pistache, oak, and honey locust, or under fruit or other smaller flowering trees. In the mountains they can also be planted in rock gardens or perennial borders. Lamb's ear and artemisias make interesting companions.

HOW TO PLANT
Seeds should be covered with 1/8 in. of soil so that they stay damp through the winter. Light seems to inhibit germination. Till 3 to 4 in. of compost into the area to be planted and set out plants in the

amended soil. A 3-in.-deep topdressing of shredded bark, pine straw, or pecan hulls as mulch will keep the soil more uniformly moist and more moderate in temperature.

ADVICE FOR CARE
To maintain a more manicured look, trim off the spent flowers when they start to look weathered. Trim off the previous year's stems in spring before new growth appears. Water to a depth of 24 in. once a week when temperatures are 85 degrees Fahrenheit or above, every 2 weeks when temperatures are 65 to 85 degrees Fahrenheit, and monthly during cooler weather. Fertilizing is usually not necessary when the soil has been composted and plants are mulched, but a granular iron-and-sulfur fertilizer can be used if leaves yellow in summer's heat.

SPECIES, CULTIVARS, OR VARIETIES
'Wargrave Pink' geranium, a cultivar of *G. endressii* from the Pyrenees, grows 15 in. tall and spreads to 24 in. wide. It produces clear, soft-pink flowers and foliage with a distinctly gray cast. 'Johnson's Blue' geranium is a cultivar of *G. himaleyense* that grows 18 in. tall and 24 in. wide with light purple-blue flowers. *Geranium macrorrhizum* is a European species cultivated since the 1600s. It spreads by rhizomes and has aromatic foliage and pink flowers. *Geranium sanguineum* grows only 10 in. high and spreads 15 in. wide with rose-pink flowers above finely divided leaves that turn red in fall. Two widespread native species of New Mexico's mountains are *Geranium caespitosum*, with red-purple flowers with darker veins; and *Geranium richardsonii*, with white flowers tinged pink on stems 24 in. or taller.

Creeping Baby's Breath

Gypsophila repens

Height: 4 in.
Color: White or pink
Bloom Period: Spring through summer
Zones: 3 to 8
Water: Moderate to low

Light Requirement:

*L*ess well-known than its bigger, potentially weedy kin, creeping baby's breath forms a mat of small, narrow, pale-green leaves that are 1/2 in. long and closely spaced on fine, low-spreading stems. Clusters of tiny white or pink flowers bloom in mid-spring, appearing just above the leaves on threadlike stems. They create a lacy veil that nearly hides the foliage. Creeping baby's breath is long-lived and trouble-free with deep fleshy roots. Much more of the plant is below ground than above, which explains its heat and drought tolerance.

WHEN TO PLANT

Creeping baby's breath can be sown outdoors in April or early May if the seed has been kept moist and refrigerated for a month prior to planting. Transplant in spring after the danger of hard freeze is past, or in fall at least 4 weeks before hard freezes recur. This is especially important in colder northern and high-elevation gardens. Summer planting also works if care is taken to keep container-grown transplants from getting too dry, especially while they are in bloom.

WHERE TO PLANT

Creeping baby's breath is a versatile filler that can be tucked into gaps between boulders in rock gardens, between flagstones in pathways, or at the edges of patios. It mixes well with dozens of plants including pineleaf penstemon, dianthus, salvias, veronicas, and sedums. Because it creeps along the soil surface, it will look fresher in Zone 8 when grown in afternoon shade.

HOW TO PLANT

Since light inhibits germination of these small seeds, rake them into tilled soil deeply enough to cover them about 1/4 to 1/2 in. deep. To transplant potted plants, dig generous holes, loosening the soil so that new roots will have an easy time breaking ground. Recent research has demonstrated that the best soil preparation for container-grown plants is to dig holes only as deep as the rootball but 4 times its diameter. In a large grouping where plants are spaced 12 to 15 in. apart, till the area to be planted and set out plants in the loosened soil. A light mulch of shredded bark, pecan hulls, or fine gravel will keep the soil more uniformly moist and more moderate in temperature, accelerating root development.

ADVICE FOR CARE

To maintain a more manicured look and limit self-sowing, trim off the seedheads when they start to dry. Rejuvenate established plants by cutting long, sprawling stems back to a few inches from the crown any time from late autumn to early spring. Water deeply once a week when temperatures are above 85 degrees Fahrenheit, every 2 weeks when temperatures are 70 to 85 degrees Fahrenheit, and monthly during cooler weather. Water should penetrate to a depth of 24 in. once plants are established. Fertilizing is usually not necessary.

SPECIES, CULTIVARS, OR VARIETIES

'Bristol Fairy' is a double cultivar of *Gypsophila paniculata*, a perennial that grows to 30 in. tall with clouds of white flowers. It is used as a filler in garden flower beds and in cut flower bouquets as well. It was introduced in 1928 and is still a very popular bedding perennial. *Gypsophila elegans* is a 12- to 18-in.-tall annual that reseeds too well, especially in good garden soil.

Dianthus

Dianthus species

	Light Requirement:
Height: 6 in.	
Color: Pink, rose, or white	
Bloom Period: Spring	
Zones: 4 to 8	
Water: Moderate to ample	

*D*ianthus naturally belong to the "color-per-square-foot" school of plant breeding, where the highest value is placed on a sheet of flower color that nearly obscures the foliage. *Dianthus deltoides* cultivars are the epitome of saturated color. Because of the heat, plants tend to be short-lived, especially at lower elevations in the southern half of New Mexico, but they are worth replacing every 3 or 4 years. The dense mounds of narrow, nearly stemless green, blue, or gray leaves set the stage for the mass of flowers, but they have a much longer-lasting presence in the garden. Their refined, grassy texture makes a nearly year-round filler, striking an interesting balance with the brief intensity of the flower display.

WHEN TO PLANT

Seeds, 25,000 per oz., germinate at 60 degrees Fahrenheit and can be sown fairly early in spring. Make divisions in spring, in late summer when the plants are not in bloom, or in fall. Potted plants also transplant best when temperatures are cooler.

WHERE TO PLANT

Dianthus prefers well-drained soil, but a small amount of organic matter worked into the mix will help retain moisture and get plants off to a strong start. In lower-elevation gardens, dianthus looks lusher and takes less water when planted in afternoon shade. It is used as edging for perennial borders, walkways, and patios, and in rock gardens. The *deltoides* cultivars produce such intense colors that even though the plants are small, they can be placed in the distance and still draw attention. Artemisias, fleabane, and woolly thyme in the foreground make good companions for the brazen *deltoides*. The cheddar pinks (*D. gratianopolitanus*) are more subtle and require a place in the foreground where their fine flowers and foliage, as well as their clovelike fragrance, can be appreciated.

How to Plant

Prepare a seedbed by tilling 3 to 4 in. of compost into the area to be planted. Rake the small seeds lightly into the surface and water gently to keep from dislodging the seeds. To transplant potted specimens, dig generous holes only as deep as the rootball, but 4 times its diameter, so that plants develop the lateral, absorbing roots they rely on for initial establishment and long-term survival. If a grouping of plants is spaced 12 in. apart, till 3 to 4 in. of compost into the area to be planted and set out plants in the amended soil. A 2-in.-deep top-dressing of compost, shredded bark, pecan hulls, composted cotton burrs, or fine gravel will hasten rooting because it keeps the soil cooler and more uniformly moist.

Advice for Care

Trim off spent flowers to maintain a more manicured look and possibly stimulate a second flush of blooms in late summer. Water to a depth of 18 in. once a week when temperatures are 85 degrees Fahrenheit or above, every 2 weeks when temperatures are 65 to 85 degrees Fahrenheit, and monthly during cooler weather. Fertilizing is usually not necessary, especially if the soil has been organically amended, but a granular iron-and-sulfur fertilizer may be needed to reverse chlorosis in summer.

Species, Cultivars, or Varieties

'Flashing Lights', 'Brilliant', and 'Zing Rose' are cultivars of *Dianthus deltoides*; they produce dark-green foliage and a profusion of small, single flowers on slender 6-in. stems in spring. 'Flashing Lights' has wine-red flowers and red-tinged leaves; 'Brilliant' is intense crimson; and 'Zing Rose' is a rich rose-pink. *Dianthus × gratianopolitanus* 'Tiny Rubies' forms a 12- to 18-in. cushion of pale blue-gray leaves and clove-scented, double, rose-pink flowers on 4-in. stems.

Gaura

Gaura lindheimeri

Height: 30 in. **Color:** White tinged with pink **Bloom Period:** May to October **Zones:** 6 to 8 **Water:** Low to moderate	**Light Requirement:**

*G*aura has become one of the horticultural darlings of the '90s, and for good reason. It produces fountains of 1-in. flowers with very little encouragement, dozens per stem, in a continuous show from late May until autumn frost. Impressive as the mass display of blooms is at a distance, up close the form of individual flowers is exotic and deceptively fragile. Four petals resembling those of an apple blossom fan out above a cascade of white stamens tipped dark pink. The petals open white and fade to pink. The coarse leaves and slender, arching stems are dark green flecked with red. Gaura is a member of the evening primrose family, which has contributed many long-blooming, elegant perennials to the Southwestern gardening palette.

WHEN TO PLANT

Sow seeds in spring when the soil has warmed to 75 degrees Fahrenheit. It is best to set out plants in spring before they begin to flower. If you transplant in late summer or autumn, be sure not to overwater plants when the weather turns cold.

WHERE TO PLANT

Gaura needs sun to flower well and prefers medium-textured soils. Gaura tends to be short-lived in rich, humusy soils, but it will self-sow with reckless abandon. Its gauzy presence blends well in mixed borders with tall penstemons, Russian sage, bubblegum mint, dwarf goldenrod, and gayfeather. Gaura and Russian sage are the constants of this group while the other flowers blaze and fade.

HOW TO PLANT

Seeds are enclosed in a woody capsule and take nearly a month to germinate in tilled, warm soil. Mixing seeds with damp vermiculite or perlite and refrigerating for a month before sowing in April will cut outdoor germination time in half. Seedlings produce a deep initial root; plants seeded where they are to grow tend to take less water. To transplant container-grown plants, dig holes only as deep as the rootball, but 4 times its diameter. A 3-in.-deep topdressing of shredded bark, pecan hulls, or fine gravel will keep the soil cooler and more uniformly moist.

ADVICE FOR CARE

To encourage self-sowing, cut stems down to the ground in autumn after seeds have fallen. To maintain flowering and limit reseeding, trim off the flower heads when they start to look weathered. Water to a depth of 24 in. once a week when temperatures are above 85 degrees Fahrenheit, every 2 weeks when temperatures are 65 to 85 degrees Fahrenheit, and monthly during cooler weather. Fertilizing is usually not necessary. Flea beetles are the most significant pest. Larvae can be controlled with the San Diego strain of *Bacillus thuringiensis*, or you may use beneficial nematodes to destroy over-wintering eggs and larvae. If the problem has gotten out of hand, apply carbaryl to eliminate adult flea beetles.

SPECIES, CULTIVARS, OR VARIETIES

'Siskiyou Pink' and 'Dolphin' are cultivars with pink flowers. The related evening primroses include Mexican evening primrose (*Oenothera speciosa* 'Rosea'), a dense, spreading groundcover 12 in. high with 2-in. cup-shaped pink flowers in spring and early summer; white-tufted evening primrose (*Oenothera caespitosa*), which forms clumps of slender green leaves 10 in. high and nearly twice as wide and has 4-in. white flowers in spring and late summer; Missouri evening primrose (*Oenothera macrocarpa*), which forms clumps of glossy, green leaves with large yellow flowers in spring; and Organ Mountain evening primrose (*Oenothera organensis*), which grows 1 ft. high and 3 to 8 ft. wide with hundreds of large yellow flowers that open each afternoon in summer.

Gayfeather

Liatris punctata

Height: 24 in. **Color:** Rose-purple **Bloom Period:** September **Zones:** 3 to 7 **Water:** Low	**Light Requirement:**

*G*ayfeather is a favorite garden perennial that, thanks to its striking form, has become a cutflower standard. The native species, *Liatris punctata*, sometimes called "dotted gayfeather," is the best garden form for New Mexico gardens. It starts the season looking very much like a clump of coarse green grass, with leaves less than 1/4 in. wide and 3 in. long. The leafy flower stems begin to emerge from the basal foliage in midsummer. After 3 or 4 growing seasons, a single plant may have 2 dozen flower spikes; in 6 years, it may have twice that number. Age is glory with this long-lived plant. The bloom time is short, typically 3 weeks in September. Monarch, swallowtail, and checkered butterflies dance above the 18-to 24-in. rose-purple flower spikes. What a grand way to celebrate the end of summer!

WHEN TO PLANT

Sow seeds in spring when the soil is 65 to 80 degrees Fahrenheit. Container-grown plants can be set out any time but will initially need more water when temperatures reach 90 degrees Fahrenheit. The starchy taproots should be kept fairly dry in winter.

WHERE TO PLANT

Gayfeather has the best form when it is grown in lean soils with modest watering. Fine-textured and neat in leaf, and stunning in bloom, the plant is controlled enough to look elegant in manicured xeric perennial borders with artemisias, Jerusalem sage, and Mexican tarragon. It is equally at home among the prairie grasses, adding a spark of color to a sweep of grama and little bluestem. It can be woven like a ribbon through plantings of sand lovegrass, dwarf fountain grass, or blue avena. If planting gayfeather in large groups, space a dozen or more plants 2 to 4 ft. apart.

How to Plant

Gayfeather is easy to grow from seed that has been kept moist and refrigerated for 2 weeks prior to planting. Seed averages 9000 per oz., which covers at least 1000 sq. ft. Rake the seeds $1/2$ in. into the surface. While recent research shows that the best soil preparation for most container-grown plants is to dig shallow but very broad planting holes, gayfeather initially grows a carrotlike taproot several feet deep. Loosening the soil more deeply will ensure that new roots have an easy time breaking ground.

Advice for Care

Trim off the seedheads when they start to look weathered. Do this before seed scatters to limit self-sowing, or after birds have harvested the seeds if the garden is also a habitat. Water to a depth of at least 2 ft. every 2 or 3 weeks when temperatures are 85 degrees Fahrenheit and above. Water monthly during cooler weather. Fertilizing will cause flower stems to grow too tall and soft; it is not recommended. Pocket gophers can decimate a planting if they aren't trapped and relocated as soon as their loose soil mounds appear.

Species, Cultivars, or Varieties

'Kobold' and 'Floristan' are two cultivars of *Liatris spicata*. 'Kobold' grows 2 to 3 ft. tall with rose-purple flower spikes, while 'Floristan' is either violet or white. *Liatris pycnostachya* is a Great Plains native with 3- to 4-ft. stems, the top halves of which are densely cloaked with rose-purple flowers. All three selections bloom in midsummer, have stout truncated flower stems that look coarse compared with our native species, and take more water to thrive here.

Regional Considerations

While gayfeather will survive in Zone 8, it lacks the vigor that gives it such impact in slightly cooler climates. It is cold hardy to at least 8000 ft. elevation if the soil is well drained.

'Goldsturm' Rudbeckia

Rudbeckia fulgida var. *sullivantii* 'Goldsturm'

Height: 24 in.	**Light Requirement:**
Color: Yellow	
Bloom Period: Summer	
Zones: 4 to 8	
Water: Moderate to ample	

'Goldsturm' is noteworthy as the only truly perennial Rudbeckia. Its longevity is even more remarkable because it blooms so prolifically. Its dark-green basal leaves are oval- to oblong-shaped, rough, and coarsely veined in dense clumps 18 in. across. By early summer, 24-in. sparsely leafed stems stand above the basal foliage bearing 3-in. single flowers with yellow rays and dark-brown, button-like eyes. New stems emerge throughout the summer and older stems branch to produce a continuing display of flowers into September. 'Goldsturm' attracts butterflies and holds up well as a cut flower.

WHEN TO PLANT

Sow seeds in early autumn for blooms the following summer, or sow in spring for blooms the following year. To establish plants faster and with less water, set out plants in spring or fall while the weather is cool.

WHERE TO PLANT

'Goldsturm' *Rudbeckia* grows best in organically amended garden soil. A bit coarse and bold, but too self-contained to be wild, it has a relaxed garden personality that blends well with blue mist, pitcher sage, and Russian sage. It is used as a filler between roses and in cottage-garden-style borders. In winter, the dark-brown seedheads contrast with the russet and blond fall colors of maiden grass or the pale foliage of blue avena.

HOW TO PLANT

Prepare for seeding or transplanting by tilling a 3- to 4-in. layer of compost into the soil of the entire area to be planted. Sow 1/8 oz. seed per 100 sq. ft. or set out plants 18 to 30 in. apart. Cluster at least three to five plants together for impact. Seeds of 'Goldsturm' and newer cultivars of *Rudbeckia hirta* are fairly expensive, take about

3 weeks to germinate, and seedlings develop slowly; most gardeners buy container-grown plants. A 3-in.-deep topdressing of compost, shredded bark, or pecan hulls as mulch will keep the soil cooler and more uniformly moist, accelerating root development.

ADVICE FOR CARE
Trim off the spent flowers to stimulate continued blooming, and cut stems close to the ground any time from autumn to early spring when the seedheads begin to look weathered. Water deeply once a week when temperatures are 80 degrees Fahrenheit or above, every 2 weeks when temperatures are 60 to 80 degrees Fahrenheit, and monthly during cooler weather. Established plants should be watered to a depth of 24 in. Apply a small amount of granular fertilizer in spring and late fall. You may use a granular iron-and-sulfur fertilizer if leaves yellow in summer's heat.

ADDITIONAL SPECIES, CULTIVARS, OR VARIETIES
Black-eyed susan (*Rudbeckia hirta*) is an annual with soft, feltlike leaves and large, single flowers with yellow rays and dark eyes. It can be included in prairie seed mixes at higher elevations. 'Goldilocks' is a compact variety with semi-double yellow rays around a dark eye. 'Irish Eyes' grows 30 in. tall and has single yellow flowers with green eyes. 'Toto' is a 10-in.-tall dwarf that has single yellow flowers with dark eyes. For hot, dry gardens and prairies, the native Mexican hat (*Ratibida columnifera*) is an even better choice. Depending on soil type and water quantity, its very finely divided leaves form either a tuft 6 in. high and wide or a mound 18 in. tall and wide. The flowers are only 1$^{1}/_{2}$ in. in diameter with distinctive, elongated central disks. Flowers may be yellow, mahogany red, or a combination of both.

REGIONAL CONSIDERATIONS
In the south and central low-desert regions, rudbeckias need ample water. Plants grown in these areas may stop blooming in very hot weather and can suffer from leaf burn on their margins unless planted in partial shade. Rudbeckias grown above 7000 ft. are moderate water users and bloom better in full sun.

Greek Germander

Teucrium aroanium

Height: 4 to 6 in.
Color: Rose-pink
Bloom Period: Intermittently throughout the
growing season
Zones: 5 to 8
Water: Low

Light Requirement:

*T*his recent immigrant from the rocky slopes of Greece forms a
dense mat of silver foliage on slender prostrate stems. It is less
than 6 in. tall but spreads to 24 in. wide in 2 or 3 years. The soft,
evergray leaves are ³/4 in. long and ¹/16 in. wide and smell like sweet
thyme. In May or June the first flush of dime-sized clusters of rose-
pink flowers nearly hides the foliage. If spent flowers are removed,
Greek germander will bloom repeatedly until frost. While it is fairly
new to gardens in New Mexico, it has been tested for 5 years in hot,
dry, wind-scoured places in a wide range of unamended native soils,
and seems to be thriving everywhere without insect or disease problems. Rabbits don't even seem interested in it.

WHEN TO PLANT

Greek germander transplants all year but does best when planted in
spring or fall. Plants transplanted in summer will initially require a
bit of extra water. In winter, set out only those plants that are hardened off, and water modestly to avoid root rot. Greek germander is
grown commercially from cuttings rooted under light mist in early
fall. The lower stems of established plants will develop roots where
they come in contact with soil and can be transplanted in spring
or fall.

WHERE TO PLANT

Greek germander is small and refined enough to be tucked into
rock gardens and between paving stones, or to be planted in borders
along walkways and patios. It is also cold, heat, and drought tolerant enough to drape the edge of retaining walls or soften the feel
of cactus gardens. Our climate is tough on evergreens, so this
newcomer's winter color and texture are particularly welcome at
entryways. A few good companions for Greek germander are

rosemary, both shrubby and herbaceous salvias, yellow pineleaf penstemon, and creeping germander.

How to Plant

To transplant, dig generous holes only as deep as the rootball but 4 times its diameter so that plants will develop lateral, absorbing roots and stems that can root where they contact soft soil. In a bed where plants are spaced 12 to 15 in. apart, till the area to be planted and set out plants in the loosened soil. A 2-in.-deep mulch of fine gravel will keep the soil more uniformly moist and more moderate in temperature, accelerating root development.

Advice for Care

To maintain a more manicured look and stimulate another flush of blooms, shear off flower heads as they dry. Water plants deeply every 2 weeks when temperatures are above 80 degrees Fahrenheit and monthly during cooler weather. Well-established plants should be watered to a depth of 24 in. Fertilizing is not necessary even in loose sand or gravelly soils. Limited watering helps to prevent weed invasion; otherwise, a bed may need monthly tending to keep invaders at bay. Established plants form such a dense network of roots that weeding becomes only an occasional chore.

Species, Cultivars, or Varieties

Creeping germander (*Teucrium chamaedrys* 'Prostrata') is described in the Groundcovers chapter. Greek germander could also be considered a groundcover, but it is not so aggressive that it requires confinement to keep it from overwhelming less vigorous companions.

Hardy African Daisy

Osteospermum baberiae 'Compactum'

Height: 12 in. **Color:** Pink-purple **Bloom Period:** Summer **Zones:** 6 to 8 **Water:** Low to moderate	**Light Requirement:**

*U*ntil the recent introduction of *Osteospermum baberiae* 'Compactum', the African daisies grown in the Southwest were too tender to survive the cold winters of the high desert. This species grows to 9200-ft. elevations in the mountains of South Africa and adapts to about 7000 ft. in south and central New Mexico. Hardy African daisy forms a compact mound of thick stems 12 in. tall and 24 in. wide. Irregularly shaped oval leaves are a lush backdrop for the mass of 2-in. flowers with pinkish purple rays and deep-purple eyes. Flowers bloom from late spring well into summer.

WHEN TO PLANT

Because hardy African daisy is so new to cultivation, the range of conditions it is known to accept is still limited. For now, it's best to plant in spring so that plants have plenty of time to establish themselves before having to cope with a harsh winter.

WHERE TO PLANT

African daisy requires sun and well-drained soil. Too much winter moisture, especially in heavy clay soils, can prove fatal.

HOW TO PLANT

When planting a large grouping or a perennial border with plants spaced 18 to 30 in. apart, till a few inches of compost into the area to be planted and set out plants in the amended soil. To transplant individual plants, dig generous holes, loosening the soil so that new roots will have an easy time breaking ground. Recent research has demonstrated that the best soil preparation, even for deeply rooted, xeric, container-grown plants, is to dig holes only as deep as the rootball but 4 times its diameter. To avoid crown rot, plant African daisy only as deeply as it was growing in the container. A 3-in.-deep topdressing of fine gravel as mulch will keep the soil more uniformly moist and more moderate in temperature, accelerating root development.

ADVICE FOR CARE

To stimulate new growth and rejuvenate established plants, cut long stems back to side shoots 12 in. from the crown in late summer or just as new leaves begin to emerge in spring. Maintain a more manicured look by trimming off the seedheads when they start to look weathered. Water deeply once a week when temperatures are 85 degrees Fahrenheit or above, every 2 weeks when temperatures are 65 to 85 degrees Fahrenheit, and monthly during cooler weather. Once plants are established, waterings will be less frequent if water penetrates to a depth of 24 in. Fertilize with a small amount of granular fertilizer in spring. An iron-and-sulfur fertilizer can be used if leaves yellow in summer's heat.

SPECIES, CULTIVARS, OR VARIETIES

Osteospermum are closely allied to *Dimorphotheca sinuata*, the African daisy profiled with the annuals.

REGIONAL CONSIDERATIONS

In the low-desert areas of southern New Mexico, hardy African daisy looks fresher and uses less water when shaded in the afternoon.

Jerusalem Sage

Phlomis species

Height: 2 to 4 ft.	**Light Requirement:**
Color: Yellow	
Bloom Period: Midsummer	
Zones: 6 to 8	
Water: Low to moderate	

*J*erusalem sage is large for an herbaceous perennial, not just because it may grow to 4 ft. tall and wide, but because it has a bold garden presence. Underlying its soft, mounded form are stout stems densely covered with woolly leaves. They are topped with whorls of large, tubular yellow flowers in July and August. Jerusalem sage is native to the coastal limestone soils of the Mediterranean and is quite at home in our gritty alkaline soils.

WHEN TO PLANT

Transplant in spring and early summer to allow plenty of root development before cold weather. In warmer gardens, acclimated plants can be set out any time.

WHERE TO PLANT

Jerusalem sage prefers well-drained soil and contrasts nicely with red yucca, Russian sage, Texas sages, English lavender, and the shrubby salvias in borders, along paths, near patios, and clustered in front of evergreens.

HOW TO PLANT

To transplant, dig generous holes, loosening the soil so that new roots will have an easy time breaking ground. Recent research has demonstrated that the best soil preparation for container-grown plants is to dig generous holes only as deep as the rootball, but 4 times its diameter. This allows plants to develop the lateral, absorbing roots they rely on for initial establishment and long-term survival. A 3-in.-deep topdressing of shredded bark, pecan hulls, or fine gravel as mulch will keep the soil more uniformly moist and more moderate in temperature, accelerating root development.

ADVICE FOR CARE

Rejuvenate established plants by cutting stems close to the ground any time before new growth emerges in early spring. Trim off the spent flower heads down into the leaf mound to maintain a more manicured look and stimulate new blooms. Water deeply once a week when temperatures are above 90 degrees Fahrenheit, every 2 weeks when temperatures are 70 to 90 degrees Fahrenheit, and monthly during cooler weather. Established plants should be watered to a depth of at least 24 in. Fertilizing is usually not necessary.

SPECIES, CULTIVARS, OR VARIETIES

There are two species of Jerusalem sage that are similar in form, differing mostly in detail. *Phlomis fruticosa* is the larger of the two in overall plant size, leaf size, and also in the size of the flowers. Its hairy leaves are rough textured, olive green on top, and woolly beneath. *Phlomis lanata* grows 2 to 3 ft. tall and spreads to 4 ft. wide. Its leaves are more rounded, gray above, and woolly white beneath. It has a softer, more refined look when the two species are compared side by side and may be slightly less cold hardy. *Phlomis russeliana* spreads by runners, making a 2-ft.-wide mat of large green heart-shaped leaves covered with soft gold hairs. Flowers are similar to those of the other species, but the stems usually grow only 2 ft. high. *P. russeliana* is cold hardy to at least Zone 5; it is less drought tolerant than the others.

REGIONAL CONSIDERATIONS

In warmer climates, Jerusalem sage is more evergreen and is often listed as a shrub, but in the southern 2/3 of New Mexico to 6500-ft. elevation it is an herbaceous perennial, regrowing from the roots each spring. At higher elevations, *Phlomis russeliana* is the best species to use; give it afternoon shade if planting at lower elevations.

Mat Daisy

Anacyclus pyrethrum var. depressus

Height: 4 in.
Color: White and red
Bloom Period: Spring
Zones: 4 to 8
Water: Moderate to low

Light Requirement:

From the Atlas Mountains in Morocco comes mat daisy, a subtle and reliable spring flower. It begins as a soft carpet of ferny gray-green leaves. By mid-spring, 1-in. white daisies dot the foliage mat. The undersides of the narrow ray petals are red, and since the flowers close in the evening and on cloudy days, flower color changes throughout the day. Blooming stops with the onset of heat in early summer, abruptly at lower elevations; as might be expected, plants growing in light shade continue to flower a little longer than those bearing the brunt of the summer sun. The lifespan of individual plants is fairly short, averaging 3 or 4 years, but if some flowers are left to produce seeds, mat daisy often develops a self-renewing colony.

When to Plant

Sow seeds in spring when the soil has warmed to 70 degrees Fahrenheit. Potted plants can be set out any time of year. The best time to transplant is in spring or fall, but with an initial bit of extra water, plants will establish well in summer. In winter, set out only those plants that have been grown outdoors and are conditioned to cold. Water mat daisy modestly to avoid root rot.

Where to Plant

Mat daisy is adapted to infertile, well-drained soil. Its low profile and fine texture make it ideal for growing nestled between boulders in rock gardens or retaining walls, between flagstones, and for early color with species tulips, starflower, and pineleaf penstemon. Although mat daisy tolerates quite a bit of shade, later-blooming companions should be compact and self-contained (for example, sedums and 'Goblin' gaillardia) so they do not overwhelm this low-lying plant.

How to Plant

To sow seeds or to establish a large group of plants spaced 12 to 15 in. apart, till 3 in. of compost into the area to be planted and set out plants in the amended soil. Recent research has demonstrated that the best soil preparation for container-grown plants is to dig holes only as deep as the rootball but several times its diameter so that plants develop the lateral absorbing roots they rely on for initial establishment and long-term survival. A light topdressing of pecan hulls or fine gravel as mulch will keep the soil more uniformly moist and more moderate in temperature, accelerating root development.

Advice for Care

Shear off the spent flower heads to maintain a more manicured look and limit reseeding. Prolific self-sowing is likely only in good garden soil that is watered frequently. Water deeply once a week while blooming and when temperatures are 85 degrees Fahrenheit or above, every 2 weeks when temperatures are 65 to 85 degrees Fahrenheit, and monthly during cooler weather. Established plants should be watered to a depth of 24 in. Because mat daisy is fine textured and does not root aggressively enough to prevent weed invasion, you may have to weed a few times each season. Fertilizer is usually not necessary, especially if the soil has been amended, but a small dose may be applied in spring if companion plants require it.

Species, Cultivars, or Varieties

There are no other species in cultivation.

Mexican Tarragon

Tagetes lucida

Height: 24 in.	**Light Requirement:**
Color: Yellow	
Bloom Period: Autumn	
Zones: 7 and 8	
Water: Moderate to low	

*M*exican tarragon is grown for its handsome anise-scented foliage. Its brief display of yellow daisies in October and November is a bonus. Strong vertical stems stand 24 in. tall and fan out 18 in. wide. The unbranched stems bear narrow, dark-green leaves that are crisp, smooth-edged, and grow less than an inch wide and 3 in. long. The individual flowers are small and daisylike but have few rays. They would not be noteworthy except that they are held in large clusters at the ends of the stems and first appear at a time of year when most plants are long past blooming. If you can't find Mexican tarragon at nurseries among the perennials, look for it among the herbs. Though it is not a replacement for French tarragon, it has a long local history of being steeped for a refreshing tea.

WHEN TO PLANT

Set out plants in spring after all chance of frost is past. Mexican tarragon needs a long, hot growing season to establish roots before it can withstand a cold winter.

WHERE TO PLANT

Mexican tarragon does best in the well-drained infertile soil so common in New Mexican gardens. Its rich, dark foliage offers an interesting contrast to other plants in herb gardens and xeric flower borders, or when clustered among desert shrubs. Lively companions include lavender sage, 'Bowles Mauve' wallflower, 'Powis Castle' and other artemisias, catmint, threadgrass, woolly and dwarf butterflybushes, and Texas sages. Mexican tarragon's wonderful scent is welcome near windows or in entryways and sitting areas.

HOW TO PLANT

To transplant, dig generous holes only as deep as the rootball, but 4 times its diameter so that plants develop the lateral absorbing roots they rely on for initial establishment and long-term survival. A 3-in. mulch of shredded bark, pecan hulls, or fine gravel will keep the soil more uniformly moist and more moderate in temperature, speeding root development.

ADVICE FOR CARE
Rejuvenate established plants by cutting stems close to the ground any time from autumn to early spring. Water to a depth of 24 in. once a week when temperatures are 85 degrees Fahrenheit or above, every 2 weeks when temperatures are 70 to 85 degrees Fahrenheit, and monthly during cooler weather. Fertilizing is usually not necessary; too much nitrogen can destroy the crisp character of the plant.

SPECIES, CULTIVARS, OR VARIETIES
Mountain marigold (*Tagetes lemmonii*, sometimes labeled *T. palmerii*) is a larger plant, 3 to 4 ft. tall and wide, with more marigold-like characteristics and strongly aromatic, dark-green, divided leaves. It produces showy clusters of yellow-orange daisies in autumn. Because of its size and the strong scent of the foliage—which people have described as both marigold-mint-lemon and "skunky"—you may want to live with the plant in a container to see how you like it before planting mountain marigold in frequently used areas.

REGIONAL CONSIDERATIONS
Both Mexican tarragon and mountain marigold can be used as annuals or tender perennials in the warmest microclimates of colder New Mexico gardening areas.

Partridge Feather

Tanacetum densum ssp. *amani*

Height: 6 in.	**Light Requirement:**
Color: Yellow	
Bloom Period: Summer	
Zones: 4 to 8	
Water: Low	

---

artridge feather is grown for its finely sculpted silver foliage rather than for its flowers. The leaves are 1/2 in. wide and 3 in. long, covered with soft silver hairs and closely set on woolly stems that form mats 15 in. in diameter. Clusters of yellow button flowers appear in summer.

WHEN TO PLANT

Container-grown plants can be transplanted any time as long as they are acclimated to sun and cold rather than transplanted directly from a greenhouse, especially in summer or winter. Stems in contact with loose soil will root and can be cut and transplanted in spring or fall.

WHERE TO PLANT

Partridge feather requires soil that drains well. It seems most at home in rock gardens and stacked stone retaining walls where the companion boulders collect extra water by recycling condensation, but the root zone of the plants is well-aerated. Because the detail of the leaves is so remarkable year round, I like to use plants where they can be seen close up, such as at entryways or in sitting areas. The pale-silver foliage blends well with Turkish speedwell, the spiky veronicas, salvias, penstemon, and rosemary. Partridge feather complements dark-leafed, bold- or fine-textured foliage as well as brightly colored xeric plants.

HOW TO PLANT

To transplant, dig generous holes only as deep as the rootball but several times as wide, loosening the soil so that new roots will have an easy time breaking ground. A 3-in.-deep topdressing of fine gravel as mulch will keep the soil more uniformly moist and more moderate in temperature, accelerating root development. Fibrous mulches can contribute to rot in heavier soils by keeping the crown too moist.

ADVICE FOR CARE

Rejuvenate established plants by cutting longer stems back to side shoots close to the crown in early spring. To maintain a more manicured look, trim off the seedheads when they start to look weathered. Water deeply every 2 weeks when temperatures are above 75 degrees Fahrenheit, and monthly during cooler weather. Water should penetrate to a depth of 24 in. once plants are established. Fertilizing is usually not necessary, but a granular iron-and-sulfur fertilizer can be used if leaves yellow in summer's heat.

SPECIES, CULTIVARS, OR VARIETIES

White bouquet or snowy tansy (*Tanacetum niveum*) is a mounding plant 18 in. high and slightly wider. Its tiny white daisies with yellow eyes cover the lacy silver foliage in early summer. It is relatively short-lived, but 3 to 4 years of its beautiful foliage and clouds of blooms seem worth any necessary replanting. Snowy daisy is not as drought tolerant as partridge feather is in loose, sandy soil, but it thrives in heavy clay soils that retain water well.

REGIONAL CONSIDERATIONS

Plants grown in the low-desert areas of central and southern New Mexico will do best in afternoon shade. In the north and at higher elevations, plants grow better in full sun.

Penstemon

Penstemon species

Height: 2 to 36 in. **Color:** Red, purple, pink, or yellow **Bloom Period:** Varies **Zones:** 3 to 8 **Water:** Low to moderate	**Light Requirement:**

*P*enstemons range in form from matlike plants that could be easily mistaken for creeping thyme or veronica, to cushions of narrow leaves or billowy mounds of slender stems. The majority of species, however, grow flower spikes 12 to 36 in. tall from basal rosettes of leaves. Some are evergreen, while others lose their basal leaves as the flower stems shoot up. Most species and a spate of recent cultivars require well-drained soil to prosper, and they all tend to self-sow to some degree. The tubular flowers attract hummingbirds. All the species described here—and at least a hundred others—are knockouts when in bloom, and well worth a try in the garden.

WHEN TO PLANT

Sow seeds in spring or fall when the soil is cool, and move seedlings in spring just as new growth begins. Both novice and seasoned gardeners often plant potted plants in bloom. New gardeners can't resist the gorgeous flowers; devotees, aware that penstemons hybridize freely, wait to be sure they're getting what they want (or something interesting they suddenly developed a need for). Though the plants do surprisingly well when transplanted in bloom, this is the most stressful time for planting. Be sure the soil stays moist enough, but don't drown new transplants with good intentions.

WHERE TO PLANT

Lean, well-drained soil is best, even for high-elevation natives. Penstemons are mixed in xeric perennial borders; the low growers are used in rock gardens; and the larger species may be grouped between dryland shrubs. Species with crisp evergreen leaves look better when shielded from drying winter winds.

How to Plant

Seeds may require a period of cool dry storage to germinate. Most germinate more uniformly if the seed is mixed with damp perlite, refrigerated for a month, and sown when the soil is between 55 and 70 degrees Fahrenheit. Loosen the soil well so that new roots have an easy time breaking ground. A 3-in. mulch of fine gravel can be used to suppress weeds, but fibrous mulches such as shredded bark and pecan hulls may keep the crowns too damp and contribute to root rot.

Advice for Care

Let the seedheads ripen and shatter to feed songbirds and encourage reseeding. To maintain a more manicured look, cut spent flower stalks down to the basal foliage when they start to look weathered. Water deeply every 2 weeks when temperatures are above 75 to 85 degrees Fahrenheit, and monthly during cooler weather. Fertilizer is usually not necessary, and too much water, fertilizer, and organic matter in the soil will shorten the lifespan of most western species.

Species, Cultivars, or Varieties

Bush, or sand, penstemon (*P. ambiguus*) loves heat and drought. It is also one of the longest lived of the penstemons. Its 2-ft.-tall stems are topped with pale-pink flowers in May and September. Cardinal penstemon (*P. cardinalis*) is one of many species with red flowers on 2-ft. stems, but it blooms in summer, later than most, and the leaves are large, gray-green, and leathery. A canyon native, desert penstemon (*P. pseudospectabilis*), has rose-pink flowers on 30-in. stems. Its flowers bloom from early spring to the heat of summer above a mound of evergreen leaves 12 in. high and 36 in. wide. It likes afternoon shade in the hottest desert gardens. Mat penstemon (*P. caespitosus*) grows a carpet of small, dark-green leaves on spreading, wiry stems. The flowers are deep blue on short spikes a few inches above the leaves; plants bloom in May or June. Pineleaf penstemon (*P. pinifolius*), one of the cushion-forming types, produces needlelike evergreen leaves and red flowers on short spikes. Flowers bloom in May and intermittently through summer if deadheaded. There are two types of pineleaf penstemon: One grows 8 in. high and 10 in. wide; the other reaches nearly twice that size. A mutation, 'Mersea Yellow', is rumored to have first appeared in a garden in England the year after the Chernobyl meltdown. It doesn't glow in the dark, but it seems even more heat tolerant than the species. Rocky Mountain penstemon (*P. strictus*) is a pinyon-juniper woodland native with narrow, glossy, dark-green basal leaves and 18-in.-tall blue-violet flower spikes that appear in May.

Prince's Plume

Stanleya pinnata

Height: 30 in. **Color:** Yellow **Bloom Period:** Late spring **Zones:** 4 to 7 **Water:** Low	**Light Requirement:**

*P*rince's plume is a tough desert wildflower with a fanciful name that reflects its elegant appearance rather than its harsh native surroundings. Pale-green basal leaves emerge from a woody crown in spring, forming clumps 12 to 18 in. across. Sturdy, wandlike stems end in showy racemes of yellow flowers. Flower size is striking. The foot-long clusters of blooms and the delicate filigree of stamens create plumes worthy of a prince. Long, slender seedpods called "siliques" droop from the stems as the flowers fade. Prince's plume grows in the wild in exposed, rocky, windswept places where soils are usually high in selenium, but it adapts readily to the drier borders of desert gardens where conditions are less severe. Though it is handsome enough to grow for early-season color in any garden, it does best in minimally cultivated settings.

WHEN TO PLANT

Seeds germinate in spring as the soil warms to 70 degrees Fahrenheit. Container-grown transplants can be set out any time, but they will establish roots most quickly when the soil is warm.

WHERE TO PLANT

Prince's plume adapts best to dry, infertile soils. It makes a striking contrast with threadgrass and Rocky Mountain penstemon in a xeric flower bed, or clustered for early color among desert penstemon, shadscale, blackfoot daisy, and prickly pear cactus.

HOW TO PLANT

Plants started from seeds tend to persist longer and grow more vigorously than potted transplants because their deep initial roots are not disturbed. To start seeds, till the area to be planted, loosening the soil so that new roots will have an easy time breaking ground. Sow the seeds and rake them lightly into the surface.

Germination takes less than a week when the soil is warm. To transplant, dig generous holes only as deep as the rootball, but 4 times its diameter. Even desert plants with deep initial roots develop lateral absorbing roots when grown in pots, and once its initial taproot is interrupted, prince's plume relies on the network of lateral roots for long-term survival. A 3-in.-mulch of fine gravel helps establish new transplants by keeping the crown aerated and the soil more uniformly moist.

ADVICE FOR CARE

To maintain a more manicured look, trim off the seedheads when they start to look weathered. Rejuvenate established plants by cutting off the previous season's growth close to the ground any time from autumn to early spring. In habitat gardens and gardens likely to be browsed by wildlife, protect young plants with wire mesh during the first season until they have rooted enough to survive being nibbled on. Once plants are established, water to a depth of 24 in. every 2 weeks when temperatures are above 75 degrees Fahrenheit, and monthly during cooler weather. Plants grown from seeds sown directly in the garden in areas that receive 10 to 12 in. annual rainfall require no supplemental water after the first year. Fertilizing is not necessary, and though prince's plume tolerates high levels of selenium in the soil, it doesn't seem to require it.

SPECIES, CULTIVARS, OR VARIETIES

There are no other species in cultivation. There are two varieties of *Stanleya pinnata*. *S. pinnata* var. *integrifolia* has slightly broader leaves; *S. pinnata* var. *bipinnata* has leaves that are more finely divided.

REGIONAL CONSIDERATIONS

Prince's plume is best adapted at elevations between 4000 and 8000 ft., and though not common, it can be found growing wild in the canyon country of northwestern New Mexico.

PERENNIALS

'Profusion' Fleabane

Erigeron karvinskianus 'Profusion'

Height: 10 in. **Color:** White and pink **Bloom Period:** Summer **Zones:** 5 to 8 **Water:** Moderate to ample	**Light Requirement:**

Fleabanes are notable among the many daisies of the aster and sunflower family because their rays are very narrow, almost threadlike, and they have many more rays surrounding their yellow centers. The unglamorous name comes from the traditional use of some species to repel fleas. 'Profusion' is a cultivar of a Mexican species with soft, green leaves on slender, sprawling stems that form airy mounds less than a foot high and 2 ft. wide. The 3/4-in. flowers, borne a little above the leaves like a lacy cloud, are white when they open and blush pink as they mature. As you might guess from the cultivar name, they bloom in *profusion* all summer.

WHEN TO PLANT
Sow seeds in spring when the soil has warmed to 70 degrees Fahrenheit. Transplant volunteers in spring and set out potted plants after frost is past. Because plants bloom heavily all summer, it is best not to plant at that time. Young plants can be frost-tender; plant them early enough to allow a full 2 months rooting time before cold weather in the fall.

WHERE TO PLANT
'Profusion' grows well in hot, sunny places with infertile-to-average garden soil. Its fine texture and tendency to sprawl make it ideal as a filler in flower borders and edging paths, where it will create a casual, cottage-garden effect.

HOW TO PLANT
Seeds are tiny, 350,000 per oz., and take about 2 weeks to sprout in warm soil. To sow seeds or start plants spaced 18 to 24 in. apart in a bed or border, till a few inches of compost into the area to be planted. Scatter seeds or set out plants in the amended soil and water lightly to settle the soil surface. A 2-in.-deep topdressing of

shredded bark, pecan hulls, composted cotton burrs, or fine gravel as mulch will keep the soil more uniformly moist and help suppress weeds, accelerating the root development of transplants.

ADVICE FOR CARE

To maintain a more manicured look or to prevent self-sowing, trim off spent flowers as needed. Cut stems close to the ground any time from autumn to early spring as a seasonal cleanup. Water deeply once a week when temperatures are 90 degrees Fahrenheit or above, every 2 weeks when temperatures are 70 to 90 degrees Fahrenheit, and monthly during cooler weather. Established plants should be watered to a depth of 12 in. Though fertilizing is not usually necessary, a small amount of granular fertilizer can be applied in spring to support the long bloom season. Apply an iron-and-sulfur fertilizer if leaves yellow in summer's heat. Excess nitrogen will produce floppy stems and few flowers.

SPECIES, CULTIVARS, OR VARIETIES

Whiplash daisy (*Erigeron flagillaris*) is native in the foothills and valleys of New Mexico. Its flowers are similar to those of 'Profusion', but it forms rosettes of leaves, like strawberry offsets, on long wiry stolons. A few plants can develop into large colonies. Whiplash daisy blooms in spring, and if mowed after the first flowering to remove the network of stolons, it will bloom again in late summer and fall. It can be used in areas above 6500 ft. that are too cold for 'Profusion'.

Rue

Ruta graveolens

Height: 24 in.	**Light Requirement:**
Color: Yellow	
Bloom Period: Summer	
Zones: 3 to 8	
Water: Moderate to low	

*R*ue has a long history as a medicinal plant known as "herb of grace," and grace under pressure is a gift in our arid climate. Modern gardens need elegant textures and muted colors to balance the bold, color-per-square-foot displays we've come to expect. Mounded in form, rue produces rather stiff, upright stems that are hidden beneath its lacy, scalloped, blue-green leaves. The leaves fade after frost to a pale tan and persist well into winter before they drop. The umbels of small yellow flowers are unimpressive, but they provide a rich source of nectar for many of the predatory insects that rid our gardens of pests. Rue is a preferred host plant for swallowtail butterflies and their larva. The woody seedpods are interesting in the garden and in dried floral arrangements.

WHEN TO PLANT

Sow seeds in spring when the soil has warmed to 70 degrees Fahrenheit. Potted plants can be set out any time of year. The best time is spring or fall, but they will establish well in summer if given a bit of extra water. In winter, set out only those plants that have been growing outdoors and are hardened off, and water sparingly to avoid root rot.

WHERE TO PLANT

Rue grows well in any garden soil. It adds a subtle texture to garden spaces combined with rosemary, artemisias, the shrubby salvias, and Greek germander. Mix it with roses, coneflowers, yarrow, and buddleia as butterfly habitat. In full sun rue forms a tighter mound with smaller leaves, while in dappled shade it grows more open with larger leaves.

HOW TO PLANT

To prepare the soil for seeding, till a few inches of compost into the soil in the area to be planted. Rake the seeds lightly into the surface. To transplant, dig generous holes, loosening the soil so that new roots will have an easy time breaking ground. Recent research has demonstrated that the best soil preparation for container-grown plants is to dig holes only as deep as, or at most a few inches deeper than, the depth of the rootball but several times its diameter. This enables plants to develop the lateral absorbing roots they rely on for initial establishment and long-term survival. A 3- to 4-in.-deep top-dressing of shredded bark, pecan hulls, or fine gravel will keep the soil more uniformly moist and more moderate in temperature, accelerating root development.

ADVICE FOR CARE

To maintain a more cultivated appearance, trim off the seedheads when they start to look weathered. Rejuvenate established plants in early spring by cutting stems down to 6 in. from the ground to stimulate a flush of new growth. Water deeply at least every 2 weeks when temperatures are above 75 degrees Fahrenheit, and monthly during cooler weather. Established plants should be watered to a depth of 24 in. Fertilizing is not usually necessary, but a granular iron-and-sulfur fertilizer can be used if leaves yellow in summer's heat.

SPECIES, CULTIVARS, OR VARIETIES

Though there are some 40 species of *Ruta*, most of which are native to the rocky hillsides bordering the Mediterranean, only rue is cultivated with any regularity.

REGIONAL CONSIDERATIONS

At high elevations and in northern gardens, rue grows best in full sun, and once established it may not need any supplemental watering. This Mediterranean native is remarkably cold hardy, but to remain vigorous it should be kept fairly dry in winter.

Russian Sage

Perovskia atriplicifolia

Height: 3 to 5 ft. **Color:** Blue **Bloom Period:** June to frost **Zones:** 4 to 8 **Water:** Low to moderate	**Light Requirement:**

*I*n the midst of water conservation controversies, Russian sage has become a star, the plant everyone seems to like. It is native to Afghanistan, Iran, Pakistan, and Tibet, which explains its tolerance of heat, cold, drought, and political conflict. Though it is often described as a shrub because it grows at least 3 ft. high and 4 ft. wide and its base becomes woody, I consider it a perennial because it looks best if cut back near its crown each fall. The silver spear-shaped leaves are $1/2$ in. wide and 3 in. long. They vary in shape; some have incised margins, while others are finely divided and lacy. The small, dusky lavender-blue flowers are borne in such abundance on the branched stems that they make up half the plant's mass. Its long and undemanding color display accounts for its present popularity, but Russian sage is a newcomer to horticulture in New Mexico. It is proving to be an avid self-sower, and some plants have begun to rootsprout aggressively. We should carefully consider its introduction into undisturbed natural areas because, beautiful as it is, we may cease to appreciate it if it runs amok.

WHEN TO PLANT

Transplant volunteer seedlings in spring or fall. Container-grown plants can be set out any time.

WHERE TO PLANT

Russian sage is not fussy about soil as long as it is not kept too wet in clay. It gets large and does so quickly; be sure to allow plants plenty of space to develop. It is also a magnet for bees, including bumblebees, which are interesting to watch at leisure but not much fun to dodge in high traffic areas or near doors or gates. Russian sage provides strong contrast for magenta and purple flowers such as giant four o'clock, purple coneflower, and purple iceplant.

How to Plant

Though recent research has demonstrated that container-grown plants should be planted in holes several times wider than the diameter of the rootball, it may be best not to do this when transplanting Russian sage. If it does prove to be an overly aggressive rootsprouter, not loosening the soil laterally may help limit its spread. Do not amend the backfill soil. A 4-in.-mulch of shredded bark, pecan hulls, or fine gravel will keep the soil more uniformly moist and more moderate in temperature. It will also help suppress weeds until the sage roots out.

Advice for Care

Trim off flower heads when they start to look weathered; trim right after flowers fade to limit reseeding. Rejuvenate established plants by cutting stems down close to the ground any time after frost. Water to a maximum depth of 24 in. every 2 weeks when temperatures are above 85 degrees Fahrenheit, and monthly during cooler weather. Fertilizing is not recommended. Avoid forcing new growth in spring, because our late frosts will blacken tender shoots.

Species, Cultivars, or Varieties

'Filigran' is a cultivar with very lacy foliage; it seems a bit less robust than the species. 'Blue Spire' is more upright with larger flower spikes.

Regional Considerations

Russian sage is hardy to 8500 ft.

Salvia

Salvia species

Height: 12 to 30 in.	**Light Requirement:**
Color: Shades of blue, purple, or pink	
Bloom Period: All season	
Zone: Varies	
Water: Moderate	

*T*here are two distinct forms of salvia: The woody sub-shrubs are included in the Shrubs chapter, and the herbaceous types are highlighted here. Because they have been in cultivation for a long time, the salvia family tree is a twiggy and somewhat tangled affair. Not only are there selected cultivars, but there are also refinements of those selections and hybrids between species. Stems are typically tall and slender; some, like those of the superbas, are rather stiff, while others, like those of meadow and pitcher sage, are more supple. Breeding has intensified color and increased flower production.

WHEN TO PLANT

Sow seeds in spring when the soil has warmed to 65 degrees Fahrenheit. Potted plants of the most cold-tolerant types can be set out any time of year. The best time for transplanting is spring or fall, but with a bit of extra water during establishment, salvia will transplant well in summer. The more tender salvias do best when transplanted into warm soil.

WHERE TO PLANT

Salvias prefer well-drained soil but are adaptable if they are not kept too wet in heavy soils, particularly during cold weather. All types make good border plants; the blue-purples are particularly striking when contrasted with 'Moonshine' yarrow or Jerusalem sage. The hybrid superbas are more formal-looking and make good companions for dianthus, candytuft, floribunda roses, and curry plant.

HOW TO PLANT

Salvia seeds need light to germinate. Broadcast seeds on tilled soil; water lightly to avoid burying them too deeply. Soil should be loosened so that new roots will have an easy time breaking ground.

Compost is not necessary when planting the species, but it will help maintain more consistent soil moisture for the hybrids.

ADVICE FOR CARE

Stimulate repeated blooming by cutting flower stems close to the ground as they start to fade. Water hybrids deeply once a week when temperatures are 80 degrees Fahrenheit or above, every 2 weeks when temperatures are 60 to 80 degrees Fahrenheit, and monthly during cooler weather. The species can be watered every 2 weeks when temperatures are above 70 degrees Fahrenheit, and monthly during cooler weather. Fertilize hybrids every spring; species usually don't need supplementing.

SPECIES, CULTIVARS, OR VARIETIES

'Blue Queen', 'Rose Queen', 'May Night', and 'Ostfriesland' salvia are cultivars of *S. nemorosa* (also known as × *superba*). They are grown for their intense color and long season of bloom. All grow to 18 in. tall and 12 in. wide. 'May Night' is an improved 'Ostfriesland' that blooms a month earlier with larger blue-violet flowers. 'Blue Queen' is dark purple-blue; 'Rose Queen' is wine-purple. 'Ostfriesland', which is hardy to Zone 4, seems to be the most cold tolerant of the superbas; the others are hardy only to Zone 5. Chaparral sage (*S. clevelandii*) is the least cold hardy, to Zone 8, with large, woolly, silver leaves and 2-ft. whorls of dusky-blue flowers. The whole plant is fragrant and is used as a culinary herb. Littleleaf sage (*S. microphylla*) has small, aromatic leaves on sprawling 3-ft. stems. It produces scarlet flowers in spring and fall. It is hardy to Zone 7. Meadow sage (*S. verticillata*) 'Purple Rain' has 18-in.-tall arching spikes of berry-purple flowers and coarse fuzzy foliage. It is hardy to Zone 4. Mealy sage (*S. farinacea*) 'Victoria' grows clumps of narrow, gray-green basal leaves and small, violet-blue flowers on slender 24- to 30-in. spikes. It may freeze out every few years except in Zone 8. Pitcher sage (*S. azurea*) is a plains native with clear-blue flowers that arch 30 in. tall when grown dry in lean soil. Plants grown in good garden soil with plenty of water may reach 60 in. high. Unfortunately, the extra size is mostly rangy stem, not flower; as with many xeric plants, less is more.

Serbian Bellflower

Campanula poscharskyana

Height: 4 in.	**Light Requirement:**
Color: Blue-purple	
Bloom Period: Spring	
Zones: 4 to 7	
Water: Moderate to ample	

*T*hese woodland wildflowers are only practical in cooler shade gardens, but even in the central desert areas of New Mexico there are places shaded by trees or walls where bellflowers can find a comfortable niche. Serbian bellfower grows a network of wiry stems that spread to form an 18-in. mat densely covered with heart-shaped leaves. Leaves are a crisp light green and grow 1 in. in diameter with finely toothed margins. The 1-in. star-shaped flowers open wider than most bellflowers and dot the leafy carpet from late spring into summer. Serbian bellflower is more heat and drought tolerant than other campanulas, but it spends a few years developing an extensive root system before it fills out above ground.

WHEN TO PLANT

Transplant and divide plants in spring or autumn because roots develop most quickly during cool weather.

WHERE TO PLANT

Adding generous amounts of compost to the soil at planting time will pay off greatly in reduced water use over the long term; it also gets new plants off to a much stronger start. Bellflower is used in rock gardens, to edge shaded flower beds and shrub borders, and to fill pockets between other plants. It loves shade and moisture too much to be used extensively as a groundcover.

HOW TO PLANT

When plants will be spaced 12 to 18 in. apart, till 4 in. of compost into the entire area to be planted and set out plants in the amended soil. A 3-in.-deep topdressing of compost, shredded bark, composted cotton burrs, or pecan hulls as mulch helps keep the soil cooler and more uniformly moist, and it will suppress weeds until the bell-flower spreads to fill the space.

ADVICE FOR CARE

Trim off the spent flowers to keep plants blooming, and mow plants down close to the ground any time from autumn to early spring as an annual cleanup. Water to a depth of 18 in. once a week when temperatures are 80 degrees Fahrenheit or above, every 2 weeks when temperatures are 60 to 80 degrees Fahrenheit, and monthly during cooler weather. Small amounts of fertilizer applied in spring for the first few years after planting will help get plants off to a strong start; this may not be necessary if the soil has been enriched with compost and if more compost is used as mulch. A granular iron-and-sulfur fertilizer can be used if leaves become chlorotic in summer's heat, but if leaves continue to yellow and leaf margins burn, the location may be too hot or dry for bellflower.

SPECIES, CULTIVARS, OR VARIETIES

Harebells (*Campanula rotundifolia*) produce clumps of heart-shaped basal leaves with bright-blue, lavender, purple, or white flowers on slender, nodding, 1-ft.-tall stems. Deadhead repeatedly to keep plants blooming, but allow some flowers to set seed at the end of the season to replace declining plants. Dalmatian bellflower (*Campanula portenschlagiana*) is very similar to Serbian bellflower but the flowers are violet-blue. They nod above the leafy carpet in clusters of 2 or 3 per 6-in. stem. The compact plants spread 10 to 12 in. wide and will require full sun if planted above 7500 ft. Roving bellflower (*Campanula rapunculoides*) is a native of the Caucasus with bright-blue flowers on nodding, one-sided racemes. It is also known as "cancer-of-the-garden" by those who have unwittingly planted it in perennial borders in good garden soil. Roving bell-flower is best planted as a groundcover in high elevation gardens by gardeners who have space to fill and who don't want to have to tend it too closely.

REGIONAL CONSIDERATIONS

Zone 8 is beyond the range of heat tolerance; campanulas are best left to the mountain gardens in southern New Mexico.

Soapwort

Saponaria ocymoides

Height: 4 to 8 in.
Color: Pink
Bloom Period: Spring
Zones: 3 to 8
Water: Moderate

Light Requirement:

*S*oapwort is a venerable rock garden plant, neat and undemanding with clusters of deep-pink flowers in April and May. Small, rounded, dark-green leaves cloak wiry stems that spread 12 in. and densely cover the soil, spilling over the edge of rock walls and creeping between paving stones. It is a bit too small and not aggressive enough to be considered a groundcover, but soapwort is pest-free and long-lived with a minimum of care. While it may reseed a little in good garden soil, don't confuse this reliable, self-contained species with bouncing bet (*Saponaria officianalis*), a rank and invasive weed that found its way into gardens long ago, but fortunately seems poorly adapted in New Mexico.

WHEN TO PLANT
Sow seeds in spring when the soil has warmed to 60 degrees Fahrenheit. Potted plants can be set out any time of year. The best time is spring or fall, but soapwort will transplant well in summer if provided a bit of extra water during establishment. In winter, set out only those plants that have been growing outdoors and are hardened off; water sparingly to avoid root rot.

WHERE TO PLANT
Soapwort is not fussy about soil, but adding compost to loose sand helps retain moisture better, and in clay it will improve drainage. Soapwort is used for contrast with spring bulbs (especially dwarf daffodils and grape hyacinths) or with perennials such as catmint and candytuft. The foliage makes a cool, green filler throughout the growing season in rock gardens or along beds and pathways.

HOW TO PLANT
Seeds are small, 12,000 per oz.; $1/3$ oz. covers 10 sq. ft. Rake seeds lightly into the surface in spring. In a perennial bed or border where

plants are spaced 12 in. apart, or to grow soapwort from seeds, till 3 to 4 in. of compost into the area to be planted and set out plants or seeds in the amended soil. Individual plants can be set out in thoroughly loosened, unamended soil, but they will develop more slowly. A 3-in.-deep mulch of compost, shredded bark, or pecan hulls helps keep the soil more uniformly moist and more moderate in temperature; it will also limit weed invasion between soapwort transplants until they fill the space.

ADVICE FOR CARE

Trim off the flower heads when they start to look weathered; since the seedheads blend into the foliage, this isn't a pressing chore. Rejuvenate established plants by cutting long, sprawling stems back to sideshoots 6 in. from the crown any time from autumn to early spring. Water deeply once a week when temperatures are 80 degrees Fahrenheit or above and while plants are blooming. Water every 2 weeks when temperatures are 60 to 80 degrees Fahrenheit, and monthly during cooler weather. Established plants should be watered to a depth of 24 in. Fertilizing is usually not necessary, but a small amount of a granular fertilizer can be applied in spring and will be especially helpful during establishment.

SPECIES, CULTIVARS, OR VARIETIES

Saponaria × lempergii might be called giant summer soapwort, since its leaves and clusters of flowers are nearly twice the size of *Saponaria ocymoides* and it blooms in midsummer. Because of its size and flowering time, this soapwort takes more water than the smaller spring bloomer, and it adapts best in gardens above 6500 ft.

Speedwell

Veronica species

Height: 2 to 10 in. **Color:** Shades of blue **Bloom Period:** Spring **Zones:** 4 to 7 **Water:** Moderate to ample	**Light Requirement:**

*T*here are nearly 300 species of *Veronica* growing native on 6 continents. A major thaw on Antarctica would probably make it unanimous. The species that grow well in New Mexico are mainly those from the Mediterranean. They are all long-lived and cultivated-looking, yet they require little care. The small individual flowers have four petals in shades of blue. They are borne on spikes ranging from less than 1 in. to 9 in. long. The foliage is fine-textured and varies from round thumbnail-sized leaves to long, narrow leaves in basal clumps. The taller species generally take more water; compact species with thick or woolly leaves are the most drought tolerant. Because veronicas have been under cultivation for so long, there are many minor variations in leaf density, flower size, and color. To get and keep the cultivars you prefer, select plants with the preferred leaf and flower form, and increase them by layering or dividing established plants.

WHEN TO PLANT

Divisions and layered stems can be transplanted in spring just as the plants begin active growth, or in late summer or fall. Potted plants can be set out any time of year. The best time is spring or fall, but with a bit of extra water during establishment the more drought-tolerant species will also transplant well in summer. In winter, set out only those plants that have been acclimated to cold.

WHERE TO PLANT

Veronicas are not fussy about soil. Their refined growth habits and intense color make them valuable fillers in rock gardens, along paths and patio edges, and in the foreground of low flower borders combined with 'Profusion' fleabane, dianthus, salvias, or penstemon.

How to Plant

When plants are to be spaced 12 to 18 in. apart, tilling a few inches of compost into the area to be planted and setting out plants in the amended soil is an easier way to plant than digging individual holes. A light mulch of shredded bark or pecan hulls will keep the soil cooler and more uniformly moist.

Advice for Care

Trimming off the spent flowers of the taller forms will prolong blooming. Water plants to a depth of 24 in. once a week when temperatures are 85 degrees Fahrenheit or above, every 2 weeks when temperatures are 60 to 85 degrees Fahrenheit, and monthly during cooler weather. A small amount of granular fertilizer can be applied in spring, or a 4-month time-release formula can be worked into the soil under drip emitters each year. An iron-and-sulfur supplement can be used if leaves yellow in summer's heat.

Species, Cultivars, or Varieties

'Goodness Grows' alpine veronica (*V. spicata*, also known as *V. alpina*) is a long-blooming cultivar that, if deadheaded repeatedly, will produce 10-in. spikes of violet-blue flowers from May through October. Foliage grows as a dense mat of linear green leaves. Silver speedwell (*Veronica incana*) is slow growing and forms compact 12-in. clumps of narrow, silver leaves and deep-blue flower spikes. It is heat tolerant and grows best in full sun. Turkish speedwell (*Veronica liwanensis*) looks like a large, glossy-leafed, evergreen creeping thyme, but the waves of gentian-blue flowers that cover the foliage in spring quickly clear up that misunderstanding. Woolly veronica (*V. pectinata*) has 1/2-in. soft, silver, wedge-shaped leaves with notched edges. Its fine, prostrate stems root at the nodes and produce short spikes of purple-blue or rose-pink flowers with white centers.

Stonecrop

Height: 15 to 18 in.
Color: Pink to rust
Bloom Period: Midsummer
Zones: 4 to 8
Water: Moderate to low

Light Requirement:

'Autumn Joy' is one of the sedums best adapted throughout New Mexico. Unlike the small mat-forming species, it is grown for its showy flowers rather than for its foliage. Thick pale-green shoots push up from the soil in spring, quickly expanding into clumps of round fleshy leaves with scalloped margins. The stems continue to elongate until midsummer when the domed flower umbels unfold. 'Autumn Joy' flowers open pale pink, mature to a deep coral, and finally dry a rich russet color that persists through winter. Plants are long-lived and attract butterflies.

WHEN TO PLANT

Divisions can be transplanted in spring just as the plants begin active growth. Cuttings can be taken in late spring when the stems are 6 in. tall and set out when well-rooted in late summer or fall. Potted plants can be set out any time of year. The best time is spring or fall, but with a bit of extra water they transplant well in summer, even when they are in bloom. In winter, set out only those plants that have been acclimated to cold; water sparingly.

WHERE TO PLANT

'Autumn Joy' adapts to most soils, even heavy clay, as long as it is not kept too wet. It is used in xeric flower and shrub borders for late-season color and winter interest, especially to provide contrast with blue avena, shadscale, lavender sage, garlic chives, or threadgrass.

HOW TO PLANT

To transplant sedum, dig generous holes, loosening the soil so that new roots will have an easy time breaking ground. In perennial beds or borders where plants are spaced 15 to 20 in. apart, till the area to be planted and set out plants in the soft soil. A 3-in.-deep topdressing of shredded bark, pecan hulls, or fine gravel as mulch will help plants root faster and suppress weeds until they do.

ADVICE FOR CARE

To tidy up established plants in spring, cut the past year's dried flower stems down close to the ground when new shoots begin to emerge. Water to a depth of 24 in. once a week when temperatures are 90 degrees Fahrenheit or above, every 2 weeks when temperatures are 70 to 90 degrees Fahrenheit, and monthly during cooler weather. Fertilizing is usually not necessary. Aphids may attack the succulent new growth in spring. The best method of control is to wash them off the leaves with a strong spray of water; insecticides can burn the waxy leaves.

SPECIES, CULTIVARS, OR VARIETIES

'Red Chief' is very similar to 'Autumn Joy'. *Sedum spectabile* as a species is also similar to *Sedum telephium*, though its foliage is a bit brighter green and its flower umbels are flat-topped rather than crowned. These old standbys bloom in white, pink, or lavender; when I was a kid, it seemed that everyone's grandmother had urns of them growing on her front porch. The cultivars 'Meteor', with burgundy-red flowers, and 'Brilliant', with carmine flowers and bronze foliage, are offered as either *spectabile* or *telephium* by various growers. Mahogany plant (*S. maximum* 'Atropurpureum') is another similar species with leathery, dark-reddish foliage that sunburns badly in full sun in the low desert.

REGIONAL CONSIDERATIONS

When planted in full sun, 'Autumn Joy' is cold hardy up to 8500 ft. in New Mexico. In the low-desert areas of the southern part of the state, plants do much better with afternoon shade.

Torch Lily

Kniphofia uvaria

Height: 30 in.
Color: Orange and yellow
Bloom Period: Early summer
Zones: 5 to 8
Water: Low

Light Requirement:

Torch lily is also known by its old botanical name, *Tritoma*, and as "poker plant" or "red hot poker." It is a South African high-altitude native with coarse, grassy leaves and flamelike flower spikes. The leaf blades are 1 in. wide but look narrower due to the lengthwise fold down their midribs. They grow to 2 ft. long, arching over so that the leafless flower spikes stand well above the clumps of leaves. The 6-in. spikes top stout 30-in. flower stems. The tightly clustered tubular flowers are soft coral-orange at the tips, blending to yellow at the base. Established plants' numerous deep, pencil-thick roots account for torch lily's drought and heat tolerance.

WHEN TO PLANT

Seeds germinate and plants root out fastest when the soil is warm. Divide or transplant torch lily from mid-spring through late summer or early fall. Seeds germinate in 3 weeks when the soil has warmed to 65 degrees Fahrenheit.

WHERE TO PLANT

Though well-drained soil is best, torch lily will grow well in heavy clay as long as it isn't kept too wet. It is one of the few showy perennials that will tolerate saline soil. Mix torch lily in xeric perennial beds with 'Moonshine' yarrow, valerian, 'Powis Castle' artemisia, salvias, and Rocky Mountain penstemon; or try it clustered in the foreground of shrub borders with dwarf or woolly butterflybush, English lavender, and rosemary.

HOW TO PLANT

To start torch lily from seeds, till the soil well so that new roots will have an easy time breaking ground. Seedlings may vary in color from bicolor to all orange or all yellow. Established clumps can be cut into several sections with a sharp spade and replanted at the same depth they were growing previously. When transplanting container-grown plants, dig holes only as deep as the rootball but 4 times its diameter. If roots are coiled around the rootball, unwind or sever the potbound roots so that new roots will branch out into the loosened soil. Plants may be spaced 2 to 3 ft. apart and mulched with 3 in. of shredded bark, pecan hulls, or fine gravel.

ADVICE FOR CARE

Trim off the flower stalks at their base as they fade. Clean up established plants by cutting leaves down close to the ground any time from autumn to early spring. Water deeply every 2 weeks when temperatures are above 75 degrees Fahrenheit, and monthly or less during cooler weather. Established plants should be watered to a depth of at least 24 in. Fertilizing is not usually necessary. When clumps become very thick, flowering declines. When this happens, plants should be lifted, divided, and reset.

SPECIES, CULTIVARS, OR VARIETIES

'Alcazar' is more cold hardy, vigorous, and deeper in color. 'Border Ballet' is shorter, to 24 in. tall, in a mix of colors including pink. 'Primrose Beauty' is an all-yellow selection.

Valerian

Centran ruber

Height: 18 to 24 in.	**Light Requirement:**
Color: Shades of coral, pink, and white	
Bloom Period: All season	
Zones: 3 to 8	
Water: Moderate to low	

*V*alerian, also known as "Jupiter's beard," is an old garden favorite whose color, adaptability, and long bloom season have brought it renewed popularity. The lance-shaped medium-green leaves are smooth and waxy in texture. Growing 1/2 in. wide and 2 to 3 in. long, they cover the limber stems to form a mound at least as wide as it is tall. Valerian's individual florets are tiny, but they are clustered together in branching flower heads above the leaves. The fragrant flowers cut well for filler in bouquets and attract both butterflies and hummingbirds to the garden.

When to Plant

Sow seeds in spring when the soil has warmed to 65 degrees Fahrenheit. Plants can be set out any time during the growing season. The best time is spring or fall, but with a bit of extra water during establishment, valerian will also transplant well in summer.

Where to Plant

Valerian is not fussy about soil, but it should not be kept too wet in heavy clay, especially in winter. The coral-pink blooms are a great contrast for the blues of English lavender, Russian sage, catmint, blue mist, and dwarf butterflybush, especially when red yuccas are added to repeat the coral tones. In perennial beds or as filler between yellow roses with salvias, gaura, and 'Profusion' fleabane, valerian will continue to flower for most of the growing season.

How to Plant

Seeds are small, 16,000 per oz., and require light to germinate. Press seeds gently into the soil surface. To amend the soil for sowing, till 3 to 4 in. of compost into the seedbed. When plants are to be set out and spaced 2 ft. apart in perennial beds or borders, tilling the area to be planted and transplanting into the loosened soil is an easier way to plant groups of perennials than digging individual holes. Amending the soil with organic matter isn't necessary, but valerian is adaptable if its companions will benefit from the added compost. A 3-in.-deep topdressing of fine gravel, shredded bark, or pecan hulls as mulch will keep the soil more uniformly moist and more moderate in temperature, accelerating root development.

ADVICE FOR CARE

Trim off spent flowers periodically to stimulate continuous blooming and to limit self-sowing. Seedheads are very fine and will not detract from the appearance of the garden, but keep in mind that volunteer seedlings tend to crop up in good garden soil with merry abandon. If you like to maintain order, deadhead often. If a bursting-at-the-seams cottage garden is more your style, be a bit slow to trim. Plants are long-lived and don't require dividing to bloom well. Cut the old stems down close to the ground any time from autumn to early spring for seasonal clean up. Water deeply once a week when temperatures are 90 degrees Fahrenheit or above, every 2 weeks when temperatures are 70 to 90 degrees Fahrenheit, and monthly during cooler weather. Water should penetrate to a depth of 18 in. once plants are established. Fertilizing is usually not necessary, but to support the long bloom season a small amount of granular or time-release fertilizer may be applied in spring. Too much nitrogen will promote lush foliage growth at the expense of flowers.

SPECIES, CULTIVARS, OR VARIETIES

Centranthus ruber var. *Albus* is a white variety. When valerian is allowed to self-sow, a few white-flowered plants may sport from a group of pink plants.

Woolly Thyme

Thymus pseudolanuginosis

Height: 2 in.
Color: Pink
Bloom Period: Summer
Zones: 4 to 8
Water: Moderate to low

Light Requirement:

*C*reeping thymes have been cultivated for a long time, and as a result there are many varieties with characteristics that make them noteworthy. Woolly thyme is the most drought tolerant of the lot. Its tiny gray leaves, covered with fine silver hairs, form a dense carpet. The wiry stems root where they touch loosened soil. A single plant will spread to cover 24 in. in 2 years, but small plants are often spaced 12 in. apart for coverage in one season. Woolly thyme's tiny rosy-pink flowers are sparsely scattered across the carpet of foliage. This plant is grown for its fine texture, its sweet aromatic fragrance, and for the subtle seasonal foliage change (to a smoky plum color) that takes place after frost.

WHEN TO PLANT

Rooted stems or plugs cut out of an established stand can be transplanted in spring or fall. Potted plants can be set out any time of year. The best time is spring or fall, but with a bit of extra water during establishment, they will also transplant well in summer.

WHERE TO PLANT

Woolly thyme prefers well-drained soil. It is used as a filler between flagstones or between boulders in rock gardens. Mix it in edging beds with chives, blue fescue, and pineleaf or mat penstemon. The pale color and fine texture can be blended with complementary plants such as woolly veronica, mat daisy, pussytoes, partridge feather, or Greek yarrow to create a subtle brocade effect. Gourmands that they are, rabbits love woolly thyme, so be sure to plant it in an area enclosed by a wall or fine-mesh fencing.

HOW TO PLANT

If plants are spaced 12 to 18 in. apart, tilling 3 to 4 in. of compost into the area to be planted and setting plants out in the amended soil is a more efficient way to plant than digging individual holes. Because woolly thyme roots where the stems contact loosened soil, planting in tilled soil reduces the time it takes plants to fill in gaps.

ADVICE FOR CARE

To rejuvenate established plants that are beginning to look ragged, shear them down close to the ground in early spring. Water deeply once a week when temperatures are 85 degrees Fahrenheit or above, every 2 weeks when temperatures are 65 to 85 degrees Fahrenheit, and monthly during cooler weather. At higher elevations and in shade, watering every 2 weeks (with an extra watering when temperatures peak) may be sufficient. Established plants should be watered to a depth of 18 in. Fertilizing is not usually necessary. Woolly thyme never becomes thick enough to exclude weeds, but weed invasion decreases as plants develop a denser network of roots.

SPECIES, CULTIVARS, OR VARIETIES

Thymes can be classified as either ornamentals or culinary herbs, though even the herb forms are attractive garden plants. The culinary varieties are mostly selections of English thyme (*Thymus vulgaris*), which grows 10 in. tall and nearly as wide with rose-pink flowers and small, very pungent evergreen leaves. 'Pinewood' smells strongly of pine. 'Narrow-leaf French' has needlelike gray leaves and a very pleasant flavor. Lemon thyme (*Thymus citriodorus*) has small green leaves and is valued both for its usefulness as a fine-textured filler, and for its strong lemon scent and flavor. *Thymus serpyllum* is an ornamental selection with bright-green foliage; var. *albus* blooms white, and *coccineus* blooms magenta. 'Minor' has the smallest leaves and forms the tightest mats to 12 in. in diameter. Juniper thyme (*T. neiceffii*) has long, fine leaves that resemble juniper foliage.

Yarrow

Achillea × 'Moonshine'

Height: 18 to 24 in. **Color:** Yellow **Bloom Period:** May to October **Zones:** 5 to 8 **Water:** Moderate	**Light Requirement:**

'Moonshine' is the most versatile and trouble-free of the yarrows. Its finely divided silver foliage grows in 18-in.-wide self-contained clumps that will not outgrow their space or overwhelm companions. The flat-topped, lemon-yellow flower umbels make long-lasting cut flowers. They dry well if cut early in the day; choose flowers that have just begun to show color.

WHEN TO PLANT

Potted plants can be set out any time of year. The best time is spring or fall, but with a bit of extra water while it is in bloom, yarrow can also be transplanted in summer. In winter, set out only those plants that have been acclimated to cold; water sparingly until the soil warms in spring.

WHERE TO PLANT

Though yarrow adapts to most soils, it will require less frequent watering in sandy soils that have been amended with compost. 'Moonshine' flowers are a chameleon color that appears hot when mixed with valerian, blanketflower, and cardinal or desert penstemon. The color is strong but more subdued when combined with salvias, blue flax, Rocky Mountain penstemon, or Russian sage. The plant is large enough to hold its own in borders among roses, dwarf butterflybush, or other flowering shrubs.

HOW TO PLANT

Dig generous holes, loosening the soil so that plants can develop the lateral, absorbing roots they rely on for initial establishment and long-term survival. If plants are spaced 18 to 30 in. apart, tilling 3 to 4 in. of compost into the area to be planted and setting plants out in the amended soil is easier than digging individual holes. A 3-in. mulch of shredded bark, composted cotton burrs, or pecan hulls keeps the soil cooler and more uniformly moist; it will also help suppress weeds.

ADVICE FOR CARE

Remove spent flowers regularly to keep plants blooming continuously. At the end of the season, cut the dried flower stems down close to the ground any time they start to look weathered. Trim away dead foliage to rejuvenate established plants. Water deeply once a week when temperatures are 85 degrees Fahrenheit or above, every 2 weeks when temperatures are 60 to 85 degrees Fahrenheit, and monthly during cooler weather. Established plants should be watered to a depth of 18 in. A small amount of a granular or time-release fertilizer may be applied in spring to help generate new roots.

SPECIES, CULTIVARS, OR VARIETIES

Greek yarrow (*Achillea ageratifolia*) has small, linear, pale-gray leaves that are deeply incised and clustered on short, soft stems. The foliage forms dense mounds 6 in. high and 12 to 15 in. across. Umbels of small white flowers appear in late spring. Greek yarrow requires well-drained soil. It is used in rock gardens or for edging paths and xeric flower beds. It is especially effective when mixed with the low-growing veronicas or pineleaf penstemon. There are many color selections of *Achillea millefolium* that work especially well as groundcovers in partial to full shade. 'Red Beauty' has red flowers that fade to pale yellow; 'Cerise Queen' blooms carmine-rose; and 'Salmon Beauty' produces peachy apricot flowers that fade to pale yellow. All produce 12- to 18-in.-high flower stems above a dense mat of green fernlike foliage. In the southern low-desert areas, all species and varieties of yarrow will use less water if grown in the shade.

"...it was New Mexico that liberated me from the present era of civilization."

—D.H. Lawrence

African Daisy
Dimorphotheca sinuata

California Poppy
Eschscholzia californica

Cosmos
Cosmos bipinnatus

Cowpen Daisy
Verbesina encelioides

Creeping Zinnia
Sanvitalia procumbens

Desert Marigold
Baileya multiradiata

Gazania
Gazania splendens

Globe Amaranth
Gomphrena globosa

Hollyhocks
Alcea rosea

Moss Rose
Portulaca grandiflora

Mullein
Verbascum bombyciferum
'Arctic Summer'

Nolana
Nolana paradoxa

ANNUALS AND BIENNIALS

Pansy
Viola × wittrockiana cultivars

Skyrocket
Ipomopsis rubra

Sweet Alyssum
Lobularia maritima

BULBS, CORMS AND RHIZOMES

Verbena
Verbena tenuisecta 'Imagination Purple'

Crocus
Crocus species and hybrids

Daffodils
Narcissus species and hybrids

Grape Hyacinth
Muscari armeniacum

Iris
Iris species and hybrids

Meadow Saffron
Colchium autumnale

Ornamental Onions
Allium species

Rainlily
Zephyranthes longiflora

Starflower
Ipheion uniflorum

Tulips
Tulipa species and hybrids

Beargrass
Nolina species

Century Plant
Agave species

Cholla and Prickly Pear
Opuntia species

Hardy Tiger Jaws
Chasmatophyllum musculinum

Hedgehog Cactus
Echinocereus species

Ocotillo
Fouqueria splendens

Pincushion Cactus
Escobaria species

Purple Iceplant
Delosperma cooperi

Sotol
Dasylirion wheelerii

Yucca
Yucca species

Creeping Dalea
Dalea greggii

Creeping Germander
Teucrium chamaedrys 'Prostrata'

Daylily
Hemerocallus hybrids

Desert Zinnia
Zinnia grandiflora

Dwarf Plumbago
Ceratostigma plumbaginoides

Giant Four O'Clock
Mirabilis multiflora

'Gro-low' Sumac
Rhus aromatica 'Gro-low'

Himalayan Fleeceflower
Persicaria affinis

'New Gold' Lantana
Lantana × 'New Gold'

Periwinkle
Vinca minor

Prairie Grasses

Prairie Sage
Artemisia ludoviciana

Spreading Cotoneaster
Cotoneaster species

Yerba Mansa
Anemopsis californica

Blue Avena
Helictotrichon sempervirens

Blue Fescue
Festuca ovina 'Glauca'

Blue Lyme Grass
Elymus arenarius 'Glaucus'

Dwarf Fountain Grass
Pennisetum alopecuroides

Dwarf Pampas Grass
Cortaderia selloana 'Pumila'

Feather Reed Grass
Calamagrostis arundinacea 'Karl Foerster'

Maiden Grass
Miscanthus sinensis

Muhly Grass
Muhlenbergia capillaris

Prairie Dropseed
Sporobolus heterolepis

Sand Lovegrass
Eragrostis trichodes

Threadgrass
Stipa tenuissima

Tufted Hairgrass
Deschampsia caespitosa

Artemisia
Artemisia species

Blackfoot Daisy
Melampodium leucanthum

Blanketflower
Gaillardia grandiflora

Blue Spurge
Euphorbia myrsinites

'Bowles Mauve' Wallflower
Erysimum linifolium 'Bowles Mauve'

Bubblegum Mint
Agastache cana

Candytuft
Iberis sempervirens

Catmint
Nepeta × *faassenii* and *Nepeta mussinii*

Columbine
Aquilegia species

Cranesbill
Geranium species

Creeping Baby's Breath
Gypsophila repens

Dianthus
Dianthus species

Gaura
Gaura lindheimeri

Gayfeather
Liatris punctata

'Goldsturm' Rudbeckia
Rudbeckia fulgida var. *sullivantii* 'Goldsturm'

Greek Germander
Teucrium aroanium

Hardy African Daisy
Osteospermum baberiae 'Compactum'

Jerusalem Sage
Phlomis species

Mat Daisy
Anacyclus pyrethrum var. *depressus*

Mexican Tarragon
Tagetes lucida

Partridge Feather
Tanacetum densum ssp. *amani*

Penstemon
Penstemon species

Prince's Plume
Stanleya pinnata

'Profusion' Fleabane
Erigeron karvinskianus 'Profusion'

Rue
Ruta graveolens

Russian Sage
Perovskia atriplicifolia

Salvia
Salvia species

Serbian Bellflower
Campanula poscharskyana

Soapwort
Saponaria ocymoides

Speedwell
Veronica species

Stonecrop
Sedum × 'Autumn Joy'

Torch Lily
Kniphofia uvaria

Valerian
Centran ruber

Woolly Thyme
Thymus pseudolanuginosis

Yarrow
Achillea × 'Moonshine'

Climbing and Pillar Roses
Rosa

Floribunda Roses
Rosa

Hybrid Tea Roses
Rosa

Shrub Roses
Rosa

Species and Native Roses
Rosa

Barberry
Berberis species and cultivars

Blue Mist
Caryopteris × *clandonensis*

Butterfly Bush
Buddleia species and cultivars

'Centennial' Broom
Baccharis × 'Centennial'

Cotoneaster
Cotoneaster species and cultivars

Curry Plant
Helichrysum angustifolium

Fairy Duster
Calliandra eriophylla

Firethorn
Pyracantha species and cultivars

'Hancock' Dwarf Coralberry
Symphoriacarpos × chenaultii 'Hancock'

Lavender
Lavandula species and cultivars

Lilac
Syringa species and hybrids

Mahonia
Mahonia species

Manzanita
Arctostaphylos species and cultivars

Mexican Buckeye
Ungnadia speciosa

'Moonlight' Broom
Cytisus scoparius 'Moonlight'

Ornamental Cherries
Prunus species

Pomegranate
Punica granatum

Redtwig Dogwood
Cornus sericea

Rosemary
Rosmarinus officinalis

Rose-of-Sharon
Hibiscus syriacus

Salvia
Salvia species

Santolina
Santolina species

Shadscale
Atriplex confertifolia

Silverberry
Elaeagnus pungens

Spanish Broom
Spartium junceum

Sumac
Rhus species

Texas Mountain Laurel
Sophora secundiflora

Texas Sage
Leucophyllum species and cultivars

Turpentine Bush
Ericameria laricifolia

Viburnum
Viburnum species

Yellow Bells
Tecoma stans

TREES

Ash
Fraxinus species

Bigtooth Maple
Acer grandidentatum

Blue Spruce
Picea pungens f. *glauca*

Catclaw Acacia
Acacia greggii

Cedar
Cedrus species

Chaste Tree
Vitex agnus-castus

Chinese Pistache
Pistacia chinensis

Desert Willow
Chilopsis linearis

Flowering Fruit Trees
Prunus and *Malus* species

Golden Raintree
Koelreuteria paniculata

Hawthorn
Crataegus species and cultivars

Honey Mesquite
Prosopis glandulosa

Japanese Scholar Tree
Styphnolobium japonica

Jujube
Zizyphus jujuba

Juniper
Juniperus species and cultivars

Kentucky Coffee Tree
Gymnocladus dioica

Linden
Tilia species

Netleaf Hackberry
Celtis reticulata

New Mexico Olive
Forestiera neomexicana

Oak
Quercus species

Pine
Pinus species

Poplar
Populus species

Redbud
Cercis species

Smoke Tree
Cotinus coggygria

Thornless Honey Locust
Gleditsia triacanthos var. *inermis*

Western Catalpa
Catalpa speciosa

Boston Ivy
Parthenocissus tricuspidata

Carolina Jessamine
Gelsemium sempervirens

Clematis
Clematis species and cultivars

Coral Honeysuckle
Lonicera sempervirens

English Ivy
Hedera helix

Queen's Wreath
Antigonon leptopus

Silk Vine
Periploca graeca

Silver Lace Vine
Fallopia aubertii

Trumpet Vine
Campsis radicans

Wisteria
Wisteria sinensis

COLD HARDINESS ZONE MAP

Modified for New Mexico

ZONE	4
ZONE	5
ZONE	6
ZONE	7
ZONE	8

This map is based on the USDA Cold Hardiness Zone Map adjusted for elevation and for average cold temperatures based on National Weather Service climate records.

HEAT ZONE MAP

Modified for New Mexico

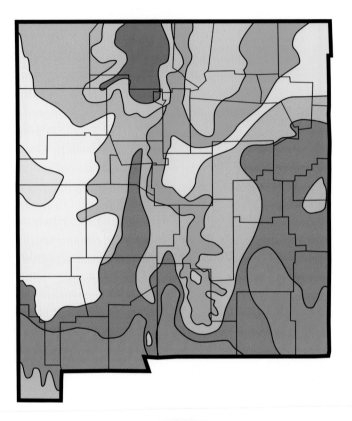

ZONE	2
ZONE	3
ZONE	4
ZONE	5
ZONE	6
ZONE	7
ZONE	8
ZONE	9

This map is based on the American Horticultural Society Heat Zone Map
adjusted for elevation and for average cold temperatures based on
National Weather Service climate records.

*Isn't it the
wealth of
possibility
that keeps
us growing?*

CHAPTER SEVEN

Roses

*R*OSES EVOKE STRONG FEELINGS. Devoted rosarians may doubt there can be a garden without roses. But many of us impulsively purchase packaged roses because of the photo on the wrapper, or plant potted roses in bloom because they are too gorgeous to leave in the nursery—only to have waves of aphids and mildew enjoy them more than we do. Such experiences might lead a casual gardener to believe that all roses are more trouble than they're worth. Please think again! Select the right roses, give them the care they need, and they will be among the longest-lived and most productive plants in your garden.

The rose profiles are grouped by category as climbers, floribundas, hybrid teas, shrub roses, and species and native roses. The native roses are typically the most rugged and the species roses are nearly as tough, but in every category there are cultivars that have proven themselves garden-worthy in New Mexico. The cultivars included in the profiles are by no means the only ones that will grow well here, but they are a starting point for success with roses.

Be selective. It is a better garden that has a half dozen superb specimens than twenty ailing ones that need constant nursing. Because nurseries pay royalty fees on patented varieties, the most expensive cultivars are the newest ones, though they are not necessarily the best roses for high-desert gardens. Roses are graded for quality: No.1 grade indicates the strongest plants. Starting with the most robust specimens makes sense in a climate that makes crumbs of the weak. Whether the rose is grafted or grown on its own roots also influences its vigor. High-elevation and northern gardeners prefer own-root plants since grafts are vulnerable in extremely cold areas.

All types but the native roses prefer a somewhat sheltered location where they are buffered from the winds that scorch leaves and blossoms. Roses need at least six hours of sun daily. Because temperatures above 95 degrees Fahrenheit can keep flower buds from

Chapter Seven

forming, afternoon shade is beneficial, especially in the low deserts of southern New Mexico.

Most roses prefer a well-drained soil that has a neutral pH and is rich in organic matter; this is far from the status quo in the Southwest. Prepare the soil well before planting, and your roses will reward your efforts handsomely. Thoroughly mix a 6-inch layer of compost at least 18 in. deep into the soil of a new bed to increase the water-holding capacity, improve drainage, and help reduce alkalinity. One cubic yard of compost is enough to amend the soil for four to six individual roses, amending the soil 18 in. deep and 3 to 4 ft. in diameter for each plant. If you are planting bareroot roses, soak the roots or submerge the whole plant in water overnight in a warm room. Dormant bareroot plants are best transplanted in February or early March in the central part of the state at elevations between 4000 and 6500 ft.; in the north and at higher elevations, transplant up to a month later; and plant a few weeks earlier in the low desert and in the south. Potted roses should have two or three strong canes that are 6 to 12 in. long. Be sure that plants do not settle deeper than they were originally planted, and that the bud union on grafted plants is about 2 in. above soil level.

Roses can be used in a variety of ways, and spacing depends on the size of mature plants. If you are a traditionalist who views garden life as a bed of roses, that bed should be 3 to 4 ft. wide if it can be worked only from one side, and 6 to 8 ft. wide if it can be worked from both sides. Stagger plants in a zigzag pattern to fit in the most plants without limiting air circulation and access for pruning. Water immediately after planting and whenever the leaves become a little dull and slightly droopy. Once roses are established, water should penetrate to a depth of 2 ft., and occasionally a bit deeper, to leach salts beyond the root zone. Roses may need water weekly when temperatures are above 85 degrees Fahrenheit and when plants are in bloom, every two weeks when temperatures are 65 to 85 degrees Fahrenheit, and monthly during cooler weather. Blooming roses growing in sandy soil, in sunny exposed locations, or in raised beds may need water every three or four days. Plants growing in heavier soils, or in sheltered spaces that are mulched deeply, may be able to go longer than a week between deep waterings. If roots dry out too much, or if plants are fertilized too heavily, the leaves will turn brown on the margins. Mulches help maintain more uniform soil temperature and moisture. Bark, pecan hulls, pine straw, compost, grass clippings, or other fibrous mulches are better than gravels because they stay cooler and reflect less heat. Grafts can be buried with loose mulch to protect them from both heat and cold.

Roses, especially varieties that bloom repeatedly, are heavy feeders. There are almost as many preferences for fertilizers among rose growers as there are favorite rose cultivars. To maintain the best soil conditions, work cottonseed meal, compost, or alfalfa pellets into the soil surface in early spring to get plants off to a good start. Alfalfa pellets are a favorite way to steadily improve the soil and are recommended by many New Mexican gardeners. Look for them at feed stores rather than at garden centers, since their primary use is as feed for livestock, especially for domestic rabbits. There's delicious irony in feeding rabbit food to roses instead of having to defend the roses from hungry rabbits. To satisfy the extra fertilizer needs of recurrent-blooming rose varieties, apply 1/4 cup of a granular 10-10-10 formula after the probability of frost is past, again after the first blooms fade, and monthly until 8 weeks before the first average frost date in autumn.

Pruning goals vary with different types of roses. Climbers are pruned to induce the lateral branching that produces flower buds. Floribundas, shrub, and species roses are similar to other flowering shrubs that need pruning to even out growth and remove the oldest stems to keep plants young and vigorous. Hybrid teas need the most extensive pruning, especially if you want to produce large show-quality blooms. The native roses need the least pruning; they require only occasional thinning to enhance form and rejuvenate maturing plants. Regardless of the purpose or the extent of pruning required, the basic cut is the same: using sharp shears, cut at a 60-degree angle 1/4 in. above the buds or lateral shoots that point out from the center of the plant. To seal cane-boring carpenter bees out of the stems, paint the cuts of all types but the natives with liquid wood glue or clear nail polish.

Aphids are the most common garden pest, and roses are not immune. These insects congregate on the soft new growth and flower buds. Control aphids by washing them off regularly. Thrips are an insidiously tiny pest most damaging to white and pale-yellow rose cultivars. Thrips distort the flower buds but don't really interfere with the overall health and vigor of the plant. The damage may be only cosmetic, but most roses aren't grown for their leaves! The best prevention is planting resistant, brightly colored cultivars, and the best control is removing the affected flowers as soon as they are noticed. To stifle overwintering pests and limit insect and disease damage later in the season, use a light horticultural oil spray before buds begin expanding. While our dry climate makes the incidence of diseases such as black spot mercifully rare, in certain circumstances susceptible cultivars may be bothered by rust or mildew. Rusts produce small yellow or orange bumps on the leaves as well as soft stems that can lead to major leaf drop, weakening the plant. Rust is more common at elevations above 6500 ft. and in cooler, damper northern New Mexico. Ornamental grasses may serve as an alternate host for rusts on roses, so it's best not to interplant the two. Mildew, a white powdery film on the leaves, is most likely to develop in shaded areas that have poor air circulation. It is most widespread late in the monsoon season when the days are warm and the nights are much cooler. Spraying with a dormant lime-sulfur spray just as leaf buds begin opening in spring will help suppress these diseases, but sulfur sprays can't be used once the air temperature is 90 degrees Fahrenheit or above. Crown gall is a soil bacteria common in the Southwest. Pithy nodules form on roots and at the root crown. The gall reduces sap flow through the infected plant, which declines in vigor and eventually dies. There is no chemical control. Remove affected plants and the soil around them, and don't replant roses in the same area for at least three years.

When roses are planted in appropriate locations, in the soil they prefer, and watered and fertilized according to their individual needs, disease problems are of minor concern. Roses can be chosen for their flowers or fragrances, their jewellike hips, their size and shape, or their fine foliage. Few plants can rival them for versatility and beauty.

Climbing and Pillar Roses

Rosa

Height: 7 ft. to more than 20 ft. **Color:** Varies **Bloom Period:** Spring; some are recurrent **Zone:** Varies **Water:** Moderate to ample	**Light Requirement:**

*C*limbing and pillar roses have long, limber canes with blooms on shorter stems along their length. Pillars are naturally shorter than the climbers, but both types need support to control their sprawl. Both also require pruning to stimulate the growth of vigorous new canes and to remove shoots growing away from the supporting structure. Because bending the canes induces the production of hormones that push the development of the blooming laterals, climbers bloom most heavily when canes are arched, and pillars trained as columns tend to bloom more lightly at the ends of the stems. There are hundreds of cultivars in a rainbow of colors. The ones described below have proven themselves in this climate.

WHEN TO PLANT
Plant in spring after hard freezes are past, and before hot weather creates heat and moisture stress.

WHERE TO PLANT
Climbers are used to trail along the edge of portals and porches, cover arbors and ramadas for shade, drape over walls and gate archways, and cover trellises for screening as tall living fences. They impart a feeling of lush abundance as do few other plants. Pillar roses are used where space is more limited and a more controlled plant is called for.

HOW TO PLANT
For soil preparation and early care of climbers and pillars, see the guidelines in the introduction to this chapter. Because these plants become much larger than many of the shrub roses, climbers often share an extended area of soil and water with annuals, bulbs, and perennials as they mature.

ROSES

ADVICE FOR CARE

Allow new roses a few years to establish enough growth to begin training. Tie long canes horizontally along the trellis framework, or bundle canes against posts and arch long shoots across arbors or ramadas. Most climbers bloom on 1- or 2-year-old wood. Their canes grow from the base of the plant or branch from older canes. Prune after the first flowering, cutting lateral shoots back to 10 or 12 buds. When rejuvenating older plants that haven't been pruned in years, begin while plants are dormant, removing the weakest canes and leaving ⅔ of the most vigorous wood. Then prune the newest lateral shoots back by ⅔ their length after the roses have flowered.

SPECIES, CULTIVARS, OR VARIETIES

Lady Banks' Rose (*Rosa banksia*) 'Lutea' and 'Alba' are yellow- and white-flowering forms, respectively, of a plant introduced to European horticulture more than 200 years ago. Lady Banks has been at home in Southwestern gardens for the past century, where it has proven to be very drought and heat tolerant. The finely divided leaves persist through most winters if plants are watered deeply each month in winter, and every 2 to 4 weeks while actively growing. Large clusters of 2-in., lightly fragrant, double flowers appear only in spring. Lady Banks can spread 20 ft. in 3 or 4 years' time, and should be pruned sparingly since it flowers on old wood. It is hardy in Zones 6, 7, and 8. 'Blaze Improved' is of hybrid perpetual parentage and was introduced in 1932. It is a heavily blooming cultivar with 3-in., semi-double, lightly fragrant, medium-red flowers in mid-spring. Blooms repeat through summer except when temperatures remain in the '90s. 'Blazed Improved' averages 9 ft. tall and requires only light pruning. It is hardy in Zones 5 through 8. 'Dortmund' is a Kordes cultivar introduced in 1955. It grows 10 to 12 ft. high and bears 3-in. red flowers with a white ring circling gold stamens. 'Dortmund' is disease free, repeats well, and produces red rose hips late in the season. It is hardy to Zone 4. 'Altissimo' is a pillar rose introduced in 1966. Its clusters of single, 4-in., deep lustrous-red flowers with yellow stamens produce a light clove fragrance and recur well throughout the growing season. It grows 10 to 12 ft. high and will flower elegantly at the branch tips if trained upright, or flower more profusely if canes arch horizontally. It is hardy in Zones 5 through 8.

Floribunda Roses

Rosa

Height: 2 to 4 ft.	**Light Requirement:**
Color: Varies	
Bloom Period: Late spring to frost	
Zones: 5 to 8	
Water: Moderate to ample	

*F*irst introduced in 1909, floribunda roses are crosses of hybrid teas and polyanthas. They possess the excellent repeat blooming and wide color range characteristic of the hybrid teas, but have smaller flowers in clusters, are more cold hardy, and are generally easier to grow. The original floribundas were small plants as a result of their polyantha parentage, but by the 1940s the average plant and flower size had increased. By the 1950s many cultivars had also attained the tapered buds and high-centered blooms of their tea parents. As a class, they are some of the best landscape roses because their blooms are so colorful and their forms are compact and mounded. There are many cultivars both old and new that are worth growing; those listed below hold up well in summer heat, and the flowers remain colorful and fresh despite our intense sunlight.

WHEN TO PLANT
Plant in spring after hard freezes are past and before hot weather creates heat and moisture stress.

WHERE TO PLANT
Floribundas have the greatest impact when planted in groups of the same cultivar in borders with artemisias, salvias, gaura, and 'Moonshine' yarrow, or when planted as informal hedges edged with dianthus, candytuft, or creeping baby's breath.

HOW TO PLANT
Plant floribundas following the general guidelines given in the introduction.

ADVICE FOR CARE
Since floribundas are bred for compact size and mass color, the canes are thinner and need less pruning. When new growth begins

in spring, remove any shoots that sprout below the graft on budded cultivars, any old flower stems from the previous year, and a few of the oldest, least productive canes. During the growing season, cut back any overly vigorous shoots to even out growth, especially when plants are clustered. Occasionally remove spent flowers to clear the way for the next flush of color. Rejuvenate older plants while they are dormant by removing entirely some of the oldest canes, leaving well-spaced, vigorous, newer canes.

SPECIES, CULTIVARS, OR VARIETIES

'Amber Queen' is a 1988 AARS (All-America Rose Selections, Inc.) award winner with large, very fragrant, double, apricot-blend flowers that repeat well. 'Europeana' is the 1968 AARS award winner with lightly fragrant clusters of dark-red, semi-double, 3-in. flowers on plants that grow 30 in. tall and 48 in. wide. Foliage is dark green with bronzy new growth. Blooming starts in late spring and repeats until frost. 'Poulsen's Pearl' was the first floribunda purposely bred as a floribunda. It produces clusters of fragrant, single, pale pink flowers with dark coral stamens above glossy green foliage; plants grows 2 ft. high and 3 ft. wide. Flowers appear in late spring and continue until frost. 'Traumerei' is an orange blend with small, obviously double flowers on 2-ft.-tall plants. Like most Kordes hybrids, it is exceptionally cold hardy. 'Trumpeter' was introduced in 1977 from parentage including 'Satchmo'. It has 3-in., double, lightly fragrant, neon orange flowers borne singly and in clusters on compact, bushy plants that grow 2 ft. high and 4 ft. wide. The flowers are high centered and very ruffled when open; leaves are dark and glossy.

Hybrid Tea Roses

Rosa

Height: 4 to 6 ft.	**Light Requirement:**
Color: Varies	
Bloom Period: Varies	
Zones: 5 to 8	
Water: Ample	

The first hybrid teas appeared in the latter half of the 1800s as a result of crossing hybrid perpetuals with China teas. The aim was to combine the vigor of the perpetuals with the clean-shattering, repeat blooming, and smaller stature of the teas. I may as well admit that I have a strong bias against the later hybrid teas. The modern single-minded breeding for enormous flowers on stiff tall stems at the expense of fragrance and disease resistance has created plants without balance or grace. They require the most water and work, and the flowers themselves are rather overblown. When they were first marketed, hybrid teas were touted as "the aristocrats of roses," leading some to speculate on whether that meant they were tender and difficult, or more positively, that they shed their petals and had a knack for dying gracefully. Hybrid teas need at least 6 hours of sun and repeated pruning to produce large blooms. Despite the shortcomings of the group as a whole, there are several cultivars that are hard to resist.

WHEN TO PLANT
Plant in spring after hard freezes are past, and before hot weather creates heat and moisture stress.

WHERE TO PLANT
Most hybrid teas are best in a utility cutting garden where their awkward shapes will be hidden by southernwood, pitcher sage, hollyhocks, garlic chives, Russian sage, or rudbeckias.

HOW TO PLANT
General planting techniques for hybrid teas are the same as those outlined in the introduction. Deep mulch helps buffer the heat in low-desert gardens and insulates against cold at higher elevations.

ADVICE FOR CARE

Vigorous canes bloom for 6 years or longer. The most casual approach to pruning hybrid teas is to remove exhausted canes when the quality and number of flowers decline. In late winter, remove any shoots that emerge from below the graft. The most extreme pruning technique you can use to produce show-quality blooms is to select 3 to 5 canes of the previous year's growth which form a bowl with an open center, and remove all small twiggy growth and most laterals. Cut 4- to 5-ft. shrubs to 2 ft., larger shrubs to 3 ft., and exhibition plants to 1 ft. above the grafts. When older plants don't produce new growth from the crown, select strong laterals instead. To maintain large single blooms on long cutting stems, remove spent flower stems down low on the stem where leaves have five leaflets. If spent blooms are not removed, most hybrid teas will revert to producing several smaller flowers per stem.

SPECIES, CULTIVARS, OR VARIETIES

'Peace', a Meilland introduction celebrating the end of World War II, has set the standard for 20th-century hybrid tea roses. Its huge double flowers are lemon yellow blushed with pink and have a fruity fragrance. Plants are very vigorous and long-lived, growing 6 ft. tall and 4 ft. wide with disease-resistant, leathery green leaves. There is also a climbing form with 12- to 14-ft. canes. 'Pink Peace', a sweet-scented, clear-pink selection, was introduced in 1959. In 1962 a sport with a much deeper pink blush appeared in a Chicago garden and was introduced as 'Chicago Peace'. Neither of the selections is as robust as the original. 'Olympiad', introduced in 1984, has large, velvety, double-red flowers that hold up in intense sunlight. It has a light fruity scent and a strongly upright form, growing 5 ft. tall and 4 ft. wide with dark gray-green foliage. 'Mrs. Oakley Fisher' is a yellow single with dark-orange stamens on 3-ft. plants. 'Tropicana' is a robust, 4-ft.-tall plant with large, fragrant, grenadine coral flowers suffused with pink. The color is rich, holds up well in intense sunlight, and has real south-of-the-border zest when mixed with violet blue-purple flowers such as English lavender, dwarf buddleia, and salvias.

Shrub Roses

Rosa

Height: 10 in. to 7 ft.	**Light Requirement:**
Color: Varies	
Bloom Period: Varies	
Zone: Varies	
Water: Moderate to ample	

The shrub rose group is a catchall category that includes miniatures, groundcovers, hybrid musks, hybrid rugosas, polyanthas,
and a relatively new focus in rose breeding known as "landscape
roses." The definition of landscape roses fits all the shrub roses: adaptable, colorful, long-blooming plants with graceful forms and attractive
foliage. These are plants that look good in the garden, require less
pruning, and are more disease resistant. Philosophically, I reject the
notion that a plant is more precious if it is demanding, if it is rare
because it lacks the ability to survive without pampering. I believe in
reciprocity, a balance of give and take. Along with the natives, the
roses described below are some of my favorites because they don't
demand more than they offer.

WHEN TO PLANT

Plant in spring after hard freezes are past, and before hot weather
creates heat and moisture stress. Most shrub roses are own-root,
not grafted, and they are cold hardy enough to be planted in fall. If
given plenty of water during establishment, they can also be planted
in bloom in summer, especially in Zones 4 through 6.

WHERE TO PLANT

The miniatures and polyanthas are used in large pots and in low
borders with creeping baby's breath, candytuft, veronicas, salvias,
and Roman wormwood. The groundcovers are low spreading and
thorny, effective barriers to foot traffic. The hybrid musks and
hybrid rugosas make excellent informal hedges and screens, and
they may also be interwoven in mixed borders with conifers such
as blue atlas cedar and blue spruce. The landscape roses can be used
in mixed shrub and perennial borders, or as tall groundcovers and
barrier plantings.

How to Plant

The general planting guidelines for roses in the introduction apply to shrub roses.

Advice for Care

The most intensive approach to pruning is to remove the oldest $1/4$ of canes each year in spring when temperatures moderate. A less aggressive approach is to remove the old flower stems back to a leaf node, and remove $1/3$ of the oldest canes every 4 or 5 years.

Species, Cultivars, or Varieties

The miniature roses were introduced in the early 1800s. They are generally own-root, and cold hardy to Zone 5. Their small size—most average 12 to 18 in. high, spreading slightly wider—tends to make them more water conservative and heat tolerant. There are only a few thousand to choose from, including 'Winsome', which grows 16 in. high and 20 in. wide with large, pointed buds opening to deep wine-colored, cupped flowers; and 'Summer Butter', an abundant producer of fragrant, clear-yellow flowers on plants growing 12 in. high and 18 in. wide.

Groundcover roses include 'Red Cascade', a very thorny cross of *R. wichuriana* and 'Floradora' that was introduced in 1976. It is adapted to partial shade and grows 1 ft. high and 3 to 8 ft. wide with clusters of 1-in. double-red flowers from May to frost. 'Red Ribbons' is another groundcover rose, a Kordes introduction that grows 2 ft. high and spreads 5 ft. wide with medium-red, semi-double flowers even in the 95-degrees-Fahrenheit heat of midsummer. 'Bassino' is another Kordes cultivar that grows 2 ft. high and spreads 5 ft. wide; it produces large clusters of small, single, medium-red flowers and fine-textured foliage. 'Ferdy' grows 3 ft. tall and 5 to 7 ft. wide with clusters of 1-in., semi-double, coral-pink flowers. It usually has one extended period of bloom in early summer and a strong repeat in autumn.

Hybrid musks are more accurately oversized floribundas than they are musks. They bloom profusely but repeat best in full sun. 'Ballerina' grows 3 ft. high and 4 ft. wide with clusters of 2-in. single flowers that shade from white at the center stamens to pale pink tinged with darker pink at the petal edges. It is lightly fragrant, blooms repeatedly even in the heat, and has glossy, light-green, disease-resistant foliage on nearly thornless, arching stems.

Hybrid rugosas are 20th-century introductions that are not as cold hardy as the species, but possess the same ribbed, disease-resistant foliage. They include 'Frau Dagmar Hartopp' and

'Delicata', which both grow 3 ft. high and 4 ft. wide and have 3-in. clove-scented flowers—'Frau Dagmar Hartopp' produces single, light-pink blooms followed by huge red rose hips, and the flowers of 'Delicata' are semi-double mauve. 'Hansa' grows 5 ft. tall and wide with large, double, violet-red flowers. It is hardy to Zone 3 and has large, red rose hips and very thorny stems. 'Topaz Jewel', introduced in 1987, grows 5 ft. tall and wide with 4-in. double yellow flowers that are blushed with coral. It produces a strong fruity scent and light-green foliage.

Polyanthas are derived from multiflora and China roses. They begin to bloom in early summer and repeat well. 'The Fairy' and 'Margo Koster' were both introduced in the early 1930s and have dense, glossy, light-green leaves and large clusters of small flowers. 'The Fairy' has double, medium-pink, ruffled flowers; the form varies from low and sprawling to 2 ft. tall, upright, and bushy. 'Margo Koster' grows 12 in. high and wide with semi-double, cupped, coral flowers. There is also a climbing form that reaches 12 to 15 ft. tall.

The French House of Meilland is a front runner in the breeding of landscape roses. Most selections are worth trying here, though the double-pink 'Bonica' fades and browns in the sun, and a rose with a suntan is not a pretty sight. 'Scarlet Meidiland' is wonderful, with supple canes that grow 3 ft. high and arch 5 ft. wide. It produces clean, bright-green foliage and clusters of small, double flowers that repeat well. 'First Light' is the 1998 AARS (All-America Rose Selections, Inc.) winner. It reaches 18 in. high and 24 in. wide. The flowers grow in clusters and have five to seven peach-pink petals around a frilly center of dark stamens. The 'First Light' planted in Albuquerque's Prospect Park Rose Garden looked fresh and was blooming vigorously after weeks of weather above 90 degrees Fahrenheit.

Species and Native Roses

Rosa

Height: 4 to 10 ft.	**Light Requirement:**
Color: Shades of white, yellow, or pink	
Bloom Period: Varies	
Zones: 3 to 7	
Water: Moderate to low	

*B*ecause roses have been cultivated for nearly 5000 years, most so-called "species" roses are hybrids. Clues to their past can be found in their distinctive characteristics—fragrance, heat and drought tolerance, and growth form—and flower features such as color range, size, clustering, and bud form. The native roses, as yet unhybridized, are handsome shrubs with showy flowers and interesting foliage. Flowering is usually profuse but seasonal, and plants are valued for their form and foliage as much as for their blossoms. When growing within their normal elevation ranges, they require little supplemental watering and are rarely bothered by disease or pests. All provide cover or food for birds and nectar for butterflies.

WHEN TO PLANT

Even species roses native to the Middle East can grow in moist niches within that arid climate. Because species roses are not xeric plants, it is best to set out new plants or transplant established ones before hot weather creates heat and moisture stress. Species roses are own-root, not grafted, and they are cold hardy enough to be planted in fall. If given plenty of water during establishment, they can also be planted in summer, especially in Zones 4 and 5. Since most native roses are well adapted to both heat and cold, container-grown plants can be transplanted any time the soil can be worked. Shrubby cinquefoil, best adapted at higher elevations, benefits from fall planting in low-desert gardens. Planting at this time allows it to develop new roots before the heat of summer. The best time to transplant volunteer seedlings is just as growth begins in spring, or in early autumn when topgrowth is semi-dormant but roots are growing.

WHERE TO PLANT

These are all large, densely branched shrubs used for screening and informal hedges. Those producing rose hips contrast nicely in early winter with dark-green conifers or the larger artemisias. Some of their extra water needs can be met by planting them in storm drainage catchments. With the exception of cinquefoil, which is native to wet meadows at high elevations and prefers humusy soil and shade in the lowlands, most native roses prefer well-drained, infertile soils.

How to Plant

Plant species roses according to the guidelines given in the introduction. A 3- to 4-in. mulch of shredded bark, pecan hulls, or pine straw helps buffer the heat in low-desert gardens and insulates against cold at higher elevations. Use coarse gravel mulch on plants growing in runoff areas, because lighter mulches will float when the areas flood. The native roses prefer unamended soil, loosened well so that new roots can break ground easily.

Advice for Care

In comparison to other roses, the species and natives are not heavy feeders. Apply a granular iron-and-sulfur fertilizer in summer if plants show signs of chlorosis (as rugosas are likely to do). Maintain a more manicured appearance by cutting weathered flower stems back to a leaf node. To rejuvenate older plants, remove 1/3 of the oldest stems every 4 or 5 years. Water cinquefoil and species roses weekly when temperatures are above 85 degrees Fahrenheit and when plants are in bloom; every 2 weeks when temperatures are 65 to 85 degrees Fahrenheit; and monthly during cooler weather. Once they are well established, the more xeric natives look best when watered monthly to a depth of 3 ft. Sprays burn rugosa foliage, but the species and native roses are seldom bothered by pests.

Species, Cultivars, or Varieties

Cultivated since 1590, 'Austrian Copper' (*Rosa foetida* 'Bicolor') grows 6 to 8 ft. tall and wide and is cold hardy to 9000 ft. It bears clusters of single flowers in spring that are copper red on the upper surface and yellow on the lower. One of the parents of many of the modern yellow roses is 'Persian Yellow' (*Rosa foetida* 'Persiana'), which is smaller, 4 to 6 ft. tall and wide, with 2-in. double chrome-yellow flowers in small clusters. 'Harison's Yellow', better known to most as the "yellow rose of Texas," was brought west by early settlers. It produces arching canes to 7 ft., finely divided foliage, and 2-in. deep-yellow double flowers in spring that are followed by small black rose hips. It is a natural sport that appeared in a New York garden in the mid-1800s and is considered a hybrid of 'Persian Yellow' and the Scotch rose (*R. spinosissima*).

The species *Rosa rugosa* grows 5 ft. tall and 6 ft. wide with fragrant 3-in. single flowers and red 1-in. rose hips. 'Rubra' is dark mauve; 'Alba' is white.

The New Mexican native roses include Apache plume (*Fallugia paradoxa*), which is most often found growing below 8000 ft. in arroyos. Its glory is the cloud of feathery pink seedheads that follow each flush of bloom. Plants are semievergreen and densely branched, growing 3 to 6 ft. tall and wide with small dark-green leaves. The white 1-in. flowers are most profuse in spring, recurring after summer rains. Apache plume is hardy in Zones 5 through 8.

Arizona rosewood (*Vauquelinia californica*) grows upright limber stems that are 6 to 12 ft. tall and 3 to 8 ft. wide. The crisp, dark, evergreen leaves are 3/4 in. wide and 3 in. long with finely toothed margins. Umbels of tiny white flowers appear in early summer. Arizona rosewood is cold hardy to 6000 ft. in central and southern New Mexico (Zones 6 through 8).

Cliffrose (*Cowania mexicana*) initially produces long vertical stems, but the branches twist and arch with age to form interesting gnarled specimens that grow 4 to 10 ft. tall and 3 to 8 ft. wide. The evergreen leaves are small and dark. Sweetly scented, pale-yellow flowers crowd the new growth in spring and bloom again in late summer if temperatures persist in the mid-90s Fahrenheit. Cliffrose is hardy to 7500 ft. in Zones 4 through 8.

Fernbush (*Chamaebatieria millefolium*) grows 3 to 8 ft. tall and 4 to 6 ft. wide. Its pale-green, finely divided foliage resembles woolly fern leaves. Butterflies are attracted to the white 1/2-in. flowers that grow clustered in candelabra-like spikes, turning a deep russet brown as they go to seed. The whole plant has a pleasant, spicy aroma. Fernbush is hardy to 7500 ft. in Zones 5 through 8.

Shrubby cinquefoil (*Potentilla fruticosa*) is most cold hardy in Zones 3 through 7 and is native above 8000 ft. in elevation. It grows 2 to 4 ft. tall and wide in a compact vase shape. The dark-green deciduous leaves are a cool backdrop for the flushes of 1-in. flowers that repeat throughout the growing season. The species is yellow but there are many cultivars, including the white 'Abbotswood'. The red-orange 'Tangerine' and 'Red Ace' fade out in bright sunlight. Spider mites are an ongoing problem when cinquefoil is planted in hot, dusty locations.

Wood's rose (*R. woodsii*) forms thickets along streams in the mountains. It grows 3 to 5 ft. tall and at least as wide, producing fragrant, single pink flowers in spring and round, 1/2-in. rose hips in late summer and fall. In gardens it is valued for erosion control near gutters and canales and as habitat for butterflies and songbirds. The red stems and hips are striking against the snow.

CHAPTER EIGHT

Shrubs

$\mathcal{S}$HRUBS ARE ONE OF THE DOMINANT FEATURES of the wild New Mexico landscape. With their compact forms and deep roots, shrubs thrive where it is too dry for trees, and even where it is too dry for many wildflowers and grasses. In traditional garden design, shrubs set the boundaries of the garden. While trees form the ceiling, shrubs create the walls, and may even carpet the floor of garden spaces. Their distinct personalities determine the roles they play. Some flower brilliantly but briefly, while others flower most of the growing season. Their blossoms may enliven the garden by luring hummingbirds or butterflies, and an abundance of colorful fruit may attract songbirds.

Some shrubs are evergreen, and others have leaves that are interesting for their color or texture. Their stems may be rich tones of green, yellow, red, copper, or chalk. But color, whether offered by annual flowers or shrub foliage, is seasonal; the more enduring value of shrubs is the wide range of forms they exhibit, forms that become stronger and more impressive with time. Some shrubs are densely twiggy; others have fewer but stouter stems and open branch patterns. Those that are adapted to dry climates often have rounded silhouettes that reduce their evaporative surface. The more stylized design of Japanese and desert gardens relies on trees and shrubs with sculptural forms used as focal points, as well as on shrubs with less defined profiles that are used as space fillers between accent plants.

Working with shrubs is partly art and partly science. You need to appreciate the natural shapes of the plants in order to know whether to cut; and you need to know when, where, and how to prune to enhance the natural forms. Barberry, mahonia, manzanita, cotoneaster, coralberry, rosemary, shadscale, and sumac are among the shrubs that rarely need pruning if given enough space to develop their natural size. The new growth of brooms, sages, butterfly bush, Apache plume, and sand cherry is the most attractive, and these plants look best in cultivated settings if the oldest stems are removed entirely, a few at a time each year to keep the plants youthful and vigorous. Shrubs such as viburnum, lilac, rose-of-Sharon, mountain mahogany, cliffrose, pomegranate, cherry laurel, Mexican buckeye, and mountain laurel are plants that have sculptural quality. The goal in pruning them should be to clear away anything that detracts from the essential beauty of their form. This kind of pruning is a pleasure because we get to know the plants better in the process. Shearing, on the other hand, is mindless exercise, and when you commit the crime, you do the time. Too many shrubs with beautiful natural shapes are tortured into gumdrops and cubes in the name of horticulture, and once the severe form is created, it requires consistent effort to maintain. If you prefer the closely clipped, uniform appearance of sheared plants, fill your garden with shrubs like curry plant, santolina, lavender, and turpentine bush, whose forms are naturally very dense and compact. Trim them annually to stimulate new growth and remove spent flowers. The better we match our expectations and interests to nature's patterns, the more rewarding gardening becomes.

By relying heavily on shrubs, a garden can be an easy balance of well-kept appearance and low maintenance. Unlike lawn mowing, pruning is a seasonal chore that can be done a few plants at a time as your schedule allows and growth cycles require. If you can spend only a few hours a month on garden chores, concentrate on plants that grow more slowly and require little pruning. If you like to putter, exercise no restraint at all when it comes to blooming plants; removing spent flowers and cutting fresh flowers for the house can absorb as much of your time as you want to devote. The perfect garden is not necessarily the most labor intensive; it is a place that encourages you to linger, and that gives you the option of doing so with either clean hands or with shears and shovel as your mood and time allow. Shrubs are the mainstay of such a balance.

Barberry

Berberis species and cultivars

Height: 2 to 7 ft. **Flowers:** Yellow **Foliage:** Mostly evergreen **Bloom Period:** Spring **Zones:** Varies **Water:** Varies	**Light Requirement:**

The handsome barberries are prickly shrubs. Some species have thorns along their stems; others have barbed leaf margins. All bear honey-scented clusters of small yellow flowers in spring, and some produce showy, berry-like fruits later in the season. Rather than focus on one species, I have chosen to describe six species with interesting foliage textures and colors. All are long-lived and easy to grow, but they do require a little patience—it takes some time to establish roots before much top growth is produced.

WHEN TO PLANT

Container-grown plants may be set out any time from spring through early autumn. Plants establish roots more quickly when the soil is cool, but in Zones 4 to 6, dry freezing winds can scorch the evergreen foliage, so it's best to forego planting in winter.

WHERE TO PLANT

Although barberries prefer well-drained soil, they will adapt to heavy clay if not kept too wet. They blend well with other evergreens and with deciduous shrubs in borders and screen plantings. Their prickly nature makes them effective barrier and security plantings, and their seasonal fruits make them excellent songbird habitat.

HOW TO PLANT

Dig holes only as deep as the rootball but four to six times its diameter, loosening the unamended soil well so that roots can penetrate easily.

ADVICE FOR CARE

None of the barberries require much pruning if they are spaced to allow for their mature size. Because they grow slowly and steadily, a small amount of a time-release fertilizer applied in spring for the first few years after planting can help get plants off to a faster start. In the long term, no fertilizer is necessary. Once they are well rooted, the native algeritas need watering only once a month year round. When watering, water should penetrate to a depth of 3 feet. Other barberries may require water weekly when temperatures are above 90 degrees Fahrenheit, every two weeks when temperatures are 65 to 90 degrees Fahrenheit, and monthly during cooler weather. Plants grown in the shade usually need less water.

SPECIES, CULTIVARS, OR VARIETIES

'William Penn' barberry (*B. × gladwynensis*) grows 4 ft. high and 6 ft. wide and has leathery, spine-tipped, evergreen leaves that are 2 to 3 in. long and less than 1 in. wide. 'William Penn' takes heat well and is hardy in Zones 5 through 8. Algerita (*B. fremontii*) grows 4 ft. high and 5 ft. wide with a very dense, compact form. The stiff frosted-blue leaves are evergreen and grow 2 in. long and ³/₄ in. wide. They are barbed at the tips. Fragrant yellow flowers in spring yield an abundance of ¹/₂-in. fleshy red fruits late in summer. Algerita is a Southwestern native and is extremely heat and drought tolerant once deeply rooted. It is cold hardy to Zone 4. There are two other barberries called algerita: *B. haematocarpa*, native to central New Mexico, and *B. trifoliata*, native to the southern foothills. They grow twice as large as *B. fremontii* and have grayer, more finely incised leaves. *B. haematocarpa* is hardy in Zones 5 through 8, and *B. trifoliata* is best in Zones 6 through 8. Mentor barberry (*B. × mentorensis*) is semievergreen in Zones 4 to 7 and evergreen in Zone 8. It is an old standard that is not planted much anymore, but I include it here because mentor barberry is a plant that is worth keeping if you are renovating an older landscape. As a dense barrier or screen planting, it grows 5 to 7 ft. tall and wide and produces small leathery leaves and spiny stems. 'Crimson Pygmy' barberry (*B. thunbergii* 'Atropurpurea Nana') is the least drought tolerant of the barberries listed here, but it is popular for its small rounded purple leaves, and compact 2-ft. mounded form. In the southern desert, it is more water efficient but less colorful when grown in partial shade. Although it is deciduous briefly, its thorny dark-red stems are interesting in winter. It is cold hardy to Zone 4.

Blue Mist

Caryopteris × clandonensis

Height: 3 ft. **Flowers:** Blue **Foliage:** Deciduous **Bloom Period:** Summer **Zones:** 5 to 8 **Water:** Moderate to low	**Light Requirement:**

*B*lue mist is popular in New Mexican gardens because it is colorful and easy to grow. The slender stems form a mound 3 ft. high and 4 ft. wide. Its pleasantly aromatic pale-green leaves are 2 in. long and 1/4 in. wide with irregular margins. In midsummer, the small blue flowers clustered on short spikes at the ends of the stems give blue mist the dusky look its common name suggests. After frost the tiered seedheads bleach to a pale tan color and persist into winter.

WHEN TO PLANT

Move volunteer seedlings in spring just as new growth begins, or in late summer 6 to 8 weeks before hard freezes occur. Potted plants can be set out any time, but since plants bloom in summer's heat, transplanting then can be stressful. In Zone 5, spring planting allows time for plants to root extensively before the return of cold weather.

WHERE TO PLANT

Blue mist prefers well-drained soil. It can be used as a large perennial in flower borders. Group it in front of conifers, cliffrose, or Arizona rosewood, where its compact size and abundance of flowers will add seasonal color. It also attracts butterflies. Blue mist's flowers contrast well with the coral blooms of red yucca in sunny xeric plantings. In shadier spaces it can be combined with coral honeysuckle. The flower color takes on added depth when blue mist is mixed with purple pinks such as bubblegum mint or giant four o'clock, and it provides a cooling contrast for yellow evening primroses and brassy blanketflowers. Because the blue flowers also attract bees, it's best to site plants away from paths and doorways.

HOW TO PLANT

Dig generous holes, loosening the soil so that new roots will have an easy time breaking ground. Recent research has demonstrated that the best soil preparation for container-grown shrubs is to dig holes only as deep as, or at most a few inches deeper than, the depth of the rootball, but four to six times its diameter. This will allow plants to develop the lateral absorbing roots they rely on for initial establishment and long-term survival. Backfill soil requires no amendment, but a generous mulch seems to accelerate root development.

ADVICE FOR CARE

A small amount of a time-release fertilizer applied in spring for the first few years after planting can help get plants off to a stronger start, especially in very sandy soils. Keep in mind that too much nitrogen will produce floppy stems and lush foliage at the expense of flowers. Trim the stems down to 1 ft. from the ground when the seedheads begin to look weathered. To prevent self-sowing, cut plants back as soon as the flowers fade. When plants are in bloom and temperatures are above 90 degrees Fahrenheit, water blue mist every two weeks to maintain flowering. Water monthly during the rest of the year. Well-established plants should be watered to a depth of 2 ft. Plants growing in the shade usually need less water. Root rot can develop if plants are kept too wet in heavy clay soils, especially during extreme periods of heat or cold.

SPECIES, CULTIVARS, OR VARIETIES

'Dark Knight' has deep-violet-blue flowers. 'Longwood Blue' has lavender-blue flowers.

Butterfly Bush

Buddleia species and cultivars

Height: 3 to 5 ft.
Flowers: Blue, purple, pink, or orange
Foliage: Varies
Bloom Period: Summer
Zones: 5 to 8
Water: Moderate to low

Light Requirement:

There are four buddleias that grow well in New Mexico. They are all butterfly magnets, but each has its own distinctive character. Dwarf buddleia is the most widely planted because its compact size, lacy winter presence, and profusion of color from June until frost make it desirable in even the smallest garden. Woolly butterfly bush is limited to the low desert in southern New Mexico because it cannot tolerate prolonged cold. The intensity of the spring color of fountain buddleia is enhanced by its the graceful arching branches.

WHEN TO PLANT

All the buddleias are best transplanted in spring so they will have plenty of rooting time before cold weather returns. Blooming specimens that have been transplanted should be provided consistently with water, even if they are of the more drought-tolerant species.

WHERE TO PLANT

Buddleias prefer well-drained, infertile soil. Dwarf buddleia is useful where some height is needed but space is limited. The fragrance and butterfly activity can be best appreciated near windows, entryways, and patios. Standard buddleia needs the company of evergreens to compensate for the large gap it leaves in winter. Fountain butterfly bush requires plenty of space. It is best used in the distance—while it is glorious enough to command attention when in bloom, the plant is rather nondescript in winter and when out of bloom in other seasons. Woolly buddleia is a soft companion for cacti and other spiky desert plants.

HOW TO PLANT

Dig generous holes that are only as deep as the rootball but four to six times its diameter, loosening the soil so that new roots will have an easy time breaking ground. Backfill soil requires no amendment, but a generous topdressing of mulch will keep the soil more uniformly moist and more moderate in temperature.

ADVICE FOR CARE

Trim off the brown seedheads for a neater look. The woolly and dwarf buddleias may be pruned back or thinned by $1/3$ every few years to rejuvenate the plants. Fountain butterfly bush may be thinned by $1/4$ or less every two years to keep it vigorous. The standard buddleia should be cut back to the ground each winter. Watering varies by species. Fountain and standard buddleias need water weekly when temperatures are above 85 degrees Fahrenheit, every two weeks when temperatures are 65 to 85 degrees Fahrenheit, and monthly during colder weather. Dwarf buddleia should be watered every two weeks when temperatures are above 70 degrees Fahrenheit, and monthly during colder weather. Well-established woolly buddleia should be watered monthly year round.

SPECIES, CULTIVARS, OR VARIETIES

Dwarf butterfly bush (*B. davidii* var. *nanhoensis*) grows 5 ft. tall and spreads 4 ft. wide. It has slender branches and small, linear leaves that are dark green on top and pale silver beneath. Sprays of purple or blue flowers on arching stems appear in summer. 'Nanho Blue' has lavender-blue flowers; 'Nanho Purple' has royal-purple flowers; 'Petite Plum' has wine-colored blooms. The standard butterfly bush (*B. davidii*) has larger leaves and stouter stems twice the height of the dwarf cultivars. It is coarser and needs to be cut back to the ground each year. There are more color selections, including pink and white. Fountain buddleia (*B. alternifolia*) grows 12 ft. tall and wide with slender, arching stems bearing sprays of pink-purple blossoms in spring. It is best adapted above 6500 ft. Woolly butterfly bush (*B. marrubifolia*) is a Chihuahuan desert native that is cold hardy only in Zones 7 and 8. It is the most heat and drought loving of all the buddleias. It grows 3 to 5 ft. high and wide with round white leaves and stiff arching stems. Compressed globes of tiny orange flowers bloom from March through August.

'Centennial' Broom

Baccharis × 'Centennial'

> **Height:** 2 to 3 ft.
> **Flowers:** Inconspicuous
> **Foliage:** Semievergreen
> **Bloom Period:** Summer
> **Zones:** 6 (with protection) to 8
> **Water:** Low to moderate
>
> **Light Requirement:**
>

'Centennial' is a hybrid of coyotebush (*Baccharis pilularis*) and desert broom (*Baccharis sarathroides*); it has the best qualities of both. It is larger and more vigorous than coyotebush, but it doesn't grow as fast or self-sow as invasively as desert broom. 'Centennial' has slender vibrant-green stems and small pale-green leaves that form a dense mound 2 to 3 ft. high and twice as wide. It is grown for its bright leaf and stem color rather than for its flowers.

WHEN TO PLANT

Plants root out faster in warm soil, so it is best to transplant during the growing season. In the low desert, 'Centennial' can be planted any time, as long as water is available in summer and plants have been acclimated to the cold in winter. At the northern and high-elevation limits of its cold-hardiness range, 'Centennial' is best started in spring so that it will have ample rooting time before the return of cold weather.

WHERE TO PLANT

'Centennial' adapts to a wide range of soils. Its vivid green hue and fine texture provide a strong contrast for silver-leafed plants such as Jerusalem sage and artemisias. The evergreen stems provide winter interest when grouped with mesquite, acacia, Mexican buckeye, or fairy duster.

HOW TO PLANT

'Centennial' is not a sterile hybrid, but seedlings tend to resemble desert broom rather than being true to type, so it should be propagated by cuttings. The cuttings root easily almost any time during the growing season. Lower stems can be pinned to the soil, then severed and replanted after they have taken root. When transplanting, dig generous holes only as deep as the rootball but at least 4 times as wide, loosening the soil so that new roots will have an easy time breaking ground. Even xeric plants develop lateral absorbing roots, which they rely on for initial establishment and long-term survival. Backfill soil requires no amendment, but a generous topdressing of mulch will keep the soil more uniformly moist and more moderate in temperature, accelerating root development.

ADVICE FOR CARE

Once plants are well-rooted and have filled their garden space, sustain plant vigor by watering once a month to a depth of 2 ft. Fertilizer and frequent watering induce rampant growth. 'Centennial' may be pruned back every few years or thinned by 1/3 to rejuvenate the plants.

SPECIES, CULTIVARS, OR VARIETIES

Coyotebush (*Baccharis pilularis*) grows 1 ft. high and spreads 5 ft. wide with small, pale-green, wedge-shaped leaves and wiry, green stems. It is native along the coast of California and seems to decline in the cold desert, especially if the soil is kept too moist during extreme periods of heat and cold. Desert broom (*Baccharis sarathroides*) grows 5 ft. high and 6 ft. wide and is very similar to 'Centennial' in color and texture, but it is more upright in form. In autumn, the fluffy white seedheads give female plants added impact, but seeds drift into gardens dandelion-style and can become a nuisance. Unwanted seedlings are easy to uproot when they are small.

REGIONAL CONSIDERATIONS

'Centennial' is not hardy in central and northern New Mexico above 6500 ft.

Cotoneaster

Height: 2 to 3 ft.
Flowers: White
Foliage: Varies
Bloom Period: Spring
Zones: 5 to 8
Water: Moderate

Light Requirement:

*T*here are many worthwhile cotoneasters, varying considerably in size and shape. Those that are most used in New Mexico gardens are small leafed and generally evergreen. The graceful arch of their stems and the dense cover of small, round leaves make cotoneasters rather elegant plants. Their white flowers are small but clustered in tight umbels that have a lacy look against the dark foliage. Bright-red fruits add color later in the season. The low-spreading evergreen species are described in the section on groundcovers.

WHEN TO PLANT

Cotoneaster is planted any time from fall through spring in warmer parts of the state, and spring through fall in the colder parts of the state.

WHERE TO PLANT

Cotoneasters prefer well-drained soil but will grow in most soils if not watered excessively. They are most often used as fillers for contrast between flowering and deciduous plants.

HOW TO PLANT

Recent research has demonstrated that the best soil preparation for container-grown shrubs is to dig holes only as deep as the rootball but 4 to 6 times its diameter. Backfill soil requires no amendment. Cotoneasters become potbound when they are held in containers. If a tight mass of roots circles the base of the container when the plants are unpotted, the rootballs should be scored in several places with a sharp knife or shears to encourage roots to branch outward.

SHRUBS

ADVICE FOR CARE

Most cotoneasters have a dense self-contained growth habit that can be maintained with little pruning or fertilizing. It takes a few years to develop an extensive root system; during this time, plants do best if fertilized lightly in spring and watered once a week when the temperature is above 85 degrees Fahrenheit. To sustain established plants, water every 2 weeks when the temperature is above 70 degrees Fahrenheit, and monthly during cooler weather. A 3- to 4-in. layer of mulch helps suppress weeds until the plants fill in. Coton-easters can be susceptible to fireblight, especially in the cooler parts of the state where spring weather is damp. This disease makes whole stems appear to have been burnt. Cut infected stems back to healthy wood, and disinfect shears after every cut to prevent spreading the bacteria.

SPECIES, CULTIVARS, OR VARIETIES

Grayleaf cotoneaster (*C. buxifolius*) grows 2 to 3 ft. high and 6 ft. wide. The stiff branches may arch taller until the weight of their lengthening stems bows them downward. This shrub is the most unruly looking of the group, as well as the most heat and drought tolerant, so it is the species best suited to the low-desert areas. Grayleaf has 1/4-in. evergreen leaves that are steel gray during the growing season and turn a deep plum gray during cold weather. Pyrennes cotoneaster (*C. congestus*) grows slowly to 3 ft. high and wide with dark evergreen leaves. It is a reliable filler for small spaces and requires only deep watering to thrive. Rockspray (*C. horizontalis*) grows 2 to 3 feet high and 10 ft. wide. It loses its leaves briefly in winter and has the showiest red fruit in autumn and early winter. The long branches produce an interesting fishbone pattern of lateral shoots that gives the plant a distinctive texture and form. It is cold hardy to Zone 3 and a good choice for the colder areas of New Mexico.

Curry Plant

Helichrysum angustifolium

Height: 1 ft.	**Light Requirement:**
Flowers: Yellow	
Foliage: Evergreen	
Bloom Period: Summer	
Zones: 5 to 8	
Water: Low	

*P*lants adapt to hot, dry conditions by reducing their evaporative surfaces, assuming compact, mounded forms, and by producing small leaves covered with silky hairs that reflect sunlight. Curry employs all those tactics to thrive in New Mexico's gardens. Its thready leaves are a soft sage green, and it forms a cushion 1 ft. high and nearly twice as wide. Curry is grown primarily for its leaf color and texture, though the umbels of tiny flowers stand several inches above the foliage mound and add a golden halo above the pale-silver cushion of foliage. This plant also foils a harsh environment with its strong aroma. Insect pests and rabbits won't touch it, though you may experience sudden cravings for East Indian food when you encounter its rich aroma.

WHEN TO PLANT

When planting in northern and higher elevation gardens, curry can be transplanted any time from spring through late summer. It is best to avoid midsummer planting in the low desert; plant from fall through late spring instead.

WHERE TO PLANT

Curry grows in any infertile soil, but it is unusual among xeric subshrubs in that it seems to prefer heavier, clay-based soils as long as they are allowed to dry between waterings. It can be used for a strong contrast with green foliage and colorful flowers such as Mexican tarragon, superba salvias, torch lily, and veronicas. The repetition of the mounding shape contrasted with the stronger colors of pineleaf penstemon and turpentine bush creates an interesting rhythm in border plantings. For a more subtle tone-on-tone color variation, mix curry with fernbush and Roman wormwood against a backdrop of silverberry. Such muted plant groupings create serene islands that offset bold flower displays.

How to Plant

Curry cuttings root easily when the plant is not in bloom. If transplanting, dig generous holes, loosening the soil so that new roots will have an easy time breaking ground. Recent research has demonstrated that the best soil preparation for container-grown shrubs is to dig holes only as deep as the rootball but several times its diameter. This allows even deeply rooted plants to develop the lateral absorbing roots they will rely on for initial establishment and long-term survival. Backfill soil requires no amendment. Rich, humusy soil may be too high in carbon dioxide and too low in oxygen to allow the vigorous rooting of curry plant.

Advice for Care

Though curry foliage remains attractive throughout most winters, it should be trimmed back 4 to 6 in. from the ground in early spring so that the winter-weathered stems can be replaced with soft new growth. In summer, trim the finished flower stems down into the foliage to tidy up the plants and stimulate a flush of new growth. Water every 2 weeks when temperatures are above 80 degrees Fahrenheit; water monthly the rest of the year. Water should penetrate to a depth of at least 18 in. In light, sandy soils, curry may need weekly watering during peak summer heat, especially when plants are in bloom. Fertilizer is generally not needed.

Species, Cultivars, or Varieties

Curry plant is sometimes offered for sale as *Helichrysum italicum*. Strawflower (*Helichrysum bracteatum*) is a well-known dried flower that is grown from seed as a summer annual.

Fairy Duster

Calliandra eriophylla

Height: 3 ft.
Flowers: Pale to deep pink
Foliage: Deciduous
Bloom Period: Spring and summer
Zones: 6 to 8
Water: Low

Light Requirement:

*F*airy duster is a Chihuahuan desert native with an open twiggy form and fine leaf texture. It emblemizes the paradox of resilience and fragility that characterizes the most drought- and heat-loving plants. Very finely divided leaves shade the network of slender arching stems that grow 3 ft. high and spread 4 ft. wide. Fairy duster is fancifully named for its pink powder puff flowers and 1-in. bundles of stamens that from a distance look like a soft pink haze. It blooms most heavily in spring, providing a welcome home for returning humming-birds. Flowering recurs sporadically throughout the summer.

WHEN TO PLANT

Spring planting, when the soil has warmed to 70 degrees Fahrenheit, is ideal for both seeds and container-grown plants. Planting at this time allows a long season for root growth before the return of cold weather. In Zone 8, fairy duster can be planted year round.

WHERE TO PLANT

Fairy duster requires well-drained sandy or gravelly soil. It is used as accent along dry streambed pathways and between the boulders that stabilize slopes in xeric gardens. The best complements to the featherlight appearance of fairy duster are offered by strongly defined plants such as prickly pear, yuccas, and century plants.

HOW TO PLANT

Seeds have a hard seedcoat and germinate quickly if soaked in hot water before planting. Loosen the soil so that new roots will have an easy time breaking ground. Recent research has demonstrated that the best soil preparation for container-grown shrubs is to dig holes only as deep as, or at most a few inches deeper than, the depth of the rootball, but several times its diameter. Even deeply rooted plants develop lateral absorbing roots, which they rely on for initial establishment and long-term survival. This is especially true of nursery-grown desert plants, because their deep initial root development is interrupted by confinement in a container, which initiates lateral rooting. Backfill soil requires no amendment; gritty, infertile soil is fairy duster's preferred growing medium.

ADVICE FOR CARE

Protect new plants from rabbits until the plants are well established. Fairy duster needs no pruning or fertilizing. To keep plants leafy and encourage flowering, water established plants once a month (especially from March through August) to a depth of 2 to 3 ft..

SPECIES, CULTIVARS, OR VARIETIES

Baja fairy duster (*Calliandra californica*) has larger scarlet flowers, but it is not reliably cold hardy in even the hottest protected microclimates in southern New Mexico.

REGIONAL CONSIDERATIONS

Fairy duster is best adapted below 6000 ft. in the southern half of the state. Creosotebush and ocotillo are good local indicators of where fairy duster will thrive.

Firethorn

Pyracantha species and cultivars

Height: 4 to 12 ft.	**Light Requirement:**
Flowers: White	
Foliage: Evergreen	
Bloom Period: Spring	
Zones: 5 to 8	
Water: Moderate	

*P*yracantha has been used extensively in New Mexico because it is adaptable, lush looking, and reliably evergreen. Its narrow, oval dark-green leaves densely cloak the stiff, thorny arching stems. In spring, clusters of small white flowers foretell the real glory of firethorn, its autumn display of brilliant red-orange berries. The older cultivars grow large, often much too large for the small spaces in which they have been planted; as a result, frequent pruning is required to keep them contained. The cultivars described below are more restrained in growth habit, though it's best not to underestimate the vigor of well-established pyracantha.

WHEN TO PLANT
Set plants out after temperatures moderate in spring through summer and early autumn. Though pyracantha survives summer transplanting, it is best to wait until temperatures are below 90 degrees Fahrenheit to reduce the chance of heat stress. Planting during winter is hard on the evergreen leaves.

WHERE TO PLANT
Pyracantha adapts to most soils. The thorns make pruning an unpleasant chore, so choosing the cultivar that fits the space available is important. The thorns create an excellent security barrier. The strong leafy branches espalier nicely against walls and fences in tall, narrow spaces. The low-spreading cultivars are a colorful foreground for blue and silver evergreens.

HOW TO PLANT
Dig generous holes only as deep as the rootball, but 4 to 6 times its diameter. Backfill soil requires no amendment, but 3 to 4 in. of mulch will keep the soil cooler and more uniformly moist.

ADVICE FOR CARE

If pyracantha must be pruned, cut vigorous new stems back to short lateral branches after plants have flowered and daytime temperatures begin to soar. This will limit regrowth and help prevent the spread of fireblight, a bacterial disease that is most likely to occur during cool, wet weather. Shearing pyracantha is particularly self-defeating, because it also reduces the fruit color to small patches scattered within the stubble. Firethorn takes a few years to establish an extensive root system; during establishment, water once a week when the temperature is above 85 degrees Fahrenheit. To sustain established plants, water every 2 weeks when the temperature is above 70 degrees Fahrenheit, and monthly during cooler weather. A deep layer of mulch helps suppress weeds until the plants fill in. Fertilizer is usually not needed once plants are established, but plants grown in strongly alkaline soils may need an application of granular iron-and-sulfur fertilizer to prevent or reverse summer yellowing.

SPECIES, CULTIVARS, OR VARIETIES

'Gnome' and 'Yukon Belle', cultivars of *P. angustifolia*, are the most cold hardy (to Zone 4). 'Gnome' grows 4 ft. high and 6 ft. wide; 'Yukon Belle' grows 6 to 8 ft. high and wide. Both produce orange berries. 'Fiery Cascade' and 'Low Boy' are cultivars of *P. coccinea* that are cold hardy in Zones 6 to 8. 'Fiery Cascade' grows 4 ft. high and 6 ft. wide with red berries. 'Low Boy' grows 2 to 3 ft. high and spreads 6 to 8 ft. wide with orange berries. 'Santa Cruz', a *P. koidzumii* cultivar, is the least cold tolerant in Zones 7 and 8. It grows 3 ft. high and 4 feet wide with red berries. The hybrid 'Red Elf', a trademarked cultivar that is also hardy only in Zones 7 and 8, grows 2 ft. high and wide with red berries. It was bred for fireblight resistance.

REGIONAL CONSIDERATIONS

Cultivars grown in Zone 6 may freeze to the ground in colder areas, but they regrow rapidly in spring. Since fruit production is heaviest on year-old wood, plants that freeze back aren't as colorful.

'Hancock' Dwarf Coralberry

Symphoricarpos × chenaultii 'Hancock'

Height: 2 ft.
Flowers: Pale pink
Foliage: Deciduous
Bloom Period: Spring
Zones: 4 to 7
Water: Moderate

Light Requirement:

In cooler microclimates, 'Hancock' coralberry is an elegant filler grown for its subdued color and refined foliage and form. Slender, closely spaced stems arch from the crown and root where they touch ground, creating a dense thicket. Pairs of 1/2-in. rounded leaves line the limber stems. Tiny pink flowers appear at the leaf nodes in late spring, followed by pairs of small pink berries. The leaves are pale green with a bronze tinge. Individual plants will need about 6 ft. of space in 3 or 4 years, but for faster coverage small plants may be spaced 4 ft. apart to cover in 2 years.

WHEN TO PLANT

Root sprouts can be divided from the base of established plants in spring or fall. Coralberry transplants best when the weather is cool, but it can be set out any time as long as it is watered consistently during hot weather.

WHERE TO PLANT

'Hancock' coralberry prefers humusy well-drained soil. It is planted in drainage swales and basins for erosion control and as a low foundation planting on north or east exposures; it can be grouped with evergreens for contrast. It is a good companion for aspens, as the shade provided by the coralberry keeps the aspen roots cooler, and the white trunks of the aspen compliment the nodding stems and pink fruit of the coralberry in winter.

HOW TO PLANT

'Hancock' coralberry can be rooted by pinning branches to loosened soil. To transplant container-grown shrubs, dig holes only as deep as, or at most a few inches deeper than, the rootball, but several times its diameter. This allows plants to develop the lateral absorbing roots they rely on for initial establishment and long-term survival. Compost can be worked into the backfill; if several 1-gallon plants are to be set out 4 to 6 ft. apart, a 4-in. layer of compost may be tilled into the entire area prior to planting. Three or 4 in. of mulch will accelerate layering by keeping the soil more uniformly moist and more moderate in temperature.

ADVICE FOR CARE

Coralberry is long-lived and pest-free. Every 3 to 5 years, $1/3$ of the oldest stems can be cut down to the ground in early spring to rejuvenate the planting. It takes a few years to establish an extensive root system; during establishment, plants should be watered once a week when the temperature is above 85 degrees Fahrenheit. To sustain established plants, water every 2 weeks when the temperature is above 70 degrees Fahrenheit, and monthly during cooler weather. A 3- to 4-in. layer of mulch helps suppress weeds until the plants fill in. Fertilizer is usually not needed once the plants are well rooted. In strongly alkaline soils, an application of a granular iron-and-sulfur fertilizer will prevent or reverse summer yellowing.

SPECIES, CULTIVARS, OR VARIETIES

Coralberry (*S. orbiculatus*) is a taller, coarser plant with limber stems that are weighted at the ends with clusters of small rose-pink fruits. It forms a thicket 3 to 4 ft. tall and at least 5 ft. wide.

REGIONAL CONSIDERATIONS

Though dwarf coralberry will survive in Zone 8 if planted in shade with ample water, it is best adapted to elevations between 5500 and 8000 ft. in the northern half of the state.

Lavender

Lavandula species and cultivars

Height: 1 to 3 ft.	**Light Requirement:**
Flowers: Blue-purple	
Foliage: Semievergreen	
Bloom Period: Spring and summer	
Zones: 5 to 8	
Water: Low to moderate	

The rich color, compact form, and wonderful fragrance of lavender has made it a favorite garden plant for centuries. The narrow leaves vary in color from silver-green to blue-gray. They are crowded on the wiry stems, forming a dense mound 2 ft. high and wide. Lavender flowers come in a range of shades of blue and purple. Small florets grow clustered 1 ft. or more above the mound of foliage at the ends of slender, leafless stems.

WHEN TO PLANT

Lavender roots quickly in warm soil and is best seeded or transplanted when the soil has warmed to 65 degrees Fahrenheit in spring. It can be transplanted throughout the summer as long as plants are watered regularly.

WHERE TO PLANT

Plants grow best in well-drained, infertile soil. Lavender blends well with cherry sage, Jerusalem sage, bubblegum mint, licorice mint, dianthus, gaura, and golden columbine in sunny or partly shaded beds and borders. Lavender seems to prefer being nestled between boulders, where reflected heat and recycled moisture from condensation create a comfortable niche for this Mediterranean native.

HOW TO PLANT

Lavender is easily grown from seed (28,000 per oz.) sown on a seedbed that has been prepared thoroughly. Two to 3 in. of compost should be tilled into the soil, ensuring that new roots will have an easy time breaking ground. When transplanting container-grown plants, dig holes only as deep as the rootball, but 4 to 6 times its diameter, so that plants develop the lateral absorbing roots they rely on for initial establishment and long-term survival. Backfill soil requires no amendment, but a generous topdressing of mulch keeps the soil more uniformly moist and more moderate in temperature.

ADVICE FOR CARE

In early spring, trim lavender back by half so that soft new growth can replace the winter-weathered stems. In summer, trim the finished flower stems down into the foliage to tidy up the plants and stimulate another flush of blooms. Water once a week when plants are in bloom and temperatures are above 90 degrees Fahrenheit. Water twice a month when temperatures are between 70 and 90 degrees Fahrenheit; water monthly during the rest of the year. Water should penetrate to a depth of 24 in. In heavier soils, lavender might need watering only every 10 to 14 days during peak summer heat.

SPECIES, CULTIVARS, OR VARIETIES

English lavender (*L. angustifolia*) is the most cold tolerant of the species; it is hardy to 6500 ft. in northern New Mexico. Its many cultivars include 'Hidcote', which is slow growing to 2 ft. high and wide with dark-purple flowers; 'Munstead', which grows 12 to 18 in. high and wide with blue-purple flowers; and 'Nana', which is compact, 6 to 8 in. tall, with deep-blue flowers. French lavender (*L. dentata*) is one of the most fragrant lavenders. It grows 2 to 3 ft. high and wide and is hardy only in Zones 7 and 8. Spanish lavender (*L. stoechas*) grows 2 to 3 ft. high and wide. Its foliage is a darker gray and the flowers are wine purple with large winged bracts. French and Spanish lavenders are more tender; they need protection in the central part of the state and above 5500 ft. in the south.

Lilac

Syringa species and hybrids

Height: 8 to 15 ft.
Flowers: Shades of purple or white
Foliage: Deciduous
Bloom Period: Spring
Zones: 3 to 8
Water: Moderate to ample

Light Requirement:

Lilacs are native to southeastern Europe and Asia, but it's hard to imagine the winding streets of Santa Fe and Taos without them overhanging the adobe walls. Popular for their early color and fragrance, lilacs are large plants with strong stems growing up to 15 ft. tall and spreading nearly as wide. Leaves are medium green and heart-shaped; flowers grow in large panicles of blue, purple, pink, or white. Lilacs prefer alkaline soils, root deeply, and are very long-lived. Since they have been cultivated for centuries, it is probably safe to say that all the plants cultivated today are hybrids. The Persian, Chinese, and Korean varieties are the most drought tolerant.

WHEN TO PLANT

Lilacs can be planted any time the soil can be worked, but they root most quickly when the soil is cool. If planted in the heat of summer, they will require ample water to get by until the soil cools down.

WHERE TO PLANT

Lilacs need spaces large enough to accommodate their mature girth, and they must have good air circulation to minimize mildew problems in summer. They are used as tall informal hedges, low windbreaks in large gardens, or multi-trunk specimen trees in small gardens.

HOW TO PLANT

Dig holes only as deep as the rootball, but 4 to 6 times its diameter so that plants develop the lateral absorbing roots they rely on for initial establishment and long-term survival. Compost added to the backfill can improve the drainage in heavy soils and retain moisture in loose, sandy soils, but it is not strictly necessary. A 3- to 4-in.

mulch of compost or shredded bark keeps the soil cooler and more uniformly moist.

ADVICE FOR CARE

Prune lilacs by removing the spent flowers as they fade; buds for the following year are set soon after plants finish blooming. To rejuvenate an older plant, remove all dead wood immediately after the shrub flowers, cutting 1/3 of the oldest stems and most of the suckers down to the ground. Repeat the process each spring for 3 years, at which time all the topgrowth will be young and vigorous. Lilacs need fertilizer only every few years in spring. Establishment of an extensive root system may take up to 5 years; during this time, water once a week when the temperature is above 85 degrees Fahrenheit. To sustain established plants, water every 2 weeks when the temperature is above 70 degrees Fahrenheit, and monthly during cooler weather.

SPECIES, CULTIVARS, OR VARIETIES

Common lilac (*S. vulgaris*) is native from the Caucasus to Afghanistan. The French hybrids grown today were bred originally for the European floral trade nearly two centuries ago. Their flowers are stiffer and bulkier than those of the species. Persian lilac (*S. persica*) is native in the same region as the common lilac, but it is smaller (5 to 10 ft. tall), its leaves are narrower, its branches are more limber, and its flower panicles are looser and more spreading. Chinese lilac (*S. rothomagensis*) is thought to be a hybrid of common and Persian lilacs. It grows to 12 ft. tall and wide with pale-violet flowers. It is more mildew resistant than *S. vulgaris* and takes heat well. Korean lilac (*S. patula*) is dense and twiggy, growing slowly to 7 ft. tall and 4 ft. wide with dark-purple flowers that fade to blue. The small leaves turn red in fall and rarely mildew. 'Miss Kim' is a compact selection that grows only 3 ft. tall. Dwarf Korean lilac (*S. meyeri*) grows 6 ft. tall. Its leaves are slightly hairy, don't mildew, and turn peachy orange in autumn. The fragrant flower buds are deep violet-purple and open a paler lavender. *S. meyeri* is the most drought and heat tolerant of all the lilacs.

Mahonia

Mahonia species

Height: 1 to 6 ft. **Flowers:** Yellow **Foliage:** Evergreen **Bloom Period:** Spring **Zones:** 5 to 8 **Water:** Moderate	**Light Requirement:**

One trend in horticulture is toward more compact forms of plants that require less pruning and fit smaller garden spaces. The increased popularity of compact mahonia over the old standby Oregon grape holly is an example. All three of the mahonias described below are similar in that they have leathery, evergreen holly-shaped leaves and fragrant yellow flowers in spring. Leaf color changes subtly through the year: the new growth in spring is copper-colored, summer leaves are a deep blue-green, and foliage turns a rich plum-purple after frost.

WHEN TO PLANT

Container-grown plants may be set out any time in spring through early autumn. Plants establish roots more quickly when the soil is cool, but freezing dry winds can scorch the evergreen foliage, so it's best to forego planting during winter. Even if the garden is protected from wind, most nurseries keep their broadleafed evergreens sheltered in winter. Exposing them to outdoor winter temperatures can be fatal.

WHERE TO PLANT

Although mahonia prefers rich, well-drained garden soil, it will adapt to heavy clay if not kept too wet. It is used as a filler between flowering shrubs such as viburnum or blue mist, and as a tall groundcover under redbuds, golden rain tree, or Japanese scholar tree. The plum-colored winter foliage blends well with 'Powis Castle' artemisia.

HOW TO PLANT

Dig holes only as deep as the rootball, but 4 to 6 times its diameter, so that plants can easily develop the lateral absorbing roots they rely on for initial establishment and long-term survival. Backfill soil requires no amendment, but a generous topdressing of composted cotton burrs, shredded bark, or pecan hulls as mulch will keep the soil more uniformly moist and more moderate in temperature.

ADVICE FOR CARE

Mahonia requires little pruning. Because it grows slowly and steadily, this shrub does not generally need fertilizing, but a small amount of a time-release fertilizer applied in spring for the first few years after planting can help get plants off to a faster start. It takes 3 to 4 years to establish an extensive root system; during establishment, mahonia should be watered once a week when the temperature is above 85 degrees Fahrenheit. To sustain established plants, water every 2 weeks when the temperature is above 70 degrees Fahrenheit, and monthly during cooler weather. A 3- to 4-in. layer of mulch helps suppress weeds until the plants fill in. Plants growing in the sun may need water once a week in summer.

SPECIES, CULTIVARS, OR VARIETIES

Oregon grape holly (*M. aquifolium*) grows 6 ft. tall and 5 ft. wide, rootsprouting at the base to form a dense thicket. Compact mahonia (*M. aquifolium* 'Compacta') is a smaller form of Oregon grape, growing 2 ft. high and spreading 4 ft. wide. It is the most versatile of the three. Creeping mahonia (*M. repens*) is native above 7500 ft. in mountains throughout the West and is slower to establish. It is less heat tolerant than the others. When combined with blue avena, it makes a handsome groundcover in the shade.

REGIONAL CONSIDERATIONS

In southern New Mexico, mahonia is practical only above 7500 ft. and in full shade.

Manzanita

Arctostaphylos species and cultivars

Height: 3 to 6 ft. **Flowers:** Pink **Foliage:** Evergreen **Bloom Period:** Spring **Zones:** 5 to 8 **Water:** Low to moderate	**Light Requirement:**

*M*anzanita is an exceptional plant with stiff, leathery evergreen leaves on smooth copper-colored branches. Depending on light and exposure, the stems arch as tall as they are widespread or sprawl much wider than they grow tall. Sheltered, shaded plants grow 6 ft. high and wide. On exposed sunny slopes, manzanita may reach 4 ft. tall and 12 ft. wide. Its clusters of pendulous, pale-pink, droplet-shaped flowers are pretty, but manzanita is valued more for its handsome sculptural branches and evergreen foliage. If you decide you want to grow it in your garden, be prepared to search for this horticultural holy grail. Because it is difficult to propagate and is not the easiest plant to transplant, manzanita is usually available only through specialty nurseries, those cherished growers who have the patience and persistence to bring this shrub to the marketplace.

WHEN TO PLANT

Because intense heat and cold, drying winds are particularly hard on newly transplanted broadleaf evergreens, it is best to transplant manzanita in spring, late summer, or early autumn.

WHERE TO PLANT

Manzanita grows on highly permeable volcanic soils and should be planted where soil has excellent drainage. It is especially effective when interplanted with blue-leafed conifers such as 'Blue Haven' juniper, blue spruce, and blue atlas cedar, or with dark-leaved plants such as silverleaf oak and curlleaf mountain mahogany. Manzanita can be used as a screen, mass planted as a clean, green slope cover, or grown as filler between flowering shrubs such as the native roses.

How to Plant

Manzanita can be rooted by layering: Pin stems of the current year's growth to the soil in late summer and cut off the rooted sections. Transplant cuttings the second spring after they have been pinned. Loosen the soil well so that new roots will have an easy time breaking ground. Dig holes only as deep as the rootball, but 4 to 6 times its diameter; this enables plants to develop the lateral absorbing roots they rely on for initial establishment and long-term survival. In well-drained areas, the backfill soil will require no amendment. Disturb the roots as little as possible while transplanting. A generous mulch of pine straw, shredded bark, or fine gravel will keep the soil more uniformly moist and more moderate in temperature.

Advice for Care

Manzanita needs water twice monthly when the temperature is above 75 degrees Fahrenheit; water monthly the rest of the year. Time-released fertilizer worked into the soil under drip emitters for the first few springs after transplanting can give plants a more vigorous start.

Species, Cultivars, or Varieties

Greenleaf manzanita (*A. patula*) has bright-green leathery leaves on smooth mahogany stems with small red fruits in summer. It grows 5 ft. tall and 10 ft. wide. Kinnikinnick (*A. uva-ursi*) is native to the acidic soils of conifer forests at high elevations and is less heat and drought tolerant than the others. It has small, round, evergreen leaves on wiry, prostrate, mat-forming stems 6 in. high and 24 to 36 in. wide. Kinnikinnick is adapted to protected shady niches in gardens below 7000 ft. and more open rock gardens at higher elevations. It needs weekly watering when temperatures are above 85 degrees Fahrenheit; it is cold hardy to Zone 3. 'Emerald Carpet' is a hybrid of *A. uva-ursi* and *A. nummularia* that has glossy dark-green leaves on low, arching branches mounding 1 ft. high and 3 ft. wide. It is cold hardy to Zone 6 if given protection from drying winds. Pointleaf manzanita (*A. pungens*) is the most xeric of the group with paler-green leaves and bronzy pea-sized fruits in summer. It grows 3 to 6 ft. high and 5 to 12 ft. wide.

Mexican Buckeye

Ungnadia speciosa

Height: 8 ft.
Flowers: Rose-pink
Foliage: Deciduous
Bloom Period: Spring
Zones: 7 and 8
Water: Low to moderate

Light Requirement:

This stoutly branched native shrub has interesting features year round. In spring, clusters of 1-in. deep-pink flowers with long, dark stamens cover the rounded canopy so densely that the plants are often mistaken for redbuds. As the flowers fade, compound leaves appear, each with five to seven leaflets 3 in. long and 1 1/2 in. wide, tapering to points at the tips. The leaves are dark green on the upper surface; the underside is paler and covered with fine hairs. When the leaves drop in autumn, 2-in. rust-colored, woody seed capsules shaped like heads of garlic hang from the branches. As they dry, the pods split open, exposing large round black seeds.

WHEN TO PLANT

Mexican buckeye roots fastest when the soil is warm, so it is best to transplant in spring and summer. Seeds germinate best once the soil has warmed to 70 degrees Fahrenheit.

WHERE TO PLANT

Use Mexican buckeye as nature does, planted along dry streambeds as an accent plant. Use it to shade a large boulder that also serves as a seat, or as a focal point against a wall or evergreen screen. Mexican buckeye blends well with Apache plume, littleleaf sumac, beargrass, Texas sage, evergreen oaks, and pinyon.

HOW TO PLANT

Sow seeds 1/2 in. deep in spring, loosening the soil so that new roots will have an easy time breaking ground; or sow in deep pots where the long initial root will have enough depth to develop. Recent research has demonstrated that the best soil preparation for container-grown shrubs is to dig holes only as deep as, or at most a few inches deeper than, the depth of the rootball, but 4 to 6 times its diameter. When the deep initial root is interrupted by being pot-grown, even deeply rooted plants like Mexican buckeye develop the lateral absorbing roots that they rely on for initial establishment and long-term survival. Backfill soil requires no amendment, but a generous topdressing of composted cotton burrs, pecan hulls, or gravel as mulch will accelerate root development by keeping the soil more uniformly moist and more moderate in temperature. Use coarse gravel as mulch on plants in drainage swales and basins; lighter mulches will float when the basins flood during storms.

ADVICE FOR CARE

Once established, Mexican buckeye needs no fertilizing, but for the first few years in the garden a mild-dose fertilizer will help get it off to a strong start. Little pruning is required if the plant is allowed the 8 to 12 ft. of space a mature plant will need. Water established plants monthly to a depth of 3 ft., or twice a month when the temperature is above 85 degrees Fahrenheit to maintain a denser leaf canopy.

SPECIES, CULTIVARS, OR VARIETIES

There are no other species in cultivation.

REGIONAL CONSIDERATIONS

I suspect that Mexican buckeye has been growing in New Mexican gardens since gardening pioneers fell in love with the plant growing wild along southern arroyos. They are sure to have noticed its blooms or its curious seedpods, and carried seeds back to the hacienda or ranch. It is growing in gardens in Truth or Consequences and further south, but there are even warm microclimates in Albuquerque where it would be worth a try.

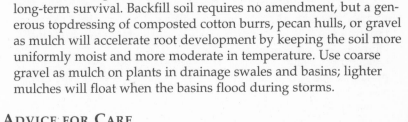

Moonlight' Broom

Cytisus scoparius 'Moonlight'

Height: 4 to 6 ft.	**Light Requirement:**
Flowers: Pale yellow	
Foliage: Deciduous	
Bloom Period: Spring	
Zones: 5 to 8	
Water: Moderate	

'Moonlight' is one of the Scotch brooms whose invasive reseeding has become an ecological problem in warmer, moister climates. For once, the severity of our climate is a blessing, since only well-tended plants survive here. Not that 'Moonlight' broom is difficult or fussy. It rewards a minimum of care with a profusion of 1-in., pale-yellow, pea-shaped flowers in late spring. The slender stems also bear small, narrow leaves that add to the refined character of the plant. The leaves drop during drought and after frost, leaving the newest stems, which remain green in winter, to do most of the plant's photosynthesizing.

WHEN TO PLANT

'Moonlight' broom roots out faster in warm soil, so it is best to transplant during the growing season. It can be planted in the low desert at any time; be sure that water is available in summer, and that plants have been acclimated to the cold in winter. At the northern and high-elevation limits of its cold-hardiness range, plants are best started in spring so that they will have ample rooting time before the return of cold weather.

WHERE TO PLANT

Plants grow best in well-drained gravelly soil that has had some organic matter thoroughly incorporated into it. The soft-yellow flowers contrast well with blue flax, salvias, lavender, and Russian sage; the fine green stems blend well with artemisias. 'Moonlight' broom is used as a filler in shrub borders. It can be grown spilling over a low retaining wall, or used to stabilize soil on slopes where moisture is consistently available.

How to Plant

'Moonlight' broom responds poorly to root disturbance; even cuttings are usually rooted in individual containers to minimize losses during handling. When transplanting, dig holes only as deep as the rootball, but 4 to 6 times its diameter, so that plants will develop the lateral absorbing roots they rely on for initial establishment and long-term survival. When several plants will be grouped 4 to 6 ft. apart, tilling 4 in. of compost into the area to be planted and setting plants out in the loosened soil is easier than digging individual holes would be. A 3- to 4-in. mulch of composted cotton burrs, shredded bark, pine straw, pecan hulls, or fine gravel will keep the soil cooler and more uniformly moist; it will also reduce weed invasion.

Advice for Care

Apply a granular iron-and-sulfur fertilizer each spring to prevent yellowing later in the season; or use chelated iron in summer as needed. Severe cold, especially if plants are not hardened off, can cause dieback of the stems. To keep plants in their prime, it's best to remove 1/3 of the oldest woody stems (including any winter dieback) each spring as the new growth emerges. Broom takes a few years to establish an extensive root system; during establishment, it should be watered once a week when the temperature is above 85 degrees Fahrenheit. To sustain established plants, water every 2 weeks when the temperature is above 70 degrees Fahrenheit, and monthly during cooler weather. Plants grown in the south may need a bit more water; brooms grown in low-desert areas will be lusher if given afternoon shade.

Species, Cultivars, or Varieties

Cytisus scoparius 'Lilac Time' grows 3 ft. high and 4 ft. wide with rose-purple flowers. It is less cold tolerant than 'Moonlight' and is hardy to Zone 6. 'Warminster Broom' (*Cytisus praecox*) is more cold hardy; it grows 3 to 5 ft. high and wide and has foul-smelling pale-yellow flowers. 'Allgold' is a cultivar with brighter yellow blooms; the flowers of 'Hollandia' are cream and wine-red.

Ornamental Cherries

Prunus species

Height: 4 ft. to 10 ft.
Flowers: White
Foliage: Varies
Bloom Period: Spring
Zones: Varies
Water: Moderate to ample

Light Requirement:

The ornamental cherries are a diverse group of shrubs. Some are evergreen, but most are deciduous and under ideal conditions will grow quite large. All bloom in the spring, producing clusters of small white flowers at the ends of their branches. Their succulent fruit and dense cover provide valuable habitat for wildlife, yet they possess good garden qualities: showy flowers, attractive forms, and refined foliage. The individual species described here adapt to very different garden niches.

WHEN TO PLANT

Plants root out faster in cool soil, so it is best to transplant the evergreen species in spring, and the deciduous species in spring or fall.

WHERE TO PLANT

The evergreen cherries need wind protection; plant against walls or on the lee side of larger evergreens such as blue spruce, Austrian pine, and cedar. Chokecherry grows well in storm runoff catchments and is most water efficient in cooler microclimates. Sand cherry is a versatile midsized plant used as a filler in shrub borders. All the cherries can be messy while fruiting because of the birds they attract, but planting them away from sidewalks and patio paving minimizes this inconvenience.

HOW TO PLANT

Dig holes only as deep as the rootball, but 4 to 6 times its diameter, so that plants can root out easily. Backfill soil requires no amendment, but a generous mulch of composted cotton burrs, shredded bark, pine straw, or pecan hulls will keep the soil cooler and more uniformly moist, and it will help suppress weeds until the cherries fill in.

ADVICE FOR CARE

The ornamental cherries take a few years to establish an extensive root system; during establishment, plants should be watered once a week when the temperature is above 85 degrees Fahrenheit. To sustain established plants, water every 2 weeks when the temperature is above 70 degrees Fahrenheit, and monthly during cooler weather. Chokecherry may need more water; sand cherry may take a little less.

SPECIES, CULTIVARS, OR VARIETIES

Carolina cherry laurel (*P. caroliniana*) is a handsome plant that grows 10 ft. tall and wide, producing large black cherries in summer. Its glossy dark-evergreen leaves are 3 in. long and 1 in. wide. It is cold hardy to Zone 6 and is best adapted in the shade of north- or east-facing walls or in sheltered courtyards. Schipka cherry laurel (*P. laurocerasus* 'Schipkaensis') is similar to Carolina cherry laurel but is more cold tolerant. It grows 12 ft. tall and 8 ft. wide. 'Zabeliana' is a dwarf form 6 ft. tall and wide with narrow lance-shaped leaves. Western chokecherry (*P. virginiana* var. *melanocarpa*) is the most cold hardy, growing best in Zones 3 to 7. It is also the most moisture loving, growing native in drainage areas and along streams in the West. It grows 8 to 12 ft. tall and suckers to 10 ft. wide with many limber, upright branches that form a rounded canopy. In spring, the 5-in.-long racemes crowded with small, white flowers are striking. The small purple fruits that follow are favorites of many songbirds. Chokecherry leaves are deciduous, large, and dark green, turning shades of red and yellow in autumn. Western sand cherry (*P. besseyi*) is the smallest of the lot, growing 4 ft. tall and up to 6 ft. wide. Its limber stems are sheathed in fragrant white flowers in spring, large black cherries in summer, and red foliage in fall. It is hardy from Zones 4 through 7 and at elevations up to 8500 ft.

Pomegranate

Punica granatum

Height: 8 to 10 ft. **Flowers:** Red **Foliage:** Deciduous **Bloom Period:** Summer **Zones:** 6 to 8 **Water:** Moderate	**Light Requirement:**

*P*omegranate is a heat-loving native of the Middle East and India that is well adapted to alkaline soils and seasonal drought. It is a handsome plant, upright while young, becoming vase-shaped as it matures, with glossy bright-green leaves 1/2 in. wide and 2 in. long. Large orange-red flowers appear in the heat of summer, followed by edible red fruits that average 4 in. in diameter and ripen late in the growing season.

WHEN TO PLANT

Plants root out faster in warm soil, so it is best to transplant during the growing season. At the cold limits of its hardiness, start pomegranate in spring so it will have ample rooting time before the return of cold weather.

WHERE TO PLANT

Choose the warmest niche in good garden soil for pomegranate, especially if you want to harvest fruit. It makes a beautiful small patio tree in courtyards where it can soak up reflected heat from walls and paving. The jewellike color of its flowers and fruit contrasts beautifully with lavender, Russian sage, pitcher sage, and blue-violet cultivars of Texas sage.

HOW TO PLANT

If pomegranate is grown as an ornamental, any well-drained soil is acceptable, but to encourage fruit production, work a generous amount of compost into the growing area so that the soil stays more evenly moist. Recent research has demonstrated that the best soil preparation for container-grown plants (even for deeply rooting shrubs) is to dig holes only as deep as, or at most a few inches deeper than, the rootball, but several times its diameter. This enables plants to develop the lateral absorbing roots they rely on for initial establishment and long-term productivity. Amending with compost is worthwhile only if the area to be improved is large enough to support much of the plant's absorbing roots. A generous topdressing of compost as mulch will keep the soil more uniformly moist and more moderate in temperature, accelerating root development.

ADVICE FOR CARE

Young pomegranates need shaping in spring to remove twiggy interior branches and to emphasize their fanlike form. In the low desert, they will grow large enough to train as small trees. Water once a week when the temperature is above 90 degrees Fahrenheit, especially when plants are in bloom or forming fruit. If fruit production isn't important, established plants can be sustained by watering so that moisture penetrates to a depth of 2 to 3 ft. every 2 weeks when the temperature is above 70 degrees Fahrenheit, and monthly during cooler weather. A 3- to 4-in. layer of mulch helps suppress weeds until the plants fill in. White fly can become a problem on plants that are stressed by excess fertilizing or by over- or underwatering.

SPECIES, CULTIVARS, OR VARIETIES

'Wonderful' is one of the most popular fruiting varieties. Dwarf pomegranate (*Punica granatum* 'Nana') grows 3 ft. high and 2 ft. wide with small single flowers and tiny, dry red fruits. It is cold hardy to Zone 7. Because of its small size, it is a bit more drought tolerant than the species.

Redtwig Dogwood

Cornus sericea

Height: 2 to 6 ft.	**Light Requirement:**
Flowers: White	
Foliage: Deciduous	
Bloom Period: Spring	
Zones: 3 to 7	
Water: Moderate to ample	

*R*edtwig dogwood is a high-elevation streambank native (not exactly the most promising plant for desert gardens), but it is also vigorous, long-lived, and adaptable enough to find a special niche here. Though its large, dark-green, rough-textured leaves and large flat umbels of tiny white flowers are elegant, this dogwood is grown for its slender stems and smooth, lustrous red bark.

When to Plant

Redtwig dogwood roots fastest when the soil is cool and can be planted any time from autumn through spring, as long as plants have been outdoors and are acclimated to cold.

Where to Plant

To reduce water needs to reasonable amounts in lowland gardens, redtwig should be grown only in the shade, planted in heavier clay soils or in garden soil generously amended with compost. It is a good choice for growing in storm runoff catchments, under cotton-woods, at the edge of ponds, or on the north and east side of walls. At higher elevations, redtwig is a striking foil for the white bark of aspens, and its red stems poking up through the snow brighten the grayest winter day.

How to Plant

Recent research has demonstrated that the best soil preparation for container-grown shrubs is to dig holes only as deep as, or at most a few inches deeper than, the depth of the rootball, but 4 to 6 times its diameter. This allows plants to develop the lateral absorbing roots they rely on most for initial establishment and long-term survival. Backfill soil requires no amendment when plants are grown at higher elevations or in heavy clay valley soils. Compost should be mixed deeply into loose sand to improve its water-holding capacity. A deep mulch of compost, pine straw, or shredded bark will keep the soil more uniformly moist and more moderate in temperature, accelerating root development. Dogwood used in catchment areas should be mulched with coarse gravel because lighter mulches will float off when the swales or basins flood.

ADVICE FOR CARE

It takes redtwig dogwood a few years to establish an extensive root system; during establishment, plants should be watered once a week when the temperature is above 85 degrees Fahrenheit. To sustain established plants, water to a depth of 24 in. every 2 weeks when the temperature is above 70 degrees Fahrenheit, and monthly during cooler weather. An iron-and-sulfur fertilizer applied in spring will help prevent chlorosis in alkaline and calcareous soils. If yellowing and scorched leaf margins persist despite iron treatments, redtwig may need more water or a cooler microclimate.

SPECIES, CULTIVARS, OR VARIETIES

'Isanti' grows 4 ft. high and 6 ft. wide. 'Kelsey Dwarf' grows 2 ft. high and 3 ft. wide. It is cold hardy only to 7000 ft. in Zone 5. 'Flaviramea' is a yellow-stemmed variety that grows 6 ft. high and 8 ft. wide.

REGIONAL CONSIDERATIONS

No amount of water can compensate for the prolonged summer heat at lower elevations. In Zone 8, even planting in shade can't keep dogwood cool enough.

Rosemary

Rosmarinus officinalis

Height: 1 to 4 ft.	**Light Requirement:**
Flowers: Blue	
Foliage: Evergreen	
Bloom Period: Early spring and autumn	
Zones: 6 to 8	
Water: Low	

osemary is a culinary herb grown for its aromatic, dark, evergreen, needlelike foliage, but it has garden appeal well beyond the kitchen. As the plant matures, its compact mounded form becomes more irregular, branches spreading as wide as the plant is tall. Rosemary's rugged form evokes the rocky slopes above the Mediterranean where it grows wild. While it is well adapted to New Mexico's heat and drought, its seaside origins don't prepare rosemary for our extreme shifts in temperature from day to night and from season to season. Rosemary begins active growth in response to the least hint of warming in spring, and its growth does not slow in response to lengthening nights and cold in autumn like high-desert natives do. It blooms in February and early March, and again in October, blue flowers cloaking the ends of the stems and attracting bees with their nectar.

WHEN TO PLANT

Plants root out faster in warm soil; it is best to transplant in spring so that rosemary will have ample rooting time before the return of cold weather. Cuttings of woody new growth root easily in summer.

WHERE TO PLANT

Rosemary prefers well-drained, infertile, alkaline soil. It tolerates some shade but is densest and most vigorous in full sun. To buffer the extreme temperature shifts, plant rosemary in courtyards where reflected heat and wind protection create a more temperate microclimate, and where its wonderful scent can be appreciated. It blends nicely with silverleafed salvias and artemisias, Greek germander, iceplants, catmint, and 'Bowles Mauve' wallflower. Rosemary provides an evergreen backdrop for any number of xeric perennials.

How to Plant

Dig holes only as deep as the rootball, but 4 to 6 times its diameter, so that plants can root out extensively. Backfill soil requires no amendment, but a generous topdressing of composted cotton burrs, shredded bark, pecan hulls, or fine gravel as mulch will keep the soil more uniformly moist and more moderate in temperature, accelerating root development; it will also help suppress weeds.

Advice for Care

Rosemary needs no fertilizer. Water every 2 weeks to a depth of 2 to 3 ft. when the temperature is above 80 degrees Fahrenheit; water monthly the rest of the year. Give plants a deep soaking in late summer, then withhold water until after a few hard freezes to limit new growth late in the season. Snipping stems for cooking and grilling keeps plants more compact. No pruning is needed if you want a windswept, irregular form. Removing 1/3 of the oldest stems or cutting 1/3 of the length of branches back to side shoots every 2 or 3 years in late spring will keep plants more mounded and controlled looking.

Species, Cultivars, or Varieties

'Arp' is the most reliably cold-hardy cultivar, usually surviving winters in Zone 5 with little dieback. 'Prostrata' is the low-spreading form often described as a groundcover, though even in warm microclimates it is not consistent enough to cover large spaces. Its leaves are smaller and smoother, and densely cover branches that arch and spread 1 ft. high and 3 ft. wide. Prostrate rosemary looks beautiful creeping between boulders or spilling over the edge of a planter or retaining wall.

Rose-of-Sharon

Hibiscus syriacus

Height: 15 ft.
Flowers: Shades of pink, purple, or white
Foliage: Deciduous
Bloom Period: Midsummer
Zones: 5 to 8
Water: Moderate to ample

Light Requirement:

ose-of-Sharon is an old garden favorite, enduring centuries of changing horticultural styles. Its stiff upright form is quite narrow when plants are young, broadening to a vase shape 2/3 the width of its height. The leaves are medium green and coarsely lobed. The 3-in.-wide funnel-shaped flowers are what have kept this plant in demand, especially since they appear in the doldrums of midsummer when few shrubs bloom profusely. Because it has been under cultivation for so long, rose-of-Sharon has produced hundreds of cultivars whose flowers are single or double in a range of pinks, purples, and bicolor blends, as well as white. Gardeners who find the large seedpods unattractive can plant the newer, sterile hybrids. The single flowers seem to hold up better in our intense sunlight and low humidity than the doubles do.

WHEN TO PLANT

Rose-of-Sharon can be transplanted from containers any time, but since water consumption peaks when plants are in bloom, it is better to forego planting in the heat of summer, especially in low-desert gardens in the southern half of the state. At the high-elevation and northern limits of their cold hardiness, it is better to set plants out before midsummer so that they will have plenty of time to root before the onset of cold weather.

WHERE TO PLANT

Rose-of-Sharon will tolerate a half-day of shade, but full sun produces the best flowering. It grows well in any soil but should not be kept constantly wet in clay. Substantial enough to be used as a single accent plant, its profile is so uniform that it is also planted as an unsheared formal hedge.

How to Plant

Dig holes only as deep as the rootball, but 4 to 6 times as wide, so that plants will develop the lateral absorbing roots they rely on for initial establishment and long-term survival. Backfill soil requires no amendment, but 3 to 4 in. of composted cotton burrs or shredded bark as mulch will keep the soil cooler and more uniformly moist, and it will also help suppress weeds.

Advice for Care

Rose-of-Sharon is an adaptable plant, but an extensive root system takes a few years to establish. During establishment, plants should be watered once a week when the temperature is above 85 degrees Fahrenheit. To sustain established plants, water every 2 weeks when the temperature is above 70 degrees Fahrenheit, and monthly during cooler weather. Apply a balanced fertilizer each spring until plants are well rooted. A granular iron-and-sulfur fertilizer will reverse summer chlorosis in strongly alkaline soils. As the canopy begins to fan out, the shade of the upper leaves limits light to the lower branches, causing the foliage to thin out at that level. Thinning the plant by removing 1/4 of the oldest branches in early spring will allow more light to filter through, or you may remove the smallest lower branches to create a tree form.

Species, Cultivars, or Varieties

Single varieties include × 'Aphrodite', which produces dark-pink flowers with red throats and no seedheads; 'Blue Bird', with violet flowers; 'Red Heart', whose flowers are white with a scarlet center; 'Woodbridge', which has rose-pink flowers with red centers; and × 'Diana', with all-white flowers and no seedheads. Double-flowered varieties include 'Collie Mullens' and 'Arden', both violet purples; 'Jeanne d'Arc', white; and 'Lucy', wine red.

Salvia

Salvia species

Height: 2 ft. **Flowers:** Pink, purple, blue, or red **Foliage:** Mostly evergreen **Bloom Period:** Spring, some all growing season **Zones:** Varies **Water:** Moderate to low	**Light Requirement:**

*L*ike people, plants don't easily fit in the neat categories we'd like to assign them. Though these salvia are not large shrubs, they are different from the herbaceous types in that they have a woody crown similar to those of lavender, santolina, and curry plant. They all produce colorful floral displays that attract hummingbirds, and most have attractive evergreen foliage as well.

WHEN TO PLANT
In the low desert, salvias can be planted any time, as long as water is available in summer, and plants have been acclimated to the cold in winter. At the northern and high-elevation limits of their cold hardiness range, it is best to start plants in spring to provide ample rooting time before the return of cold weather.

WHERE TO PLANT
Salvias grow in any well-drained infertile soil. The evergreen forms are used in xeric borders for winter interest among herbaceous plants. They can be grouped along paths, dry streambeds, and patios, or clustered in the light shade of desert willow, acacia, or mesquite.

HOW TO PLANT
If several small plants will be spaced 2 to 3 ft. apart, till 3 to 4 in. of compost into the entire area to be planted and set plants out in the amended soil. When planting single individual plants, the backfill soil requires no amendment, but a generous mulch will keep the soil more uniformly moist and help suppress weeds.

ADVICE FOR CARE

To stimulate new growth, the faster-growing salvias such as cherry sage and garden sage may be cut back 8 to 12 in. above ground each spring just as they begin releafing. The smaller, slower-growing types may need rejuvenating only every 3 to 5 years. Applying a mild dose of a granular fertilizer or a 4-month time-release formula in spring keeps long-blooming plants vigorous. Water to a depth of 2 ft. every 2 weeks when temperatures are above 80 degrees Fahrenheit; water monthly the rest of the year.

SPECIES, CULTIVARS, OR VARIETIES

Cherry sage (*S. greggii*) grows 2 ft. high and 2 to 3 ft. wide with spikes of rose-pink, red, purple, coral, or white flowers. Also called autumn sage, it flowers heavily in spring, lightly all summer, and heavily again in fall. In Zone 6 it may die back to the ground entirely some winters, but it may remain mostly evergreen in Zone 8. Chihuahuan sage (*S. chamaedryoides*) grows 18 in. high and 24 in. wide and has small, silver, evergreen leaves on limber stems. It produces gentian-blue flowers in flushes through the growing season. It is cold hardy in Zones 6 through 8 and is touchy about overwatering, especially during extremes of heat and cold. Chihuahuan sage mixes nicely with pineleaf penstemon, desert penstemon, and Greek germander. Desert sage (*S. dorrii*) forms a cushion 1 to 2 ft. high and 2 to 3 ft. wide. Its stiff stems are covered with small, silver, evergreen leaves. Tiny blue flowers in pom-pom clusters appear in late spring, persisting for 2 to 3 weeks. It is native to the Mojave desert but is cold hardy in Zones 5 through 8. Garden sage (*S. officinalis*), the culinary herb with stiff stems 2 ft. high and 3 ft. wide, has aromatic evergray leaves in Zones 5 through 8. It is deciduous but cold hardy in Zone 4. It produces showy blue-purple flower spikes in spring. Maintain a neat appearance by removing the seedheads when they start to look weathered. *S. officinalis* 'Purpurascens' is similar to garden sage except that its leaves are suffused with a purple blush that intensifies in sunlight and cooler temperatures. It is evergreen and hardy in Zones 5 to 8. Lavender sage (*S. lavandulifolia*) is also similar to garden sage, but its leaves are smooth, pale silver, and lavender scented; its small purple flowers are borne on slender leafless stems well above the mound of foliage. Lavender sage is cold hardy in Zones 5 to 8.

Santolina

Santolina species

Height: 2 ft.	Light Requirement:
Flowers: Yellow	
Foliage: Evergreen	
Bloom Period: June	
Zones: 5 to 8	
Water: Low	

*S*antolina, a native of the Middle East and drier Mediterranean areas, is quite at home in the cold desert of New Mexico. The soft, finely divided leaves on stiff stems grow into a dense mound 1 to 2 ft. high and 2 to 3 ft. wide. Yellow, button-shaped, 3/4-in. flowers appear in June on short wiry stems a few inches above the mound of foliage. The leaves have a pleasant aroma but the scent of the flowers, especially as they mature, is unpleasant to most people. Since santolina is grown primarily for its form and foliage, the blooms can be sheared off if they prove offensive.

WHEN TO PLANT

Plants root out faster in warm soil, so it is best to transplant during the growing season. In the low desert, santolina can be planted any time, as long as water is available in summer, and plants have been acclimated to the cold in winter. At the northern and high-elevation limits of their cold hardiness range, it is best to start plants in spring so they will have ample rooting time before the return of cold weather.

WHERE TO PLANT

Santolina requires well-drained infertile soil. It is used as a filler and as a colorfoil for pineleaf, Rocky Mountain penstemon, desert penstemon, gaillardia, valerian, and salvias in xeric perennial beds and borders. Its well-defined cushion shape makes an interesting counterpoint to the fountain forms of ornamental grasses.

HOW TO PLANT

Santolina may be grown by layering: Pin the lower stems to the loosened soil around established plants until the stems root. Then sever the layers from the original plant and transplant them to a new location. Dig holes only as deep as the rootball but several times its diameter so that transplants can develop the lateral absorbing roots they rely on for initial establishment and long-term survival. Backfill soil requires no amendment, but a generous mulch of fine stone, shredded bark, or pecan hulls will moderate soil temperatures and help suppress weeds.

ADVICE FOR CARE

In early spring, trim santolina back 12 in. from the ground so that soft new growth can replace the winter-weathered stems. Tidy up plants in summer by trimming the flower stems down into the foliage. Water every 2 weeks when temperatures are above 90 degrees Fahrenheit; water monthly the rest of the year. Water should penetrate to a depth of 24 in. Excess water in winter, particularly in heavy soil, can kill santolina even after it is well established.

SPECIES, CULTIVARS, OR VARIETIES

Gray santolina (*S. chamaecyparissus*, sometimes labeled *S. incana*) is the most heat tolerant, drought tolerant, and robust of the three species. Its foliage is pale silver; flowers are bright yellow. Green santolina (*S. rosmarinifolia* ssp. *rosmarinifolia*, sometimes labeled *S. virens*) has bright-green foliage and pale-yellow flowers. It seems the least vigorous of the three, and in the southern low deserts this species does best in afternoon shade. Rosemaryleaf santolina (*S. rosmarinifolia*) is slower growing and more irregular in form. Its foliage is dark gray and flowers are pale yellow.

Shadscale

Atriplex confertifolia

Height: 18 in. **Flowers:** Inconspicuous **Foliage:** Evergreen **Bloom Period:** Summer **Zones:** 5 to 8 **Water:** Low	**Light Requirement:**

*S*hadscale looks so civilized, yet it is native to the worst soils and most extreme hot, cold, dry, and windy places in all of New Mexico. Adapting to the harshness of its natural surroundings has given it a compact shape, resilient woody stems, and thumbnail-sized blue-silver reflective leaves, characteristics that make it an attractive garden plant. The leaves are clustered on the stems and blush subtle shades of pink and purple in winter, giving plants an opalescent sheen. The flowers are small and wind-pollinated, followed by clusters of winged 1/2-in. seeds that attract birds, especially quail. The plant grows about twice as wide as it is tall, forming a neat mounded cushion with unexpectedly sharp barbs at the ends of each stem.

WHEN TO PLANT

Shadscale transplants from containers any time of year, but young seedlings should be dug up and moved in spring or early fall when the soil is warm but temperatures are more moderate.

WHERE TO PLANT

Shadscale grows in a range of gravelly, sandy, silty, salty, and infertile soils without any problems, though it should be kept drier in heavy clay. It is used along dry streambeds and in dry rock gardens with rosemary, and Greek germander in more controlled circumstances, or with turpentine bush, cacti, and desert zinnia in wilder, more exposed settings. For winter interest, it can be mixed into xeric perennial borders with gayfeather, penstemon, bubblegum mint, Jerusalem sage, and torch lily.

HOW TO PLANT

The best soil preparation for transplanting container-grown shrubs is to dig holes only as deep as, or at most a few inches deeper than, the depth of the rootball, but 4 times its diameter. Even xeric plants rely on lateral absorbing roots for initial establishment and long-term survival. Backfill soil requires no amendment, but a generous mulch of fine gravel will conserve soil moisture and suppress weeds.

ADVICE FOR CARE

Shadscale requires little pruning except to trim off bare seed stems. No fertilizer is needed; the soft growth induced by added nitrogen makes shadscale more attractive to scale insects. Once established, plants should be watered to a depth of at least 24 in. once or twice a month during the growing season, and once a month or less in winter.

SPECIES, CULTIVARS, OR VARIETIES

Four wing saltbush (*Atriplex canescens*) is an excellent habitat and revegetation plant growing 5 ft. high and 6 ft. wide with small sage-green leaves. The large winged seeds, semievergreen leaves, and stems are relished by just about any creature living in proximity. The problem with using saltbush as a garden plant is that it is aggressive enough to take this kind of pressure in stride. In more cultivated settings, it runs amok, swallowing less tenacious plants in a gulp; and its copious wind-borne pollen is a potent aero-allergin. *Atriplex obovata* is a more-refined plant similar to shadscale, but it is a native of southern New Mexico.

Silverberry

Elaeagnus pungens

Height: 8 ft.	**Light Requirement:**
Flowers: Inconspicuous	
Foliage: Evergreen	
Bloom Period: Spring and fall	
Zones: 5 to 8	
Water: Moderate	

Silverberry is a very easy, versatile, large, broadleafed ever-green. Unwary gardeners plant it in spaces far too small for its mature spread of 10 ft., dooming it to a life of repeated butchery. This is especially sad because silverberry recovers quickly from heavy pruning by replacing what was cut off with whiplike shoots that have long internodes and sparse foliage. When left to develop its natural character, silverberry grows layers of graceful arching branches. The new leaves and stems are covered with bronze hairs. The 3-in.-long, 1-in.-wide mature leaves are pale olive-green flecked with fine silver scales, creating a dance of shadows and light that gives the plant a soft vibrancy. Small bell-shaped flowers droop from the stems and are hidden by the leaves; they are wonderfully fragrant.

WHEN TO PLANT

Container-grown plants may be set out any time from spring through early autumn. Because freezing, dry winds can scorch the large evergreen leaves, it's best to forego planting during winter in Zones 5 and 6.

WHERE TO PLANT

Silverberry prefers well-drained soil, but only very impermeable clay poses any real problem. It is used as a screen, hedge, and wind buffer, and is one of the most effective noise barriers because its large leaf surfaces deflect sound as well as light and wind. Silverberry provides contrast to dark-green conifers such as Austrian pine and pinyon, and it blends well with fernbush, rugosa roses, southernwood, maiden grass, and sand lovegrass.

How to Plant

Dig holes only as deep as the rootball, but 4 to 6 times its diameter, so that plants develop the lateral absorbing roots they rely on for initial establishment and long-term survival. Backfill soil requires no amendment, but a generous mulch of composted cotton burrs, shredded bark, pecan hulls, or gravel will keep the soil more uniformly moist and will help suppress weeds until the silverberry fills out.

Advice for Care

The less silverberry is pruned, the better. To increase the density of young plants, cut the longest stems back to side shoots in spring to force lateral branching. If there is enough space, severely shorn plants can be returned to a more natural state by cutting the wild whip-like growth back by half just above a leaf node. After a few years of forcing lateral branching, the unruly growth should taper off and plants will assume looser, softer contours. There is no need to fertilize unless young plants show signs of yellowing in summer. Heat chlorosis can be reversed by applying a granular iron-and-sulfur fertilizer. It takes a few years to establish an extensive root system; during establishment, plants should be watered once a week when the temperature is above 85 degrees Fahrenheit. To sustain established plants, water every 2 weeks when the temperature is above 70 degrees Fahrenheit, and monthly during cooler weather.

Species, Cultivars, or Varieties

Elaeagnus ebbingei is very similar to *E. pungens* but is more upright, growing 10 ft. high and 12 ft. wide. Russian olive (*Elaeagnus angustifolius*) was introduced in the Southwest for erosion control and has been widely planted for windbreaks. Both ideas have proven to be ill-conceived. Russian olive escaped cultivation along streams and has displaced native vegetation, degrading habitat in some areas. It is weak-wooded and short-lived and the branches crack and split in the wind, leaving wounded trees open to bacterial infection. The contrast of silver foliage and dark, shredding bark when plants are pruned as small shade trees is attractive, but Russian olive sheds flowers, fruit, leaves, and small twigs. It is weedy and messy in gardens.

Spanish Broom

Spartium junceum

Height: 8 ft. **Flowers:** Yellow **Foliage:** Deciduous **Bloom Period:** Spring **Zones:** 6 to 8 **Water:** Low to moderate	**Light Requirement:**

The bright evergreen color of Spanish broom comes from its slender stems rather than from the seasonal appearance of its small leaves. In late spring, the ends of each stem are covered with large, yellow, pea-shaped flowers, and their sweet honey fragrance drifts through neighborhoods on every breeze. Spanish broom is fast growing and produces a fountain of upright stems that spreads nearly as wide as it is tall.

WHEN TO PLANT

Plants root out faster in warm soil, so it is best to transplant during the growing season. In the low desert, Spanish broom can be planted any time, as long as water is available in summer, and plants have been acclimated to the cold in winter. At the northern and high-elevation limits of their cold hardiness range, it is best to start plants in spring so that they have ample rooting time before the return of cold weather.

WHERE TO PLANT

Spanish broom prefers well-drained soil and can die back severely in winter if kept too wet in heavy clay. It grows densely enough to be used as a screen and can be planted in xeric shrub borders mixed with chamisa and bird-of-paradise, or Arizona rosewood and Texas sage for contrast. Spanish broom makes an interesting backdrop for Russian sage, Jerusalem sage, red yucca, and torch lily.

HOW TO PLANT

When transplanting volunteer seedlings or container-grown plants, dig holes only as deep as the rootball but 4 to 6 times as wide, loosening the soil so that new roots will have an easy time breaking ground. Backfill soil requires no amendment, but a generous topdressing of mulch will keep the soil more uniformly moist and more moderate in temperature.

ADVICE FOR CARE

Spanish broom looks best if it is placed where it can reach its mature proportions without shrink-to-fit pruning. As plants mature, the new growth begins to shade the older stems, and they turn brown and dry. Removing ¼ of the oldest brown stems back to live wood or all the way back to the ground after they bloom keeps plants young and vigorous. Protect new plants from rabbits until they have rooted well and are woody enough to be less inviting. If you garden in deer country, plants will need protection for the first several years. Aphids can be persistent pests on new growth. They seldom do any real damage, usually disappearing by early summer; wash them off periodically to control infestations. In south-ern New Mexico, various caterpillars infest plants, quickly stripping the stems of all green tissue. *Bacillus thuringiensis* is an effective control. Water established plants once a month so that moisture penetrates the soil to a depth of 2 to 3 ft. Fertilizing is unnecessary and only produces more soft growth beloved by aphids.

SPECIES, CULTIVARS, OR VARIETIES

Genista hispanica, also called Spanish broom, is very similar to *Spartium* but grows only about half as tall. Dyer's woad (*Genista tinctoria* and *G. multibractea*) has very slender, limber stems that grow 4 ft. high and slightly wider. Small yellow flowers are clus-tered at the tips of the stems. 'Royal Gold' is a dwarf variety 2 ft. high and 3 ft. wide. All three types are hardy from Zone 4 to 7.

Sumac

Rhus species

Height: 5 to 8 ft.	Light Requirement:
Flowers: Inconspicuous	
Foliage: Evergreen and deciduous	
Bloom Period: Spring	
Zones: Varies	
Water: Low to moderate	

*S*umacs are among the plants gardeners can rely on as the bones of the garden. They are attractive in form and foliage, long-lived, and easy to grow. Compound leaves of dark-green leaflets and clusters of tiny white or greenish-yellow flowers in spring are followed by sticky red-orange fruits like peppercorns. None of these sumacs are poisonous; in fact, the fruits of some have been used to make a tart drink high in vitamin C, and all species provide valuable food for wildlife.

WHEN TO PLANT

Container-grown deciduous sumacs may be set out any time, and seedlings may be transplanted in spring or early autumn. Plants establish roots more quickly when the soil is cool, but freezing, dry winds can scorch the types that have evergreen leaves, so it's best to forego planting them in winter.

WHERE TO PLANT

Sumacs are adapted to a wide range of soils. The dark leaf color offers a striking contrast to blue-gray conifers, artemisias, Texas sage, Jerusalem sage, silverberry, and buddleias. Sumacs spread a few feet wider than their height, and even the root-sprouting staghorn types look controlled, though they tend to wander into moist areas in the garden. The more self-contained species can be used as informal hedges or screens, as fillers in evergreen or flower-ing shrub borders, and in habitat gardens. The thicket-forming staghorns are great slope stabilizers and make a handsome under-story with conifers, but they can be a pest in more cultivated areas.

How to Plant

Dig generous holes, loosening the soil so that new roots can break ground easily. Backfill soil requires no amendment, but a generous mulch of compost, shredded bark, pecan hulls, or gravel will keep the soil more uniformly moist and more moderate in temperature.

Advice for Care

When plants are spaced to accommodate their mature size, little pruning is needed. A modest dose of a granular fertilizer may be applied to quicken growth in spring while plants are getting established, but once sumacs are well established and fill the allotted space, they are best left to their own resources. Water to a depth of 3 ft. once a month year round to maintain established plants. At lower elevations, the staghorn species may need water every 2 weeks when the temperature is above 85 degrees Fahrenheit.

Species, Cultivars, or Varieties

Evergreen sumac (*Rhus virens*) is native to the southern foothills of New Mexico at 3500 to 7000 ft. It is hardy in Zones 7 and 8 and grows 8 ft. high and 10 ft. wide with glossy 1 1/2-in. oval leaflets. Littleleaf sumac (*R. microphylla*) is the most drought and heat tolerant of the sumacs. It is deciduous with stiff, arching branches to 6 ft. high and 8 ft. wide. The 1-in. compound leaves and tiny individual leaflets give the plant a refined appearance. The showy clusters of red-orange fruit appear in July and August. Leaves turn deep burgundy-red in autumn, and the fine tracery of stems takes on a smoky plum cast in winter. Littleleaf sumac is hardy in Zones 5 to 8. Littleleaf and evergreen sumacs do best in the warmer low-desert and southern foothills. Smooth sumac (*R. glabra*) grows 6 to 8 ft. high and spreads indefinitely. Rocky Mountain cutleaf sumac (*R. glabra* var. *cistmontana*) is the smallest representative of the staghorn sumacs, which produce dense compressed spikes of small red fruits at the ends of stout leafless stems. The fruits persist into winter. All the staghorn sumacs rootsprout, forming thickets, and are best adapted in cooler northern and high-elevation gardens. They have brilliant red or orange fall color. Cutleaf sumac grows only 3 1/2 ft. high with a spread of at least 6 ft. Prairie flameleaf sumac (*R. lanceolata*) is a species of staghorn sumac whose size is between that of cutleaf and smooth sumac. Staghorn sumacs are cold hardy in Zones 4 to 8.

Texas Mountain Laurel

Sophora secundiflora

Height: 5 to 15 ft.
Flowers: Purple
Foliage: Evergreen
Bloom Period: Spring
Zones: 7 and 8
Water: Low to moderate

Light Requirement:

*T*exas mountain laurel doesn't look like a desert plant, especially in spring when its branches are decorated with pendulous clusters of flowers scented like grape drink. Yet it grows in the foothills of the Guadalupe Mountains in southeastern New Mexico, flourishing on the boulder-strewn slopes along the drive into Carlsbad Caverns National Park. It could be considered a small tree, but in New Mexico the extremes of heat, cold, drought, and wind keep the plants smaller than they would be under milder and moister conditions. Nestled against a warm garden wall in irrigated gardens, mountain laurel may grow 10 ft. tall and wide; in open areas it may grow only to 5 ft. high. Its crisp, shiny, dark-green, compound leaves are another anomaly, looking cool and lush in the baking sun. The flowers are followed by plump 3-in. seedpods containing hard, round, red, poisonous seeds that are still used for making rosaries and necklaces in Mexico.

WHEN TO PLANT

Plants root out faster in warm soil, so it is best to transplant early in the growing season. This will allow ample rooting time before the return of cold weather.

WHERE TO PLANT

Mountain laurel prefers well-drained soil but will adapt to most soils as long as it is not kept too wet. Reflected heat from walls and paving can provide the ideal warm, protected niche where mountain laurel thrives. It is dense and leafy enough to be effective as screening. Shadscale, cherry sage, Big Bend silverleaf, bubblegum mint, and Jerusalem sage are all good companions. The poisonous marble-sized red seeds are attractive, and though they are enclosed in a thick pod that makes them fairly difficult for children to reach, it is best to avoid planting mountain laurel near play areas.

How to Plant

Mountain laurel is grown from seed. The hard seedcoat of the
1/2-in. seeds can be nicked with a file to allow air and moisture to
penetrate to the embryo. A deep initial taproot needs loosened soil
or a deep container to develop properly. Recent research has demonstrated that the best soil preparation for container-grown plants is to
dig holes only as deep as, or at most a few inches deeper than, the
depth of the rootball, but 4 to 6 times its diameter. Once the deep
initial root of mountain laurel is disturbed by potting or transplanting, even these taprooted plants develop the lateral absorbing roots
that they rely on for long-term survival. Backfill soil requires no
amendment, but a generous topdressing of compost, shredded
bark, pecan hulls, or gravel as mulch will accelerate root development because it keeps the soil more uniformly moist and more
moderate in temperature.

Advice for Care

Mountain laurel requires very little pruning. Blooms are produced
on the previous year's growth, so thinning to enhance the naturally
handsome form is best done in early summer. Water to a depth of
2 ft. at least twice monthly when the temperature is above 85
degrees Fahrenheit. This will enhance growth and flowering and
will also maintain leaf density. When growing mountain laurel at
the northern and high-elevation limits of its cold-hardiness range,
it is particularly important that you reduce watering in late summer
and fall so that tender new growth will have time to harden before
frost. Mature established plants perform well if watered deeply
once a month.

Species, Cultivars, or Varieties

Guadalupe mountain laurel (*Sophora gypsophila*) is a small, densely
branched shrub that grows to 4 ft. tall. It produces fuzzy silver
leaves and small purple flowers. It is found only on gypsum soils
and is slow growing and difficult to propagate, so it is rarely seen in
gardens, though it would be a lovely addition.

Texas Sage

Leucophyllum species and cultivars

Height: 2 to 6 ft.	**Light Requirement:**
Flowers: A range of pinks and purples	
Foliage: Evergreen	
Bloom Period: Summer	
Zones: 7 and 8	
Water: Moderate to low	

eucophyllum are native to the Chihuahuan desert in southwest Texas, southern New Mexico, and northern Mexico, but the common name, Texas sage, is well deserved since a long-term breeding program at Texas A & M University has produced many of the trademarked cultivars. All Texas sages have small silver or green leaves clustered along the slender stems with bell-shaped blooms in summer. The plant's pioneer name, "barometer bush," refers to its tendency to flower heavily after summer downpours.

WHEN TO PLANT

Plants root out faster in warm soil, so it is best to transplant during the growing season. In the low desert, Texas sage can be planted any time, as long as water is available in summer and plants have been acclimated to the cold in winter. At the northern and high-elevation limits of its cold-hardiness range, it is best to start plants in spring so they will have ample rooting time before the return of cold weather.

WHERE TO PLANT

Texas sage grows in any soil that has reasonable drainage. It is planted as informal hedges, and is clustered with red yucca, cherry sage, rosemary, Mexican buckeye, bubblegum mint, Mexican tarragon, and muhly grass in xeric borders for patios, paths, and entryways. A backdrop of pines or other darkleafed conifers provides contrast for the silverleafed varieties.

HOW TO PLANT

Texas sage is commercially grown from cuttings. Propagation of the trademarked cultivars is licensed to Texas A & M; royalties are used to fund the university's horticultural research. Dig generous holes so that plants can root out easily. Backfill soil requires no amendment, but a generous topdressing of composted cotton burrs, pecan hulls, shredded bark, or gravel as mulch will keep the soil cooler and more uniformly moist and will also help suppress weeds.

ADVICE FOR CARE

If you want to shear Texas sage, commit the crime in early spring before flower buds form. To rejuvenate mature plants, thin out $1/3$ of the oldest stems every 3 to 5 years in early spring. Fertilizer is usually not needed; excess nitrogen can limit flowering. It takes a few years for Texas sage to root out extensively; during establishment, plants should be watered weekly when temperatures are above 85 degrees Fahrenheit. Watering established plants deeply every 2 weeks during the growing season and monthly in winter will keep them leafy and can sometimes trigger blooming.

SPECIES, CULTIVARS, OR VARIETIES

Big Bend silverleaf (*L. minus* 'Big Bend') grows 3 ft. high and wide with silver leaves and pale-violet flowers. It is the only *Leucophyllum* native to New Mexico. Chihuahuan sage (*L. laevigatum*) grows 4 to 5 ft. tall and 3 to 4 ft. wide and has small green leaves clustered closely along the stems. Flowers are lavender blue. 'Cimmaron' sage (*L. zygophyllum* 'Cimmaron') grows 2 to 3 ft. high and 3 ft. wide with small green leaves and violet-blue flowers. 'Green Cloud' sage, a cultivar of *L. frutescens*, grows 6 ft. tall and wide with silver leaves and pink flowers. 'Rio Bravo' sage (*L. langmaniae* 'Rio Bravo') grows 4 to 5 ft. tall and wide with small green leaves and blue flowers that are more open than those of other cultivars. Violet silverleaf (*L. candidum* 'Silver Cloud') grows 3 ft. tall and 4 ft. wide with silver-white leaves and dark-purple flowers; 'Thundercloud' is similar but has deep-violet flowers. These two cultivars bloom most heavily in autumn. *L. candidum*, *L. laevigatum*, and *L. frutescens* may be slightly less cold tolerant than the others.

Turpentine Bush

Ericameria laricifolia

Height: 2 ft.
Flowers: Yellow
Foliage: Evergreen
Bloom Period: Fall
Zones: 6 to 8
Water: Low

Light Requirement:

---

*T*urpentine bush gets its common name from the scent of its resinous green foliage. But our sense of smell is very individualized—how else can you explain anyone eating limburger cheese? I think the common names of turpentine bush and another Chihuahuan desert native, creosote bush, miss the mark by a wide margin. Both plants' fragrances are pungent but subtle and pleasantly fresh. The best description of creosotebush is given by Arizona ecologist and author Gary Nabhan: "The desert smells like rain." To me, turpentine bush smells faintly of pine. It is a compact cushion of a plant, with soft needlelike leaves that densely cover the wiry stems. In October, clusters of small yellow daisies bloom at the tips of the branches. The chaffy seeds disperse on the wind, leaving starlike, straw-colored dried flowers for winter interest.

WHEN TO PLANT

Plants root out faster in warm soil, so it is best to transplant during the growing season. In the low desert, turpentine bush can be planted any time as long as water is available in summer, and plants have been acclimated to the cold in winter. At the northern and high-elevation limits of its cold-hardiness range, it is best to start plants in spring so they will have ample rooting time before the return of cold weather.

WHERE TO PLANT

Turpentine bush grows along arroyos in the foothills where the soil is rocky and where gully-washer rainstorms provide several deep soakings every summer. In the garden, it may be clustered along dry streambeds that channel storm drainage from canales and gutters. It makes a fine informal hedge along paths and blends nicely in xeric borders with Texas sages, beargrass, creeping indigo, the shrubby salvias, and artemisias. It is manicured enough to use near pools and in small patio gardens yet tough enough to thrive in wilder settings with equal grace.

HOW TO PLANT

To transplant volunteer seedlings, loosen the soil so that new roots will have an easy time breaking ground. The best soil preparation for container-grown shrubs (even deeply rooting desert plants) is to dig holes only as deep as, or at most a few inches deeper than, the rootball, but several times its diameter. This enables transplants to develop the lateral absorbing roots they rely on most for establishment and long-term survival. Backfill soil requires no amendment, but a generous topdressing of gravel, shredded bark, or pecan hulls as mulch will keep the soil more uniformly moist and more moderate in temperature, accelerating root development. In runoff catchments, use coarse gravel as a mulch since lighter materials will float away.

ADVICE FOR CARE

In early spring, trim turpentine bush down close to the ground so that soft new growth replaces the winter-weathered stems; or thin out the oldest stems, leaving a naturally shaped mound of the greenest growth. Trim off the remains of the dried seedheads any time they start looking weathered in winter. Water twice a month when temperatures are above 90 degrees Fahrenheit; water monthly the rest of the year. Water should penetrate to a depth of at least 24 in. No fertilizer is needed.

SPECIES, CULTIVARS, OR VARIETIES

There are no other species in cultivation.

Viburnum

Viburnum species

Height: 4 to 6 ft.
Flowers: White
Foliage: Deciduous or semievergreen
Bloom Period: Spring
Zones: 4 to 7
Water: Moderate to ample

Light Requirement:

Viburnums are generally adapted to cooler, more temperate places than the deserts of New Mexico, but their fragrant flowers, handsome foliage, and showy fruit make them plants worth a bit of extra nurturing. To use them in this arid climate, you must provide a cooler, shaded niche and consistent watering. Gardens in the central and northern parts of the state, as well as garden at elevations above 6500 ft. in the south, often have wind-protected microclimates where the more compact forms of viburnum can be grown with a reasonable amount of water.

WHEN TO PLANT
Plant viburnum from fall through spring in warmer parts of the state; plant from spring through fall in the colder parts of the state.

WHERE TO PLANT
Viburnum grow best in good garden soil. Their controlled growth and seasonal interest earns them positions near patios and entry-ways. They benefit from the extra moisture when planted in shaded runoff catchments. The fragrance of burkwood is strong but not cloying, so place it near doors and windows where its scent can drift in on the breeze. Burkwood viburnum is a good companion for rugosa roses. Austrian or southwestern white pine make a good backdrop to shield viburnum from the southwest sun.

HOW TO PLANT
Work several inches of compost into a planting area 6 ft. in diameter. Dig generous holes, loosening the soil so that new roots will have an easy time breaking ground. Mix compost into the backfill, 1/4 by volume; this will help the soil retain moisture. Maintain a 3- to 4-in. layer of compost, shredded bark, pine straw, or pecan hulls as

mulch to suppress weeds and keep the soil cooler and more evenly moist.

ADVICE FOR CARE

Viburnums have a layered, self-contained growth habit that needs little pruning. Since they are relatively slow growing, apply a granular fertilizer each spring until plants begin to fill out. In extremely alkaline soil, use an iron-and-sulfur fertilizer to prevent yellowing. It takes a few years to establish an extensive root system; during establishment, plants should be watered once a week when the temperature is above 85 degrees Fahrenheit. To sustain established plants, water every 2 weeks when the temperature is above 70 degrees Fahrenheit, and monthly during cooler weather. In full sun or sandy soil, viburnums may always need weekly watering in summer.

SPECIES, CULTIVARS, OR VARIETIES

Dwarf cranberrybush (*V. trilobum* 'Compactum') grows 4 ft. high and 5 ft. wide with lacy clusters of small, white flowers in spring, followed by drooping clusters of red pea-sized fruits in late summer and autumn. It is deciduous with deeply lobed, dark-green leaves that turn scarlet in fall. Burkwood viburnum (*V. burkwoodii*) grows 5 ft. tall and nearly as wide with small clusters of very fragrant flowers in late spring. Its small, oblong, crinkled leaves are dark green, turning purple after frost. In sheltered locations, foliage may persist through winter.

REGIONAL CONSIDERATIONS

Even in shade with ample water, Zone 8 in New Mexico is just too hot for these plants.

Yellow Bells

Tecoma stans

Height: 5 to 8 ft. **Flowers:** Yellow **Foliage:** Deciduous **Bloom Period:** Late spring and summer **Zones:** 7 and 8 **Water:** Low	**Light Requirement:**

*Y*ellow bells is native to the southern foothills near Las Cruces. Commercial nurseries have recently begun to grow and distribute it throughout the warm desert areas of the southwest. The limber stems form an upright vase shape 5 or more ft. high. The glossy dark-green leaves are pinnately divided with toothed margins. Bright-yellow flower trumpets first appear in late spring and bloom intermittently throughout summer, drooping at the ends of the branches. Pencil-sized seedpods reminiscent of catalpa and desert willow, kin of yellow bells, follow the flowers at the end of the season.

WHEN TO PLANT

Plants root out faster in warm soil, so it is best to transplant during the growing season. In the low desert, yellow bells can be planted any time as long as water is available in summer, and as long as plants have been acclimated to the cold in winter. At the northern and high-elevation limits of its cold-hardiness range, it is best to start plants in spring so they will have ample rooting time before the return of cold weather.

WHERE TO PLANT

Yellow bells does best in well-drained soil in locations that receive reflected heat. It is deeply rooted and can be nestled up against south- and west-facing courtyard walls, or between boulders along dry streambeds and pathways. Yellow bells blends nicely with Russian sage, catmint, salvias, and Texas sage.

HOW TO PLANT

Yellow bells is grown from seed and cuttings. Fresh seeds germinate best in warm, well-drained soil. Semisoftwood cuttings are taken in late summer. A deep initial taproot needs loosened soil or a deep container in order to develop properly. Recent research has demon-strated that the best soil preparation for container-grown trees and shrubs is to dig holes only as deep as, or at most a few inches deeper than, the depth of the rootball, but 4 to 6 times its diameter. Once the initial root is interrupted by the limited space available to a potgrown plant, even desert natives like yellow bells develop lateral absorbing roots, which they rely on to harvest rainfall and irrigation. Backfill soil requires no amendment, but a generous mulch of shred-ded bark, pecan hulls, or gravel will help conserve soil moisture and suppress weeds.

ADVICE FOR CARE

During severe winters, yellow bells might freeze back to the ground, but it recovers rapidly the following summer. Remove all the deadwood as soon as regrowth begins in late spring. Since they flower on new growth, plants are more colorful if pruned fairly drastically, removing 1/3 of the oldest wood each spring regardless of winter dieback. Water deeply at least twice monthly when the temperature is above 85 degrees Fahrenheit to enhance growth and flowering, and to maintain leaf density. If you are growing yellow bells at the northern and high-elevation limits of its cold-hardiness range, it is particularly important to reduce watering in late summer and fall to prevent plants from producing soft new growth late in the season. Mature established plants perform well if watered deeply once a month.

SPECIES, CULTIVARS, OR VARIETIES

No other species is cold hardy in New Mexico.

Trees

$\mathcal{I}$F ONLY BECAUSE OF THEIR SIZE, trees are the most important plants in the garden. In our intense New Mexican sunlight, the shade of arching tree branches makes being outdoors comfortable most of the year.

Yet most large trees are not at home in the high desert. Large trees tend to be shallowly rooted forest and riverbank plants adapted to climates where rain is plentiful. Forest trees find strength in numbers and are primed for fast, upright growth because they evolved as members of a group competing for light. Planted as single specimens in our high-desert gardens, they bear the brunt of strong winds with no companions to buffer the force, and they are exposed to much more intense sunlight not only from above, but also reflected from walls, paving, and unmulched soil. Recent statewide efforts to conserve water have many New Mexicans rethinking gardens that were planted decades ago, and homeowners are unwittingly damaging trees they value. Silver maples, London plane trees, and green and velvet ash trees planted in bluegrass lawns find the cool grass peeled away and gravel dumped on their shallow roots. Sometimes plastic film is laid over the soil before the gravel is spread, shutting out the oxygen needed to keep roots healthy. These poor trees must wonder how they find themselves in hell without dying first.

You may be building a new home in the mountains or valley bosque where the health of mature native trees is at stake, or reworking a garden where established exotic trees are at risk, or planting new trees in your garden. The most important thing to consider in any of these situations is that a tree's absorbing roots usually extend far beyond the branch canopy. Maintaining the status quo within the absorbing root zone is essential to preserving the health of a tree. Soil compaction caused by repeatedly driving over the soil; changes in the land contours that expose or bury roots; trenching through the root zone to lay new irrigation pipe; not providing enough loosened soil area for new roots to grow into; and significantly altering the amount of water available will all cause trees to decline. Native trees will usually adapt to a bit more water-ing if xeric groundcovers, ornamental grasses, or perennials are added within their root zone, but greatly increasing the quantity or frequency of watering can weaken mature trees. The space within eight or ten feet of the trunk of an established shade tree can be used as a sitting area with benches or a garden swing set on a base of fine-textured mulch or paving stones set in mulch, since the tree absorbs little water in that area. Beneath the dripline of the tree, a sweep of compatible groundcovers several feet wide can be planted, with other plants clustered farther beyond the branch canopy so that water is being distributed to a balanced portion of the tree's extended roots. Mulching the surface with a nonreflective material such as bark or pecan hulls will also ease a mature tree into the new garden.

While you may not be able to reduce water use as much as you would like when retrofitting a landscape where thirsty, exotic trees will be kept, the shade that the tree provides may reduce energy consumption in the house enough to offset its water consumption. If you drip irrigate the supporting cast of new plants instead of using less efficient sprinklers, you may succeed in your conservation goals anyway, because little of the water you apply will be lost to evapo-ration before roots can absorb it. When deciding the fate of trees in your garden, remember that only healthy trees are valuable. As difficult as it is to play judge and executioner, if a mature tree is already showing dieback in the canopy, exhibiting thinning or off-color foliage, or is chronically beset with pest problems, it may be time to remove that tree and plant one that is better adapted. The trees profiled here are by no means the only trees that will grow well in New Mexican gardens, but they are some of the best choices for a range of circumstances. Most are relatively small in stature and leaf size, which contributes to their ability to thrive with less water.

You can suggest the mass of larger trees by grouping small trees in groves. Not only does grove planting share the wind load among trees, but it shades more soil area, reducing glare. Smaller trees are also less likely to create problems with overhead power lines, and their roots are less likely to lift paving and invade sewer lines. Finer leaf texture has advantages: it provides dappled shade suitable for a wide selection of companion plants, and it requires less cleanup in autumn. Even though lawn grasses, including the natives, will grow

Chapter Nine

under many of the trees, it is better to plant trees outside of mowed grass areas. Injuries from string-line trimmers and lawn mowers are common. Fertilizers used on turfgrass can be too high in nitrogen and may be applied at the wrong time of year to benefit trees.

Be sure that temperate-climate trees have enough moisture to support their expanding roots during hot weather; and be sure that the soil around newly planted desert trees is kept dry until the soil is warm enough for roots to begin absorbing moisture. Roots of container-grown trees should not be tightly coiled at the bottom of the container. If you unpot the tree and see circling roots, unwind and cut through several of them to encourage new roots to branch out into the surrounding soil. Trees that are balled and burlapped are often wrapped in heavy wire baskets to hold the soil firmly while trees are being moved. All wire or plastic twine binding the roots or trunk should be removed at planting time because it will not deteriorate in our alkaline soil the way wire does in more acidic soils. Wire and twine will interfere with sap flow, slowly killing the tree over many years' time. Large production nurseries often grow trees quickly and closely spaced; trees are forced with fertilizers and staked so they will stand upright. While this is far from ideal, these trees will survive in our wild, windy climate if handled carefully. Trees naturally develop thicker cells at the base of the trunk and progressively thinner cells up the stems. When trees are rigidly bound, their natural movement in the wind is restricted and the taper doesn't develop. When planting trees that have been staked, especially in open, windy exposures, restake the trees from opposite sides using broad straps that will not cut into the bark. Place the straps low enough on the trunks and leave enough slack in the straps to allow the trees to move in the wind, but keep them secure so they will not whip around or break. After a growing season, the trunks should have thickened enough to remove the stakes and straps.

Our warm winter afternoons hold unexpected peril for young smooth-barked trees. Sunscald, also called "southwest injury," occurs when that side of the trunk heats up, stimulating sap flow during the day. A nighttime plunge to temperatures well below freezing expands the fluids enough to rupture cell walls. The damage doesn't become evident until the following summer when the

Chapter Nine

dead sunken patches of bark stand out against the surrounding healthy tissue. At that point, there is no remedy except to keep the tree as vigorous as possible otherwise and to hope for the best. Sunscald is easy to prevent by wrapping thin-barked trunks with strips of paper or burlap in autumn until they become woody. If you have problems with wildlife browsing your garden as though it were an all-you-can-eat buffet, the wrap will also keep critters from gnawing on the bark and girdling your trees. Tree wrap, like other binding, should be removed promptly so that it does not interfere with sap flow as the trunk increases in girth. Excessive pruning contributes to sunscald. Most trees naturally begin life looking more like high-centered shrubs than the single-trunk forms we most often see in gardens. Avoid removing too much growth too early in a plant's cultivated life. A tree that will be walked under when it is mature should have any branches below 8 ft. cut back to 12 to 18 in. from the trunk. These side branches should not be removed entirely at first, because their leaves will help thicken and shade the trunk. Often the new transplant doesn't have enough side-branching to prune anything away for a year or two. Multi-trunk trees also need a few years to begin developing interesting curves. During the first few years in the garden, remove only the fast-growing suckers that sprout from the base of the trunks and sap strength from young plants. Once a tree has had time to root and begin vigorous growth throughout the canopy, prune lightly to emphasize its natural structure. On single-trunked shade trees, the canopy above head height should have branches radiating out from the trunk every foot or two at least a third of the way around the trunk from the branch below it. Multi-trunked trees often need a few extra years to develop height, after which the process for thinning out side branches is similar. If the tree is shaped carefully during its first decade in the garden, only crossing branches and minor twiggy growth will require pruning as the tree matures.

Before I came to New Mexico, I took tall trees for granted. Now I respect them as sculpture, the ceiling, the high walls, the exclamation points, the refuge and serenity of the garden. They are the elders. Cultivate them as carefully as you do your close personal friendships, because just a few trees will have as much impact in your garden as most of the other plants combined.

Ash

Height: 15 to 30 ft.	**Light Requirement:**
Flowers: Varies	
Foliage: Deciduous	
Bloom Period: Spring	
Zones: 5 to 8	
Water: Moderate	

*M*ost ashes are riverside natives of temperate climates, so they require a consistent supply of groundwater to be healthy, vigorous shade trees. They are grown primarily for their handsome foliage; the compound leaves grow up to 8 in. long with individual leaflets that are 1 to 2 in. in length. Ashes are also popular for their gold or wine-red fall color.

WHEN TO PLANT
The ideal time for planting trees is early autumn, when roots have several weeks of mild weather before and after winter dormancy to develop before the trees releaf to face the wind and heat. Fragrant ash can be grown from seeds that are collected in autumn and sown immediately; or you can refrigerate the seeds for 3 months in a damp vermiculite mixture, then sow in spring.

WHERE TO PLANT
Claret ash needs a large space to flourish and should be planted at least 15 ft. from walls and paving. Fragrant ash is ideal in small patio areas or entryways, where the scent of its lacy white flowers can be appreciated in spring. It roots deeply and can be planted 6 to 8 ft. from walls and paving. Both ashes are adapted to alkaline soils.

HOW TO PLANT
Recent research has demonstrated that the best soil preparation for container-grown or balled-and-burlapped trees is to dig holes only as deep as the rootball but 4 to 6 times its diameter. This allows them to develop the lateral absorbing roots they rely on most for initial establishment and long-term survival. Backfill soil requires no amendment, but a generous topdressing of compost as mulch will accelerate root development because it keeps the soil cooler and more uniformly moist.

ADVICE FOR CARE

Apply a balanced fertilizer when trees begin to leaf out in spring to encourage strong growth and root development. Continue this practice for the first 5 years. Water to a depth of 2 ft. every 2 weeks when temperatures are above 80 degrees Fahrenheit; water monthly the rest of the year.

SPECIES, CULTIVARS, OR VARIETIES

Claret ash (*F. oxycarpa*) is a fast-growing tree from southern Europe and the Middle East that grows 25 to 30 ft. tall with a 20- to 25-ft. canopy. Its fine-textured, dark-green leaflets keep their rich color in the heat of summer, turning a deep wine-red in autumn. 'Raywood', the most widely available variety, is a budded cultivar with a more uniform oval canopy form. Fragrant ash (*F. cuspidata*) is native to the middle elevations of central New Mexico. It is rare among ash species in that it has showy fragrant flowers. Lacy white panicles 3 to 4 in. long cover the tree in spring. Fragrant ash is a small multi-trunked tree that grows 15 to 20 ft. high and 12 to 15 ft. wide. 'Modesto', a cultivar of *F. velutina* which is native to the Southwest, and green ash (*F. pennsylvanica*), of Eastern origin, have been so heavily planted in areas where they struggle to survive that they have become hosts to a number of insects and diseases. Nature is an opportunist, making lemonade out of lemons. Where there are weakened trees, she sees food for parasites. We gardeners are rarely so egalitarian. Our gardens welcome charismatic wildlife, but only a few of my entomologist friends relish the idea of borers infesting their trees. For northern and higher-elevation gardens in the rare places where groundwater is plentiful, green ash remains a viable shade tree selection. In similar oases in southern and low-elevation gardens, cultivars of velvet ash are still a good choice. Otherwise, claret ash and fragrant ash are better options.

Bigtooth Maple

Acer grandidentatum

Height: 20 to 40 ft.	**Light Requirement:**
Flowers: Inconspicuous	
Foliage: Deciduous	
Bloom Period: Spring	
Zones: 3 to 6	
Water: Ample	

This profile of maples is a plea for mercy. Silver maples have been widely planted in New Mexico. There are precious few specimens that have been well cared for, meaning they have been given ample water and yearly iron treatments to prevent chlorosis. These few trees can meet a gardener's expectations of a large shade tree. Many more have died prematurely or spend summers a sickly yellow, leaves scorched and growth stunted by drought. After 25 years in New Mexico, I still miss the blaze of sugar maples in autumn, and the best remedy for my childhood nostalgia is a pilgrimage to one of the isolated stands of bigtooth maples that grow in moist mountain canyons in central and southern New Mexico. One colony lies just 35 miles due east of where I live, in the Manzano Mountains in Fourth of July Canyon. The canyon is named not for the summer holiday, but for the mapleleaf fireworks in fall. In theory, bigtooth maple is more adapted to alkaline soil, but no maples can tolerate the pH of 8 or above that is common in lower-elevation gardens. Because they grow along streams and in low-lying runoff catchments, maple roots are extensive but shallow. Bigtooth maple grows 20 to 40 ft. tall and half as wide. Its dark-green leaves have five bluntly toothed lobes, and they turn a range of yellow, gold, orange, rose, and scarlet in autumn. Though bigtooth maple is my first choice for New Mexico gardens, the information below applies to all maples trying to make a home here.

WHEN TO PLANT

Bigtooth maple should be planted in early fall so that it can establish roots while temperatures are coolest.

WHERE TO PLANT

Because bigtooth maple is adapted to cooler microclimates, it grows best in afternoon shade on northeastern exposures in storm drainage basins or other low-lying areas where it can be kept moist. Clematis, columbine, geraniums, candytuft, daylilies, yerba mansa, yarrow, and Serbian bellflower are good companion groundcovers.

HOW TO PLANT

Dig generous holes, loosening the soil so that new roots will have an easy time breaking ground. Backfill soil requires no amendment, but a generous topdressing of compost as mulch will accelerate root development because it keeps the soil cooler and more uniformly moist.

ADVICE FOR CARE

Apply a granular iron-and-sulfur fertilizer each spring to prevent chlorosis. Water to a depth of 18 to 24 in. weekly when temperatures are above 90 degrees Fahrenheit, every 2 weeks when temperatures are between 75 and 90 degrees Fahrenheit, and monthly during cool weather.

SPECIES, CULTIVARS, OR VARIETIES

Rocky Mountain maple (*Acer glabrum*) is also native to the mountains of New Mexico. It grows 10 to 15 ft. tall and 10 ft. wide with leaves that are more deeply cut than bigtooth leaves. Fall color is mostly yellow, sometimes suffused with rose-pink. Japanese maple (*Acer palmatum*) has finely cut leaves that are tissue-paper thin. They will sunburn and windburn to withered skeletons unless grown in a sheltered, shaded microclimate. Well-grown specimens displayed in a shaded lathhouse are hard to resist. This is a choice plant for gardeners who enjoy pampering their pets.

Blue Spruce

Picea pungens f. glauca

Height: 40 to 60 ft. **Flowers:** Inconspicuous **Foliage:** Evergreen **Bloom Period:** Spring **Zones:** 3 to 6 **Water:** Moderate to ample	**Light Requirement:**

*B*lue spruce is a tall, tapered conifer that is native to the upper elevations of the Rockies and mountain ridges throughout the West. The cultivars available in nurseries are grafted selections from plants having particularly good color, foliage density, or form. Spruce has short blue-green needles that spiral densely around the stems; the stems are in turn branched in whorls around a single slender trunk. When plants are young, the branches are rather stiff, but as trees mature their branches flex and layer elegantly. This is a useful adaptation where plants may need to shed 100 or more inches of snow in winter. Blue spruce is shallowly rooted and has evolved to thrive in cool climates that receive 30 in. of rain and snow a year, yet it grows remarkably well at 5000-ft. elevations.

WHEN TO PLANT

Blue spruce roots most quickly when the soil is cool. Drying winds in winter and extreme heat in summer are hard on new transplants, so early autumn and early spring are the ideal planting times. Larger trees should be loosely staked until they have rooted well to prevent them from blowing over during windstorms.

WHERE TO PLANT

Blue spruce are magnificent and long-lived; after a quarter century of growth, just one can swallow a small garden whole. Other trees and shrubs that are part of the framework of the garden should be planted at least 12 to 15 ft. from the spruce. Groundcovers planted at the same time as the spruce may disappear under its sweeping skirts, but the increased humidity and reduction in reflected heat afforded by groundcovers keeps the lower branches of the spruce viable. The wide spread and shallow root system of blue spruce make it a strong forest tree, but they also make mature single trees more susceptible to being blown over during windstorms. Finding a wind-protected space large enough to accommodate the mature tree can be a challenge.

How to Plant

The best soil preparation for container-grown or balled-and-burlapped trees is to dig holes only as deep as the depth of the rootball but 6 times its diameter. This allows spruce to develop the lateral absorbing roots they rely on for initial establishment and long-term survival. Backfill soil requires no amendment, but a generous topdressing of compost as mulch will help accelerate root development because it keeps the soil cooler and more uniformly moist.

Advice for Care

Blue spruce declines if kept too wet or too dry. Water to a depth of 18 to 24 in. every 2 weeks when temperatures are above 75 degrees Fahrenheit; water monthly during cooler weather. Plant a companion groundcover to provide an extended moist area for the spruce's roots, and maintain a 4-in.-deep mulch to keep plants growing vigorously.

Species, Cultivars, or Varieties

'Hoopsii' was selected for its beautiful silver-blue color. It seems to be somewhat more heat tolerant than the species and grows 40 ft. high and 25 ft. wide. 'Fat Albert' is a cultivar selected for its bright-blue color and fast, dense, symmetrical growth to 25 ft. high and 20 ft. wide. 'Montgomery' was selected for very slow growth, only 2 in. a year, and so can be used in smaller spaces with less water over the long term.

Catclaw Acacia

Acacia greggii

Height: 10 to 15 ft. **Flowers:** Yellow **Foliage:** Deciduous **Bloom Period:** Early summer **Zones:** 6 to 8 **Water:** Low	**Light Requirement:**

There are at least 450 species of acacia worldwide, and most are small trees adapted to warm winter conditions. In New Mexico, only our native species reliably survive the winters. They are plants of small stature and prickly disposition. Catclaw is fast growing, especially when drip irrigated. It has a rounded, spreading silhouette and open branch pattern. Short, curved spines are hidden in the finely divided sage-green compound leaves. Catclaw is among the desert plants nicknamed "wait-a-bit," so called because when it grabs you, a few minutes of fancy maneuvering are required to get yourself unsnagged. The perfume of the frilly, 2-in.-long, pale-yellow flower spikes is fair compensation for any run-ins with the thorns. Twisted, rust-colored pods 4 in. long and 3/4 in. wide appear in late summer.

WHEN TO PLANT

Young acacia are especially frost tender and root most quickly when the soil is warm. Set out container-grown plants in late spring or summer so that plants will have time to establish new roots before the onset of cold weather. Seeds also need warm soil to germinate.

WHERE TO PLANT

Catclaw acacia prefers well-drained rocky or gritty soil. It has a pleasing spareness when used as a barrier planting, excluding trespassers without closing in a space. Catclaw can be planted in front of windows to provide light shade and security; just be sure you can clean the windows without tangling with the catclaw. Birds use the protection of acacia for nesting, and quail collect its seeds.

HOW TO PLANT

Soak catclaw seeds in hot water until they plump up, or they may never sprout. Acacia can be sown directly where the plants are to grow, or in a deep container that will accommodate the long initial root. Transplant potted plants carefully, disturbing the roots as little as possible. Root disturbance doesn't kill young plants, but it can halt growth for the season. Dig generous holes, loosening the soil so that new roots will have an easy time breaking ground. Recent research has demonstrated that even deep-rooting native trees grown in containers develop lateral absorbing roots first after being transplanted, and rely on those roots for both initial establishment and long-term survival. Backfill soil requires no amendment.

ADVICE FOR CARE

Remove the lower branches to create a sculpted small tree. Acacia needs no fertilizer. Young plants can be watered every 2 weeks from spring through midsummer to stimulate faster growth. Established plants will thrive on deep watering once a month when the temperature is above 85 degrees Fahrenheit. Acacia growing in revegetation plantings with no supplemental watering will defoliate in response to extreme drought.

SPECIES, CULTIVARS, OR VARIETIES

Whitethorn (*Acacia neovernicosa*) grows upright to 10 ft. high and 8 ft. wide. Its tiny leaves, slender stems lined with pairs of white spines, dark-yellow globular flowers, and narrow seedpods give whitethorn a deceptively delicate appearance.

Cedar

Cedrus species

Height: 100 ft.
Flowers: Inconspicuous
Foliage: Evergreen
Bloom Period: Spring
Zones: 5 or 6 to 8
Water: Moderate

Light Requirement:

True cedars are huge trees at maturity and develop mass quickly in the garden. The only things small about these giants are the fine tufts of needles and the small cones borne on the upper side of their wide, sweeping branches. The contrast between the soft foliage texture and the bold branching pattern makes them distinctive both at a distance and close at hand. Cedars are long-lived and adapted to a broad range of rainfall, from just under 20 in. to more than 50 in. per year. In New Mexican gardens, well-rooted cedars that are watered moderately will remain a modest size, a mere 50 ft. tall, arching and thrusting half as wide.

When to Plant

Cedars are quite heat tolerant, but they are not cold tolerant until well established. They should be planted in late spring through late summer to allow adequate time to root out before the onset of cold.

Where to Plant

Cedar will adapt to almost any soil as long as it is neither soggy nor bone dry. Space is required to accommodate the mature size of the plant and to set it off from other plants so that its monumental form can be appreciated.

How to Plant

Loosen the soil in an area 4 to 6 times the diameter of the rootball so that new lateral roots will have an easy time breaking ground. Backfill soil requires no amendment, but a generous topdressing of compost as mulch will keep the soil more uniformly moist and more moderate in temperature.

ADVICE FOR CARE

It takes about 5 years before cedars become rooted well enough
to be considered drought tolerant. Fertilize during establishment
with a balanced granular or time-release formula each spring, and
water once a week when temperatures exceed 90 degrees Fahrenheit. Apply a granular iron-and-sulfur fertilizer in summer if the
foliage becomes chlorotic. Water established cedar trees to a depth
of 2 ft. every 2 weeks when temperatures are above 80 degrees
Fahrenheit, and monthly during cooler weather. Maintain at least
4 in. of shredded bark, pecan hulls, or fine gravel mulch over the
root zone. The weeping forms can be thinned to accentuate their
sinuous branches. The lower branches of mature plants should be
removed as they defoliate.

SPECIES, CULTIVARS, OR VARIETIES

Blue atlas cedar (*C. atlantica* 'Glauca') is native to the Atlas
Mountains in North Africa. It grows tall and straight when young,
then expands to a flat-topped, tiered pyramid as it matures. 'Glauca'
is a blue-needled form. 'Fastigiata' maintains a tighter, more columnar shape. 'Pendula' has a weirdly wonderful form that is elegant
when trained against a high wall or fence. 'Compacta' grows more
slowly and densely. Cedar of Lebanon (*C. libani*) grows very wide
at the base with stiff, horizontal branches that taper to a point when
the plant is young and broaden to a flat-topped crown with age.
The fine needles are dark gray-green. 'Pendula' is a slow-growing
grafted variety that is prostrate unless staked to create a tree form.
Cyprus cedar (*C. libani* ssp. *brevifolia*) is slow growing to 30 ft. tall
with an irregular profile and very small needles. Deodara cedar (*C.
deodara*) has foliage of dark silver-gray on strongly tiered branches
with drooping tips. The species is hardy only in Zones 7 and 8, but
the variety 'Kashmir' can be grown in Zones 5 and 6 as well.

Chaste Tree

Vitex agnus-castus

Height: 10 to 20 ft.	**Light Requirement:**
Flowers: Blue	
Foliage: Deciduous	
Bloom Period: Midsummer	
Zones: 6 to 8	
Water: Low to moderate	

*C*haste tree is a Mediterranean native cultivated for centuries as a medicinal herb, and more recently as a garden ornamental. Modern science is investigating the therapeutic effects of vitex on hormone production in the human body, but chastity remains an elusive prescription. Chaste tree is versatile and easy to grow in the garden. It may be used as a flowering shrub for several years before maturing to ornamental tree status. Vitex leaves are palmate, divided into five to seven slender leaflets 2 to 3 in. long, dark green on the upper surface and silver on the underside. The aromatic foliage is so dense that the plant is used for both screening and shade. In July and August, 8-in. spikes of tiny blue flowers crown the plant. Every year the display becomes more grand; a mature vitex stands at least 15 ft. tall and 12 ft. wide. The flowers are replaced by beadlike seeds the size of coriander, giving dormant vitex an interesting profile in winter.

WHEN TO PLANT

Chaste tree needs warmth to grow well. Summer transplants will require extra water to offset the heat. Volunteer seedlings transplant best just before they leaf out in spring.

WHERE TO PLANT

Vitex will grow well in almost any soil as long as it is not kept too wet in winter. Allow 12 to 15 ft. of space for plants used as accent specimens. Creeping germander, evening primrose, spreading cotoneaster, or prairie sage make good groundcovers for use with chaste tree because they will grow well in the sun while the tree is small, and adapt to the shade as chaste tree matures. It is also planted 10 to 12 ft. apart for screening or as a wind buffer. When it blooms, vitex hums with bees, so it is best to site plants in open areas or in the background. It is deeply rooted and may be planted close to walls and paving.

HOW TO PLANT

Recent research has demonstrated that even arid-adapted trees rely on their lateral absorbing roots for initial establishment and long-term survival. Dig holes only as deep as, or at most a few inches deeper than, the depth of the rootball, but 4 to 6 times its diameter. Loosen the soil so that new roots can break ground easily. Backfill soil requires no amendment, but a generous topdressing of mulch will keep the soil more uniformly moist and more moderate in temperature, accelerating root development.

ADVICE FOR CARE

To prune vitex as a small tree, leave the most shapely branches as the framework, and remove all the twiggy growth within several feet of the ground in early summer. Each year in early summer, remove any suckers or side shoots from the lower stems, exposing more of the trunks as the plant gets taller. The seedpods may be trimmed off when they begin to look weathered. Once chaste tree is well rooted, water to a depth of 2 ft. every 2 weeks when temperatures are above 90 degrees Fahrenheit and when plants are flowering. Water to a depth of 3 ft. once a month the rest of the year.

SPECIES, CULTIVARS, OR VARIETIES

Vitex agnus-castus 'Alba' is a white form; 'Rosea' has light-pink flowers.

REGIONAL CONSIDERATIONS

Chaste tree is root hardy in Zone 5 and plants will die back to the ground each winter, but since flowers are produced on new growth, it can be grown as a medium-sized shrub. Set new plants out in late spring or early summer so they will have time to root out before the return of cold weather.

Chinese Pistache

Pistacia chinensis

Height: 30 ft.	**Light Requirement:**
Flowers: Red	
Foliage: Deciduous	
Bloom Period: Spring	
Zones: 6 to 8	
Water: Moderate to low	

*C*hinese pistache is one of the best large shade trees for xeric gardens. Its dark-green compound leaves with leaflets 2 in. long and ¾ in. wide turn blazing shades of wine-red, scarlet, and orange in autumn. The small red flowers are large enough to be noticeable, but they are more curious than showy. Female trees produce small, hard, blue seeds that sprout readily if the soil is moist, though mature trees are not weedy self-sowers. Although Chinese pistache tolerates heat and drought and has few pest problems, it has only recently become sought after as a shade tree. The deep root system that makes pistache so water efficient in the garden also makes it harder to produce commercially . . . but the main reason Chinese pistache has been slow to find commercial success may be that it looks like a hat rack when it is young. After an awkward adolescence, the blunt, stiff branches form an appealing vase shape. Mature trees develop irregular spreading canopies.

WHEN TO PLANT

Chinese pistache transplants well any time, but in the heat of summer and dead of winter, root disturbance seems particularly damaging.

WHERE TO PLANT

Pistache is not a good lawn tree to plant with bluegrass or turf fescues. The water and fertilizer needed to maintain cool-season turfgrass is much more than pistache prefers. Its deep root system allows planting near foundations and paving, so pistache is an ideal street tree and shade tree for patios. Its root system doesn't interfere with the growth of other plants sharing its space, but companions need to be shade tolerant and low-to-moderate water users such as spreading cotoneasters, prairie sage, fleabane, catmint, and creeping germander.

How to Plant

Seedlings of pistache do not survive bareroot transplanting well, so move plants with a rootball intact even when they are dormant. The best soil preparation for container-grown or balled-and-burlapped trees is to dig holes only as deep as the rootball, but 4 to 6 times its diameter, because recent research has demonstrated that even tap-rooted plants rely on lateral absorbing roots for initial establishment and long-term survival. Backfill soil requires no amendment, but a generous topdressing of mulch will keep the soil more uniformly moist and more moderate in temperature, accelerating root development.

Advice for Care

Chinese pistache roots for a year or two before it produces much growth above ground. A modest dose of calcium nitrate applied in spring promotes a strong start. Once it is well rooted, pistache should be watered to a depth of 2 ft. once a month. Verticillium wilt sometimes develops when plants are watered and fertilized excessively, particularly in heavy soils. Young pistache whips should be tip pruned to promote side branching. Very little pruning is needed once a branch scaffold has been selected from the laterals that develop.

Species, Varieties, or Cultivars

Pistacia vera, the pistachio nut tree, is native to Syria and Palestine. It grows 30 ft. tall. At least 200 frost-free nights are required to ripen a crop. Pistachios are new to commercial production in New Mexico and have proven to be well adapted in the Tularosa Basin north of Alamogordo in the southeastern part of the state.

Desert Willow

Chilopsis linearis

Height: 20 ft.	**Light Requirement:**
Flowers: Pink, purple, or white	
Foliage: Deciduous	
Bloom Period: Summer	
Zones: 6 to 8	
Water: Low to moderate	

*D*esert willow is native below 6000 ft. in the southern two-thirds of New Mexico. Its slender gnarled trunks grow 10 to 20 ft. tall and spread as wide. Each plant develops its own unique pattern of sinuous branches. The narrow lineal leaves do little to conceal the form, but they are dense enough to provide cooling shade. Pairs of orchidlike flowers at the branch tips are favorite nectar-sipping places for hummingbirds and orioles. Pencil-sized seedpods persist into winter, giving even the most upright trees a weeping grace.

WHEN TO PLANT
Desert willows are heat lovers, one of the last plants to bud in spring. They can be planted in winter if watered sparingly until they begin to leaf out.

WHERE TO PLANT
Though desert willow will grow in almost any soil, root rot can be a problem in wet, heavy soils. Desert willow is used as an accent specimen, planted in groves for light shade near windows and patios, and along dry streambed paths and storm drainage channels.

HOW TO PLANT
Desert willow is easy to grow from seeds sown on warm, well-drained soil in spring. Plants with selected flower colors are grown from soft cuttings taken in summer, or from hardwood cuttings taken in spring. Dig generous holes several times wider than the rootball, loosening the soil so that new roots will have an easy time breaking ground. Desert willow has coarse roots with sponge-like surfaces without fibrous absorbing root hairs. Those roots penetrate the soil deeply while more superficial roots capture rain-fall most efficiently.

ADVICE FOR CARE

Let desert willow grow for a few years until it begins to show some character. Emphasize the most shapely trunks by removing all the twiggy growth and suckers within several feet of the ground in early summer each year. Seedpods may be trimmed off when they begin to look weathered. Desert willow needs no fertilizing; if forced to grow more than 2 ft. a year, it tends to split and crack in the wind. Until it reaches the desired height, water to a depth of 2 to 3 ft. every 2 weeks when temperatures are above 90 degrees Fahrenheit, especially when the tree is flowering. Water once a month through spring and fall, and every 6 weeks or less in winter. Watering is optional once plants have filled the space desired.

SPECIES, CULTIVARS, OR VARIETIES

There are many cultivars of desert willow, including the white-flowering 'Hope'. 'Dark Storm' has deep wine-red flowers on slow-growing plants. 'Lucretia Hamilton' flowers longer and produces fewer seedpods because it sets seeds only from late-summer blooms. *Chitalpa tashkentensis*, a hybrid of desert willow and *Catalpa bignon-ioides*, has 4-in.-long, 1-in.-wide leaves that are borne densely on stout branches. Chitalpa's leaves drop cleanly after the first frost, making it an ideal shade tree for solar gain in winter. It can be shaped as a single-trunked standard tree or as a multi-trunk speci-men 20 ft. tall and nearly as wide. It looks best when watered deeply once a month after establishment. Chitalpa is robustly cold hardy to Zone 5.

REGIONAL CONSIDERATIONS

Desert willow has been teased into growing in warm microclimates in Santa Fe and Denver, but those plants are not as vigorous as trees that have plenty of heat to bake their desert genes.

Flowering Fruit Trees

Prunus and *Malus* species

Height: 20 ft.
Flowers: Pink or white
Foliage: Deciduous
Bloom Period: Spring
Zones: 4 to 8
Water: Moderate to ample

Light Requirement:

*A*pricot, peach, plum, pear, and crab apple trees are all valued for the clouds of fragrant flowers that dispel the winter blues. Our early February warmth makes fruit production a gamble in this state. Fruit trees have shallow roots that are quickly nudged out of dormancy, but early warming in the desert is often interrupted by Arctic cold fronts blasting south along the mountains. Frigid air pools in the valleys like an icy flood, washing away every trace of spring. Shallow roots are also more vulnerable to summer heat and drought, and deep mulch can make the difference between thriving trees and those that are merely surviving.

WHEN TO PLANT
Ornamental fruit trees transplant best in spring or fall when the soil is cooler. Wrap the tender bark on the trunk of fall-planted trees to avoid sunscald in winter.

WHERE TO PLANT
Trees that are planted on cooler north and east exposures, on higher ground rather than in low spots where cold air settles, will bud a little later in spring and will be less likely to be frosted. Planting companions that share water with the developing tree roots ensure the tree's strong future. Columbine, creeping germander, chives, dwarf plumbago, candytuft, compact mahonia, spreading coton-easters, soapwort, catmint, daylilies, and 'Red Cascade' or other groundcover roses are among the many plants that work well.

HOW TO PLANT
Dig generous holes, loosening soil as deep as the rootball and 4 to 6 times its diameter. Till 4 to 6 in. of compost into the soil where the tree and its groundcover will be planted, and add a generous top-dressing of compost, shredded bark, or pecan hulls as mulch.

ADVICE FOR CARE

Prune only as much as is needed to keep the canopy open enough to allow dappled light to reach the lower branches, and remove any crossing, rubbing branches. Apricot, peach, and plum trees are susceptible to borers, especially if they are stressed for water. Generous soil preparation, mulching, and companion planting will go a long way toward preventing the appearance of borers. Check the trunks periodically for the sap nodules that cover borer holes. Using borer crystals to treat the soil around the base of the tree each fall is both a preventative and a control. Apply a granular or time-release fertilizer each spring after blooming. Peaches, and sometimes plums, need a dose of a granular iron-and-sulfur fertilizer to prevent chlorosis. Water should penetrate to 18 in. Young trees may have to be watered weekly when the temperature is above 90 degrees Fahrenheit, every 2 weeks from bloom time until the end of summer when temperatures are not extreme, and monthly in winter.

SPECIES, CULTIVARS, OR VARIETIES

Apricot (*Prunus armeniaca*) is long-lived with pale-pink flowers and coral-gold fall foliage. The earliest of spring bloomers, it may produce fruit if sited well. It is cold hardy in Zones 5 through 8 up to 7500 ft. Crab apple *Malus* varieties with small persistent fruit are the easiest to live with in the garden. Tolerant of poor soils and cold, 'Radiant', 'Hopa', and 'Spring Snow' are hardy to 9000 ft. in the southern mountains. Ornamental pear (*Pyrus calleryana*) has shiny, dark-green leaves, white flowers in spring, and deep-red fall foliage. Cultivars differ in form: 'Chanticleer' grows 25 ft. tall and 15 ft. wide; 'Capitol' forms a very narrow column; and there are a dozen varieties of intermediate width. Pears tolerate poor air quality better than most flowering trees. Standard varieties of peach (*Prunus persica*) grow 15 ft. tall and wide and provide a very low shade canopy. Trees grown for fruit need heavy pruning annually to strengthen their structure and limit fruit set to what the branches can support. The two weakest of every three new branches should be removed each spring. In addition to an iron-and-sulfur treatment, dormant spraying with a mix of lime-sulfur and light oil will help prevent and control leaf curl and scale. Purpleleaf plum (*P. cerasifera* 'Atropurpurea') grows 20 ft. tall and 15 ft. wide with a stiff, oval profile that is like a vase or a lollipop, depending on the cultivar. Every spring, I admire the dozen plums blooming on every street. Then the screaming purple leaves emerge, and I find that diversity can be visually soothing as well as ecologically sound. 'Krauter Vesuvius' is the cultivar most likely to need iron; 'Newport' produces the least fruit; and all plums may need a dormant oil and lime-sulfur spray to minimize leaf curl.

Golden Raintree

Koelreuteria paniculata

Height: 25 ft.
Flowers: Yellow
Foliage: Deciduous
Bloom Period: Summer
Zones: 5 to 8
Water: Moderate to low

Light Requirement:

*T*he first golden raintree arrived in colonial America from Asia in 1763. Well adapted to heat and drought, it has become a naturalized citizen in the Southwest. The branches curve upward and then relax outward as the plant matures, forming a rounded canopy to 25 ft. high and at least 15 ft. wide. The compound leaves have up to 15 dark-green leaflets per stem. They turn a mellow gold color in autumn, though the "golden" in the tree's name refers to the loose panicles of yellow flowers that cover the tree in early summer. Rusty, paper-thin, lanternlike seedpods appear later in the season and persist into winter, decorating the bare branches.

WHEN TO PLANT

Plants can be set out any time of year. In summer, raintree will need more water during establishment, especially if it is transplanted while in bloom. Cold-acclimated trees planted in winter should be watered well only to settle the soil around the roots when they are transplanted, and not again until spring when the soil begins to warm up.

WHERE TO PLANT

Golden raintree roots deeply in any infertile soil that is not kept too wet. It is wind resilient and smog tolerant, so it can be used in urban areas. Out in the desert, it provides dappled shade as a street or patio tree, and it blends well with conifers in windbreaks. Prairie sage, cherry sage, catmint, and spreading cotoneasters are among the many good companion plants for rain tree.

HOW TO PLANT

Dig generous holes, loosening the soil so that new roots will have an easy time breaking ground. Recent research has demonstrated that the best soil preparation for container-grown or balled-and-burlapped trees is to dig holes only as deep as the rootball but 4 to 6 times its diameter. This is because even deep-rooting plants develop lateral, absorbing roots first, and these are the roots on which they rely most for initial establishment. Backfill soil requires no amendment, but a generous topdressing of mulch can accelerate root development by keeping the soil more uniformly moist and more moderate in temperature.

ADVICE FOR CARE

Golden raintree needs little pruning. Any suckers that sprout at the base of the trunk should be removed; seedpods may be trimmed off when they begin to look weathered. Red-and-black box elder bugs are attracted to the seeds but do no harm and need no control. The only time the insect numbers increase to noticeable extremes is when large numbers of plants are grouped together near buildings or sitting areas. Interplanting compatible tree species is an ecologically sound way to avoid cultivating annoying populations of insects. Once rain tree is well-rooted, water it to a depth of 2 ft. every 2 weeks when flowering, and once a month during the rest of the year.

TREES

Hawthorn

Crataegus species and cultivars

Height: 25 ft.	**Light Requirement:**
Flowers: White	
Foliage: Deciduous	
Bloom Period: Spring	
Zones: 4 to 7	
Water: Moderate	

awthorns are handsome trees with arching stems that form a rounded crown 25 ft. tall and 15 ft. wide. Clusters of white flowers appear in late spring after most fruit trees have finished blooming. Drooping clusters of round fruits 1/4 to 1/2 in. in diameter turn red in autumn and persist until birds carry them off. Foliage is dark green, turning shades of yellow, orange, and red in fall. The thorny branches are interesting after the leaves drop.

WHEN TO PLANT

Plants can be set out any time of year. In summer, hawthorn will need more water during establishment, especially when temperatures are above 85 degrees Fahrenheit. Cold-acclimated trees planted in winter should be watered immediately to settle the soil around the roots; water monthly until spring.

WHERE TO PLANT

Hawthorns prefer well-drained, alkaline soil. They can be used singly or in groups as accent specimens and for shade in small gardens; or they can be contrasted with Austrian pines, spruce, or silverberry in a windbreak, screen, or barrier planting for large spaces. Because hawthorns are an alternate host for cedar apple rust, avoid planting them near junipers. Spreading cotoneaster, vinca, compact mahonia, creeping germander, and Organ Mountain evening primrose, as well as dwarf plumbago underplanted with grape hyacinths all make good groundcovers under hawthorns.

HOW TO PLANT

Recent research has demonstrated that the best soil preparation for container-grown or balled-and-burlapped trees is to dig holes only as deep as the rootball but 4 to 6 times its diameter. This enables

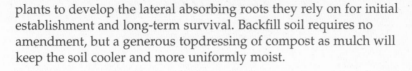

plants to develop the lateral absorbing roots they rely on for initial establishment and long-term survival. Backfill soil requires no amendment, but a generous topdressing of compost as mulch will keep the soil cooler and more uniformly moist.

ADVICE FOR CARE

Prune young hawthorns as multi-trunk or standard trees, removing any suckers, and gradually expose more of the trunks as the plants get taller and bark becomes thicker. Thin out crossing and twiggy growth to emphasize the layered branch patterns in early summer. Apply a granular or time-release fertilizer each spring after blooming. Washington hawthorns planted in strongly alkaline or calcareous soil may need a dose of granular iron-and-sulfur fertilizer to prevent chlorosis. Once hawthorns are well rooted, water to a depth of 2 ft. every 2 weeks when temperatures are above 85 degrees Fahrenheit, and once a month during cooler weather.

SPECIES, CULTIVARS, OR VARIETIES

Cockspur hawthorn (*C. persimilis* 'Prunifolia') has oval, dark-green, glossy leaves that turn bronzed red in autumn. It produces clusters of small white flowers in spring; small russet fruits appear in autumn. Four-inch-long thorns add to its habitat value as nesting cover. Thornless cockspur hawthorn has a horizontal branch structure that gives plants a distinctively tiered look, especially when they are in bloom. 'Crusader' is a trademarked thornless cultivar selected for disease resistance. The thornless selections are more people friendly, but less drought and heat tolerant. Russian hawthorn (*C. ambigua*) has deeply lobed, soft-green leaves that hide short, stiff spines on a plant that is upright and vase-shaped when young, developing a gnarled character with age. It is cold hardy to Zone 3 and 10,000-ft. elevations, and is much less heat tolerant in the lowlands. Washington hawthorn (*C. phaenopyrum*) is densely twiggy and thorny with glossy lobed leaves that turn shades of scarlet in fall. The scarlet fruits are colorful most of the winter.

REGIONAL CONSIDERATIONS

Although hawthorns can be coaxed to grow in Zone 8 heat, there are better choices among the desert trees for both color and habitat.

Honey Mesquite

Prosopis glandulosa

Height: 15 ft.
Flowers: Yellow
Foliage: Deciduous
Bloom Period: Summer
Zones: 7 and 8
Water: Low

Light Requirement:

---

*H*oney mesquite, native to New Mexico's southern and central deserts, is easy to identify any time of year by its dark-gray thorny branches that spread as wide as the plant is tall. In spring, mesquite's fresh yellow-green compound leaves brighten the hillsides; its feathery leaves and frilly yellow flowers are a sharp contrast to its dark bark and coarse thorns. Honey mesquite's starchy 6-in.-long, 1/2-in.-wide seedpods are cream-colored and flecked with red.

WHEN TO PLANT

Mesquite roots most quickly if transplanted when the soil is warm. At the cold-hardiness limits of its growing range, plant mesquite in spring so it will have plenty of time to root before the onset of cold weather.

WHERE TO PLANT

Mesquite prefers well-drained soil and is more susceptible to borers when grown in heavy clay that doesn't dry out periodically. The deep roots make it ideal for planting close to windows for light shade. Because of its thorns, mesquite is an ideal barrier and habitat plant, but it should be placed far enough from paths, play areas, and patios to avoid snags.

HOW TO PLANT

Mesquite can be grown from seeds that have been pried out of the triangular woody capsules embedded in their starchy pods. Soak the seeds in hot water until they swell, then plant in warm, loosened soil after all chance of frost has passed. To transplant container-grown plants, dig generous holes, loosening the unamended soil only as deep as or at most a few inches deeper than the depth of the rootball, but 4 to 6 times its diameter. This ensure that new roots will have an easy time breaking ground. Even this deeply rooted tree develops lateral absorbing roots, which are key to its initial establishment and long-term survival.

ADVICE FOR CARE

To prune mesquite as a small tree, leave the most shapely branches as the framework and gradually remove all the twiggy growth within several feet of the ground. Each year in early summer, remove any suckers and a few more of the side shoots from the lower stems, exposing more of the trunks as the plant gets taller. The seedpods usually drop off as they ripen and can be raked up periodically. Once mesquite is well rooted, water to a depth of 2 to 3 ft. once a month while plants are leafy, and once or twice in winter.

SPECIES, CULTIVARS, OR VARIETIES

There are several varieties of mesquite distinguished more by their point of origin and resistance to cold than by their appearance. The New Mexico native, *Prosopis glandulosa torryana*, is the most cold tolerant. *P. glandulosa* var. *glandulosa* is native to West Texas. Velvet mesquite (*P. glandulosa* var. *velutina*) is native to Arizona and is the least cold tolerant of the North American species. Chilean mesquite (*P. chilensis*) is not reliably cold hardy anywhere in New Mexico, but it is such a beautiful feathery green that gardeners can't resist trying it. Screwbean mesquite (*P. pubescens*) has slender stems 12 to 15 ft. tall spreading 8 to 10 ft. wide. Its blue-gray leaves are even smaller than those of honey mesquite, and its thorns are also smaller but just as prickly. Screwbean is so called for its clusters of coiled seedpods that decorate the branches in winter. It is the most cold hardy of all the mesquites and suffers little dieback, even in Zone 6 during the occasional polar blast.

REGIONAL CONSIDERATIONS

Native honey mesquite is root hardy in Zone 6 but doesn't grow large enough to be considered a tree except in the low-desert areas of south central New Mexico.

Japanese Scholar Tree

Styphnolobium japonica

Height: 30 ft. **Flowers:** White **Foliage:** Deciduous **Bloom Period:** Summer **Zones:** 5 to 8 **Water:** Moderate to low	**Light Requirement:**

*J*apanese scholar tree, also called pagoda tree because it is widely planted in shrine gardens in the Orient, is actually native to China and Korea. I first saw one growing near a pond in a bluegrass lawn, and I dismissed it as too thirsty to be practical here. During a recent drought, after 3 in. of rainfall in an entire year, I started noticing a small tree that stood out among the others. Its small compound leaves were dark, lustrous green while surrounding plants were dusty and scorched-looking. It was blooming profusely in parking strips and in a vacant lot where it had received no water for many months. It was the scholar tree! Young trees have shiny green bark, while the woody bark on mature trunks is striated in shades of brown. Its lacy, white, fragrant flowers stand out against the spreading canopy of dark glossy leaves in midsummer, looking cool and fresh in 100 degrees Fahrenheit heat. Small, flat, pale-green seedpods that persist through winter give it a vibrant look while dormant, and are a clue to its distant kinship with our native mesquite. Scholar tree is disease and insect resistant, tolerates heat, drought, and poor soil, and grows at a moderate 18 to 24 in. a year once it settles into a garden.

WHEN TO PLANT

Plants can be set out any time of year. In summer, scholar tree will need more water during establishment, especially when temperatures are above 90 degrees Fahrenheit. Cold-acclimated trees planted in winter should be watered immediately to settle the soil around the roots; water monthly or less often until spring.

WHERE TO PLANT

Japanese scholar tree is not fussy about soil as long as it is not kept wet in poorly drained clay. It is used to shade patios and other outdoor living spaces. Smooth surfaces such as scored concrete are easier to sweep clear of the flowers, leaves, and seedpods that scholar tree sheds seasonally than are flagstones or other rough paving.

HOW TO PLANT

Japanese scholar tree is available in a range of sizes, from 5-gallon specimens to large boxed trees. Recent research has demonstrated that the best soil preparation for container-grown or balled-and-burlapped trees is to dig holes only as deep as the rootball but 4 to 6 times its diameter. This enables plants to quickly develop the lateral absorbing roots they rely on for initial establishment and long-term survival. Backfill soil requires no amendment, but a generous topdressing of shredded bark or fine gravel mulch helps accelerate root development by keeping the soil more uniformly moist and more moderate in temperature.

ADVICE FOR CARE

Scholar tree needs little pruning. Remove suckers that sprout at the base of the trunk as well as any crossing or rubbing branches. Trees are usually 10 years old before they flower; fertilizing and pruning tend to delay blooming. Once scholar tree is well-rooted, water it to a depth of 2 ft. every 2 weeks when flowering, and once a month during the rest of the year.

SPECIES, CULTIVARS, OR VARIETIES

'Regent' blooms earlier, in 6 or 7 years, and has a narrower canopy. It tends to be a Zone less cold hardy.

Jujube

Zizyphus jujuba

Height: 20 to 30 ft.	**Light Requirement:**
Flowers: Greenish yellow	
Foliage: Deciduous	
Bloom Period: Summer	
Zones: 6 to 8	
Water: Low to moderate	

*J*ujube is also called "Chinese date" for the sweet, edible fruits it produces in autumn. It has been cultivated for so long that its native origin is questionable. While the Chinese claim it and have developed the cultivars used for candy-making, jujube may actually be native to the Mediterranean from Persia to North Africa. It forms thickets naturally. Rootsprouts create a grove of thorny stems where songbirds find inviting cover. Its stems arch and curve stiffly downward; branches zigzag at the spiny nodes, making a very interesting profile when trees are dormant. Jujube has small, glossy, light-green leaves that turn a clear, pale yellow in autumn. The small yellow-green flowers are not conspicuous, but the smooth bronze skin of the datelike fruits provides an interesting contrast for the airy foliage.

When to Plant

Because seedling production is erratic, plants are grown from root divisions, and shoots of established trees can be transplanted in spring or autumn. Nursery-grown plants are usually grafted cultivars selected for fruit quality. They can be set out any time of year, as long as winter-planted specimens have been acclimated to cold, and trees planted in summer get plenty of water during establishment.

Where to Plant

Jujube grows well in most soils. One of the easiest ways to accommodate its rootsprouting nature is to mix jujube with evergreens in screen, windbreak, or barrier plantings. Their dormant silhouette is attractive highlighted against a high wall. Spreading cotoneaster, Mexican evening primrose, yerba mansa, and prairie sage are all good companion groundcovers.

How to Plant

Dig generous holes, loosening soil so that new roots will have an easy time breaking ground. Recent research has demonstrated that the best soil preparation for container-grown trees is to dig holes only as deep as the rootball but 4 to 6 times its diameter. Root-sprouting can be contained by surrounding the planting with a wide band of unirrigated, compacted soil such as a wide path.

Advice for Care

It is easiest to plant jujube where there is space available for a grove, letting it grow naturally. To grow jujube as a single tree, remove all the twiggy growth within several feet of the ground and cut root sprouts and suckers out in early summer, exposing more of the trunk as the plant gets taller and the bark thickens. Use a double layer of geotextile under 4 in. of mulch to suppress rootsprouting. To maintain established plants, water jujube to a depth of 2 ft. once a month. Plants are heat loving, alkali tolerant, and seem to bear well without fertilizer.

Species, Cultivars, or Varieties

'Lang' is a cultivar of jujube selected for early bearing of nearly round, plump fruit. 'Li' is the other commercial cultivar, with oblong fruit 2 in. long. Graythorn (*Zizyphus obtusifolia*) is native to southern New Mexico. Its stiff, waxy, thorny stems grow slowly to 6 ft. tall. Graythorn has small blue fruit relished by wildlife.

Juniper

Juniperus species and cultivars

Height: 15 to 30 ft. **Flowers:** Inconspicuous **Foliage:** Evergreen **Bloom Period:** Spring **Zones:** 3 to 7 **Water:** Moderate to low	**Light Requirement:**

Junipers are among the evergreens used extensively in New
Mexico gardens. Drought adapted, they root deeply and extensively in search of moisture and have thready resinous foliage that
limits evaporation. All junipers are fine-textured and upright, though
they vary in form from densely columnar to broadly conical, and they
range in color from soft silver to ice-blue, deep green, and gray-green.
Sex is an important variable because the pollen of male junipers is a
major aero-allergen. Luckily, many juniper species bear male and
female flowers on separate plants, and by planting only female cultivars, gardeners can reduce the allergy potential on their home ground.
The female junipers also produce small, waxy, blue berrylike cones
that are greatly appreciated by songbirds . . . and gin distillers.

WHEN TO PLANT

Junipers can be planted all year in Zones 5 through 7, but plants set
out in winter should be acclimated to cold or they may burn badly.
Plants set out in summer will need extra water during establishment. Junipers don't show moisture stress by wilting. They fade
slowly from green to brown, and once dried out seldom recover.

WHERE TO PLANT

Junipers prefer well-drained soil, but they adapt to most soils that
are not excessively wet. They are used for screening or windbreaks,
as a backdrop for flowering shrubs, and as habitat for songbirds.
Use bright-green cultivars to contrast with the silver sages and fernbush. Blue and gray cultivars contrast well with rugosa and woods
roses, Arizona rosewood, cliffrose, and sumacs.

How to Plant

Dig generous holes, loosening soil only as deep as the rootball but 4 to 6 times its diameter so that new roots will have an easy time breaking ground. Cut the circling roots of potbound plants, scoring the rootball in several places; or cut through the bottom half of the rootball and splay the halves open in a technique called "butterflying" to stimulate new roots and prevent root-girdling. Backfill soil requires no amendment, but a generous topdressing of mulch accelerates root development by keeping the soil more uniformly moist and more moderate in temperature.

Advice for Care

Tolerant plants, junipers are tortured into all kinds of strange shapes from corkscrews to sombreros. When left unsheared, the American species have soft tapered profiles, and the Chinese species develop interesting tiered silhouettes. Varieties that look controlled without pruning include 'Skyrocket' and 'Welchii', with naturally narrow columns; and the densely leafy 'Spearmint'. Dusty dry foliage attracts spider mites. Hosing the plants off with a strong spray of water a few times a season is usually enough to limit damage. Water established plants to a depth of 2 to 3 ft. once a month in gardens below 7000 ft. in elevation.

Species, Cultivars, or Varieties

Among the Chinese junipers, *J. chinensis* 'Keteeleri' grows quickly to 20 ft. in a loose open pyramid that spreads 10 ft. wide; *J. chinensis* 'Spearmint' is a dense deep-green column 15 ft. high and 8 ft. wide. 'Hillspire' juniper (*J. virginiana* 'Cupressifolia') is deep green year-round, growing 15 ft. high and 6 ft. wide. Rocky Mountain juniper (*J. scopulorum*) is the native western species and the source of many useful female cultivars, including metallic 'Blue Haven', 20 ft. tall and 10 ft. wide; vivid 'Cologreen', 20 ft. tall and 10 ft. wide; steely 'Gray Gleam', 12 to 15 ft. high and 6 to 9 ft. wide; silver-gray 'Skyrocket', a column up to 15 ft. tall and 4 ft. wide; 'Table Top Blue', a flat-topped silver-blue form 6 to 8 ft. high and 8 to 10 ft. wide; and 'Welchii', a slow-growing silver column 12 ft. high and 4 to 6 ft. wide.

TREES

Kentucky Coffee Tree

Gymnocladus dioica

Height: 40 ft.
Flowers: White
Foliage: Deciduous
Bloom Period: Summer
Zones: 3 to 7
Water: Moderate to low

Light Requirement:

Kentucky coffee tree pioneered its way to the desert Southwest from the Midwestern plains long ago, and though it has proven well suited to drier surroundings, it is still not commonly grown in gardens here. Perhaps it doesn't fit the typical image of a shade tree. Kentucky coffee grows at a moderate pace to 30 or 40 ft. tall; its canopy eventually spreads 25 ft. wide. After relaxing in its dense summer shade, seeing a coffee tree for the first time in winter can be a bit of a shock. Not only does it shed its leaves in the fall, Kentucky coffee tree sheds 3-ft.-long leaf stems as well, reducing an impressive shade tree to a silhouette of bare bones. This stark appearance is quite in character in desert gardens, but there is also practical value in having an incredible shrinking tree. Home owners can enjoy cooling shade in summer and gain the most solar warming in winter. Mountain gardeners needn't fear the limb breakage that heavy wet snows can inflict on their trees. Coffee tree has no network of twiggy stems to build up a snow load. It is late to leaf out in spring, because its deep roots respond slowly to the surface warming that can be the undoing of early-flowering trees. The leaves hide clusters of fragrant white flowers that later develop into thick, pulpy, brown seedpods. A coffee substitute was once brewed from the ground seeds, but these days the curious pods are more likely to find their way into dried floral arrangements than into espresso machines.

WHEN TO PLANT

Containerized Kentucky coffee trees can be planted any time of year, as long as they are kept consistently moist when transplanted in summer. Bareroot or balled-and-burlapped trees are planted in autumn or in spring.

WHERE TO PLANT

Coffee tree prefers good drainage, but it will adapt to a wide range of soils. A good choice for an urban street tree, it tolerates smog, and companion plants grow well in its dappled shade.

HOW TO PLANT

Dig generous holes, loosening the soil so that new roots will have an easy time breaking ground. Recent research has demonstrated that the best soil preparation for container-grown or balled-and-burlapped trees is to dig holes only as deep as or at most a few inches deeper than the depth of the rootball, but 4 to 6 times its diameter. Even deeply rooted plants like coffee tree rely on the lateral absorbing roots formed when their deep initial roots are confined to containers, or when roots are cut during transplanting. Backfill soil requires no amendment, but a generous topdressing of compost, shredded bark, pecan hulls, or fine gravel as mulch will accelerate root development by keeping the soil cooler and more uniformly moist.

ADVICE FOR CARE

Coffee tree prunes itself, so your main gardening chore will be raking up the leaf, stem, and seed litter in autumn. Establishment takes a few years; a mild dose of a granular or time-release fertilizer in spring or after frost in fall can help along the process. In strongly alkaline clay soil, a young coffee tree may need an application of a granular iron-and-sulfur fertilizer to maintain its deep foliage color in summer. Once plants are well rooted, they rarely need fertilizing. Avoid digging around the mature trees, because disturbing the roots can cause them to rootsprout.

SPECIES, CULTIVARS, OR VARIETIES

There are no other species in cultivation.

Linden

Tilia species

Height: 30 ft. **Flowers:** Pale yellow **Foliage:** Deciduous **Bloom Period:** Early summer **Zones:** 4 to 6 **Water:** Moderate to ample	**Light Requirement:**

inden is the consummate street and garden tree. It is long-lived with a slow-to-moderate growth rate and will not overstep its bounds. Linden has a dense, uniform, pyramidal profile and small heart-shaped leaves. The slender stems and soft foliage are refined. Leaves are darker on the upper surfaces and paler on the undersides, giving linden a translucent quality in our bright sunlight. Loose clusters of sweetly fragrant pale-yellow flowers enhance the impression of lightness in early summer. Leaves turn a clear yellow in autumn.

WHEN TO PLANT

If growing linden in Zone 6, transplant in winter, spring, or fall when temperatures are cooler. If planting above 7000 ft. or in Zones 4 and 5, you may transplant linden in summer, but it will require more water during establishment.

WHERE TO PLANT

Linden grows faster in well-drained soil. Its dense canopy is good shade near lawns and patios, especially in small gardens. Geraniums, columbine, candytuft, dwarf plumbago, and vinca are just a few of the perennials that grow well in its dappled shade.

HOW TO PLANT

Consistent watering when the plant is young is essential to linden's thriving over the long term. Dig generous holes only as deep as the rootball but several times its diameter, loosening the soil so that new roots will have an easy time breaking ground. Backfill soil requires no amendment, but a 4-in.-deep mulch of compost or shredded bark will accelerate root development by keeping the soil cooler and more uniformly moist.

ADVICE FOR CARE

Linden requires little pruning except for the removal of any suckering growth or crossing branches. Apply a granular or time-release fertilizer each spring. In strongly alkaline soil, linden needs a dose of granular iron-and-sulfur fertilizer to prevent chlorosis in summer. Water should penetrate to 24 in. and may be required weekly when the temperature is above 85 degrees Fahrenheit for more than a few days at a time. When temperatures are less extreme, linden can be watered every 2 weeks from bud break until the end of summer; water monthly in winter.

SPECIES, CULTIVARS, OR VARIETIES

Littleleaf linden (*T. cordata*) grows 30 ft. tall with slender upturned branches that form a rounded canopy 25 ft. wide. 'Greenspire' is a highly regarded and widely available selection. Silver linden (*T. tomentosa*) grows larger, to 40 ft. tall and 30 ft. wide, and is more tolerant of periodic drought and erratic cold. Its dark-green leaves are silver on the undersides, and their sticky surface can collect dust and grime, making silver linden less smog tolerant than littleleaf linden. 'Sterling Silver' is a good selection.

REGIONAL CONSIDERATIONS

Linden will tolerate drier alkaline soils in the cooler northern and high-elevation gardens in New Mexico, but no amount of water can compensate for the heat in low-desert areas.

Netleaf Hackberry

Celtis reticulata

Height: 25 ft. **Flowers:** Inconspicuous **Foliage:** Deciduous **Bloom Period:** Spring **Zones:** 6 to 8 **Water:** Moderate to low	**Light Requirement:**

*L*ike their close allies the elms, hackberries have a long history of use as street trees—but the hackberry has proven to be the more resilient of the two. Smaller in stature and deeply rooted (but not invasive like Siberian elm), the Southwestern native netleaf hackberry is the most drought tolerant of the Celtis. Like many drought-resistant trees, it spends a few years developing an extensive root system before it expends energy on topgrowth, experiencing a brief awkward adolescence in the garden before developing a rounded canopy of slender drooping branches. Its 2- to 3-in. oval leaves have finely serrated margins and are dark green and sandpaper-rough on the top surface, paler with a network of veining on the lower surface. Netleaf hackberry produces small orange fruits that attract songbirds to the garden.

WHEN TO PLANT

Container-grown hackberry can be planted any time of year, as long as it is kept consistently moist if planted in the heat of summer. Bareroot or balled-and-burlapped trees are planted in autumn or in spring.

WHERE TO PLANT

Netleaf hackberry adapts to most alkaline soils, even the compacted ones typical of New Mexico construction sites. It is a handsome street tree or xeric shade tree near lawns and patios, and all but the most sun-worshipping perennials and groundcovers will thrive in its dappled light.

HOW TO PLANT

Dig a generous hole, loosening soil only as deep as or at most a few inches deeper than the depth of the rootball, but 4 to 6 times its diameter. This ensures that new roots will have an easy time

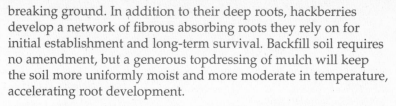

breaking ground. In addition to their deep roots, hackberries develop a network of fibrous absorbing roots they rely on for initial establishment and long-term survival. Backfill soil requires no amendment, but a generous topdressing of mulch will keep the soil more uniformly moist and more moderate in temperature, accelerating root development.

Advice for Care

The handsome foliage of hackberry may become disfigured with clusters of nipple galls. These are caused by psyllid insects that don't harm the tree except to mar its leaves. Galls are usually a problem when there are wild hackberries nearby that host a thriving insect colony. Since the effect is only cosmetic and is not noticeable from a distance, avoid planting hackberry in sitting areas or near paths where the psyllids' handiwork is likely to be noticed. Water trees twice a month during the growing season until plants approach the desired size, then cut back to deep watering once a month year-round to maintain good leaf density and general tree health. Hackberry needs no fertilizing.

Species, Cultivars, or Varieties

Desert hackberry (*Celtis pallida*) is a large shrub native to the arroyos of southern New Mexico that grows up to 10 ft. tall and wide with stiff thorny branches. Its rough oval leaves are shed during periods of drought and when temperatures drop below 20 degrees Fahrenheit. Its small orange fruits are a magnet for birds in autumn. Eastern hackberry (*Celtis occidentallis*) grows from 40 to 90 ft. high during its long lifetime, developing a broad rounded canopy 30 ft. wide. The leaves that cloak its upright arching branches are oval, 3 in. long, and a rough dull green with fine-toothed margins. Eastern hackberry prefers rich, moist soil, but it grows in northern New Mexico in relatively dry alkaline soil with little trouble. It is cold hardy to at least 7500 ft. and to Zone 4.

New Mexico Olive

Forestiera neomexicana

Height: 18 ft. **Flowers:** Greenish yellow **Foliage:** Deciduous **Bloom Period:** Spring **Zones:** 5 to 8 **Water:** Low to moderate	**Light Requirement:**

*B*ecause it is such an accommodating plant, it's easy to take New Mexico olive for granted. If you need a sculptural focal point for an entryway, or shade for a small patio or sitting area, prune out all but the most interesting branches to form a multi-trunked tree. If you need it to provide screening, leave it branched and leafy to the ground. Either way, the smooth gray bark, the branches that crook and curve in interesting ways, and the small bright-green leaves make it a pleasant companion for other plants. It roots deeply, sharing its space with low shrubs or wildflowers, and after a year or two in the garden, it grows a consistent 12 to 18 in. a year until it nears its mature height. New Mexico olive's clusters of small greenish yellow flowers in early spring aren't showy, but they smell like honey; apparently bees think so, too, because a tree hums with their activity. Female trees produce clusters of blue fruits the size of small capers that are relished by a number of songbirds. Depending on how it is managed, New Mexico olive can look lush or stark, cultivated or wild.

WHEN TO PLANT
Plant container-grown trees any time. Bareroot or balled-and-burlapped trees can be transplanted any time but summer.

WHERE TO PLANT
New Mexico olive adapts to most soils, but it grows most quickly in well-drained clay loam or decomposed granite. New Mexico olive makes a lovely small accent specimen or shade tree; or it can be left unpruned as a screen or habitat thicket; or sheared as a Southwestern version of a privet hedge. Shearing is an insult to the natural character of this fine plant, and I mention it only to illustrate how forgiving New Mexico olive can be.

How to Plant

Dig generous holes, loosening the soil so that new roots will have an easy time breaking ground. Recent research has demonstrated that the best soil preparation for container-grown or balled-and-burlapped trees is to dig holes only as deep as the rootball but several times its diameter. Like most plants, New Mexico olive develops lateral absorbing roots first, and relies on those roots most for initial establishment and long-term survival. Backfill soil requires no amendment, but a generous topdressing of mulch will accelerate root development by keeping the soil more uniformly moist and more moderate in temperature.

Advice for Care

To prune New Mexico olive as a small tree, leave the most shapely branches as the framework, and gradually remove all the twiggy growth within several feet of the ground. Each year in early summer, remove any suckers or side shoots from the lower stems, exposing more of the trunks as the plant gets taller. As the olive matures, it will require less pruning. Water well-rooted plants to a depth of 2 ft. once a month year-round. Plants growing in storm runoff catchments or other low-lying areas with shallow groundwater may not need supplemental watering. New Mexico olive will defoliate in response to severe drought, and the foliage and tender bark may mildew if plants are kept too wet.

Species, Cultivars, or Varieties

There are no other species in cultivation.

Regional Considerations

New Mexico olive is one of the few plants adaptable enough to thrive in colder northern and mountain gardens as well as in low-desert locations.

Oak

Quercus species

Height: 20 to 50 ft. **Flowers:** Inconspicuous **Foliage:** Varies with species **Bloom Period:** Spring **Zones:** Varies with species **Water:** Moderate	**Light Requirement:**

*E*ven smaller oaks have a solidity that is reassuring, and the larger species are nothing short of majestic. They develop a broad canopy, massive trunk, and thick spreading branches. Oaks root deeply and extensively, mining a large area of soil for moisture, and their crisp or leathery leaves minimize evaporation. "Evergreen" and "deciduous" are terms with much room for interpretation when it comes to describing oaks. The evergreens hold their leaves green through winter and defoliate just as they begin to sprout new leaves in spring. Some of the deciduous species' leaves turn brown or russet in autumn, but hang on the tree nearly until spring. Still others defoliate cleanly in fall and releaf in spring. No matter where you garden in New Mexico, there are oaks that you can grow easily.

WHEN TO PLANT
Generally, the evergreens transplant best in spring and summer, and the deciduous types are best planted in fall, winter, and spring.

WHERE TO PLANT
Oaks prefer well-drained, sandy loam or gravelly soils. They make good street and patio trees and are superb accent specimens. The evergreens are used for screening; their strong resilient wood makes them great wind buffers. To prevent root rot, avoid planting ground-covers that need regular watering close to oak trunks.

HOW TO PLANT
Oaks develop a deep taproot first, but container-grown plants soon abandon the initial root for a strong network of both deep and shallow laterals. Dig holes only as deep as, or at most a few inches deeper than, the depth of the rootball, but 4 to 6 times its diameter. Loosen the soil so that new roots will have an easy time breaking

ground. Backfill soil requires no amendment. A generous topdressing of mulch will encourage root development.

Advice for Care

Establishment takes 4 or 5 years; during that time, plants will benefit from low doses of a granular or time-release fertilizer applied in spring. Oaks need little pruning. Leave all the large shapely branches as the framework; each year in early summer, remove only suckers and small twiggy shoots from the lower stems, exposing more of the trunks as the plant matures. Water well-rooted specimens to a depth of 2 to 3 ft. once a month year-round.

Species, Cultivars, or Varieties

Adapted deciduous oaks include bur oak (*Q. macrocarpa*), which grows at a moderate rate to 50 ft. tall, spreading equally as wide. Its large sweet acorns are 1 in. in diameter with a mossy cup. Bur oak grows best in Zones 3 through 6. Chinkapin oak (*Q. muhlenbergii*) is fast growing with a narrow rounded canopy 50 ft. tall and 20 ft. wide. It produces 3/4-in. sweet acorns and is best adapted in Zones 6 through 8. Gambel oak (*Quercus gambelii*) tends to form shrubby thickets 12 ft. high and twice as wide in drier locations at lower elevations; in cooler, moister gardens it can grow 50 ft. high with 12-in.-diameter trunks. It is best adapted in Zones 4 through 7, from 4000 to 8000 ft. Texas red oak (*Q. texana*, sometimes labeled *Q. buckleyi*) grows moderately fast to 35 ft. tall with an irregular wide-spreading canopy, red fall foliage, and small, biennial, oblong acorns. It is best adapted in Zones 5 through 8. Evergreen oaks include cork oak (*Q. suber*), which is fast growing to 40 ft. high and 30 ft. wide with thick spongy bark and small leaves with serrated margins. It is best adapted in Zones 6 through 8. Escarpment live oak (*Q. fusiformis*) is moderately fast growing to 25 ft. tall with an irregular wide-spreading canopy and small acorns half-enclosed in the caps. It is best adapted in Zones 6 through 8. Southern live oak (*Q. virginiana*) looks like escarpment live oak except that it requires more water and grows much larger, to 60 ft., with wide, horizontally spreading branches. It is less cold hardy (Zones 7 and 8).

Pine

Pinus species

Height: 25 to 60 ft. **Flowers:** Inconspicuous **Foliage:** Evergreen **Bloom Period:** Spring **Zones:** Varies **Water:** Moderate	**Light Requirement:**

*P*ines are long-lived conifers. All 90 species are native to the northern hemisphere, but their distribution ranges from arctic to subtropical mountain slopes, and from inland plains to coastal cliffs. It is no surprise, then, that pines vary considerably in size, form, needle color, needle length, and in their adaptation to heat, cold, and drought.

WHEN TO PLANT

Balled-and-burlapped trees are planted in spring and fall. Container-grown plants can be set out any time of year. In the heat of summer the soil should not be allowed to dry out completely, nor should it be kept soggy wet. Spraying the needles of winter transplants with an anti-transpirant will help prevent windburnt foliage.

WHERE TO PLANT

One of the common traits of all pines is a strong preference for well-drained soil. They are used as screens or windbreaks, and singly or in groups as accent specimens.

HOW TO PLANT

Dig generous holes so that new roots will have an easy time breaking ground. Backfill soil requires no amendment, but a generous fibrous mulch will help keep the soil cooler and more uniformly moist. Larger trees should be staked loosely until they root out to keep them from blowing over in the wind.

ADVICE FOR CARE

Once they are well rooted, pines need watering to a depth of 2 ft. once a month. Pinetip moth has become a problem in some urban areas. Control requires carefully timed applications of systemic insecticides; the Cooperative Extension Service issues alerts each year when spraying is most effective. The size of young trees can be controlled by cutting the central candles in half before the needles start emerging in spring. As plants mature, bare lower and interior branches can be removed to emphasize their elegant natural forms. Pines rarely need fertilizing.

SPECIES, CULTIVARS, OR VARIETIES

The non-native pines include Aleppo pine (*P. halapensis*), which is native to the Middle East in areas receiving 16 to 20 in. of annual rainfall. Rather wispy when young, it develops a thick trunk and rounded canopy with age. It is fast growing from 30 to 60 ft. high and 20 to 40 ft. wide. Afghan pine (*P. eldarica*) is also fast growing to 40 ft. tall and 25 ft. wide with soft light-green needles 3 in. long. It is very narrow when young and develops an irregular tapering shape with age. Afghan pine is heat loving and is adapted to areas that receive 8 to 16 in. annual rainfall. Both Aleppo pine and Afghan pine are cold hardy to Zone 6. Austrian pine (*P. nigra*) has a dense pyramidal shape when young. It is fast growing and develops a rounded crown 30 to 50 ft. tall and half as wide. *P. nigra* 'Compacta' is a denser, slower-growing variety 18 ft. tall and 10 ft. wide. Austrian pines are best adapted to Zones 4 through 7. Bosnian pine (*P. leucodermis*) has a conical form with heavy curving branches bearing pairs of dense bright-green needles. It is slow growing to 25 ft. tall and 15 ft. wide, tolerates moderately salty soils and afternoon shade, and is best adapted in Zones 3 to 7. The native pines include the very long-lived bristlecone pine (*P. aristata*). Growing slowly and irregularly to 20 ft. tall, bristlecone pine is remarkably heat and drought tolerant for a tree native to regions above 10,000 ft. in elevation. It is adapted to gardens in Zones 2 to 7. Limber pine (*P. flexilis*) develops an irregular crown 20 to 30 ft. high and 20 ft. wide. It has a thick trunk and flexible drooping branches. 'Vanderwulf's Pyramid' grows 20 ft. tall but only 7 to 10 ft. wide; the upright branches bear soft blue-green needles 3 in. long. Limber pines are hardy in Zones 2 to 7. Pinyon (*P. edulis*) grows 10 to 25 ft. high and nearly as wide. It is the most heat and drought hardy of the native pines and grows well in Zones 4 through 8. Southwestern white pine (*P. strobiformis*) is considered by some authorities to be a southern subspecies of limber pine. It is distinct in that it grows taller, to 40 ft., with a slender, tapered mature silhouette. It is hardy in Zones 3 to 7.

REGIONAL CONSIDERATIONS

Pines are easy and undemanding if they are matched to the environment they prefer. Only Aleppo, Afghan, and pinyon are heat tolerant enough for Zone 8; in Zone 7, all other species should be planted in cooler niches and mulched well.

Poplar

Populus species

Height: 20 to 80 ft.	**Light Requirement:**
Flowers: Red	
Foliage: Deciduous	
Bloom Period: Spring	
Zones: Varies	
Water: Moderate to ample	

ottonwoods and aspens, both native Western poplars, have been prized by Southwestern people as long as humans have lived in their shade. The ancestors of the modern Pueblo peoples settled within sight of the cottonwood bosques lining the flood plains of New Mexico's rivers where groundwater is most abundant. Colonial Spanish and Eastern pioneers followed the same pattern of settling where cottonwoods made frontier life easier. Aspens, high-elevation natives that reclaim mountainsides after wildfires, rely on deep snowpack and streams fed by snowmelt to fuel their rapid growth. While native poplars occupy moist niches in desert ecosystems, they are adapted to periodic drought. No tall tree can escape the intense Southwestern sun, but the poplars' flexible leaf stems angle their leaves away from the sun during the hottest part of the day, and their waxy leaf surfaces resist evaporation. Cottonwoods and aspens are most practical as garden trees in regions where they might also be found growing wild.

WHEN TO PLANT

Aspens need cool soil to root well, so they transplant best in fall through early spring. Cottonwoods can be planted any time, but ample water will be required to sustain new roots in summer.

WHERE TO PLANT

Aspens will survive at elevations as low as 6000 ft. if they are planted on north and east exposures where the soil is shaded in the afternoon. They are grouped as accent specimens with contrasting groundcovers of dwarf coralberry, dwarf redtwig dogwood, roses, spreading cotoneasters, or compact mahonia to shade the soil. Cottonwoods are large trees that need space to root. They can invade sewer lines and septic leach fields, and they can heave wall footings and pavement if planted within 20 feet of them. They shed small branches and leaves throughout autumn and winter, so companion plants such as yerba mansa and yarrow must tolerate being buried and must also be easy to rake through.

How to Plant

Dig generous holes, loosening soil only as deep as or at most a few inches deeper than the depth of the rootball, but 4 to 6 times its diameter. This ensures that new roots will have an easy time breaking ground. Aspens and cultivated cottonwoods develop lateral absorbing roots first, and rely on those roots most for initial establishment and long-term survival. Backfill soil requires no amendment, but a generous topdressing of compost or shredded bark as mulch will keep the soil cooler and more uniformly moist. Native poplars planted in storm drainage catchments should be mulched with cobblestone, because light fibrous mulches will float away.

Advice for Care

Cottonwoods require a few years of watering at least twice a month in summer to establish an extensive root system. Once established, they can be watered monthly to a depth of 2 ft. year-round; in heavier valley soils where groundwater is shallow, cottonwoods may become self-sustaining. Aspens may need watering once a week when the temperature is above 90 degrees Fahrenheit, every 2 weeks throughout the summer when temperatures are less extreme, and monthly the rest of the year. There are several insects and a few diseases that attack cottonwoods, but vigorous trees outgrow any ill effects quickly. A perpetually ailing tree is a tree in the wrong place.

Species, Cultivars, or Varieties

Mountain cottonwood (*P. acuminata*) develops an upright rounded canopy 45 ft. high and 35 ft. wide. It grows as high as 8000 ft. in elevation. Quaking aspen (*P. tremuloides*) grows rootsprouting colonies of slender plants 20 to 40 ft. tall in clumps at least 10 ft. wide. Its smooth, white, fast-growing trunks and luminous gold autumn leaves have great garden appeal, but it is best adapted between 7500 and 10,000 ft. and suffers in hot lowland landscapes. Valley cottonwood (*P. wislizenii*) is the granddaddy of native trees. Unsurpassed in its adaptability and majesty, it grows quickly from 40 to 80 ft. tall and branches nearly as wide.

Redbud

Cercis species

*R*edbud is an old favorite spring-blooming tree. The intense-purple flowers bloom before the leaves unfold, lighting up gardens that are still mostly dormant in the wake of winter. Redbud grows as a single-trunk or a multi-stemmed specimen. The rounded leaves define an umbrellalike canopy that spreads as wide as the tree is tall. Flat rust-brown seedpods 2¹/₂ in. long and ¹/₂ in. wide persist into winter.

WHEN TO PLANT

Plants can be set out any time of year. Redbud transplanted in summer will need more water during establishment. Cold-acclimated trees set out in winter should be watered immediately after planting to settle the soil around the roots, and not again until spring when the soil begins to warm up.

WHERE TO PLANT

Redbud prefers well-drained soil, but it can be grown in heavy soils if not kept too wet. The deep non-invasive roots make it an ideal tree for planting in narrow beds or near paving. Eastern redbud grows large enough to use as a shade tree in courtyards, and it looks best when grown in such protected microclimates. Oklahoma and western redbuds can be mixed with conifers to add vibrant color to borders and screens, or they can be planted singly or in groups as accent plants. Dwarf plumbago underplanted with white grape hyacinths and dwarf daffodils makes a strong seasonal color display. Compact mahonia, spreading cotoneaster, or creeping germander are other good groundcovers.

How to Plant

Redbud does not develop a dense network of fibrous roots and resents any disturbance during transplanting. Avoid overwatering while a tree is adjusting to new surroundings. Topdressing with mulch keeps the soil more uniformly moist without frequent watering. Dig generous holes, loosening the soil so that new roots will have an easy time breaking ground. No soil amendment is needed.

Advice for Care

To prune redbud as a multi-trunk tree, leave the most shapely lower branches as the framework and gradually remove all the twiggy growth within several feet of the ground. Each year in early summer, remove any suckers or side shoots from the lower stems, exposing more of the trunks as the plant matures. The seedpods may be trimmed off when they begin to look weathered. Once redbud is well rooted, water to a depth of 2 to 3 ft. every 2 weeks when temperatures are above 85 degrees Fahrenheit, and once a month during cooler weather.

Species, Cultivars, or Varieties

Eastern redbud (*Cercis canadensis*) is most commonly available in nurseries, and is best adapted to the cooler northern third of the state. Tender new leaves will burn on the margins if it is planted in open windy locations. Eastern redbud grows slowly to 25 ft. tall and 15 ft. wide. It is best adapted in Zones 5 to 7. Oklahoma redbud (*C. reniformis*) is considered a natural hybrid of Mexican and eastern redbuds and is better adapted to hot windy climates than its eastern parent. It grows slowly to 15 ft. high and 10 ft. wide. The leaves are round, thick, and glossy. They rarely burn along the margins, even in exposed locations. Oklahoma redbud is hardy in Zones 6 through 8. Western redbud (*C. occidentalis*) grows 12 ft. high and wide, usually as a multi-stemmed clump. The leaves are smaller and blue-green, and seedpods persist most of the winter if not removed. Western redbud is reliably hardy in Zones 6 to 8.

TREES

Smoke Tree

Cotinus coggygria

Height: 15 ft.
Flowers: Inconspicuous
Foliage: Deciduous
Bloom Period: Summer
Zones: 5 to 8
Water: Moderate

Light Requirement:

*S*moke tree is grown for its handsome foliage and the cloud of seedheads that give it its common name. The seeds are a little larger than sesame seeds but are rough surfaced and hard, attached to slender branched filaments that form a silken haze. The smoky seedheads are emphasized by the backdrop of 2-in. oval leaves. The natural form has dark blue-green foliage, but the purple-leafed cultivar is more readily available. Both have a harlequin mix of fall color in gold, scarlet, and burgundy.

WHEN TO PLANT

Spring or fall planting is least stressful, but container-grown plants that have been acclimated to heat or cold can be set out any time.

WHERE TO PLANT

Smoke tree grows faster in well-drained soil, but it will grow in any soil as long as it isn't kept too wet, especially when the soil is cold. It can be used as a small specimen tree surrounded with a sweep of artemisia, chives, Jerusalem sage, or fleabane, and it is outstanding against a backdrop of fine-textured foliage such as cedar or blue spruce.

HOW TO PLANT

Dig a generous hole, loosening the soil so that new roots will have an easy time breaking ground. Recent research has demonstrated that the best soil preparation for container-grown trees is to dig holes no deeper than the rootball, but 4 to 6 times its diameter, so that plants quickly develop the lateral absorbing roots they rely on for initial establishment and long-term survival. Backfill soil requires no amendment, but a generous topdressing of mulch accelerates root development by keeping the soil more uniformly moist and more moderate in temperature.

ADVICE FOR CARE
To prune smoke tree, leave the most shapely branches as the framework; early each summer, remove any suckers as well as the twiggy offshoots from the lower stems, exposing more of the trunks as the plant matures. Shaping plants when spring growth slows with the onset of hot weather will limit the amount of regrowth. It takes a few years for smoke tree to root out and develop some character. Fertilizing with a balanced granular or time-release fertilizer each spring for the first three or four years after planting will give plants a strong start. When you begin shaping smoke tree, reduce or eliminate the fertilizing. Water established plants to a depth of 2 ft. every 2 weeks when temperatures are above 90 degrees Fahrenheit, especially when the plants are flowering. Water once a month during cooler weather.

SPECIES, CULTIVARS, OR VARIETIES
Cotinus coggygria 'Purpurea' produces new growth that is tinged with purple, turning green as the leaves mature. 'Royal Purple' is a cultivar whose foliage is a deep red-purple throughout the growing season. Its seedheads are dusky pink. Seeds of 'Royal Purple' produce plants in a range of colors from deep purple to green.

Thornless Honey Locust

Gleditsia triacanthos var. *inermis*

Height: 30 to 50 ft.	**Light Requirement:**
Flowers: Inconspicuous	
Foliage: Deciduous	
Bloom Period: Spring	
Zones: 5 to 8	
Water: Moderate to ample	

*O*f the large shade trees commonly grown in New Mexico, thornless honey locust is one of the best adapted. Although it is native to moist, fertile soil along streams, it has traits that allow it to grow in drier places. Its extensive root system, often 50 ft. beyond the canopy spread, can tap distant sources of moisture. Compound leaves with individual leaflets 1 in. long and 1/2 in. wide have less evaporative surface than the foliage of large-leafed trees. Leaves turn yellow gold in autumn, and when they drop, they reveal a strong framework of arching horizontal branches. The native species is thorny; as the species name, *triacanthos*, indicates, it is three-thorned: the thorns themselves have thorns. The wild honey locust produces a bumper crop of 10-in.-long, 1-in.-wide, curved, chocolate-brown seedpods that deer find irresistible. The horticultural cultivars are mostly thornless and seedless, making them much easier to live with in the garden.

WHEN TO PLANT

Honey locust can be planted any time of year. Fall is the best time to get trees rooted under cooler, milder conditions. In summer, honey locust may need watering once a week until it establishes new roots.

WHERE TO PLANT

Honey locust will grow in just about any soil, but it will root much faster in well-drained soils. Lawn grasses grow well in its filtered light, and it is grown extensively as a shade and street tree. Trees growing near sidewalks should be watered deeply to keep surface roots from heaving the paving.

HOW TO PLANT

Dig generous holes that are only as deep as or at most a few inches deeper than the depth of the rootball, but 4 to 6 times its diameter.

This ensures that new roots will have an easy time breaking ground. Backfill soil requires no amendment, but a generous topdressing of compost or shredded bark as mulch will keep the soil cooler and more uniformly moist, accelerating root development. Planting a groundcover in a tilled 100-sq.-ft. area surrounding a newly planted tree is an ideal way to provide moisture to the locust as its roots expand. If given a strong start, the tree will eventually share moisture with most of the plants in the garden.

ADVICE FOR CARE

The only pruning honey locust needs is the removal of an occasional crossing branch. It naturally develops a well-spaced scaffold of strong stems. Young trees can go through an awkward adolescence, but patience, not pruning, is the best remedy. Apply a granular or time-release fertilizer each spring for the first few years after planting. In strongly alkaline soil, honey locust sometimes needs a dose of granular iron-and-sulfur fertilizer to prevent chlorosis. Water to a depth of 24 in. every 2 weeks while the tree is leafy; water monthly in winter.

SPECIES, CULTIVARS, OR VARIETIES

'Imperial' grows 30 ft. high and spreads equally wide. It was selected for its deep color and dense foliage. 'Moraine', one of the oldest cultivars, produces a broad open canopy. 'Shademaster' grows 40 ft. tall and 30 ft. wide. It was selected for fast growth and because it holds its leaves longer in autumn. 'Skyline' grows 40 ft. tall and 30 ft. wide with a more pyramidal profile and larger leaflets. 'Sunburst', the yellow-leafed cultivar, suffers a much higher incidence of insect and disease attack than any of the other cultivars. In our harsh climate, plants can ill afford to sacrifice chloroplasts for chic garden color. Yellow foliage doesn't manufacture food for a large tree efficiently enough to keep it robust.

Western Catalpa

Catalpa speciosa

Height: 40 ft.	**Light Requirement:**
Flowers: White	
Foliage: Deciduous	
Bloom Period: Spring	
Zones: 4 to 8	
Water: Moderate	

*C*atalpa grows quickly, developing a thick trunk and stout branches that curve upward and outward. Plants growing in windy open areas tend to be more pyramidal, spreading half as wide as they are tall, while plants in more buffered microclimates spread 25 ft. wide. Though the branch scaffold is open and stately, catalpa's 10-in.-long, 8-in.-wide, heart-shaped leaves are so large and abundant that it produces deep shade beneath their canopy. In June, large trusses of fragrant, white, orchidlike flowers with maroon-speckled throats cover the tree. As impressive as the flower show is, catalpa seedpods—dark brown, 1/2 in. thick, and 12 in. long hanging in clusters—are the feature people seem to remember best. Catalpa has been cultivated for so long and in so many places that it seems we all played with the pods when we were children; it may be fond memories of a versatile toy, not our sophisticated horticultural sense, that keeps catalpa dear. Its ability to grow quickly and yet remain resilient in the wind, resist rot and drought, tolerate alkaline soil and salinity, and bloom profusely has earned catalpa the respect of desert gardeners.

WHEN TO PLANT
Catalpa is heat loving, one of the last plants to leaf out in spring. It can be planted in winter but should be kept fairly dry until it begins to leaf out. If it is planted in the heat of summer, water catalpa well to encourage rooting.

WHERE TO PLANT
Catalpa will grow in almost any soil, but it will root faster in warm, well-drained soil. It is used as a shade tree or an accent specimen, and to attract hummingbirds. Since catalpa sheds flowers, large leaves, and seedpods, you will have to clean up after it several times

during the growing season. Though the branches are strong in the wind, the large leaves can become tattered when catalpa is planted in very exposed areas.

How to Plant

Dig generous holes, loosening the soil so that new roots will have an easy time breaking ground. Recent research has demonstrated that the best soil preparation for container-grown or balled-and-burlapped trees is to dig holes only as deep as or at most a few inches deeper than the depth of the rootball, but 4 to 6 times its diameter. Even deeply rooted plants like catalpa abandon their initial taproots and develop lateral roots that they rely on for initial establishment and long-term survival. Backfill soil requires no amendment, but a generous topdressing of mulch accelerates root development by keeping the soil more uniformly moist and more moderate in temperature.

Advice for Care

Catalpa develops a strong framework of branches that requires little pruning except for the removal of occasional rubbing stems or suckers that sprout along the trunk. Once it has rooted out in the garden, catalpa will thrive if watered every 2 weeks while the temperature is above 85 degrees Fahrenheit. Water monthly the rest of the year.

Species, Cultivars, or Varieties

Southern catalpa (*C. bignonioides*) is very similar to western catalpa but may be less cold hardy. Its large leaves have a rather unpleasant odor when crushed, but its flower clusters are fuller than those of western catalpa.

CHAPTER TEN

Turfgrasses

*W*HEN WATER CONSERVATION IS THE SUBJECT, almost nothing causes more uproar than the suggestion that lawns are a problem. Since that fellow in England invented the lawn mower, lawns have been the solution. Lawns are great places to play. They're cool and visually refreshing in a climate where such relief is precious. Their uniform sweep is the glue that holds the garden's bold design elements together. Lawns are a simple and relatively fast way to cover the soil and suppress weeds, and they are also relatively inexpensive to start. It is their continued maintenance that makes them dear.

The concept of lawn is a paradox. The only way lawns are pleasing and useful is if they are uniform and cropped routinely, yet that rigidity is inconsistent with the nature of grasses. Lawns are one of the few instances where monotony is a virtue, and to that end we pour water, fertilizer, and weed killers on the soil so that only the mix of grasses we planted will grow. Then we shave off the grass so we can force it to regrow so we can shave it off again every weekend April through September. In the high desert, our soil, heat, and aridity thwart the process. There's something noble about the pursuit of an ideal, and if only human energy were being wasted there'd be little reason to seek a change. Let Sisyphus continue to push his mower uphill. Unfortunately, bluegrass lawns use more water than any other landscape feature in New Mexico. Turf isn't the problem, but where we put it and how we manage it needs rethinking. Since the other simple landscape solution has been to "rock it," it's no wonder that lawns prevail. Covering acres of soil with plastic and gravel is a crime against nature, and the penalty is having to live in a gravel pit.

There are better options. The first compromise is to plant only as much lawn as we need: a play space in the backyard for the family, maybe a small oasis near the front entrance as a welcoming gesture to our neighbors and guests. Any planting that will be irrigated with

Chapter Ten

sprinklers should be kept at least four feet from walls or low windows to prevent alkali from staining those surfaces. To prevent water being wasted as runoff onto pavement, keep a mulched border between the lawn and nearby hard paved surface unless the pavement drains into a planted area where the water can be captured and used. The second step is to shape the lawn so that a workable pattern of sprinklers can water it efficiently without overspraying walls and windows, or creating runoff onto pavement. Place the sprinklers so that if some of the grass is in the sun most of the day and some is shaded, those areas can be watered independently. Use low-spray-angle sprinklers that deliver water as droplets rather than as mist, and water early in the day to minimize evaporation. Use low-precipitation-rate sprinkler heads if the lawn is on a slope, or cycle the sprinklers on and off so that water is applied at a rate the soil can absorb. Better still, avoid planting spray-irrigated plants on slopes. The lawn grass you choose can make a great difference in water use.

Bluegrass is not included in the profiles because it is so poorly adapted to the heat. Its shallow roots afford it no buffer. The recommended grasses offer a range in color, texture, and reasonable water consumption. Because grass seed and sod producers have to defend their turf more often these days, research is being conducted to select increasingly water-efficient and pest-resistant cultivars of all the turfgrasses. As a result, new varieties are becoming available all the time. Separating the hype from the real advances will take time and trial.

Grasses are very accommodating plants. They slough off roots seasonally, improving the soil they occupy as those roots decompose and regenerate. New Mexico soils are inconsistent. In the foothills, soil is gritty decomposed granite or limestone-based material only a wink away from Portland cement. In the desert and High Plains grasslands, soils vary from loose sand to clay loam. In the river valleys, centuries of seasonal flooding have deposited ribbons of sugar sand, loam, and clay alongside and on top of each other. Because rainfall is scarce, mineral salts build up in the soil. Hardpan layers of calcium carbonate known as *caliche* form below the surface, impeding drainage and limiting root growth. Where groundwater is shallow, capillary action brings salts to the soil surface, forming a crust that limits plant growth. On new construction sites, lime-laden broken concrete, stucco, and sheet rock may litter the surface and lie

Chapter Ten

buried in the soil, becoming covered over when the final grading is done. All these variations will show up in the color, texture, and density of the lawn. Careful soil preparation at planting time will pay big dividends over the life of the lawn no matter what type of lawn grass you choose.

The first step in planting a new lawn is to clean the slate. Cut any annual weeds. Control perennial weeds such as bindweed and bermudagrass with repeated applications of herbicide. Nonselective herbicides containing gyphosate are an effective, minimally toxic means of control because they act systemically and affect only actively growing plants that absorb the chemical through their leaves or green bark. Established trees and shrubs that may have roots in the area will not be damaged unless spray drifts onto their leaves.

Once the area is cleared, install the sprinkler lines. Level the lawn area as much as possible to eliminate high spots that will dry out more quickly, and low spots that will stay too wet, promoting disease. Turn on the sprinklers to check the coverage and make any adjustments needed. Till compost into the surface as deeply as possible. Since our soils are completely lacking, be generous with the organic matter: 1 cubic yard of compost per 50 to 80 square feet of lawn area. Peat moss is a poor soil amendment in our climate. It dries out quickly, is difficult to rewet, and repels water when dry. When used as a topdressing, it usually blows away. Peat is also a nonrenewable resource unless you think in terms of millennia, while well-made compost is alive with beneficial micro-organisms, and it recycles waste products that would otherwise clog landfills. After tilling, relevel the surface, smoothing out any uneven spots. Then run the sprinklers again to settle the soil.

Finally it's time to plant. Divide the seed into two portions. Use a spreader (or broadcast the seed by hand if you can be consistent enough) and cover the whole area with half the seed. Start where you finished the first seeding and backtrack, sowing the second half of the seed. Lightly rake the seed into the soil. You can topdress lightly with compost, roll the surface with a half-filled roller, or just water lightly to settle the seed into the soil. Starting a lawn from sod, sprigs, or plugs involves the same soil preparation. Sprigging is very similar to seeding: broadcast the sprigs and rake them lightly into the surface. Sod strips should be laid snugly against each other with successive rows alternating the same way bricks are laid, in a basketweave pattern. Plugs are usually planted in a checkerboard pattern. Keep the newly planted surface as consistently moist as our sun and wind allow. New lawns usually need to be watered lightly at least twice a day until the seed germinates, or once a day until the sod or plugs begin to root. Gradually decrease the frequency and increase the depth of watering to encourage the grass to root as deeply as possible.

Once the lawn is growing, there are ways to manage it that will conserve resources. Leave grasses as tall as possible: 3 in. for fescue, and 4 to 6 in. for buffalograss or blue grama. Taller grass develops deeper roots, and the shade at the soil surface keeps weed seeds from sprouting. If you have persistent problems with crabgrass or spurge, you may be mowing too short. Either mow often and leave the clippings to enrich the soil, or collect the clippings to use as mulch in other parts of the garden. (Bermudagrass clippings can't be used as mulch because they may root and grow.) Keep the mower blade sharp so that grass is clipped, not torn. Water grass as deeply as the type of grass can potentially root—a minimum of 12 in. for fescue, and twice that for warm-season grasses. Experiment with different watering schedules to see how infrequently you can water. If the lawn can go 10 days when the water penetrates to 18 in., but still needs water after 10 days when watered to 24 in., the deeper application is a waste of water. If water runs off before it can soak in, run the sprinkler in cycles. Aerate and remove thatch as often as needed to help water penetrate.

Fertilizers should promote root growth; the stronger the root system, the more vigorous the lawn will be. Too much nitrogen favors mildew. Our dry climate does give us one advantage in growing lawns: Most lawn diseases flourish when temperatures are above 80 degrees Fahrenheit, and when humidity is above 70 percent. It's difficult to raise the humidity to 50 percent here. Rather than stimulating topgrowth in summer, keep turfgrasses green with a granular iron-and-sulfur fertilizer. The grass will have richer color, without the new growth that requires more water and mowing. Avoid lawn fertilizers that contain weed killers, especially if tree and shrub roots extend under the lawn.

Bermudagrass

Cynodon species

Height: Mow to 2 in.	**Light Requirement:**
Color: Bright green	
Zones: 6 to 8	
Water: Moderate	

*B*ermudagrass tolerates desert heat better than any other conventional turfgrass. Water is required to keep it lush, but it will survive with no supplemental watering and regrow vigorously after long periods of neglect. In the central part of the state where it is cool enough for other grasses to be viable lawn options, the ability of bermudagrass to rise from the dead and relentlessly invade flower beds makes it a target for herbicides rather than an object of desire. But the very toughness that makes it a formidable weed also makes it a viable lawn. The roots of this long-lived turfgrass may penetrate up to 6 ft. of soil in search of shallow groundwater. The roots also have the ability to branch deep below ground and regrow, so it fills in bare spots easily and tolerates heavy wear. Bermuda is rich green, thick and carpet-like, low-growing, and salt and alkali tolerant. Aside from being high maintenance and potentially invasive, its main drawback is its long dormant season, browning out with the first hard freezes and remaining dormant until the soil warms again late in spring.

WHEN TO PLANT
Bermudagrass is planted in late spring and summer. Allow at least 8 weeks of establishment time before frost.

WHERE TO PLANT
To minimize its wayward tendencies, locate bermudagrass lawns well away from flower beds, vegetable gardens, and any other heavily irrigated planting that you don't want overtaken.

HOW TO PLANT
The best lawn-quality bermudas have been bred for fine texture, a more moderate growth rate, and limited sterile flowering. Because the hybrids produce little or no seed, they are grown from sprigs. Cut stolons are broadcast on prepared soil and topdressed lightly to

cover, or the soil is crimped with a roller to push the cuttings into the surface. A bushel of stolon sprigs covers 200 sq. ft. of lawn bed.

ADVICE FOR CARE

In southern New Mexico, bermudagrass is often flood irrigated. This can be less wasteful than sprinklers, since water is applied less often and less is lost to evaporation. Lawns more than 1 year old should be watered to a depth of 18 to 24 in. Extra-close mowing and heavy raking at the beginning of the growing season helps warm the soil and allows water to penetrate better. Power-raking may be needed every few years. Bermuda should be fertilized in spring and once or twice in summer, depending on cultivar and care. It should be kept mowed a short 2 in. high.

SPECIES, CULTIVARS, OR VARIETIES

Common bermuda (*Cynodon dactylon*) is coarse, very aggressive, and flowers and reseeds prodigiously, making it even more invasive as well as a potent allergen. Two lbs. of hulled seed cover 1000 sq. ft. of lawn. 'Sahara' and 'Sultan' are newer cultivars for lawn use that are finer textured. The sterile hybrids of African bermuda are the finest. 'Tifway II' and 'Midirion' are propagated by sprigging.

BERMUDAGRASS CONTROL

Because glyphosate, the preferred control, is a systemic herbicide, the grass must be actively growing when the chemical is applied so that it will be absorbed by the green tissue. Target application times for weakening bermuda are just as the grass begins active growth and just as it starts to flower; at these times the grass has expended some of its stored reserves. Late summer is another optimum time because the herbicide will be absorbed more deeply into the roots as plants store carbohydrates before dormancy. Spray according to label recommendations, and a week later the grass will suddenly turn brown and look dead. Don't be fooled. You have succeeded in killing off the top and hopefully a few feet of roots. It will be back. Water occasionally to encourage regrowth, then repeat the process as soon as enough green is showing to absorb a significant dose. Usually it takes 3 applications and followup spot treatments to control robust bermudagrass.

Blue Grama

Bouteloua gracilis

Height: 4 to 18 in.
Color: Pale green
Zones: 4 to 8
Water: Low to moderate

Light Requirement:

---

*B*lue grama, native throughout most of the low and mid-elevation Southwest and Great Plains, is fast growing and long lived on most soils. It is one of the best native grasses for lawn use. After many years of cultivating native and desert-adaptive plants, the dark, lush green of conventional lawngrasses now seems intrusive and garish to me when compared with the soft texture and pale-green tones of blue grama. It is classified as a modified bunchgrass; if given no supplemental watering, it grows in discrete flat-topped clumps. When seeded heavily and watered modestly, it forms a dense, even sod. Blue grama survives with as little as 6 in. of annual rainfall, but it needs about 1 in. of water a week from May through August to maintain lawn density. It goes dormant with the first hard freezes in fall, and greens up when the soil warms in spring. Close mowing, to 2 in., and heavy raking in late March remove thatch and expose the soil to more sun, accelerating the recovery process.

WHEN TO PLANT

Blue grama is sown in late spring and summer, allowing at least 6 weeks of establishment time before the first frost in autumn. Seed sown when the soil is 70 degrees Fahrenheit or warmer germinates in 5 to 10 days.

WHERE TO PLANT

Use blue grama either as a groomed lawn or as a wilder prairie groundcover. In small gardens self-sowing can be a nuisance if the grass goes to seed. People sensitive to grass pollens should mow often enough to keep the grass from flowering.

HOW TO PLANT

Sow blue grama on prepared soil at a rate of 4 lbs. live seed per 1000 sq. ft. Rake the seed ¼ to ½ in. into the soil. Native grasses are sold either by bulk weight or PLS (percentage of live seed). Blue grama

seed is very chaffy, and is not usually cleaned more than 50 percent
by weight. If you buy bulk seed, you may need twice the bulk quantity to equal the pure live seed count.

ADVICE FOR CARE

Once the grass is 4 to 5 in. tall, you will have to decide whether you
prefer the graceful sweep of blue grama unmowed, or whether you
want a more traditional lawn. The grass will be healthiest and have
the best color and density if it is kept long by lawn standards: 3 in.
is minimum, 4 in. is better. It may need mowing every 3 weeks in
June, July, and August. Water deeply once a week when temperatures are 85 degrees Fahrenheit or above, every 2 weeks when
temperatures are 70 to 85 degrees Fahrenheit, and monthly during
cooler weather. Lawns more than 1 year old should be watered to a
minimum depth of 24 in. Apply 1 to 2 lbs. of nitrogen fertilizer in
April. In early August a granular iron-and-sulfur fertilizer can be
applied to deepen the green color. Do not fertilize in fall or winter. I
prefer the softer look of blue grama when it is left unmowed in early
fall, not shaved uniformly as it goes into dormancy. But if the grass
is a play space for children and pets, you may want to cut it to 3 in.;
when it dries in winter, it becomes brittle and will be tracked into
the house on clothes and pet fur.

SPECIES, CULTIVARS, OR VARIETIES

'Hachita', 'Lovington', and 'Alma' are selections made from wild
stands near New Mexico locations of the same names. 'Hachita' is
the cultivar favored for lawn use.

REGIONAL CONSIDERATIONS

Although blue grama grows to 8500 ft., cool-season grasses make
better lawns above 7500 ft. in elevation.

Buffalograss

Buchloe dactyloides

	Light Requirement:
Height: 4 to 8 in.	
Color: Pale green	
Zones: 4 to 7	
Water: Low to moderate	

*B*uffalograss is a Great Plains native of the shortgrass prairie that extends into northeastern New Mexico. It is naturally pale green while actively growing and a blend of warm brown tones when dormant due to frost or drought. It is slower growing during establishment and is similar in color but not quite as fine-textured as blue grama, which is the grass most often mixed with buffalo for lawns. The mix is a good marriage, since buffalograss produces stolons to fill in bare spots once the lawn is established, while the grama covers faster to begin with, making a usable lawn more quickly. Buffalograss seems to spread fastest on heavier soils. Because it is short enough to never need mowing, buffalograss is often planted solo, especially if a soft-textured "wild" lawn is preferred. Male and female flowers are borne on separate plants, the fringe of male flowers topping the leaf blades by an inch or two, while the female flowers bloom and produce their hulled seeds near the ground. An all-female lawn is more uniform on the surface; it is also pollenless, which is a boon to allergy sufferers.

WHEN TO PLANT

Buffalograss is planted in late spring and summer, allowing at least a month of establishment time before the first frost in autumn.

WHERE TO PLANT

Use buffalograss as a groomed lawn or as an unmowed groundcover. Because the large seeds form near the soil surface, weedy self-sowing is not usually a problem. Buffalograss does spread by stolons and can invade flower beds, though not nearly as aggressively as bermuda. People sensitive to grass pollens can plant the all-female cultivars, especially in courtyards, around patios, and outside windows.

How to Plant

Sow buffalograss on prepared soil at a rate of 4 lbs. of seed per 1000 sq. ft. Rake the seed $1/4$ to $1/2$ in. into the soil. Buffalograss seed is usually more than 90 percent pure, so the weights of bulk seed and percentage of live seed (often noted as PLS) are similar. Buffalo is also sold as treated or untreated seed. Treated seed has been soaked in potassium nitrate and germinates much faster, requiring only a week or two in warm soil. Untreated seed can take a year or two to germinate, which is not much of a deal even at half price.

Advice for Care

Once the grass is 4 in. tall you need to decide whether you prefer the soft texture of unmowed buffalograss or whether you want a more traditional lawn. If buffalograss is not mowed at all, it should be raked heavily in early spring to remove dried growth and expose the soil to more sun, accelerating the regreening. If the grass is underplanted with spring bulbs, careful raking makes the bulb display more emphatic. General care of buffalograss is the same as for blue grama, whether they are mixed or grown as monocultures.

Species, Cultivars, or Varieties

'Prairie' and '609' are two all-female cultivars that are propagated by plugs or sod. Unlike cool-season grasses, buffalo is usually not sodded as full surface cover, but is either plugged 1 plant per sq. ft. (1150 plugs needed per 1000 sq. ft.) or sodded checkerboard fashion with bare soil gaps between sod pieces. This reduces cost but requires regular weeding until the stolons fill the gaps. 'Topgun' and 'Plains' are two newer seed varieties selected for lawn use because they are denser, shorter leafed, and darker in color. Until recently, buffalograss was bred for range use, so older cultivars such as 'Texoka' and 'Comanche' grow taller and reseed more heavily.

Regional Considerations

Grubs have been a problem for buffalograss grown in the southern desert. As buffalograss and blue grama are more commonly grown as lawns in New Mexico, it is becoming evident that buffalograss is better adapted to the eastern plains and northern third of the state. Blue grama is more widely adapted throughout the state and is definitely more drought tolerant.

Sheep's Fescue

Festuca pseudovina 'Covar'

Height: 3 to 10 in. **Color:** Dark green **Zones:** 3 to 7 **Water:** Moderate to high	**Light Requirement:**

Sheep's fescue is a cool-season grass with the dark-green color and fine leaf blades of bluegrass, but it clumps tightly so that unmowed plantings have an interesting swirled and tufted surface. Cowlick sod is definitely not a traditional lawn. If your definition of lawn includes regular mowing, consider sheep's fescue a groundcover. If you're looking for grass with the color and texture of bluegrass, but would rather not have to mow regularly, sheep's fescue may be the lawn of your dreams. The variability and wide native range of the fine fescues generate much debate among taxonomists about the origins and specific names in this group. For gardening purposes, the cultivar name based on recent performance characteristics is more important than blueblood lineage—how the youngster behaves is more important than who her grandmother was. Apparently the European strains tend to have firmer, rougher blades, while the North American side of the family has slender, wiry leaves. 'Covar' is a selection from Turkey that seems quite heat tolerant and is adapted to 12 to 14 in. of annual precipitation. If it is to take any wear or grow thickly enough to exclude weeds, sheep's fescue will require additional watering.

WHEN TO PLANT

Cool-season grasses should be sown in mid-spring in the north, and in late summer or fall in central New Mexico. Sheep's fescue has one of the coldest germination temperature tolerances: it will germinate when temperatures are near freezing. Young seedlings also tolerate extreme cold well.

WHERE TO PLANT

Sheep's fescue is a mountain or oasis plant, and while it will grow in full sun above 8000 ft., it is more water efficient and lusher in shade at lower elevations.

How to Plant

While uniformity is not as important for sheep's fescue as it is for conventional lawns, for best results prepare the seed bed well. Improving the water-holding capacity of the soil will produce a healthier stand of grass. Sow 5 lbs. of seed per 1000 sq. ft., raking the seeds $1/4$ to $1/2$ in. into the surface. Water morning and evening until the seed germinates, then cut back to once daily, then to every other day, while increasing the depth of watering.

Advice for Care

Sheep's fescue will be healthiest and have the best color and density if it is kept long by lawn standards and mowed to 4 in. seasonally to rejuvenate it each spring and late summer. Water deeply once or twice a week when temperatures are above 85 degrees Fahrenheit, at least twice a month when temperatures are 60 to 85 degrees Fahrenheit, and monthly during cooler weather. Grass more than 1 year old should be watered to a depth of 18 in. Apply a balanced lawn fertilizer in fall and again in spring if the grass needs a boost. A granular iron-and-sulfur fertilizer can be applied in summer to maintain a deep green color without forcing the soft new growth that will require more water in the heat.

Species, Cultivars, or Varieties

'Reliant' is an endophyte-enhanced cultivar. Endophytes are microorganisms that improve nutrient and water absorption for the host plant.

Regional Considerations

Cool-season grasses prefer the higher elevations and northern foothills in New Mexico. When it comes to coaxing temperate-zone plants to grow in the desert, there comes a point at which you cannot compensate for heat with extra water. Geographically speaking, that point is near Truth or Consequences in central New Mexico. The truth is that there are consequences beyond water use that determine if a plant is worth a space in our gardens; in the desert, heat is the ultimate test.

TURFGRASSES

Tall Turf-Type Fescue

Festuca arundinacea cultivars

Height: 18 in. mowed to 4 in. **Color:** Dark green **Zones:** 4 to 7 **Water:** Moderate to high	**Light Requirement:**

*T*all turf-type fescues have been undergoing a tremendous change in response to the demand for more resource-efficient turfgrass. The old varieties grow to 3 ft. high if unmowed, form a high-centered clump, are medium green in color, and tend to be coarse with leaf blades 1/4 in. wide. The effective rooting depth of tall fescue is about 18 in., which gives it greater reserves to draw on. The newer cultivars, especially those that have been endophyte-enhanced, tend to be finer textured, deeper green, and more pest resistant. They are reasonable water users if managed well. In central New Mexico, tall fescue lawns can be kept green all year if watered and fertilized, but most people appreciate a winter break from mowing, and they reduce watering so that the lawn goes dormant. Tall fescue's one remaining drawback as a lawngrass is its inability to close over dead spots, as a rhizomatous grass does by growing underground stems which form new roots and buds at the nodes.

WHEN TO PLANT
Cool-season grasses should be sown in April or May in the north, and in late summer or fall in the central, mid-elevation parts of New Mexico.

WHERE TO PLANT
Tall fescue cultivars are the best conventional turfgrass choice for the northern 2/3 and the high-elevation areas of New Mexico. Fescue lawns take children's play wear in stride, and have the dark color that fits the traditional lawn paradigm.

HOW TO PLANT
Creating a good seed bed and supplying enough water are the prime requirements for a tall fescue lawn. If the soil is not amended and consistent, no amount of water will compensate. Broadcast 7 to 10 lbs. of tall fescue seed per 1000 sq. ft. of lawn area. Rake the seed in 1/2 in. deep and begin watering morning and evening until the

seed germinates, cutting back the frequency to once daily, then to
every other day while increasing the depth of watering. During the
first summer you may need to continue watering every 2 days. Tall
fescue blends are also available as sod; soil preparation and care are
the same as for seed. Water should initially penetrate the sod and a
few inches into the soil below to take full advantage of fescue's ability to root quickly and deeply.

ADVICE FOR CARE

Tall fescue will be healthiest and have the best color and density if
it is mowed to 4 in. from April through October. Mow often enough
that you cut only 1 in. or less off the top. Once tall fescue is established, you should water deeply twice a week when temperatures
are 85 degrees Fahrenheit and above, once a week at 65 to 85
degrees Fahrenheit, at least twice a month when temperatures are
50 to 65 degrees Fahrenheit, and monthly during cooler weather.
Lawns more than 1 year old should be watered to a depth of 18 in.
Apply a balanced lawn fertilizer in fall and again in spring if the
grass needs a boost. A granular iron-and-sulfur fertilizer can be
applied in summer to maintain a deep green color without forcing
the soft new growth that will require more water in the heat.

SPECIES, CULTIVARS, OR VARIETIES

Prior to 1980, 'Alta' and 'K31' were the commonly grown cultivars
of tall fescue. A turfgrass revolution began with the introduction
of 'Rebel' and 'Falcon' in 1980. These cultivars were distinctly
finer bladed and darker green than the old pasture-grass varieties.
'Olympic', 'Jaguar', 'Mustang', and 'Apache' followed, and the race
was on to develop selections of tall fescue that look as much like
bluegrass as possible. 'Triathalawn' is a blend of several of the newer
cultivars; the individual components change from crop to crop.
'Titan', Shenandoah, 'Tribute', and 'Mesa' are endophyte-enhanced
cultivars. Endophytes, fungal microorganisms within plant tissues,
improve nutrient and water absorption for the host plant. Endophytes are toxic to livestock, and enhanced cultivars are not intended
for pasture use. The newest trend in fescue is the dwarf cultivars,
which are finer leaved, slower growing, and the most like bluegrass.
Unfortunately, this similarity extends to greater water consumption.
In other parts of the country, its greater disease resistance means
dwarf fescue is unquestionably a better choice than bluegrass. In
New Mexico, 'Silverado' seems to be the best cultivar, a bit more
water conservative that the others. 'Rebel Jr.' is similar. 'Bonsai' has
a reputation for being harder to establish and for needing more
water. 'Crewcut', 'El Dorado', and 'Short Stop' are a few others;
there will probably continue to be refinements of these.

CHAPTER ELEVEN

Vines

*V*INES LEND A FEELING OF LUSHNESS to the landscape, and in desert gardens they mark the oases, the spaces designed for human comfort. Vines are shrubs that just don't seem to know when to quit, but in New Mexico they are less likely to swallow a garden whole. For once, our harsh climate is an advantage, limiting the rampant overgrowth of these otherwise useful plants. At higher elevations, the short growing season and cold winters contain the growth of even the hardiest vines; in the low desert, heat and aridity apply brakes to luxuriant growth. Vines have distinctive characteristics, and getting to know their personalities ensures a good match of plant and garden space. Clematis are light and deceptively fragile-looking, while wisteria and silkvine grow large and heavy with age. In time, their thick stems become living sculpture. The ivies are grown for their foliage, while coral honeysuckle and trumpet vine are valued for their colorful flowers and the hummingbirds they invite. Queen's wreath and silver lace vine can take the heat, while English ivy will grow well only in deep shade.

Vines are most often grown on trellises as screens, used to hide wire fences, and planted to provide greenery in spaces too narrow for large shrubs. In dry, windy climates like ours, vines' greatest value may be their use as substitutes for large trees, providing fast shade for patios and window overhangs. The large trees most often used as shade trees are difficult to establish and maintain in the desert. They are native to low-lying stream and lakeside environments or to forests where trees grow in large colonies. Abundant moisture is available and the force of the wind is borne by the sheltering mass. Even when enough time and water are invested to grow such trees in the desert, wind batters lone specimens that become more vulnerable as they grow larger. Vines grown on open lattice ramadas, pergolas, or arbors can provide leafy green shade with a fraction of the water and none of the wind stress—and they

Chapter Eleven

can do it faster than a large tree can. Ironically, trees themselves supply the timbers used to build many of the supports for vines.

Because there is such great variety in the mature size of vines, it's important to provide a trellis of complementary proportions. Clematis and coral honeysuckle need light support to match their fine stems, while wisteria, silk vine, and trumpet vine need sturdy support such as 5- or 6-in.-diameter wooden posts or 3- or 4-in. ironwork. It is not uncommon to see a forty-year-old wisteria holding up the arbor that is supposed to be supporting it. To keep them looking fresh and vigorous, vines such as clematis, queen's wreath, and silver lace vine need to be cut back severely every few years to remove layers of twiggy growth. They are easier to remove from an open post-and-rail support than from wire fencing or latticework where the stems and trellis will become thoroughly entangled.

Boston Ivy

Parthenocissus tricuspidata

Height: 30 ft. **Flowers:** Inconspicuous **Foliage:** Deciduous **Bloom Period:** Spring **Zones:** 4 to 7 **Water:** Moderate	**Light Requirement:**

*B*oston ivy is grown for its brilliant red fall color, but it is never unattractive. In spring, large, glossy bright-green leaves emerge along slender wiry stems that cling to walls and other surfaces with small suction disks. The lustrous green foliage is a refreshing respite throughout summer. In autumn, blasts of arctic air pushed into the high desert by fast-moving cold fronts can turn 80-degrees-Fahrenheit sunshine into hoarfrost that freeze-dries tender foliage. Two days later the temperatures may rebound, but the garden looks like winter. Regardless of this erratic weather, Boston ivy's blaze of autumn glory comes off as planned year after year, and when the leaves finally drop, a network of fine stems decorated with blue berries makes an interesting winter pattern.

WHEN TO PLANT

Boston ivy can be planted almost any time of year. Early spring and late summer or autumn are least stressful, but well-rooted plants that have been acclimated to cold can be set out in winter wherever the ground is not frozen. Since Boston ivy should be grown in the shade, it is buffered from the most extreme summer conditions, but it will require more water during establishment if transplanted when temperatures are above 85 degrees Fahrenheit.

WHERE TO PLANT

Though not fussy about soil, Boston ivy strongly prefers shade. When started against a northeast-facing wall or solid wooden fence, it will sometimes eventually grow into full sun, but the large leaf surfaces may sunscald. Space plants 8 to 10 ft. apart for solid cover in 2 to 3 years, or use a single plant highlighted against an expanse of wall to create a filigree affect.

How to Plant

Dig generous holes, loosening the soil so that new roots will have an easy time breaking ground. Recent research has demonstrated that the best soil preparation for container-grown plants is to dig holes only as deep as, or at most a few inches deeper than, the depth of the rootball, but 4 to 6 times its diameter. This enables plants to develop the lateral absorbing roots they rely on for initial establishment and long-term survival. Backfill soil requires no amendment, but a generous topdressing of composted cotton burrs or shredded bark as mulch will keep the soil cooler and more uniformly moist, accelerating root development.

Advice for Care

It takes a few years for Boston ivy to root extensively; water frequently and fertilize lightly during that time. Established plants should be watered to a depth of 2 ft. every 2 weeks when temperatures are above 75 degrees Fahrenheit; water monthly during cooler weather.

Species, Cultivars, or Varieties

Parthenocissus tricuspidata 'Veitchii' is a cultivar with smaller, finer-textured foliage. Woodbine (*Parthenocissus inserta*) is the Southwestern native species of Virginia creeper. Like Boston ivy, it produces reliable red fall foliage. Woodbine clings with tendrils on stems that are smooth and woody, and its blue fruits attract roadrunners and songbirds in autumn. It is fast growing to 20 ft. and does well in sun or shade.

VINES

Carolina Jessamine

Gelsemium sempervirens

Height: 10 ft.	Light Requirement:
Flowers: Yellow	
Foliage: Evergreen	
Bloom Period: Spring	
Zones: 6 to 8	
Water: Moderate	

*C*arolina jessamine is a nicely controlled and fresh-looking vine. Its shiny medium-green leaves are 1 in. wide and 2 in. long, borne opposite each other on smooth green or reddish brown climbing stems. Fragrant tubular yellow flowers appear in spring, growing most profusely on plants that receive reflected heat from walls and paving. Carolina jessamine's roots are rhizomatous, but because they won't extend into dry soil, they are easy to contain in our desert gardens.

WHEN TO PLANT

Because jessamine is evergreen and heat-loving, it is best to plant it in late spring and summer, when plants will root quickly. Dehydrating winter winds can damage plants set out during cold weather.

WHERE TO PLANT

Carolina jessamine isn't particular about soil, but it does prefer warmth. In Zone 6 gardens, it needs the warmest position possible, and will rarely grow large enough to cover even a small arbor. At lower elevations in southern New Mexico it can be grown on a ramada or larger trellis, but still is not aggressive enough to be used for shading.

HOW TO PLANT

Dig generous holes, loosening the soil so that new roots will have an easy time breaking ground. Recent research has demonstrated that the best soil preparation for container-grown plants is to dig holes only as deep as, or at most a few inches deeper than, the depth of the rootball, but 4 to 6 times its diameter. Most plants develop lateral absorbing roots first, and rely on those roots most for initial establishment and long-term survival. Backfill soil requires no amendment, but a generous topdressing of compost, pecan hulls, shredded bark, or fine gravel as mulch will keep the soil more uniformly moist and more even in temperature, hastening root development.

ADVICE FOR CARE
Though Carolina jessamine doesn't need frequent pruning, young plants may be tip pruned lightly to induce branching, and mature plants may have the oldest stems removed after flowering in spring to stimulate new growth. It takes a few years for Carolina jessamine to root extensively; water frequently and fertilize lightly during this time. Established plants should be watered to a depth of 2 ft. every 2 weeks when temperatures are above 80 degrees Fahrenheit; water monthly during cooler weather.

SPECIES, CULTIVARS, OR VARIETIES
Gelsemium sempervirens 'Plena' is a cultivar with double flowers.

Clematis

Clematis species and cultivars

Height: 20 ft.	**Light Requirement:**
Flowers: Varies with cultivar	
Foliage: Deciduous	
Bloom Period: Varies with species	
Zones: 4 to 7	
Water: Moderate to ample	

*T*here are 200 species of clematis, many with flowers so abundant and so beautiful in form and color that they were moved from their native habitats into gardens centuries ago. The advent of *Clematis × jackmanii* and other hybrids of the Chinese species *C. lanuginosa* made clematis one of the most popular garden vines worldwide. Slender stems climb by means of tendrils on the leaf stalks. New growth is rather brittle. Clematis produces elegant compound leaves and flowers that provide nectar for many types of butterflies.

WHEN TO PLANT
Clematis are best planted in spring. Avoid transplanting while plants are in bloom or when temperatures are above 85 degrees Fahrenheit; it is difficult to keep new plants adequately moist at these times.

WHERE TO PLANT
Clematis are oasis plants in dry-climate gardens. The hybrids prefer to have their roots kept cool, moist, and shaded, while topgrowth receives at least a half-day of full sun. All clematis will require less water if given some shade in the afternoon. They can be planted on the north or east side of a fence as a backdrop for a rosebed with compatible perennials such as golden columbine and cranesbill; or you can underplant clematis with shrubs such as 'Red Cascade' rose, compact mahonia, or cotoneaster.

HOW TO PLANT
Dig generous holes only as deep as the rootball, but 4 to 6 times its diameter, loosening the soil so that new roots will have an easy time breaking ground. The hybrids are heavy feeders and need consistent

moisture, especially while blooming. Tilling 4 in. of compost into the soil where they will be planted and working more organic matter into the backfill will give hybrids a strong start and keep them productive. No amendment is needed for anemone, golden bells, scarlet clematis, or western virgin's bower, but a generous compost mulch will enhance growth by keeping the soil cooler and more evenly moist.

ADVICE FOR CARE

Remove the oldest woody stems each year to keep plants flowering heavily. Clematis may need water once a week when the temperatures are above 85 degrees Fahrenheit, every 2 weeks when temperatures are 65 to 85 degrees Fahrenheit, and monthly during cooler weather. Because they bloom so profusely, fertilize the hybrids monthly from April to August. The species usually don't require fertilizer once they are established, but in very alkaline soils, a granular iron-and-sulfur fertilizer in summer will help prevent chlorosis.

SPECIES, CULTIVARS, OR VARIETIES

Anemone clematis (*C. montana* var. *rubens*) is a Himalayan native that is cold hardy to Zone 5. It grows 15 ft. tall and produces fragrant pink flowers in spring. Because it blooms most heavily on the previous year's growth, it should be thinned after flowering to promote new growth. *C. tanguitica* 'Golden Bells' is a Mongolian native also hardy to Zone 5. It grows stems 15 ft. long and has gray-green leaves, nodding bell-shaped yellow flowers in summer, and silver seedheads in autumn. The Jackman hybrid, a cross of *C. lanuginosa* and *C. viticella*, is one of the oldest and most heavily blooming cultivars with 4-in. deep-purple flowers. Chinese clematis (*C. lanuginosa*) has several cultivars with very large flowers including 'Candida', white; 'Nelly Moser', pink with darker markings in the center; and 'Ramona', lavender blue. They typically grow less than 10 ft. high, but 'Nelly Moser' can grow to 15 ft. in good soil with ample water. Scarlet clematis (*C. texensis*) is a more drought-tolerant species with red urn-shaped flowers in summer. It grows 8 ft. high, has dense blue-green foliage, and is best in Zones 6 to 8. Western virgin's bower (*C. ligusticifolius*) is native along rivers in New Mexico to 8500 ft. It twines 20 ft. high and has clusters of fragrant white flowers in summer followed by silver seed plumes in autumn.

Coral Honeysuckle

Lonicera sempervirens

Height: 8 ft.
Flowers: Orange-scarlet, yellow inside
Foliage: Briefly deciduous
Bloom Period: Intermittent throughout
the growing season
Zones: 3 to 8
Water: Moderate

Light Requirement:

Coral honeysuckle is a contradictory plant. Honeysuckles are renowned for their sweet scent, but coral honeysuckle is an oddity among *Lonicera* since the species and most of the cultivars are not fragrant. Most honeysuckles are rampant growers, but coral honeysuckle is very compact, rarely growing more than 10 ft. long. It tolerates heat, yet is also surprisingly cold hardy. There are several cultivars and hybrids, all with similar rounded, leatherlike, blue-gray leaves paired along slender twining stems. All produce large clusters of tubular flowers that range in color from apricot orange to pink-infused coral with a yellow throat. Hummingbirds find the nectar impossible to ignore.

WHEN TO PLANT

Coral honeysuckle can be planted from containers any time of year, but it roots most quickly in spring or late summer and autumn. Stems that are just beginning to become woody can be pinned to moist soil and rooted in summer.

WHERE TO PLANT

Although it is not fussy about soil, coral honeysuckle should not be kept too wet in heavy clay. In sun or shade, the flowers contrast with the blues and purples of buddleias, salvias, Russian sage, flax, blue mist, English lavender, and catmint. Coral honeysuckle blooms well in the shade, and placing it where the roots and most of the topgrowth are screened from the sun, especially in the afternoon, can greatly reduce its water demand.

HOW TO PLANT

Dig generous holes only as deep as the rootball, but several times wider, loosening the soil so that new roots will have an easy time breaking ground. Backfill soil requires no amendment, but plants root faster with a generous mulch of composted cotton burrs, shredded bark, or pecan hulls because it keeps the soil more uniformly moist and moderate in temperature.

ADVICE FOR CARE

Because of its controlled growth habit, coral honeysuckle needs to be thinned only every 3 or 4 years. Remove the oldest stems to encourage new growth. It takes a few years to establish an extensive root system; plants should be watered weekly in summer, especially while in bloom. Deep watering every 2 weeks when the temperature is above 85 degrees Fahrenheit and monthly during cooler weather is enough to maintain established plants. Fertilizer is usually not needed, but a small amount of fertilizer applied to companion plants will not cause coral honeysuckle to run amok. Aphids may appear on new growth but are easily controlled: Wash them off with a strong spray of water.

SPECIES, CULTIVARS, OR VARIETIES

'Goldflame' honeysuckle (*L. × heckrottii*) is the fragrant exception among coral honeysuckles. It bears large clusters of flowers in coral-pink and yellow on stems 6 to 12 ft. long. It is less cold tolerant than the others and is hardy only to Zone 5. 'Magnifica' and 'Dropmore Scarlet' are two other large-flowered cultivars; both produce orange-coral flowers and neither is fragrant.

English Ivy

Hedera helix

Height: Slowly to 30 ft.
Flowers: Greenish yellow
Foliage: Evergreen
Bloom Period: Summer
Zones: 3 to 7
Water: Moderate

Light Requirement:

*I*n the English tradition of assimilating good things from wherever they had the misadventure of originating, English ivy, like English oak and English lavender, is a Mediterranean native. For persistent, trouble-free cover in shade, English ivy is a very good find. A person's overall attitude toward vines often stems from his or her experience with English ivy. In moist climates, it is as much a force of nature as erosion. It crumbles the mortar in brick walls, swallowing unfortunate plants in its path. Even in high-desert gardens where light intensity, infertile soil, and aridity help contain its vigor, English ivy needs plenty of space and should be matched with companions of equal tenacity. The dark, evergreen, lobed leaves are closely spaced on stout stems and endowed with aerial rootlets that adhere to rough surfaces, allowing ivy to scale high walls, fences, trees, and posts.

WHEN TO PLANT

English ivy can be planted from early spring through autumn. Because winter winds can freeze-dry the leaves of new plants, it is better not to set out new plants in winter. English ivy should be grown in the shade where it will be buffered from the most extreme summer conditions. It will require more water during establishment if transplanted when temperatures are above 85 degrees Fahrenheit.

WHERE TO PLANT

English ivy is adapted to most soils and strongly prefers shade. If started against a northeast-facing wall or solid wooden fence where it eventually extends into full sun, the large leaf surfaces may sun-burn. Space plants 8 to 10 ft. apart for solid cover in 3 years, or use a single plant highlighted against an expanse of wall to avoid ivy overload as plants mature. English ivy can be used as a groundcover in the shade of large trees, but the choice of tree is important—

vigorous ivy can overwhelm a small or slow-growing tree. Fast-growing valley cottonwood, bur oak, or chinkapin oak can compete with the ivy if the tree has had a few years head start. English ivy's green winter color is attractive, highlighting the form of the tree.

How to Plant

Dig generous holes only as deep as the rootball but 4 to 6 times its diameter, loosening the soil so that new roots will have an easy time breaking ground. If a group of small plants will be used as a groundcover, till 4 in. of compost into the soil over the entire area to be planted. Backfill soil requires no amendment if only a few plants are being set out. A generous topdressing of compost as mulch will keep the soil more uniformly moist and more moderate in temperature, accelerating root development.

Advice for Care

Once English ivy takes hold, manage its growth by watering only as much as is needed to maintain health. Watering deeply twice a month when temperatures are above 80 degrees Fahrenheit, and monthly during cooler weather, will keep plants healthy without promoting excess growth. Fertilizer applied each spring for the first 3 to 5 years will speed coverage and can be stopped when plants begin to fill their desired space.

Species, Cultivars, or Varieties

'Baltica' is a tough cultivar that is very cold tolerant. 'Hahn' is more compact and produces more side branches on stems to 15 ft. It is cold hardy to Zone 6. 'Pixie' has small leaves with prominent white veining and crinkled margins. The stems extend only 5 to 10 ft.

Queen's Wreath

Antigonon leptopus

Height: 40 ft.	**Light Requirement:**
Flowers: Coral or rose-red	
Foliage: Deciduous	
Bloom Period: Midsummer to frost	
Zone: 8	
Water: Moderate	

The fast-growing wiry stems of queen's wreath are hidden by lush green heart-shaped leaves 3 to 4 in. wide. Its growth accelerates when less heat-loving plants begin the struggle to survive the sweltering 90 degrees Fahrenheit heat. The stems climb by means of tendrils, and sprays of small grenadine-colored flowers cascade from the branches by midsummer. The roots of queen's wreath, large moisture-storing tubers, are the key to its drought resistance. Also called coral vine, this native of Baja and Sonora in Old Mexico displays a range of flower color from deep coral to dark reddish pink, the shades of brilliant desert sunsets.

WHEN TO PLANT

Because it needs warm soil to develop healthy roots, it is best to set out new plants in late spring or early summer so they will have plenty of time to root before the onset of cold weather.

WHERE TO PLANT

Queen's wreath prefers a garden spot where heat radiates from walls and paving. It is a perfect cover for courtyard ramadas or portals where its rapid dense growth provides summer shade, and where the maximum solar gain is allowed in winter after queen's wreath has frozen back with the first cold. Plant it in a niche of its own or with companion plants that can be kept dry in winter. Because most of the twining topgrowth should be removed each autumn, an open post-and-rail fence or trellis, or a post-and-beam ramada or arbor are better support than more intricate mesh fencing; it is much easier to remove the stems from an open framework.

HOW TO PLANT

Dig generous holes, loosening the soil so that new roots will have an easy time breaking ground. Backfill soil requires no amendment, but a generous topdressing of pecan hulls or fine gravel as mulch in winter will help keep the soil more moderate in temperature.

ADVICE FOR CARE

Prune off most of the frost-killed topgrowth each year to keep layers of dead stems from building up and to allow sunlight to penetrate. This cleanup can be done any time after frost in fall and before new growth begins again in spring. Queen's wreath needs ample water during the first few summers to develop its deep fleshy roots. Once well established, it may require deep watering every 2 weeks during active growth. Dormant vines do not need to be watered. Fertilizer is not recommended because even modest doses promote leafy growth at the expense of flowering.

SPECIES, CULTIVARS, OR VARIETIES

'Baja Red' produces flowers of deep carmine-rose.

REGIONAL CONSIDERATIONS

Queen's wreath is hardy in only the warmest areas in the low desert of southern New Mexico.

Silk Vine

Periploca graeca

Height: To 30 ft.	**Light Requirement:**
Flowers: Maroon	
Foliage: Deciduous	
Bloom Period: Summer	
Zones: 5 to 8	
Water: Moderate	

*S*ilk vine is a Mediterranean native that is well adapted to our heat, cold, and aridity. The original plants in New Mexico may have been brought by Spanish colonists who settled along the Rio Grande nearly three centuries ago. Silk vine stems are slender and twine around fencing wire or posts, easily growing 10 ft. a year when young. Handsome dark, glossy leaves 4 in. long and 1 in. wide are paired at nodes 3 to 6 in. apart along the stems. Loose clusters of star-like, velvety, maroon flowers appear in summer, sometimes followed by paired seedpods that are inconspicuous amidst the leaves. The silken seed parachutes and milky sap are clues to silk vine's kinship with the milkweeds, and its flowers supply nectar for butterflies as well. Silk vine defoliates cleanly in autumn, leaving a sculptured skeleton of smooth coiled stems for winter interest.

WHEN TO PLANT

Acclimated plants can be set out any time of year. Silk vine transplanted in the heat of summer will require more water during establishment. Layered cuttings survive best when transplanted the spring after they were rooted.

WHERE TO PLANT

Silk vine prefers well-drained soil, but it will grow in heavy clay if not kept too wet. It is an ideal vine for covering ramadas and arbors because it provides dense shade in summer and allows sun to penetrate in winter.

HOW TO PLANT

Silk vine is propagated by cuttings or by layering (pinning the semi-soft stems to loosened moist soil until they form roots). To transplant rooted layers or container-grown plants, dig generous holes only as deep as, or at most a few inches deeper than, the depth of the rootball, but 4 to 6 times its diameter, loosening the soil so that new roots will have an easy time breaking ground. Even deeply rooted plants like silk vine plants develop lateral absorbing roots first, and rely on those roots most for initial establishment and long-term survival. Backfill soil requires no amendment, but a generous topdressing of mulch will enhance root development by keeping the soil more uniformly moist.

ADVICE FOR CARE

If given adequate room to grow, silk vine will require little pruning. Established plants should be watered to a depth of 2 to 3 ft. twice a month when leafy, and monthly while dormant.

SPECIES, CULTIVARS, OR VARIETIES

There are no other species in cultivation.

REGIONAL CONSIDERATIONS

Silk vine has a long history in the middle Rio Grande valley, but it is heat-tolerant enough to adapt to gardens further south.

Silver Lace Vine

Fallopia aubertii

Height: 25 to 40 ft.
Flowers: White
Foliage: Deciduous
Bloom Period: Early summer to frost
Zones: 4 to 8
Water: Moderate to low

Light Requirement:

Silver lace vine is arguably the fastest-growing and most drought-tolerant perennial vine for central and northern New Mexico. Its wiry stems twine around fencing or posts, scrambling to the tops of arbors and rambling across ramadas. The stems are cloaked in small medium-green leaves, which are in turn frosted with a covering of lacy, lightly scented flowers for most of the growing season. Silver lace vine is tolerant of a wide range of moisture, and its spread can be controlled somewhat by limiting the water available. Regardless of watering and pruning procedures, 20 to 25 ft. is probably the least amount of space the plant will cover. Most vines that are as twiggy as it is look rather ragged in winter, but the previous year's growth on silver lace vine turns golden brown after frost, creating a finely wrought filigree that drapes over the vine's supporting framework.

When to Plant

Because silver lace vine roots most quickly when the soil is warm, it is best transplanted in spring, summer, and early autumn. Consistent watering during establishment will be required for vines transplanted in the heat of summer. Seeds also germinate best when the soil has warmed to 70 degrees Fahrenheit.

Where to Plant

Silver lace vine will grow in any well-drained infertile soil. It is used as fast cover for fencing, and for screening and shade on arbors and ramadas.

How to Plant

Silver lace vine is grown from seeds, semi-softwood cuttings or layers, and by root division. Recent research has demonstrated that the best soil preparation for container-grown plants is to dig holes only as deep as, or at most a few inches deeper than, the depth of the rootball, but 4 to 6 times its diameter. Even deeply rooted plants develop lateral absorbing roots, which they rely on most for initial establishment and long-term survival. Backfill soil requires no amendment, but a generous mulch of compost, shredded bark, or pecan hulls will keep the soil more uniformly moist and more moderate in temperature, accelerating root development.

ADVICE FOR CARE

Silver lace vine is difficult to thin because the stems intertwine; it is easiest to rejuvenate a mature plant by cutting it back nearly to the ground when it has built up enough weathered twiggy growth to be unsightly. Depending on how much the plant is watered, this extreme pruning may be required every few years or once in a decade. To keep plants contained but vigorous, water deeply (to a depth of at least 2 ft.) once a month year round. Water larger plants every 2 weeks during the growing season. No fertilizing is needed.

SPECIES, CULTIVARS, OR VARIETIES

Pink fleeceflower (*P. baldschuanicum*) produces large sprays of pink flowers on plants that are otherwise very similar to silver lace vine.

REGIONAL CONSIDERATIONS

In the high-elevation and northern limits of its range, silver lace vine should be grown in the warmest, driest position available; once established, it will rarely need supplemental watering.

VINES

Trumpet Vine

Campsis radicans

Height: 25 to 40 ft.
Flowers: Orange
Foliage: Deciduous
Bloom Period: Summer
Zones: 5 to 8
Water: Moderate to low

Light Requirement:

With its large clusters of brilliant-orange trumpet-shaped flowers cascading down a dark-green backdrop of lush foliage, trumpet vine is a sight to behold. During the growing season, hummingbirds and orioles sip its nectar daily. But this vine can become a force to contend with, especially in enriched, well-watered garden soil, because it rootsprouts and self-sows unless efforts are made to control it. Our gritty infertile soils, heat, and aridity are an asset in managing its rampant growth. Even when treated carelessly, trumpet vine will become a very large plant in need of sturdy support and ample space as it matures. It adheres to posts, fences, and walls with aerial roots.

When to Plant

Because trumpet vine roots most quickly when the soil is warm, it is best transplanted in spring, summer, and early autumn. Vines transplanted in the heat of summer will require more water during establishment. Seeds also germinate best when the soil has warmed to 70 degrees Fahrenheit.

Where to Plant

Trumpet vine will grow in any well-drained infertile soil. It is used as fast cover for fencing, screening, and shade on arbors and ramadas. Because it can rootsprout, it is also used for erosion control on slopes, especially above retaining walls where it will cascade over the edge of the wall. The orange flowers are a striking contrast for buddleia or chaste tree in summer. An evergreen groundcover of cotoneaster, or a heavily mulched companion grouping of one of the evergray artemesias for contrast, provides interest when the vine is dormant. The most handsomely displayed plants in New Mexico are those growing on huge roughhewn timber posts, on crossbeam driveway-entrance archways, and on telephone poles—all of which make adequate stakes.

How to Plant

Dig generous holes, loosening the soil so that new roots will have an easy time breaking ground. Backfill soil requires no amendment, but a 4- to 6-in. mulch of shredded bark will enhance root development and suppress self-sowing. Geotextile used under a deep mulch will suppress most rootsprouting.

Advice for Care

If given adequate room to grow, trumpet vine will require little pruning. It is not particularly attractive when dormant. Individual plants used in highly visible places can be made more interesting by removing most of the lower twiggy stems once the main stems thicken. This will create a more trunklike base. To promote growth, water plants to a depth of 2 to 3 ft. twice a month when leafy, and monthly while dormant. To limit growth and maintain vigor, water monthly year round. In clay soil that is very alkaline, an annual application of a granular iron-and-sulfur fertilizer may be needed to prevent yellowing foliage in summer.

Species, Cultivars, or Varieties

'Madame Galen' (*C.* × *tagliabuana*) has salmon flowers deeply infused with red. It is more tender than the species during establishment. *Campsis radicans* 'Flava' is a selection with bright-yellow flowers.

Wisteria

Wisteria sinensis

Height: 25 to 40 ft. **Flowers:** Purple or white **Foliage:** Deciduous **Bloom Period:** Spring **Zones:** 5 to 7 **Water:** Moderate	**Light Requirement:**

*W*isteria is the Methuselah of vines, an adolescent at 50 years old. When plants don't bloom, it is often because they are juvenile seedlings rather than plants grown from cuttings of mature flowering stock. Wisteria is always elegant, with smooth gray stems that circle around posts and wrap around each other. The light-green compound leaves unfold early in spring and gradually expand to make a dense canopy. Leaves are still soft and translucent when the pendulous violet-blue or white flowers appear, hanging in 12-in. clusters from the stems. Because wisteria blooms early in spring when our weather is still unsettled, flowers are sometimes nipped in the bud; but if Mother Nature is kind, wisteria provides one of the finest displays of color in the spring garden.

WHEN TO PLANT

Acclimated plants can be set out any time of year, but because wisteria roots more quickly in cooler soil, it is best transplanted in spring or autumn. Summer transplants will require more water during establishment.

WHERE TO PLANT

Wisteria prefers well-drained soil. It will otherwise tolerate all but very alkaline clay soils. Because of its mature size and weight, it needs the sturdy support of an arbor or ramada; or it can be trained to drape a high garden wall. Vines can be twined up the post of a porch or portal and across the edge of the roof. Training the branches laterally across a high support shows off the pendulous flowers to full advantage. Wisteria will take hold and grow faster on a cooler north or east exposure, and the delayed warmup in spring may also keep its early blooms from being blackened by frost. The foliage will look better if plants are somewhat protected from wind.

How to Plant

Dig generous holes only as deep as the rootball but 4 to 6 times its diameter, loosening soil so that new roots will have an easy time breaking ground. Backfill soil requires no amendment, but a 4- to 6-in. mulch of compost or shredded bark will keep the soil cooler and more evenly moist, accelerating root development.

Advice for Care

Wisteria develops a deep and extensive root system in the first 3 to 5 years and will not produce much aboveground growth during this time. A dose of a granular iron-and-sulfur fertilizer worked into the soil in late spring will prevent summer chlorosis and get plants off to a strong start. If given enough room, wisteria will require little pruning, although the slender stems will have to be firmly attached to the support structure. If plants are trained as free-standing shrubs, with young stems twined around stakes until they become self-supporting, allow at least 12 ft. for spreading branches. If adequate space is not provided, new growth will have to be cut back severely several times a year. While plants are becoming established, water weekly when temperatures are 85 degrees Fahrenheit or higher, every 2 weeks when temperatures are between 70 and 85 degrees Fahrenheit, and monthly during cooler weather. Established vines should be watered to a depth of 2 to 3 ft. every 2 weeks when plants are leafy, and monthly during cooler weather.

Species, Cultivars, or Varieties

Japanese wisteria (*W. floribunda*) has flower clusters 18 in. long in a broader range of colors including white, pink, and violet-purple. The flowers are produced more sparsely over a longer season, so they do not make as strong a color impact as the Chinese species, but they are somewhat less vulnerable to late-spring frosts.

RESOURCES

Precipitation Statistics for Selected Communities in New Mexico

Name of Community	Elevation	Recorded Extremes	Typical Year
Chama	7850 ft.	14 to 31 in.	21 in.
Los Alamos	7400 ft.	8 to 28 in.	18 in.
Ruidoso	7000 ft.	12 to 34 in.	21 in.
Santa Fe	7000 ft.	8 to 20 in.	14 in.
Taos	7000 ft.	8 to 22 in.	12 in.
Raton	6900 ft.	10 to 21 in.	17 in.
Las Vegas	6800 ft.	6 to 21 in.	15 in.
Grants	6500 ft.	4 to 17 in.	10 in.
Gallup	6500 ft.	6 to 15 in.	11 in.
Estancia	6100 ft.	8 to 21 in.	13 in.
Farmington	5500 ft.	6 to 14 in.	8 to 12 in.
Silver City	5300 ft.	8 to 22 in.	14 in.
Clayton	4970 ft.	10 to 37 in.	15 in.
Albuquerque	4900 to 6000 ft.	6 to 16 in.	8 in.
Santa Rosa	4600 ft.	6 to 22 in.	14 in.
Truth or Consequences	4600 ft.	4 to 18 in.	10 in.
Socorro	4585 ft.	4 to 17 in.	9 in.
Alamogordo	4350 ft.	7 to 18 in.	11 in.
Deming	4300 ft.	4 to 22 in.	10 in.
Clovis	4250 ft.	12 to 47 in.	18 in.
Lordsburg	4250 ft.	5 to 19 in.	11 in.
Tucumcari	4100 ft.	6 to 35 in.	16 in.
Fort Sumner	4025 ft.	9 to 27 in.	14 in.
Portales	4000 ft.	7 to 26 in.	16 in.
Las Cruces	3880 ft.	4 to 12 in.	7 in.
El Paso	3775 ft.	3 to 18 in.	9 in.
Roswell	3640 ft.	4 to 33 in.	12 in.
Hobbs	3615 ft.	6 to 29 in.	16 in.
Artesia	3350 ft.	6 to 26 in.	12 in.
Carlsbad	3100 ft.	5 to 24 in.	13 in.

New Mexico stretches 370 miles from north to south and 343 miles from east to west. Eighty-five percent of the state is over 4000 ft. in elevation. The recorded extremes of precipitation are given in contrast to the typical-year estimates to illustrate that "normal" is not a concept that applies to weather in our state.

Climate data was collected from the records library of the Albuquerque and El Paso Offices of the National Weather Service. The recorded extremes and typical-year precipitation amounts reflect data spanning at least 20 years.

Temperature Statistics for Selected Communities in New Mexico

Name of Community	Elevation	Nights Below 32	Days Above 90	Extreme Low	Extreme High	Hardiness Zones Cold	Hardiness Zones Heat
Chama	7850 ft.	224	4	-29F	99F	4	2
Los Alamos	7400 ft.	172	1	-18F	95F	4 to 5	2
Ruidoso	7000 ft.	275	6	-26F	98F	4	3
Santa Fe	7000 ft.	163	8	-17F	99F	5	4
Taos	7000 ft.	191	19	-27F	98F	4 to 5	4
Raton	6900 ft.	184	18	-24F	98F	4 to 5	4
Las Vegas	6800 ft.	169	8	-39F	100F	4	4
Grants	6500 ft.	175	24	-33F	101F	4	5
Gallup	6500 ft.	187	24	-40F	99F	4	5
Estancia	6100 ft.	179	38	-37F	104F	4	6
Farmington	5500 ft.	171	61	-34F	105F	5 to 6	7
Silver City	5300 ft.	129	27	-13F	103F	6 to 7	5
Clayton	4970 ft.	143	41	-21F	105F	4	6
Albuquerque	4900 to 6000 ft.	107	66	-17F	107F	5 to 7	7 to 8
Santa Rosa	4600 ft.	110	80	-25F	109F	6	8
Truth or Consequences	4600 ft.	88	74	-4F	112F	7 to 8	8
Socorro	4585 ft.	115	89	-13F	109F	6	8
Alamogordo	4350 ft.	105	105	-14F	110F	7 to 8	9
Deming	4300 ft.	99	102	-4F	110F	8	9
Clovis	4250 ft.	116	68	-17F	110F	5 to 6	7
Lordsburg	4250 ft.	94	113	-14F	114F	7 to 8	9
Tucumcari	4100 ft.	112	83	-22F	110F	6	8
Fort Sumner	4025 ft.	112	80	-27F	109F	6	8
Portales	4000 ft.	124	77	-17F	109F	6	7
Las Cruces	3880 ft.	111	101	-10F	110F	8	9
El Paso	3775 ft.	65	104	-8F	114F	8	8 to 9
Roswell	3640 ft.	108	108	-29F	110F	6 to 7	9
Hobbs	3615 ft.	85	95	-7F	111F	7 to 8	8 to 9
Artesia	3350 ft.	103	111	-20F	113F	7 to 8	8 to 9
Carlsbad	3100 ft.	81	118	-16F	111F	7 to 8	9

Climate data was collected from the records library of the Albuquerque and El Paso Offices of the National Weather Service. Records vary from community to community, but all the places listed have records reflecting a span of at least 20 years. A few locations have data spanning nearly 100 years. This data illustrates quite dramatically the extremes that New Mexico gardeners face. Bear in mind that the extreme lows may reflect cold events that occur only once in 10 or more years, and the ultimate low may last only a few hours.

Maps for New Mexico Gardeners

While the USDA Cold Hardiness Zone Map and the American Horticultural Society Plant Heat Zone Map are always useful tools when judging potential adaptations of plants, adjustments must be made in the West to account for the sharp changes in elevation. The maps in this book have been modified to better represent New Mexico climate zones by overlaying the USDA and AHS maps on a New Mexico topographical map and adjusting for climate data from our local offices of the National Weather Service. The statistics for individual communities are given to further clarify conditions within zones. On a microclimate level, the following adjustments can be made to gain a more precise picture:

- Subtract 3 degrees Fahrenheit for every 1000-ft. rise in elevation.
- Add 3 degrees Fahrenheit for every 1000-ft. drop in elevation.
- On slopes that have a rise of 2 ft. for every 10 ft. of distance, the top of a 50-ft. incline may be a zone warmer than the base.
- The area within 10 ft. of a heated wall may be a zone warmer than the surrounding area.
- A northeast-facing wall may be a zone colder than a south-facing exposure.
- Day-to-night temperature fluctuations on a southern exposure may damage plants, while the more consistent cold on a northeast exposure may buffer sensitive plants from damage.

Great gardens are built on experimentation. If you really admire a plant that is a zone less hardy than your garden, try it in a few protected places in a courtyard, against a heat-storing wall, or against boulders. Plant your cold-tender experiments as soon as the temperatures moderate in late spring so they will have plenty of time to root out before being subjected to extreme cold. If the plant you crave is less heat tolerant than the toaster oven you call home, try a few well-rooted specimens in your coolest niches. Plant your heat-sensitive experiments in autumn so that they will have a long cool period to root out before the next onslaught of summer heat.

A Cold Hardiness Zone Map and a Heat Zone Map, both modified for climatic conditions in New Mexico, may be found on the last two pages of the color insert, just before page 225.

New Mexico
Elevation Map

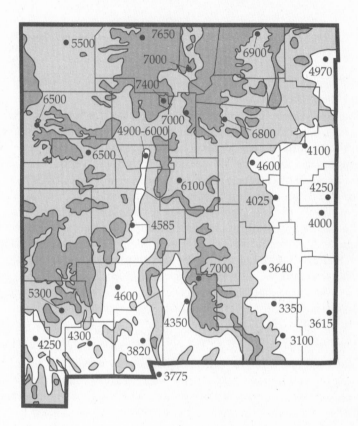

Elevation in feet

New Mexico Gardening Basics

Conserving Water and Making Gardening Easier and More Rewarding

SOIL PREPARATION

When building in an undisturbed natural area or remodeling an existing house and garden, fence off a building envelope to define the limits of the construction zone and prevent soil compaction and unnecessary destruction of existing vegetation. Contour the garden area to enhance drainage, capture runoff, and make slopes less extreme. By scooping out basins and swales to direct roof and pavement runoff into planting areas, storm drainage becomes a resource instead of a potential problem. Drainage in heavier soils can be improved by mounding soil in raised beds or berms. Gently sloped berms densely planted with trees and shrubs can create privacy and buffer street noise. Where slopes incline more than 2 ft. for every 10 ft. of distance, terracing with rock, building stone, or timbers will help reduce runoff and erosion. Loosen the soil well for all new planting. Many local soils have the texture of concrete when dry. Softening the soil enables new roots to gain ground more easily.

Add soil amendments only where they are needed by the plants; enrich the soil in most of the potential root zone. Plants that require amended soil tend to have limited and shallow root systems compared with the root systems of plants that are well adapted to local soils and climate. Desert natives need soils rich in oxygen; the carbon dioxide released by compost as it breaks down can displace soil oxygen, causing a decline in the vigor of plants adapted to gritty desert soils.

When soil amendment is appropriate, compost is the best means of adding organic matter to the soil. Peat moss tends to dry out quickly, is difficult to rewet once dry, and doesn't harbor as many soil microorganisms beneficial to plant growth as does well-made compost. Manures are often high in salts that can burn tender new roots. Uncomposted wood fiber needs nitrogen to decompose and can cause nitrogen deficiencies in plants that are growing in the soil beneath it.

Resources

PLANT SELECTION

Choose plants based on how well adapted they are as well as on how they look. Group plants of similar water use and soil preference so they can be watered efficiently.

IRRIGATION

Apply water as deeply as individual plants require and as slowly as possible to prevent runoff. New transplants will initially require smaller amounts of water applied more frequently. As the plants root out, decrease the frequency gradually and increase the depth of watering to promote deep rooting. Once established, low-water-use plants are generally able to survive without supplemental watering, but they look best if watered deeply once a month. Moderate water users may decline if they don't receive deep watering twice monthly during the growing season. Ample-use plants may require watering as often as once a week when temperatures reach the mid-nineties.

Zone irrigation lines according to plant needs. Plants that require frequent shallow watering should be zoned separately from those that will grow best when watered deeply and infrequently once they are well established. Use low-flow equipment such as drip emitters to water trees, shrubs, and shrubby groundcovers, and use soaker hoses for perennial beds or other plants that are closely spaced. Use spray heads only for close plantings of relatively low-growing plants such as grasses as well as some annual and perennial flowers. Sprinklers for lawn areas should provide uniform coverage and should be valved separately from drip emitters since they require very different pressure, volume, and run times. Be sure the sprinkler heads used have a spray angle high enough to clear the groundcover when it has grown to its mature height. Areas that will be spray watered should be at least 10 ft. wide and fairly uniform in shape. Avoid using sprays in narrow spaces or raised areas that dry out quickly and are difficult to water without creating overspray or runoff. The soil in sprinkler zones should be fairly level in grade, and as uniform as possible in absorbency. Use low-precipitation-rate sprinkler heads on slopes. In spray-irrigated areas that are sloped, place plants that can make use of the runoff at the base of the slope. Check routinely to ensure that irrigation equipment is working properly. Clean the filters, check emitters and spray heads, and regulate the water pressure so that spray heads don't mist up and low-flow systems work properly.

Change the program of automatic timers seasonally and as plants become established so that water is applied as deeply and only as often as needed to keep the plants healthy. Override automatic timers to compensate for weather changes. Timers on irrigation systems can help you use water efficiently because they make it easy to determine how long it takes to apply water to a given depth. The best way to find out how deeply water is actually penetrating is to dig down under a drip emitter before planting, or at the edge of a spray-irrigated area a few hours after watering. If the soil is moist to a depth of 12 in. after a 30-min. irrigation cycle, you can then set the timer to run as long as needed for the depth the plants require. When watering plants on slopes, you may find that repeating shorter cycles rather than using one long one prevents runoff, especially when you are using sprinklers or other high-volume irrigation equipment.

MULCHES

Choose mulches that are compatible with the plants and conditions in the garden. Organic mulches can improve the soil quality for plants that prefer humusy soil. Gravel mulches can help prevent crown rot in plants that require well-drained soil. Mulches in runoff areas should be heavy and coarse enough to withstand the flow of water during storms. In windy areas, mulches should be coarse or shredded to limit blowouts.

Apply mulches as deeply as possible to reduce evaporation, buffer heat and cold, and suppress weeds. When applying to open areas, 4 to 6 in. of mulch is ideal. Apply 4 in. around larger trees and shrubs; when applying mulch around smaller plants, start with 2 to 3 in. and renew the mulch as plants grow.

MAINTENANCE

To maintain your lawn, mow as often as needed to keep the grass at its most robust height without cutting more than $1/3$ off at one mowing. Native warm-season grasses such as blue grama and buffalograss should be kept at least 4 in. tall during the growing season. Tall turf-type fescue should be mowed 3 in. high; Bermudagrass can be kept $1^1/2$ to 2 in. high.

Fertilize, water, and prune all plants only as much as needed to keep plants healthy and blooming. Excess watering and unnecessarily severe pruning will force rampant growth that increases the

Resources

plant's demand for fertilizer. Fertilizing to satisfy the demands of excess watering will prompt more growth, which will in turn require more moisture. Avoid the costly merry-go-round by watering plants as often as needed to acclimate them to the garden and encourage vigorous root growth. Work toward establishing balanced growth by gradually decreasing the frequency of watering and increasing the depth that the water penetrates. This will encourage plants to root as extensively as possible.

Nitrogen and iron are the elements most likely to be unavailable in New Mexico soils. Xeric plants that are well adapted to our native soils may need small amounts of supplemental nitrogen until they develop an extensive root system. Plants that are not as well adapted as desert natives may require regular nutrient supplements, especially for nitrogen and iron, throughout their garden life.

While compost is not a direct source of plant nutrients, it is alive with microorganisms that support plant growth and make nutrients more available. I use small amounts of calcium nitrate as a spring nitrogen supplement for establishing xeric plants. I use potassium nitrate and a granular iron-and-sulfur fertilizer or chelated iron on plants that are less adapted. The high pH and calcium carbonate content of our soils makes iron unavailable to plants. In high-desert areas, granular iron-and-sulfur blends work well, but in the hottest, driest areas it is necessary to use iron buffered with a chelating agent. This agent surrounds the iron molecules and keeps them available to plants. I also use blood meal or time-release fertilizer on both xeric and less-adaptable plants.

Monitor pest activity and intervene only when there is potential for damage. Introduce biological controls to limit pest populations. Use chemical controls as a last resort, and choose controls specific to the pest. Routine use of broad-spectrum pesticides will destroy the beneficial insects that help balance harmful parasites.

Bibliography

Barr, Claude A. *Jewels of the Plains: Wildflowers of the Great Plains Grasslands and Hills.* Minneapolis, Minnesota: University of Minnesota Press, 1983.

Brooklyn Botanic Garden. *Natural Insect Control: The Ecological Gardener's Guide to Foiling Pests.* Brooklyn, New York: Brooklyn Botanic Garden Publications, 1994.

Carter, Jack L. *Trees and Shrubs of New Mexico.* Silver City, New Mexico: Mimbres Publishing, 1997.

Denver Water Department. *Xeriscape Plant Guide.* Golden, Colorado: Fulcrum Publishing, 1996.

Dick-Peddie, William A. *New Mexico Vegetation: Past, Present and Future.* Albuquerque, New Mexico: University of New Mexico Press, 1993.

Dunmire, William W., and Gail D. Tierney. *Wild Plants of the Pueblo Province.* Santa Fe, New Mexico: Museum of New Mexico Press, 1995.

——. *Wild Plants and Native Peoples of the Four Corners.* Santa Fe, New Mexico: Museum of New Mexico Press, 1997.

Heflin, Jean. *Penstemons, the Beautiful Beardtongues of New Mexico.* Albuquerque, New Mexico: Jack Rabbit Press, 1997.

Hodoba, Theodore B. *Growing Desert Plants from Windowsill to Garden.* Santa Fe, New Mexico: Red Crane Books, 1995.

Ivy, Robert DeWitt. *Flowering Plants of New Mexico,* 3rd edition. Albuquerque, New Mexico: Published by author, 1995.

Knopf, Jim. *The Xeriscape Flower Gardener.* Boulder, Colorado: Johnson Publishing Co., 1991.

Mielke, Judy. *Native Plants for Southwestern Landscapes.* Austin, Texas: University of Texas Press, 1993.

Morrow, Baker H. *Best Plants for New Mexico Gardens and Landscapes.* Albuquerque, New Mexico: University of New Mexico Press, 1995.

Resources

Olkowski, William, Helga Olkowski, and Sheila Daar. *Common-Sense Pest Control: Least-Toxic Solutions for Your Home, Garden, Pets and Community*. Newtown, Connecticut: The Taunton Press, 1991.

Phillips, Judith. *Natural By Design*. Santa Fe, New Mexico: Museum of New Mexico Press, 1995.

———. *Plants For Natural Gardens*. Santa Fe, New Mexico: Museum of New Mexico Press, 1995.

———. *Southwestern Landscaping with Native Plants*. Santa Fe, New Mexico: Museum of New Mexico Press, 1987.

Shigo, Alex L. *Modern Arboriculture*. Durham, New Hampshire: Shigo and Trees, Associates, 1991.

Western Society of Weed Science and Cooperative Extension Service. *Weeds of the West*. Jackson, Wyoming: University of Wyoming, 1991.

INDEX

Index

Index

Index

Index

Index

Index

Index

ABOUT THE AUTHOR

 udith Phillips is a landscape designer, horticulturist, and writer. She has designed more than 600 residential landscapes in central New Mexico as well as public landscapes including the Visitors' Center Habitat Garden at Bosque del Apache National Wildlife Refuge near Socorro. Judith and her husband Roland are partners in a nursery specializing in high-desert native and adaptive trees, shrubs, wildflowers, and ornamental grasses. Judith is the author of *Southwestern Landscaping with Native Plants* (1987), *Natural by Design* (1995), and *Plants for Natural Gardens* (1995), all published by the Museum of New Mexico Press. She contributed essays for several gardening *Taylor's Guides* published by Houghton Mifflin and has contributed to publications for the Brooklyn Botanic Garden and written numerous journal and magazine articles.

GARDENING TITLES
FROM COOL SPRINGS PRESS

The What, Where, When, How & Why
of Gardening in Your State

Alabama Gardener's Guide	ISBN 1-888608-28-5
Colorado Gardener's Guide	ISBN 1-888608-48-X
Florida Gardener's Guide	ISBN 1-888608-31-5
Georgia Gardener's Guide	ISBN 1-888608-08-0
Illinois Gardener's Guide	ISBN 1-888608-41-2
Indiana Gardener's Guide	ISBN 1-888608-40-4
Louisiana Gardener's Guide	ISBN 1-888608-33-1
Michigan Gardener's Guide	ISBN 1-888608-29-3
Missouri Gardener's Guide	ISBN 1-888608-50-1
New Jersey Gardener's Guide	ISBN 1-888608-47-1
New Mexico Gardener's Guide	ISBN 1-888608-55-2
North Carolina Gardener's Guide	ISBN 1-888608-09-9
Philadelphia Gardener's Guide	ISBN 1-888608-46-3
South Carolina Gardener's Guide	ISBN 1-888608-10-2
Tennessee Gardener's Guide	ISBN 1-888608-38-2
Texas Gardener's Guide	ISBN 1-888608-30-7
Virginia Gardener's Guide	ISBN 1-888608-11-0

Coming Soon!

Arizona Gardener's Guide	ISBN 1-888608-42-0
California Gardener's Guide	ISBN 1-888608-43-9
Kentucky Gardener's Guide	ISBN 1-888608-17-X
Mississippi Gardener's Guide	ISBN 1-888608-44-7
New York Gardener's Guide	ISBN 1-888608-45-5
Ohio Gardener's Guide	ISBN 1-888608-39-0
Oklahoma Gardener's Guide	ISBN 1-888608-56-0